THE POLITICAL SCIENCE
OF JOHN ADAMS

A STUDY IN THE THEORY OF MIXED GOVERNMENT
AND THE BICAMERAL SYSTEM

BY

CORREA MOYLAN WALSH

" *I know not how it is, but mankind
have an aversion to the study of the
science of government. To me no
romance is more entertaining.*"

J. ADAMS, ix. 567.

G. P. PUTNAM'S SONS
NEW YORK AND LONDON
The Knickerbocker Press
1915

The Knickerbocker Press, New York

PREFACE

THE theory reviewed in this work is obsolete, but it was extensively in vogue at the time of the framing of our American constitutions. In fact, we live under arrangements produced by a modified form of it. Our State and Federal systems of two chambers and veto-possessing governors or presidents, are remnants of the old theory of mixed government. Luckily the entire theory was not carried out of having all the elements equal in the mixture; yet, unfortunately, it was applied to the extent of making two of them nearly so. Although the balance was not brought up to its ideal, the opportunity for obstruction was suffered to remain.

It is submitted that a theory which has passed away but which has left its effect, is highly deserving of study, and in its most perfect manifestation.

The study may also lead to practical results. The theory which presided at their birth being a thing of the past, the form still lasting of our governments is an anachronism, and the question arises whether it should longer continue. If there is no agitation on the subject among us at present, the recent experience through which Great Britain has passed—of a revival, first, of the power of the upper House, the troubles thereby caused, and the final relegation by law of that House to the place it had formerly sunk to by custom,—may

iii

serve as a warning to us of what may happen when our people seriously arouse themselves to shake off some of the banes that mar our blessings, and find to their surprise that they themselves have granted to the greatest abuses a means of hindering the cure.

Before many months, is coming the period for revising the constitution of the largest State of the Union, and interest may again be awakened in constitutional questions.

The ensuing work, therefore, though written mainly about the past, is directed toward the future. The time for taking thought precedes the time for taking action.

C. M. W.

October, 1914.

CONTENTS

CHAPTER I

INTRODUCTION

THE FIRST PERIOD

CHAPTER II

EARLY DEMOCRATIC VIEWS

THE SECOND PERIOD

CHAPTER III

WRITINGS OF THIS PERIOD

Contents

I. DEVELOPMENT OF THE THEORY

CHAPTER IV

DIVISION AND CLASSIFICATION OF GOVERNMENTS

CHAPTER V

BADNESS OF SIMPLE GOVERNMENTS, AND NEED OF A BALANCE

CHAPTER VI

THE ORDERS AND CLASSES IN GOVERNMENT AND SOCIETY

CHAPTER VII

CONTROL OF THE ARISTOCRATS IN MIXED GOVERNMENT

II. THE PLAN OF GOVERNMENT

CHAPTER VIII

THE GENERAL STRUCTURE

CHAPTER IX

THE EXECUTIVE

Contents

CHAPTER X

THE SENATE

CHAPTER XI

THE HOUSE OF REPRESENTATIVES

CHAPTER XII

THE TWO HOUSES AND THE EXECUTIVE

Contents

CHAPTER XIII

THE JUDICIARY

CHAPTER XIV

NEGLECT OF THE CONSTITUTION

III. SOURCES AND ORIGINALITY OF ADAMS'S DOCTRINES

CHAPTER XV

CONTEMPORARY EXPOSITORS OF THE ENGLISH CONSTITUTION AND UNNOTICED CHANGES

CHAPTER XVI

EARLIER SPECULATIVE AUTHORITIES AND ADAMS'S DEVELOPMENT

IV. ATTITUDE TOWARD THE AMERICAN GOVERNMENTS

CHAPTER XVII

CRITICISM OF THE FEDERAL CONSTITUTION

CHAPTER XVIII

HIS MONARCHISM

THE THIRD PERIOD

CHAPTER XIX

SUBSEQUENT HISTORY OF THE THEORY

CHAPTER XXI

Contents

CHAPTER XXIII

THE GENERAL ARGUMENT FOR BICAMERALISM

CHAPTER XXIV

TENDENCY OF THE UNITED STATES SENATE, AND SUGGESTIONS

THE POLITICAL SCIENCE OF JOHN ADAMS

The Political Science of John Adams

CHAPTER I

INTRODUCTION

AT the two periods when the American people had
the unusual opportunity of instituting governments to suit themselves, no man had studied constitutional lore so deeply or reached such definite conclusions in regard to what he called "the true elements
of the science of government,"[1] as John Adams. To
John Adams politics was "the art of securing human
happiness," "the divine science";[2] and with the duties
of the hour he was fully impressed. "No people ever
had a finer opportunity to settle things upon the best
foundations," he wrote in 1776[3]; and when the next
occasion was approaching in 1787, he repeated that
"the people in America have now the best opportunity
and the greatest trust in their hands, that Providence
ever committed to so small a number, since the trans-

---

[1] *Works*, ed. by C. F. Adams, Boston, 1856, iv., 290.
[2] IV., 203, ix., 339, 512.
[3] IX., 434, *cf*. 391, iv., 200.

gression of the first pair"; and, he added, as "the constitutions now made in America will not wholly wear out for thousands of years," "it is of the last importance that they should begin right."[1]

To start them right he did all that he could, and he was satisfied that he did much; for not free from conceit was John Adams. He boasted that his early thoughts had influenced those who framed the constitutions of North Carolina and New York in 1776 and 1777; that he was treated as "the putative father" of the Massachusetts constitution of 1780, which he had himself drafted; and that his later opinions not only determined the remodeling of the constitutions of South Carolina, Georgia, and Pennsylvania, but through their influence upon the State governments, affected also the composition of the Federal Government.[2] With due allowance for the exaggeration of egotism, in these claims lurks a fair amount of truth. His views, however, passed beyond what was acceptable to the people, and because he insisted upon them "in season and out of season" (cf. ix. 451), hardly had the Federal Constitution been put into working order, he fell from grace, and since then less attention has been paid to his doctrines than they deserve. He developed a system for which he took no pride as inventor, but which he thoroughly made his own; for, while other political philosophers have touched upon its parts and investigated its details here and there, more than any did he minutely analyze it into its elements and carry it back to its principles, elaborately draw it out into its corollaries, symmetrically clothe it in a complete form, and trenchantly

[1] IV., 290, 298, cf. 587.
[2] II., 508, iii., 59, x., 410, cf. i., 209; vi., 463, cf. iii., 361, ix., 106; iii., 23, vi., 458, viii., 508, x., 392, cf. ix., 556.

argue for it on grounds both of experience and of reason.
To political science he thus made a contribution that is
well worthy of reconsideration. The examination of it
not only is of historical interest, giving insight into the
causes of our constitutions being what they are, but
may lead to lessons in the valuation of their merits and
defects.

In Adams's career as a political writer may be discerned three distinct periods. He began to write on
public questions in 1765, and this first period continued
down to the summer of 1786, when it came to an abrupt
end. He was occupied with practical affairs, first with
discussing our relations to England, then with advocating independence and union, and lastly with urging the
establishment, and outlining the plan, of State governments and the Confederation.

The second was a theoretical period, during which, at
its beginning already long absent from the country and
its practical affairs, he was engaged in defending the
State constitutions against the criticism of radical
writers like Price and Priestley in England, Turgot,
Condorcet, and others in France, and against the spread
of the ideas of Franklin and Thomas Paine, already
embodied in the unicameral constitution of Pennsylvania, which was imitated by South Carolina, Georgia,
and Vermont, and in advocating improvements of a
directly contrary nature. Also, after the adoption of
the Federal Constitution and the establishment of the
new government, he welcomed this as containing features he had recommended, and took it under his wing,
but subjected it to criticism where he thought it fell
short and suggested what he believed would be inevitable future amendments. This was, too, a dogmatic
period, in which from the high vantage of his fuller

studies and meditations he looked back upon his earlier
efforts as put forth at a time when he "understood very
little of the subject" (ix. 566).   He flattered himself
that now he had studied government as the astronomer
does the stars, "by facts, observations, and experiments," or as the carpenter does shipbuilding, learning
the principles of nature before constructing a machine
subject to their sway (*cf.* vi. 479, 481); and he was "as
clearly satisfied of the infallible truth of the doctrines
maintained" in his book, as "of any demonstration in
Euclid," so much so as to "think them as eternal and
unchangeable as the earth and its inhabitants," and to
know "with infallible certainty" that future experience
will   confirm   them.[1]   Accordingly,   the   system   he
expounded he pronounced to be "the only scientific
government; the only plan which takes into consideration all the principles in nature, and provides for all
cases that occur" (vi. 44).   This period, the fullest,
was the shortest.

It was followed by a third period of recantation from
his advanced and solitary position, in which he showed
himself submissive to the American constitutions as
they were and are, and renounced and denounced the
extraneous views which had rendered him unpopular,
retaining most of his opinions, however, in some sort of
shape, to save his face.

[1] J., 432 (*cf.* vi., 252); ix., 568 (*cf.* 571); vi., 300.

THE FIRST PERIOD

CHAPTER II

EARLY DEMOCRATIC VIEWS

THE first period need not detain us long. It was a period of democratic revolt, in which Adams with the "sons of liberty" and other "patriots," held what were called "revolutionary principles," that had been struck out by the English revolutionists of 1640 and 1688,—"the principles of nature and eternal reason," as he called them (iv. 15, *cf.* 55). He had read, he tells us,[1] the early republican writers, Harrington, Milton, Sydney, Nedham, Nevill, as well as the perverted Hobbes, and, chief authority of the Whigs, Locke, and the expounder of the English Constitution, Bolingbroke, a Tory, but in many respects liberal through being in opposition, and the admirer of that constitution, Montesquieu. He claimed English liberties for Americans, both as Englishmen who had not lost them by emigrating and to whom they had been promised in the charters, and as natural rights, belonging to all men, anterior to government, and not a gift from rulers.[2] He emphasized the equality of all men, required consent of the governed for the legitimacy of

[1] III., 22, vi., 492, *cf.* i., 43, iv., 194, 204, vi., 4.
[2] II., 171–2; iii., 462–3; iv., 122, 150, 159, 170.

5

government,[1] and maintained the doctrine of the "social compact" (iv. 219, vii. 196). From Harrington he borrowed the principle that dominion follows property, and, wishing to perpetuate our civil and social equality, advocated facilitating the subdivision of land-ownership,[2] at the same time, with Harrington himself, advising exclusion from the franchise of the propertiless (ix. 377). He objected to the distinction then sometimes drawn between legislation and taxation (iv. 113), but not to that between external and internal regulations, consenting to the British Parliament's control over the commerce of the empire, including the American, but not to its binding power over America "in all cases whatsoever" (52, 130–1). When the dissensions with the so-called "mother country" came to a head, he was among the first to advocate independence,[3] considering the American colonies to be absolved from allegiance because the British government was invading their rights, or as he later expressed it, "the King and Parliament committed high treason and rebellion against America."[4] Independence declared, he returned to constitution-making.

[1] III., 480; iv., 15, cf. 16; ii., 215 n., i., 193, iv., 28, 96, 99, 108, ix., 375.

[2] IX., 376–7, to be quoted later. He approved the New England laws for the distribution of intestate estates, as preventing monopolies of land, *Familiar Letters of John Adams and his Wife*, New York, 1876, p. 121.

[3] A letter written in 1755 shows that he had even then looked forward to our "setting up for ourselves" in a century or so, i., 23, cf. ix., 591–2, x., 373, 394–5. His diary reveals that he began to think of it as an imminent possibility in 1765, ii., 162, and again in 1772, ii., 308. He publicly denied wishing it in 1774, in his *Novanglus*, iv., 52, 130, 131. He began to urge it openly in the summer of 1775, ii., 412, 503 ff.

[4] X., 394, cf. ix., 598, iv., 33, 57. A similar assertion was made anent General Gage by a Boston newspaper in 1775 (Wells's *Life of Samuel Adams*, ii., 310 n.), and, in general, by Samuel Adams in 1771 (*ib.*, i., 433). Cf. Burke, *Address to the British Colonies* (*Works*, Boston,

The English government, in its form and constitution, following his teachers, he had looked up to as the best in the world. The American colonial governments, at least those of New England, he conceived to be "miniatures" of the British (ii. 330, *cf.* iv. 117). He resisted the English government because it would not suffer the colonial governments to remain such copies of itself. He still wished them to continue so. The excellence of the English Constitution lay in its being a mixed government, with balanced powers and separate departments; and in describing it he dwelt upon the popular and democratic features in it (iii. 480–2). He wished these elements to be retained in the American constitutions,— a single executive, a bicameral legislature, and judges with tenure during good behavior.[1] Defects in the model were to be corrected:—a bill of rights was to be prefixed; no hereditary powers to be introduced (iii. 17–18, 20), because of our "hereditary aversion to lordships" (iv. 54, *cf.* iii. 180); the representation to be made "an exact portrait in miniature of the people

1884, vol. vi., p. 190). The idea came from English revolutionary times. In 1215 the barons denounced John as a "regem perjurum ac baronibus rebellem" (Freeman, *Growth of the English Constitution*, p. 229). In 1642 the Long Parliament declared that Charles was making war against Parliament, against his loyal subjects, against his kingdom (Clarendon, *History of the Rebellion*, ed. of 1717, i., 534, 684, ii., 14); and this was one of the charges against him at his trial six years later (*ib.*, iii., 253). Him also Milton denounced as "disobedient and rebellious to that law by which he reigned," *Eikonoklastes*, ch. xix. The general principle was expressed by Locke, *Of Civil Government*, §§155, 222, 226, 227, and by Somers (?), *Vox Populi Vox Dei*, § 4, (who quotes the Declaration of the Nobility, Gentry, and Commonalty at Nottingham in 1689, that resistance to a tyrant is "not rebellion, but a necessary defense," §146).

[1] His plan was unfolded in several little papers written in 1775 and 1776, and in the full draft of the Massachusetts constitution prepared by him in 1779, to be found in iv., 185–7, 193–200, 203–9, 219–67. The correspondence of this period is in vol. ix.

at large,"[1] and for this purpose the electoral districts
to be equalized[2] and no parts of the country left out—
this "a first principle of liberty"[3]; elections to be
annual, at least for the popular chamber, by ballot, and
the representatives eligible only from land-holding
residents of the district—"three essential prerequisites
of a free government" (ix. 386); and the representatives to be subject to instruction from their constituents, this being a natural right reserved by the people
(iii. 481; iv. 228).   On annual elections he was insistent,
quoting an old maxim, "Where annual elections end,
there slavery begins"[4]; although for the Southern
States, which were not so democratic, he would not
condemn longer periods for "the council or middle
branch of the legislature," of three or even seven years
during the unsettled times, to be changed later (iv. 186,

---

[1] IV., 195, 205; so, later, 284, 380.   Similarly *The Essex Result*, 1778
(written by T. Parsons): the representatives should be "an exact miniature of their constituents," in Theophilus Parsons Jr.'s *Memoir of
Theophilus Parsons*, Boston, 1859, p. 376.

[2] According to the "ratable polls" of the districts for "representatives"
and according to the wealth of the districts for "senators," iv., 239, 234.
(The last was abolished in 1820.)

[3] Against the departure from it in some of the States, permitting an
equal number of representatives from unequal counties (and in Congress,
in the equal representation of unequal States), he was bitter, denouncing
it as "sowing the seeds of ignorance, corruption, and injustice in the
fairest field of liberty that ever appeared upon earth, even in the first
attempts to cultivate it," ix., 435.

[4] IV., 197, 205.   That this maxim (with "tyranny" for "slavery")
was then generally entertained, we are told by Jefferson; see his *Works*,
Washington's ed., iv., 321 (this ed. will always be referred to unless
another is specially named).   Madison in *The Federalist*, No. 53, refers
to it as "a current observation."   *Cf.* Gerry in Elliot's *Debates on the
Federal Constitution*, v., 184.   It was probably a variant made upon
Locke's "Wherever law ends, tyranny begins," *Of Civil Government*,
§ 202.   Story (*Commentaries on the Constitution*, § 588) refers it to
Montesquieu's *Esprit des Lois*, B. ii., ch. iii.; which is not to the point.

ix. 386, 398). Especially the aristocratic party in Virginia did he combat (ix. 358, 388), "the barons of the South" (i. 207), and among them a writer who recommended councillors and a governor for life (ix. 387-8; see i. 208-9, iv. 201-2), which, however, he would himself allow (iv. 197). In democratic New England he in his first thoughts would tolerate the governor being reduced to a mere president of the council, "as in Connecticut," elected by the council, itself elected by the representatives (iv. 186, 196-7, 206-7, ix. 430). But he preferred the council and governors being independently elected powers, again "as in Connecticut" (iv. 187, 197, 208-9); and soon he insisted upon this. The governor was to have an absolute negative upon the proceedings of the legislature,[1] as was each of the chambers to have upon the bills of the other.

From the very first he desired a bisection of the legislature, and asserted that a people cannot remain free under a single legislative assembly (iv. 195, 205, cf. ix. 506),—that he, at least, could "never be happy under such a government"; although he would always defend "the right of the people to establish such a government as they please," "whether they choose wisely or foolishly" (ix. 430). He argued that such an assembly would be liable to all the frailties of a single individual; that it would grow avaricious and would exempt its members from the burdens it imposed on others; that it would be ambitious and encroach upon

[1] " That he may have power to preserve the independence of the executive and judicial departments," iv., 231.—The defeat of this proposal he later attributed to the "Essex gentlemen," who "would not injure their popularity," E. Quincy's *Life of Josiah Quincy*, p. 141. The Essex Junto supported him on other points, while Th. Cushing and Samuel Adams were for a single assembly, ix., 618.

its constituents and make itself permanent or self-elective (like the Long Parliament and the Dutch States-General); and that it would contend with the executive, and, as the judiciary is not a fit mediator in this contest, another mediator must be set up in a distinct branch of the legislature itself, which should come in between the executive and the extreme popular branch.[1] These are forecasts of his later doctrines, which amplify them.

The executive was to have all appointments of officials, except sheriffs, registers of deeds, and county clerks, who were to be elected in their counties (iv. 198, 207),—so at first, but he yielded up even these to gubernatorial appointment (249). The governor and the judges were to have their salaries fixed, so as to be independent of the assemblies.[2] They were to be impeachable by the house of representatives before the council or senate,[3] and the judges also removable (as in England) by the governor upon addresses of both houses (iv. 255). Like Harrington he desired rotation in office, in order to educate as many as possible of the people in the duties of government and to distribute its burdens (ix. 339, *cf.* 426-7), recommending three years of allowable service out of six (iv. 197-8, 208);

---

[1] IV., 195-6, 205-6.

[2] IV., 186, 198, 207, 229, 251, ix., 379-80. He attached importance to salaries: the public should have too much dignity to allow itself to be served *gratis*; want of salaries is the beginning of corruption, etc., ix., 533-6, 538-44. In this period he probably agreed with Penn, who put into the *Concessions* granted in 1677 to the settlers of West New Jersey that every member of the assembly should be paid a shilling a day during the session, "that thereby he may be known to be the servant of the people." (Grahame, *History of the United States*, Boston ed., ii., 283.)

[3] IV., 238-9, 244. At first only the judges, "before the governor and council," 198-9, 207. For the commencement of this, in imitation of the English, see ii., 329-30, x., 237-8.

and he tried to introduce this principle into the Massachusetts constitution for the governor and treasurer,
but obtained it only for the latter (250–1, 254).   Electors and elected were to be circumscribed by a small
property-qualification, higher for the latter, and in their
case rising in gradation with the importance of the
office, being higher for the senators than for the representatives, and highest for the governor and lieutenant-
governor.[1]   There was also to be a religious test for
eligibility, confining certain offices to Christians.[2]
In general, Adams was for religious toleration, but not
for complete religious freedom and equality, not for
entire separation of State and Church,[3] until near the
close of his life.[4]

As for the "Continental constitution," he desired

[1] IV., 236 n., 243, 246; 238, 242–3; 245, 251–2.

[2] IV., 238, 241–2, 245, 251.   (Adopted only for governor and lieuten-
ant-governor; abolished in 1820.)   But the general article on religion,
iv., 221–2, alone of all the constitution, he said, was not drafted by him:
see Quincy's *Quincy*, 379.

[3] *Cf.* ix., 451, iv., 221.—He made the sophistical argument (also
found in Harrington, *Oceana and Other Works*, ed. of 1747, pp. 448, 506,
517) that respect for the liberty of conscience of the people requires their
being indulged with the right to impose observance of religion, if their
conscience dictates this as a duty, ii., 399, iv., 96,—a duty, however, he
would confine to the States, and not allow to the Congress, ix., 402.

[4] I., 627-8, *cf.* x., 392–3.—Parsons, representing the "Essex gentlemen," in *The Essex Result* closely agreed with Adams on most of these
points.   His reasons sometimes went ahead.   Thus he argued for three
branches that all government, like that of the Creator, requires goodness, wisdom, and power—power in one or very few, wisdom in the few
of the educated and the wealthy, goodness in the many, aiming at the
general happiness: goodness in the aim of the laws, wisdom in their
framing, and vigor in their execution.   Therefore the legislative body
should unite the wisdom and the firmness of aristocracy and the probity
and regard for the interests of the whole, of democracy (in Parsons's
Parsons, pp. 368–70).   Hence he opposed a single representative body,
thinking a second needed to furnish wisdom and firmness, independent,
itself to be checked by the first (379).   The executive, forming the third

merely a single Congress, such as was established (iv.
200, 208). Although he once, in 1776, spoke of the
Confederacy being designed "to form us, like separate
parcels of metal, into one common mass," and to make
us "become a single individual as to all questions submitted to the Confederacy" (ii. 500 n.), he later denied
that he at this time thought of or ever approved a
"national" and "consolidated government" for the
whole country, obliterating the States (iii. 16, x. 413).
He wished the authority of Congress to be "clearly
defined, and limited" to the conduct of the war, regulation of trade and controversies between the States,
management of the post-office, and disposal of the
common lands (ii. 390–1, iv., 200, 208, ix. 380). In
the Confederacy as it existed, till its final decay, besides
its falling short of these powers, he found fault only with
the equal representation of the States (ii. 366, ix. 435,
452, cf. 467). He had vainly urged representation
according to population (ii. 499–500 n., 501 n.). With
partial success he had urged the levying of contributions
according to population, including the slaves (ii. 497 n.).
He thus shared in the responsibility for the final partial
representation of the slaves. So republican was he during the Revolution that he even wished military offices
to receive from Congress only annual appointments.[1]

branch or department, to be one, or a small number (if single, with a
small privy council), for greater responsibility (382); to have power,
with consent of his council, to negative all bills (397). Thus the three
departments, separate, and balanced, to check each other and preserve
each its own independence (373, 374). The judges were not to be
removable by their appointers, nor to be dependent on the executive or
legislative for their salaries: they should be appointed by the executive,
and for misbehavior be removed on impeachment by one branch of the
legislature before the other (382–4). Parsons drew, if not from Adams,
from the same sources, especially from Harrington.

[1] I., 263; *Familiar Letters*, 248.

THE SECOND PERIOD

CHAPTER III

WRITINGS OF THIS PERIOD

IN the second period, though in years a brief one,
Adams composed a long three-volumed treatise and
several pamphlets and letters on political science. The
work entitled *Defense of the Constitutions of Government
of the United States* was mostly written in England, and
published in 1787 and 1788.[1] It was followed by
*Three Letters to Roger Sherman on the Constitution of the
United States*, 1789 (vi. 427–36), and supplemented by
Discourses on Davila, 1790 (vi. 227–403). Finally,
some *Correspondence with Samuel Adams on the Subject
of Government*, written in 1790, was published in 1802
(vi. 411–26). In the first he defended what he found
good in the American State constitutions, and recommended what he conceived to be necessary improvements, expounding the principles that underlay both
the praise and the censure. In the later ones, and in
his general correspondence of the period, he applied
the same treatment to the recently adopted Federal
Constitution.

[1] Vol. i., written Oct.–Dec., 1786, published in London early in 1787
(iv., 283–588); vol. ii., published later in 1787 (v., 5–332); vol. iii., in
1788 (v., 335–496, vi., 3–220).

The immediate occasion of his putting pen to paper was Price's publication of Turgot's criticism of the American constitutions for imitating the English in setting up different bodies—a house of representatives, a council, and a governor,—instead of "collecting all authority into one center, that of the nation."[1] This Adams unwarrantably interpreted as advocacy of a government with all power vested in and exercised by a single assembly (*cf.* iv. 302, etc.), although Turgot in the same letter expressly referred to the need of "separating the objects of legislation from those of general administration and from those of particular and local administration," and desired the establishment of "local assemblies" that should assume the functions of detail and dispense the general assembly therefrom.[2] Adams must have known of Turgot's project to set up communal, cantonal, and provincial assemblies, commencing with the lower and upon these erecting the higher, until finally reaching a national assembly, so that France would have become almost a federative republic (like what ours later became), as was popularly

---

[1] IV., 299. Addressed to Price in 1778, the letter in which this occurs was first published in Price's *Observations on the Importance of the American Revolution*, in America in 1784. In the first London edition, 1785, an English version was added. There, p. 113, it is so translated. The original is: "Au lieu de ramener toutes les autorités à une seule, celle de la nation," *ib.*, p. 92. The literal rendering is given by C. F. Adams in iv., 279: "Instead of bringing all the authorities into one." Possibly Turgot was paraphrasing Tacitus's statement: "omnem potentiam ad unum conferri pacis interfuit," *Histor.*, i., 1. And making a geographical application, Washington perhaps had Price's or Adams's translation in mind when, in 1788, in anticipation of the establishment of the new Federal Government, he expressed a wish that "all the advocates of the Constitution" would "combine their exertions for collecting the wisdom and virtue of the continent to one center." *Writings*, Sparks's ed., ix. 433.

[2] In Price's work, pp. 94, 115.

expounded in the writings of his disciple Condorcet.[1]
To Condorcet himself Adams paid his "first respects"
in *Davila* (vi., 272), classing him with those who would
concentrate all sovereignty in a single assembly (vi.
252). It is a strange blunder; for in the work he refers
to, the anonymous *Lettres d'un Bourgeois de New-
Heaven*, 1788,[2] in which Turgot's views probably
were reproduced, the scheme was a complicated system
for obviating the very evils of such a simple democracy
as Adams feared, by prescribing the submission of the
bills passed by the assembly to the electoral districts,
and additionally, in cases where natural rights might be
infringed, requiring high majorities for passing new
laws and imposts and low minorities for repealing old
ones, and in the bill of rights itself permitting low
minorities to impose restrictions on government and
only high majorities to revoke them, with tendency to
reduce governmental interference to the smallest
amount possible.[3]

[1] *Vie de Turgot*, which was published the same year Adams began to
write. (In Condorcet's *Œuvres complètes*, Paris, 1804, vol. v., pp. 159 ff.;
see especially p. 316, with which compare vol. xii., p. 72.) The next
year, 1787, a start was actually made to institute provincial assemblies;
and it was (according to Condorcet, *ib.*, xii., 183–90) to head off the
natural consequence of their leading to the satisfaction of the people's
demand for a national assembly, that the old and imperfect Estates-
General were demanded by the aristocrats and the parlements, and
within two years were convoked. The subsequent misfortunes of
France came from not following Turgot's plan; for when the Estates-
General did turn themselves into a National Assembly, there were no
firmly established local assemblies to check it.

[2] These were addressed to Mazzei, to whom Jefferson afterward
wrote a famous letter, and were published in his *Recherches sur les
États-Unis*. To him now also Madison sent a letter of protest against
his "plan of a single Legislature": see Madison's *Writings*, Congress ed.,
1867, vol. i., pp. 444–5.

[3] *Œuvres*, xii., 38–76; *cf.* 231. It must be added, however, that Condorcet later, in 1793, collaborating with Thomas Paine, advocated a

Apart from the last feature, this plan was not a new one, and Adams's blunder with regard to it was repeated with regard to some of its prototypes. For in the course of his *Defense* he attacks Milton and Hume for their unicameralism, as if the former, at least, would have had his country governed by a single assembly (iv. 465), notwithstanding that his plan, and Hume's too, provided a similar check upon the national assembly by making its measures dependent for ratification upon county assemblies.[1] In all these schemes, a little analysis would show that the national assembly is the upper house or senate, endowed with the "probouleutic function," and the lower house, instead of being a single body, is the collection of local assemblies,—for the original of all which we must, of course, go back to

constitutional plan in which the single assembly was not thus dependent for its law-making upon local bodies, *ib.*, xviii., 184–200, though he retained the principle of a single assembly (or convention) for drawing up or amending a constitution, to be of force only when ratified by local assemblies, 165–81.

[1] Milton's plan, in his *Divisions of the Commonwealth*, *Easy Way to Establish a Free Commonwealth*, and *Brief Delineation of a Free Commonwealth*, was to place the executive power in a council of state elected out of and by the grand council, which has the legislative power and is elected by landowners for life or during good behavior; but its bills, to become laws, must be ratified, not by another single representative body, but by the assemblies of the counties, which manage their own local affairs. If life tenure was too much feared, Milton allowed for rotation of one third of the grand council annually, biennially, or triennially, making the terms for three, six, or nine years. (Condorcet desired such rotation of a third every year in his provincial assemblies, *Œuvres*, xiii., 90.) Similar is Hume's in his essay on the *Idea of a Perfect Commonwealth*, with the principal difference that the single executive council is replaced by several executive committees of the senatorial council, and the senators and magistrates are annually elected (with permission, if found needful, to set a restriction upon renewals), and the lower bodies may propose laws. In reviewing these, although noticing the local assemblies of Hume, Adams omitted mention of those of Milton, iv., 464–8.

the Roman Senate and Comitia. If they are not exactly bicameral, at all events they are not unicameral: rather are they multicameral. They even have the effect of giving preponderance to the aristocracy by uniting their forces in the single assembly and scattering those of the democracy in the many.[1] Down to a few years *after* Adams wrote, when the French established a unicameral government not that advocated by Turgot, perhaps the only instance that can be found, at least in modern times (and it would be difficult to find one in ancient), of a government with all power concentrated in one assembly, was the Rump of the Long Parliament after the execution of Charles I. (*cf.* vi. 135); which, however, was a temporary usurpation, and not truly representative of the people. During its continuance some ignorant publicists advocated—and perhaps are the only ones that have advocated—permanently adopting such a system. For instance, some of the Levellers put forth on May 1, 1649, a revision of the mooted *Agreement of the People*, for establishing "a popular form, or a government by the people," with supreme authority in "a Representative" of the people, to consist of four hundred persons eligible by and from all persons above twenty-one, not servants and vagabonds.[2]

[1] Milton's scheme is evidently that of a would-be aristocrat (*cf. Paradise Regained*, iii., 49–59). Hume was a Tory, but shows advance in that his is even less aristocratic. Condorcet does not seem to have perceived this effect. Perhaps Turgot did. Adams himself did, in the case of Rome, iv., 544.

[2] The plan also contained provision for the intervals between sessions, the government then to be conducted by a committee of its own members, instead of a standing council of state. But even this appears to have contained some reservations, as did the original *Agreements* of 1647 and 1648. An account of it may be found in Marchamont Nedham's *The Case of the Commonwealth of England Stated*, London (1650), p. 70.

To contend against this kind of single-chambered
supreme government was not worth while; and to
carry out the sub-title of his *Defense*, "against the
attack of M. Turgot,"[1] Adams should have directed his
fire against the particular form of central and local
governments recommended by that statesman. But
probably his readers drew the distinction between
Turgot's and that other kind of unicameralism as little
as he did,—and as little as the French a few years later
drew it. And because he likewise did not distinguish
between Turgot's and still other possible kinds of unicameralism (that of Pennsylvania, for instance), we
need not cavil at his selecting Turgot as the butt of his
animadversions. He reprobated unicameralism in any
form and shape in which he conceived of its appear-
ing, and was alarmed at symptons of such a system
being favored in America more widely and even spread-
ing to Massachusetts.[2] Against it in general, then, he

Nedham, himself a mercurial politician, condemned it because the
people are "too brutish," pp. 71–9. It seems to have been drawn up by
Lilburne: see Gardiner, *The Commonwealth and the Protectorate*, London,
1894, vol. i., p. 53. Among its advocates Nedham mentions an extreme
faction called Diggers (*cf.* Gardiner, *ib.*, p. 47), who wished to return to
the land and enjoy all things in common, *The Case*, etc., p. 79. These
were the communists, as the others were the socialists, of the democratic party. Adams does not seem to have been acquainted with this
pamphlet; and he treats Nedham's own later plan, in his *The Excellency
of a Free State, or the Right Constitution of a Commonwealth*, 1656, as if it
were little else than the plan Nedham condemned, although his quotations, vi., 170–1, show it to have been considerably different.

[1] This seems to have been a later addition, see ix., 573. But the
design was declared on the first page, iv., 299.

[2] IV., 299–300, ix., 623. In June, 1787, in the Convention at Philadelphia, Gerry (from Massachusetts) remarked: "The people in that
quarter [the Eastern States] have at this time the wildest ideas of government in the world. They were for abolishing the Senate in Massachusetts, and giving all the other powers of government to the other branch
of the legislature." Elliot's *Debates*, v., 158.

delivered a counter attack in defense of the bicameral system, with a single executive, the existence of which he believed to be menaced. Hence the greater part of his work loses sight of Turgot, and ranges over almost the whole field of the science of government. Through its mazes we shall follow him; and, therefore, the writings of this period are the principal subject of our study.

I. DEVELOPMENT OF THE THEORY

CHAPTER IV

DIVISION AND CLASSIFICATION OF GOVERNMENTS

ADAMS commences his work by declaring that since antiquity there have been three great discoveries in the constitution of a free government—representation, separation of three departments, and threefold division of the legislative department (iv. 284). These three elements in a free government he seems to regard as equally important and equally essential, the presence of any one or two without the third being ineffectual (*cf.* 523). But he does not consider that they call for equal emphasis in his treatment of them. On the contrary, in his treatment they are of rising importance. The first, representation, is taken as such a matter of course that very little is said about it—in fact, too little, as we shall have occasion to lament. Remain, then, two principal features in Adams's description of a free government: the separation of three departments, and within one of them what he calls the separation of three orders. To defend these two principles, he said in the midst of his labors, was the object of his writing.[1]

[1] IX., 552 (*cf.*, later, 624). Repeated reference to them: iv., 382, 398, 440, 521, 544, 559, 578, v., 89, 112, 180, 220–1, 228, 257, 426, 450, vi., 44, 50, 168, 189, 488.

Here again the first is regarded as a matter little in dispute, and therefore calling for little attention. Under it comes the principle, still always maintained, that the judges must have an estate in their offices during good behavior (v. 180). But as they are to be appointed by the executive, the separation of the judiciary does not seem to fulfill Adams's demand for completeness. Nor again is there completeness in the separation of the executive from the legislative, since the executive chief is made an essential branch of the legislative. The scheme is an involved one, described as existing "where the executive is in one hand, the legislative in three, and the judicial in hands different from both" (vi. 189), but in which the one executive hand is itself one of the three legislative hands. This he calls a "political trinity in unity, trinity of legislative, and unity of executive power, which in politics is no mystery."[1] But the unity is rather inside the trinity, and at the same time outside it; which would be mysterious even in religion. The executive chief, however, both as such and as a branch of the legislative, is to be independent of the other two branches, and (if these together be called the legislature proper) independent of the legislature; yet, as we shall see, not completely even so, since through requirement of ministers and responsibility of these to the legislature, even this separation of the executive from the legislature is seriously impaired. The great principle, then, almost singly harped upon by Adams, is the "triple"

[1] VI., 128, cf. v., 316. The phrase "a trinity in unity" had been used in the same connection by W. D. Douglass, *A Summary, Historical and Political, of the first planting, progressive improvement, and present state, of the British Settlements in North America*, Boston, 1755, vol. i., p. 214. It was later ridiculed by Bentham, *To his Fellow-Citizens of France*, Sect. xii., § 8.

or "tripartite" composition or combination of a "triple-headed" legislative,[1] or, more simply, the division of the legislative department into three branches.

These three branches he furthermore requires to be equal and independent.[2] Two of them are solely legislative, the one other is a single executive first magistrate, endowed with legislative power in the right of proposing or recommending laws and in the authority to veto bills passed by the legislative chambers. It is the bicameral system in close conjunction with a single independent executive; in which system, as we shall see, the saving principle is a balance, not between the two departments, but between the three branches,— a "perfect balance" (iv. 354), which requires their triplicity and their equality. The feature perhaps the most insisted upon, because the most often denied and refused, is the negative, or absolute veto, in the hands of the executive chief, the absolute negative of each chamber upon the other being in his day conceded. "The noble invention of the negative of an executive upon a legislature in two branches" (v. 44), is one description of his plan. Another is, "the necessity of a strong and independent executive in a single person, and of three branches in the legislature [=legislative] instead of two, and of an equality among the three" (iv. 559). "So simple an invention" (v. 45), so "obvious" a remedy (23), he wondered had not early been hit upon (vi. 323, cf. v. 121), instead of being reserved for the English to reduce to practice.[3] He himself, how-

---

[1] VI., 96, 99, 108, 127, 215.

[2] IV., 497, 521, 559; 371, vi., 127, cf. iv., 296.

[3] IV., 296, 447, 497, 528, 559.—The Lacedæmonians came nearest, 553, the Romans next, 541; the Carthaginian government was most like our State governments, 470; also Rhodes in antiquity, and Neuchatel in his

ever, added complexity to it at times, by mixing up this with the other part of his plan, and requiring four things, "an independent executive authority, an independent senate, and an independent judiciary power, as well as an independent house of representatives" (vi. 399).

The great point contended for, once more, is the division of the legislative department into "three equiponderant, independent branches" (vi. 323), the equiponderance being obtained by giving to each equal power, at least in the final disposition of any legislative matter (for in taxation he apparently would allow origination to be confined to the lower house), that is, by arming each with a negative upon the motions of the others before their enactment into laws. The executive must have this absolute veto as well as each of the chambers. Only thereby can be obtained an equalization of the three branches and a balance between them, only thereby the entrance of the executive into the legislative and so into the supreme body in the nation, only thereby what he calls "an equal, independent mixture of all" the three elemental kinds of government.[1]

For Adams accepts the classical division of simple government into monarchy, aristocracy, and democracy, which he defines as the governments respectively of one, of few, and of all.[2] And he does so in spite of

own day, he treated as fairly good, 377. The whole plan was never thought of in antiquity, 474, 497, 503, nor in the Italian republics— Genoa, vi., 102, *cf.* 112; Siena, v., 220–1; Florence, 121. Possibly Epaminondas might have discovered it, had he lived longer, iv., 515. Machiavelli did not think of it, v., 44, but came near to it, 67, 183.

[1] VI., 272, similarly 108, 124, iv., 474, v., 108.

[2] IV., 328; v., 460–2, vi., 470, 448.—Ancient writers who distinguished the three kinds without speaking of the mixture, using various terms, are Herodotus, iii., §§ 80–2; Xenophon (of Socrates), *Memorabilia*, IV., vi., 12; Isocrates, *Panathenaicum*, § 50; Æschines, *Adv. Timarchum*, § 4,

maintaining that no such simple governments, by themselves, have ever existed (vi. 470), or at least two of them rarely (448), but, he insists, simple democracy never, or for the briefest periods[1]; and most governments have been very imperfect mixtures, until the English hit upon the equal mixture. He defines simple government as "a power without a check, whether in one, a few, or many" (iv. 440)—that is, a single power, in either of these three forms, entirely unchecked by either of the other two; but he does not keep strictly to this definition, and applies the term to governments in which one of the powers is very slightly checked by the others,—lopsided mixtures that present the predominance of one element. These he admits to have existed, and in abundance.[2] On the other hand, mixed governments also admit of degrees, ranging down from that in which the mixture is perfectly equal, to less

---

Adv. Ctesiphontem, § 6; Strabo, *Geographia*, p. 7 (Casaubon's ed.); Seneca, *Epist.*, 15; Quintilian, *Instit. Orat.*, v., 10; Plutarch, *De unius in repub. domin.*, § 3 (with the three perversions); Pseudo-Plutarch, *De vita et poesi Homeri*, c. 182; Sallustius, *De Diis et Mundo*, c. 10.

[1] IV., 301, 303 (not even among the gods), vi., 111 (the Italian the nearest). Never did or can, vi., 210; no examples of, iv., 379, v., 5, vi., 198; never has been tried, vi., 157, *cf.* 122; impracticable, iv., 488 (Athens but "a transient glare of glory"); commits suicide, 484 (in a later writing); merely a nation without government (= anarchy), vi., 211.—The non-existence of truly simple governments (except at least the monarchical) had been taught before by Thomas Smith, *The Commonwealth of England*, 1584, I., vi. (ed. of 1640, p. 9); Harrington, *Oceana*, etc., pp. 48, 393; Algernon Sydney, *Discourses Concerning Government*, III., xxi., II., xix., *cf.* I., x., II., xvi.; Paley, *Principles of Moral and Political Philosophy*, VI., vi.: and since by Dugald Stewart, *Lectures on Political Economy* (ed. by W. Hamilton), vol. ii., pp. 354, 355; Mackintosh (as we shall see later); Brougham, *Political Philosophy*, vol. ii., pp. 2–4 (Sparta and Venice the only pure aristocracies that lasted, the United States the only permanent pure democracy).

[2] He speaks of "near two hundred simple monarchs in Europe," vi., 121.

perfect mixtures, but always such that no one element is essentially and preëminently, distinctly and indisputably predominant. They therefore run down by insensible degrees into the laxly-called simple governments. Strictly speaking, at each extreme, the perfectly mixed and the perfectly simple governments are only of ideal existence, unless the English, and following them the Americans, have realized the former.[1]

---

[1] The idea of the superiority of the mixed system has come down from antiquity, Adams quoting to this effect Polybius, vi., §§ 3–18; Dionysius of Halicarnassus, ii., § 7, vii., 55; Cicero, *De Re Publica* (i., §§ 45, 54, 69, ii., 41, 65), (these three found it in Lacedæmon and in Rome); and Tacitus, *Annales*, iv., § 33 (who, however, despaired of its realization). He might have added Plato, *Laws*, iv., 712 D–E (for what he quotes from *The Republic*, iv. and viii., is about the simple governments only, as also *The Statesman*, 291 D–292A, 301A–303B, which doubles the three and leaves over a seventh); Aristotle, *Politics*, II., ix. (or xii.), 2, IV., x. (or xii.), 4, *cf.* II., vi. (or ix.), 15, [who found it at Athens, and to whom the term "mixed" is due, but who did not, in his list of polities, *ib.*, III., v. (or vii.), *Nic. Ethics*, VIII., x. (or xii.), and *Eud. Ethics*, VII., ix., 4, cf. *Pol.*, IV., vi. (or viii.), vii. (or ix.), clearly distinguish and separate the mixed from the three, or six, simple kinds, which was left for Polybius to do. Adams never quotes Aristotle on this subject, but he does quote Portenari, who followed Aristotle closely, v., 453 ff.]; the Stoics (in Diogenes Laërtius, VII., i., 131), among them Dicæarchus, who wrote a work entitled *Tripoliticus* (see Zeller, *Philosophie der Griechen*, iii., 892–3); and Cato (who found it at Carthage, according to Servius, *ad Virgilii Æn.*, iv., 682). In early modern times the mixed state was accepted and praised by Machiavelli, *Discorsi sopra Tito Livio*, I., ii. (merely paraphrazed Polybius); Contarini, *De Magistratibus et Republica Venetorum*, 1544, p. 25 (found it in Venice, pp. 28, 96); John Poynet, *Short Treatise of Politicke Power*, 1556 (quoted by Adams, vi., 4); Hotman, *Franco-Gallia*, 1573, c. 12 (*Opera*, 1600, vol. iii., cols., 40–1, found it anciently in France); Henry Nevill, *Plato Redivivus, or Dialogues Concerning Government*, 2d ed. 1681 (found it in England, p. 139); Mrs. Hutchinson, *Memoirs of Colonel Hutchinson*, p. 5 (ditto); W. D. Douglass, *op. cit.* (found it in the American colonies, vol. i., pp. 213–14); J. Entick, *Present State of the British Empire*, London, 1774 (ditto, vol. iv., p. 302, copying the preceding). Other English advocates of it will be noticed later. It was rejected by Bodin, *De la Republique*, II., i. (ed. of 1583, pp. 253–70, *cf.*, 272–3, 339, not even in England, which is a

On the subject of the kinds of government and their definitions, Adams is not altogether uniform. Besides the division into three simple and one mixed form, yielding in all only four conceivable kinds of government, as he later expressly said (vi. 467, 474), he sometimes divides governments into despotism, where one man holds all the three departments, monarchy, where one man holds the executive and the legislative, but not the judicial, and republic, where the three departments are separate; and as sovereignty is said to follow the legislative department, and therefore in both despotism and monarchy one man is sovereign, "republic" is left over as any government in which the sovereign is "vested in more than one" (428). Here the use of "monarchy" simply so-called is peculiar, differentiating this from "simple monarchy," which has already been defined in a way that identifies it with what is here called "despotism," and from "limited monarchy," which we shall presently see defined in a way that subsumes it under "republic."[1] Little use, however, is made of the terms "despotism" and "monarchy" simply so-called.[2]

---

monarchy, 139–42), and by Hobbes, *Leviathan*, chs. 19, 29, and 42; discountenanced by Pufendorf as an "irregular state," *De Jure Naturæ et Gentium*, VII., v., 2, 12–15, *De Officiis Hominis*, II., viii., 2, 12; allowed by Heineccius, *Elementa Juris Naturæ et Gentium*, II., vi., 118, 126; and preferred by Burlamaqui, *Principes du Droit de la Nature et des Gens*, Droit des Gens, II., ii. (ed. of 1820, vol. iv., pp. 169, 189–206 (especially that of England, p. 194). Again praised by Mably, *Entretiens de Phocion*, 1783, vol. i., p. 74, it was again rejected by Tocqueville, *De la Démocratie en Amérique*, vol. i., ch. vii., sect. 3.

[1] The above division of governments was taken probably from Montesquieu, *Esprit des Lois*, II., i.; and the peculiar definition of "monarchy" was suggested possibly by the same writer, *ib.*, XI., vi. (near beginning). Influential also may have been Paley, *loc. cit.*

[2] Yet in two passages his fourfold division of governments is made up of these: "despotism, monarchy, aristocracy, and every mixture,"

"Republic," is the important word. And the definition of this as a government in which "the sovereignty resides in more than one man" he later called the "strict definition of a republic."[1] Again, however, he defines it, at least when using the term "with approbation," as "a government in which the people have collectively, or by representation, an essential share in the sovereignty (vi. 415, cf. 454),—not necessarily the whole sovereignty, which is the attribute of simple democracy (448, 470). Indeed, he particularly objected to the definition of "republic" in such a shape as to mean nothing but simple democracy (v. 454). Yet, as in our American States, than which "governments more democratical never existed," it is possible, in his opinion, for the people to retain the whole sovereignty, the right of which is "in all nations unalienable and indivisible," without being solely and simply democratical, by admitting also monarchical and aristocratical branches in the "legislature" (iv. 308–9). Once more, he defines the term as the empire, not of men, but of laws,—of fixed and equal laws, or where all men are equally subject to the laws; and emphatically pronounces this "the true and only true definition of a Republic."[2] Then again he predicates this definition only of "free republics" (iv. 371), leaving over republics that are not free (v. 37), that is, not subject to fixed laws (cf. iv. 403), such as Poland (x. 378), which he considered worse even than an absolute monarchy (iv. 367), and Venice, nearly as bad, and Holland and Bern, very little better.[3]

leaving out democracy, which then is added separately, making five, vi., 145–6, 469.

[1] X., 378. Yet he had rejected this definition in v., 453, and treated it dubiously, 37.   [2] V., 453; so in his early period, iv., 106, 194, 204.

[3] VI., 415. Cf. The Essex Result, where Parsons says not all republics are free, and instances Venice and Holland, Parsons's Parsons, 365, 366.

Here a light is thrown upon his meaning. "Republic," when used "with approbation," and "free republic," evidently are the same; for he conceived that only where the people have an essential share in legislation are they all equally subject to fixed laws and consequently free,[1] and only there did he give his approval. But beyond this free and approved republic, he used the term of any government in which any number of men share in the actual sovereignty, even a few, down to two, and therefore included under it such aristocratical and oligarchical governments as the ones mentioned. And it was only a slip when he once applied one of the narrower definitions to "republic" in general.[2] The wider definition, however, is so comprehensive that it includes practically all governments, and we are not surprised, therefore, when he later tells us that the word "republic" "may signify anything, everything, or

[1] *Cf.* Penn's *Preface* to the *Frame of Government of Pennsylvania* (which, by the way, was in many parts modeled on Harrington's *Oceana*): "Any government is free to the people under it (whatever be the frame) where the laws rule, and the people are a party to those laws" (Poore's *Charters and Constitutions*, p. 1519). Franklin in 1768 demanded as much without expressing contentment with it, *Works*, Sparks's ed., vol. ii., p. 372. It is all that was claimed by B. Church, Boston Massacre oration, 1773, in Niles's *Principles and Acts of the Revolution*, 2d ed., 1876, p. 36A, and by the Congress in 1774 in their *Declaration of Rights*, which was drafted by Adams, ii., 538, 377, vi., 278 and n. It satisfied even Price, *On Civil Liberty*, 1776, 11th ed., p. 10. It was, of course, considered sufficient by such an English statesman as Lord John Russell, *The English Government and Constitution*, 2d ed., 1866, p. 87. And direct election by the people in one branch of the legislative was all that the framers of our Federal Constitution desired: see Gerry, Madison, and Dickinson, in Elliot's *Debates*, v., 137, 160, 161, 163. Sherman did not even want so much, *ib.*, 136. *Cf.* Cabot (quoted by H. Adams, *History of the United States*, i., 86); Jay, *Correspondence*, iv., 337; Story, *Commentaries*, §§ 572, 586.

[2] Except in the early period, when he did not have the wider definition, and "republic" alone regularly meant what "free republic" now means.

nothing"[1]; and we do not learn much when he affirms that republican are the only good governments,[2] although he is a little more definite when saying "a free republic is the best of governments."[3]

Now, further, he divides republics, like simple governments, into monarchical, aristocratical, and democratical, the first (also called limited monarchy) existing where "the supreme executive" is "a branch of the legislature,"[4] the other two, though distinguished from each other (x. 378), being nowhere defined or distinguished from simple aristocracy and simple democracy (whose definitions bring them under the broad definition of "republic," and the last apparently even under the narrow, at least in theory, if not in practice). A limited monarchy is a republic because a government of laws (iv. 296), in the making of which the people have a share. So England is a republic, but a monarchical republic.[5] So, too, the ancient Lacedæmon he considered a republic, in spite of its kings, and a monarchical republic because of them (and somehow in spite of there being two of them), the only reason apparent for its being called a republic being that "it was a mixture of monarchy, aristocracy, and democracy," although badly balanced, too much power being assigned to the aristocratical element (iv. 553).

---

[1] X., 378 below, cf. 377-8; apparently referring to iv., 370 or v., 453.

[2] Not only in his early period, iv., 194, 204, vii., 593, when the statement meant something, but also now, vi., 415.

[3] IV., 370. He had said this in his early period simply of "a republic," 194, 204, with the same meaning.

[4] VI., 428; i. e., a limited monarchy, as we shall see more fully as we proceed, is where the king or first magistrate, whatever his title, has the whole executive power and a part (an undivided third) of the legislative power.

[5] IV., 462, vi., 428; cf., in the early period, iv., 106, 194, 209.

Toward the end of this period he raised the question
whether our new Federal Government was not a monarchical republic (vi. 429), because of the great power
entrusted to a single executive chief, greater than that of
any archon, consul, avoyer, or stadtholder, nay, than
of many a king[1]; and concluded, as he later expressed
himself, that it "has some resemblance to a monarchy"
(vi. 470), only not enough, since it allows, like our
State governments [and like the Lacedæmonian] too
much authority to the aristocratical element in the
Senate (430–1).   There is perceptible here an inclination to identify republican with mixed government, and
in badly mixed governments, at least in cases where the
aristocratical or democratical element predominates,
to designate the republic according to the predominant
element.[2]   It is significant that when he divided "government" into the three kinds, he added a fourth mixed
of them, but when he divided "republic," into the three
kinds, he did not add a fourth mixed of them. This was
probably because he already conceived all the three
kinds of republics as mixed of all the three kinds of
simple government, and differing only in the prominence of one or another element.   But in the case of
"monarchical republic," he would use the term wherever
the first magistrate, with a negative upon the legislature, happens to be named a king and by old tradition is
looked upon as a monarch.   Yet if the English government were really mixed in exactly equal proportions,
as he conceived it to be, it would no more deserve to be
called a monarchical than an aristocratical or democratical republic.   And as our governments have not a

[1] VI., 430, viii., 493, later vi., 470.
[2] E. g., iv., 469, 542, 561 (in the headings,—or were these added by
the editor?).

king even in name, they would not deserve to be called monarchical, unless the first magistrate's authority exceeded that of the other elements, which he has expressly said it does not. Moreover, the fact that our first magistrates are not hereditary, but elective, gives our people participation also in the executive department, as they further have in our elective senates, and thus in all the branches of the legislative power, or sovereignty: which is a condition so entirely different from having only one share in the government, that our form of government would seem to be properly distinguished from the English by saying that the one is a republic and the other not, or at least that if the latter is, the former is not, a monarchical republic.

On the whole, it must be admitted there is much confusion in Adams's terminology on this subject. His broad definition of "republic" is absurdly broad, almost identifying "republic" with "government" itself. His narrow definition of it as "free republic," is still too broad, being proper enough as a definition of "free government," but "free republic" is still something less comprehensive than that. Also his first definition of "democracy," as the government of *all*, seems to have been a mistake, even from his own point of view, though required by sentiment. For we shall see him frequently treating the democratical element[1] in mixed government as the share in the sovereignty belonging to the *many*.[2] Had he in the beginning

---

[1] This term "element" he never used, and in his later period objected to its use by some one else in application to the simple governments in mixed government which he himself described as compounded of them, vi., 474, 475. He here merely rejected common usage.

[2] *E. g.*, iv., 508. In vi., 448, it is, ambiguously, "sovereignty in the many, that is, in the whole nation, the whole body, assemblage, congregation."

defined "democracy" as the government of many and
"republic" as the government of all, he would not only
have abided by the original meaning of the term, but
have made a more symmetrical arrangement. Then
every mixed government would have been brought
under the definition of "republic," since every mixed
government includes all the elements that make up
society[1]; and an imperfectly mixed government would
have been avowedly designated a monarchical, an
aristocratical, or a democratical republic, merely accord-

---

[1] In the Greek nomenclature the mixture or combination of the three
partial governments was necessary to make up the complete government
of all. Democracy could not enter the mixture if it were already the
government of all. Unfortunately Aristotle did not add his "mixed"
government as a seventh, but apparently treated the perfect form as one
of the three good forms, the "timocracy" or "polity" proper (*i. e.*,
republic); and yet he made this the government of "the many" (and of
this, for him, "democracy" was a perverted form), *Pol.*, III., v. (or vii.),
cf. *Nic. Ethics*, VIII., x. (or xii). The responsibility for mixing the
government of the whole with the governments of the parts, belongs to
Cicero, who, however, did not use the term "democracy," but appro-
priately called it the government of the whole people, "res publica
popularis," *De Re Publica*, i., § 42. Hence "all" instead of "many" has
been not uncommonly used by modern writers, and most ineptly connected with "democracy" (perhaps also being misled by Thucydides,
who made democracy government by the whole *demos*, vi., § 39, which
of course is not the whole people, but only the many, *cf.*, ii. § 37). Thus
Hobbes, *Leviathan*, ch. 19; Pufendorf, *De Jure*, etc., VII., v., 3 and 12,
De Officiis, II., viii., 3; Heineccius, *Elementa Juris*, II., vi., 116, 117, 130;
Burlamaqui, *Principes*, vol. iv., p. 145. Ambiguous had been, *e. g.*,
Bodin, *De la Republique*, all or the large part of the people, indifferently,
II., i. (p. 252, again pp. 338, 937; "all the people," p. 251; "the larger
part," pp. 313, 329, 332, 339); Harrington, *Oceana*, "the whole people,"
p. 38, "the many," p. 387; Paley, "the people at large," either republic
or democracy, *loc. cit.* The right definition had been given by, *e. g.*,
Poynet, "the multitude" (quoted by Adams, vi., 4); Th. Smith, *Commonwealth of England*, "the multitude," "the people," "many and the
most part," I., i., iii., xiv. (with mistake of identifying "democracy"
with "republic" or "commonwealth").

ing to the feature that is most prominent.[1] But this, while excluding from "mixed government," would have included under "republic" the government of all collected in one assembly, and would have prevented such a government from being called a "democracy." To avoid such an unpleasant collocation and separation, Adams might have identified this kind of government more effectually with "democracy" and have distinguished it more effectually from "republic," than he did, by expressly defining "democracy" as a government in which all the departments are collected into one and this one is or represents and is dependent upon many or all of the people, and by defining "republic" as a government in which the departments are separate and each separately represents and is dependent upon the whole people[2]; or, in other words, by defining "democracy" as a simple government of the many or of all, and "republic" as a mixed government of all, but so thoroughly mixed that the mixture enters into every department (and really disappears, they becoming homogeneous), instead of its being confined to the popular branch of one department, as is the case with monarchical and aristocratical mixed "free governments," where certain entire departments and one or another branch of the third are monopolized by the one and the few, holding in their own independent right. But, again, such a use of terms would have excluded from being called a republic the model government of

[1] As was done, for instance, by Th. Smith, *op. cit.*, I., vi., and by Sydney, *Discourses*, I., x., II., xvi., xviii., xxx.

[2] Such a definition of "republic" was presented to Adams by Sherman, vi., 437; but Adams did not accept it. *Cf.* Jefferson's later statement, which expresses the opinion now prevalent: "It is a misnomer to call a government republican, in which a branch of the supreme power is independent of the nation" (= people), *Works*, Ford's ed., x., 199.

England. To include this, he had to make it sufficient, to constitute a republic, that one alone of several branches of one department should represent and be dependent upon the people,—a definition which he maintained notwithstanding its demerit of letting in democracy to be a species of republic.[1] For there is apparent on Adams's part a propensity to manipulate his definitions so as to fasten the, in his day, disreputable term "democracy" upon the kind of government he was specially impugning, and while feeling constrained to admit such a government also into the circle of "republics," to stretch this respectable term to cover all the governments he approved, especially the English, even at the price of including, beside that reprobated government, other governments which he condemned, such as those of Poland and Venice, which latter two, however, he still kept out of the inner circle of "free republics,"—and practically the former one also.[2]

Through the labyrinth of this subject a clue had a couple of centuries before been provided by Bodin in his treatise *De la Republique*, wherein he invented an illuminative distinction, which has been undeservedly neglected, and seems unfortunately to have been unknown to Adams. This is the distinction between the nature of the *state* and the nature of the *government*, the former being determined by the location of the sovereignty, the latter by the derivation of the adminis-

[1] So in x., 378, condemning Madison's distinction between democracy and republic as two kinds. According to Adams, "republic" connotes less and denotes more than "democracy."

[2] In his early period he had been bolder. He then advised the colonies, upon becoming independent, "manfully" to adopt the name of "Commonwealth," ix., 425, 430, in spite of its being "unpopular and odious," *cf.* iv., 462. In the present period no more use is made of this term.

trators.[1] Bodin himself applied this distinction only to the three forms, monarchy, aristocracy, and democracy (concerning which a neat use of words would be to call the *governments* monarchic, aristarchic, or demarchic, and the *states* monocratic, aristocratic, or democratic); and he did not mark off the mixed state (though he did allow compound, if not mixed governments).[2] We, however, may extend the distinction. When there are two or more divisions in the government equal and collateral with each other, the government, composed of these, may properly be allowed to be mixed (and if there are three such, it may be called triarchic). And now if these divisions (at least two of them) extend down into the people, each division in the government resting upon, or representative of, a class or order in the people, (and the king himself being the greatest land-lord in the country), then each of these classes is equal to another, and the sovereignty is equally possessed by each in undivided shares, and the state, consisting of the whole people, which is heterogeneous, is compounded of these three elements, and may properly be likewise allowed to be mixed (and tricratic). But if the divisions in government each rest upon or is representative of the whole people, then the government alone is mixed, the people is homogeneous, and the state is simple. This simple state differs from the simple states monocratic, aristocratic, or democratic, in that in it the sovereignty resides in the whole people (it is panto-cratic), whereas in them it resides in the one, the few, or the many. In the mixed state, also, which is composed of the one, the few, and the many, and thus made up of all, the sovereignty resides in all, but differently,

---

[1] *De la Republique*, pp. 272, 330, 338–9, 1050.
[2] *Ib.*, pp. 339, 1013–14.

because it is shared by three separate divisions of the whole people. Thus, beside the three simple states, there is left over, not only a mixed state of all, but also another simple state, of all; and this last is properly, in modern parlance, the republican'state. For example, while France before the Revolution, like every absolute one-man constitution, was both monarchic and mono-cratic (the Russian Czar still being both a monarch and an autocrat), England (in Adams's conception and actually at one time) was both triarchic and tricratic; but America is slightly triarchic and almost wholly pantocratic,—and because of this last feature it alone of the three is republican (though England to-day hangs on the edge of being such, and the France of to-day of course is). In the mixed state the government ought likewise to be mixed; but of a republican state the government need not be mixed; and to make it truly (or equally) mixed, is to introduce a tendency to bring about a mixture also in the state, and for it a division of classes or orders among the people. And this we shall find recognized by Adams, and to be aimed at by him; for we shall find him wishing to bring the same orders into the American people that he wished to establish in our governments. And his wish being father to his thought, we shall soon find him asseverat-ing that the American people, and all wealthy peoples, necessarily are already divided into such orders; whereby he will be enabled to turn the argument around and say that because the people is heterogeneous and mixed, the government ought to be so too. Still, before coming to this, we must notice his treatment of the simple governments so far as, in his opinion, mixed states have mistakenly tried to set them up, without ever succeeding.

CHAPTER V

BADNESS OF SIMPLE GOVERNMENTS, AND NEED OF A BALANCE

SIMPLE governments, in Adams's opinion, are bad governments; that is, governments are worse the closer they approach to the limit of simplicity, in any of its three forms. Only mixed governments are good governments; and only as they approach the proper scheme of equal mixture already sketched, do they approach perfection. All this Adams thinks he proves both by experience and by reason (*cf.* viii. 650).

His appeal to experience does not call for much attention, although it forms the bulk of his work. He runs through the small republics left over in Europe— "on a barren rock, a paltry fen, an inaccessible mountain, or an impenetrable forest" (iv. 290, *cf.* 380, vi. 109)—San Marino, Biscay, some Swiss cantons—that have been praised as models of democracy, to show that they are not simple democracies; and he devotes many pages to surveying ancient and mediæval (Italian) republics, to show that they were not properly mixed governments; in all cases endeavoring to show that the best and longest-lived were and are those that approach nearest to his model, the English (iv. 469, 542, *cf.* vi. 108)—almost the only one that he does not historically or analytically investigate. English history has been as tumultuous as any; but, Adams says, its civil dissensions occurred before its government received the equal balance (vi. 398–9, *cf.* 488–9). Exactly when the balance was instituted, he does not tell in his polemical works of this period, and so avoids the confession that its short duration is insufficient to prove the permanence of this form of government; and yet in a later apologetical writing he says the balance was not established till the revolution of 1688, nor fully even then, and was not completed "till the present reign" (vi. 489), referring to an act in the first year of George III., less than thirty years before the composition of his principal work. The emptiness of his position becomes still more manifest, if we reflect that, as will be pointed out more fully hereafter, the very period he names for the introduction of his system into England was in reality the beginning of its extrusion. His argument is at times ludicrously lame. Though upholding a positive, he sometimes puts the burden of disproof upon his opponents, as in gravely declaring that if the Romans, upon the expulsion of the kings, had adopted his plan of government, "it is impossible for any man to prove that the republic would not have remained in vigor and in glory at this hour."[1] In general, whenever he came across an incident that agrees with his principles, he immediately universalized it, thus jumping to his conclusions, instead of gradually building up to them. His reasoning *à priori* concerns us most. It is scattered throughout his works, and its parts must be assembled piecemeal.

Simple governments, then, are bad, because either they are contentious, the seat of sovereignty being ill-defined,[2] or, this being settled, the ruling classes whichever they be, are intolerant, oppressive, imperious. They will not brook criticism, and therefore are hostile to the freedom of the press, to enlightenment, and to

---

[1] IV., 521. For another instance, not quite so flagrant, see 497; and *cf.* v., 180. A similar assertion about the continued duration of the Roman republic, had it but observed the agrarian law of Licinius Stolo, was made by Nevill, *Plato Redivivus*, p. 57.

[2] VI., 228, 230, 251, *cf.* 328, 335, 347, 392.

education, the popular party not the least (vi. 59, 88, 198, 273). They all run into tyranny—monarchy into despotism, aristocracy into oligarchy, democracy into anarchy (iv. 328, *cf.* v. 460–1). The diabolicalness of all "unlimited sovereignty, or absolute power," whether "in a majority of a popular assembly, an aristocratical council," or "a single emperor," he later said, was "the fundamental article" of his "political creed" (x. 174).

Simple democracy, or government collected in one popular assembly, he especially insisted, is as dangerous as any simple aristocracy (vi. 39), as arbitrary, aggressive, and domineering as any kings or nobles,[1] as full of passion—intemperance, ambition, favoritism—as any single individual or small body of individuals.[2] Gradually he concentrated his denunciation upon simple democracy, and in the third volume of his *Defense* it was described as the worst of all—the worst keeper of the public liberties (vi. 87–8, *cf.* 7), the most factious (50), the most corrupt (*cf.* 62), the least constant (157),—in sum, "the most ignoble, unjust, and detestable form of government," its only excellence being that it is the quickest to pass away.[3] In it, the majority will always maltreat the minority—confiscate their property, ex-

---

[1] IV., 480, vi., 252 (*cf.* 114), 417, 380–1 (from Aristotle).

[2] IV., 407, 388 (from Swift), v., 39, 230, vi., 10, 484; already in 1776, x., 405.

[3] VI., 70. In his last period, he set this off against its demerits, and concluded that on the whole it is not more pernicious, being briefest, though bloodiest while it lasts, vi., 477, 483. Still he is reported to have said: "No writer has ever yet displayed all the terrors of democracy in our language. . . . In the history of Naples and of the Italian republics the truest picture of its progress and fate is drawn," Quincy's *Quincy*, 70. In his first period he had expressed a similar opinion, but qualified: "A popular government is the worst curse to which human nature can be devoted, when it is thoroughly corrupted. Despotism is better," ix., 435.

clude them from office, drive them into exile[1]; the poor
will rob the rich[2]; to put these in the power of those is to
confide the lamb, the few, to the care of the wolf, the
many[3]; in its last stages, human "brutality" and "devil-
ism" reach the lowest degrees of depravity (vi. 90).
Next in badness to simple democracy comes simple
aristocracy. This is more safe, peaceful, and durable
(v. 238). It is more austere (vi. 62), preferring merit
to wealth (v. 289), and preserving the morals of the
people (vi. 62). But it is harsh, repressive, crushing
(*cf*. vi. 64). Not so bad, and more liked by the people,
is simple monarchy.[4] In it there is generally some
balance, some check to tyranny, in the nobility and in
the judicature (vi. 281); and the king must favor the
people, to gain their assistance against the nobles.
Apparently, in Adams's opinion, it is, of the three, the
least liable to simplicity. We shall again come across
reference to its superiority over the other kinds of
simple government.

Simple power, unchecked, unbalanced, is bad, because of the badness of human nature. If men were
good without restraint, if of themselves they always
observed the golden rule, there would be no need of
government.[5] The legislator must presuppose their
natural badness.[6] In a general way, men are "a very

[1] V., 228, 232, 485, vi., 7, 10, 109–11, 114.

[2] VI., 9, 66, 89–90, 418, 516; so, later, x., 268.

[3] V., 345 n., ix., 571. But in vi., 512, in his later period, he inverts this,
taking the many for the lamb and the few for the wolf. In vi., 68, he
speaks of either the many plundering the few or the few fleecing the
many; *cf*. ix., 562; and in vi., 280, each in turn is treated as lamb or wolf.

[4] VI., 121, 415. Example of Rome: the regal government better
than the senatorial which followed it, vi., 73, *cf*. 61, iv., 546–7.

[5] So Machiavelli, quoted iv., 410; himself, v., 273.

[6] From Machiavelli, iv., 408; from Hume, vi., 415.

good kind of creatures" (iv. 407); but this applies to
them under the constraint of government; when they
are in the government, controlling others, not controlled
themselves, their weakness rather than their wicked-
ness is at fault (cf. 406), and they fall under the sway
of their passions, which are unlimited.[1] The love of
liberty, benevolence for the public good, the influence of
religion, cannot be relied upon.[2] The "aristocratic"
passions—love of gold, love of praise, love of power
(iv. 406)—impel some men to override others. This is
true of all classes. The passions, unbridled, are the
same in all men, whether king, nobility, or popular
assembly.[3] No portion of society is "honester or
wiser" than the rest; "they are all of the same clay";
in "usurping others' rights" they are all "equally
guilty, when unlimited in power" (vi. 10). Hence the
common badness of the simple governments. Hence
the need of checks—upon the multitude as well as upon
the nobles (418, cf. 48). Emulation—the love of distinction, the hunger for esteem—is the cause of all
rivalries; but at the same time it is the great driving
force that propels to exertion and accomplishment.[4]
It has by "God and nature" been "implanted in the
human heart for the wisest and best purposes"; and
sound policy requires that our efforts should be directed
not at cooling, extinguishing, or eradicating it, which is
impossible and the attempt impious, but at regulating
it, directing it to honor and virtue, and then stimulating,
cherishing, and cultivating it.[5] "Universal in the

---

[1] The passions unlimited, from Machiavelli, v., 236; from Swift, iv.,
387, 408; himself, 406, vi., 262.

[2] VI., 418; 208, 234; iv., 263; cf. v., 289, 432.

[3] IV., 407, v., 9–10, 39, vi., 484.

[4] VI., 234, cf. v., 40; so, later, viii., 560.

[5] VI., 397, cf. v., 488; vi., 271–2; 246, 397–8.

human heart," he maintained that this passion "is a great spring of generous action, when wisely regulated, but the never-failing source of anarchy and tyranny, when uncontrolled by the constitution of the state."[1] In fact, with regard to the well-known doctrine about the connection between virtue and republican states, he inclined to invert its usual form and to believe that "the virtues have been the effect of the well-ordered constitution, rather than the cause."[2]

"Government is intended to set bounds to passions which nature has not limited" (vi. 276)—especially the passion of emulation. Accordingly, he held, "it is the principal end of government," "the great art, " in which his "philosophy of government" consisted, and to which "the science of government" reduces, "to regulate this passion, which in its turn becomes a principal means of government," by setting up "a form of government in which every passion has an adequate counterpoise," and in which emulation is used as "the only defense against its own excesses."[3] This is to be effected by "scientifically" concerting "that balance of passions and interests, which alone can give authority to reason" (vi. 252, 399), and, in the state, provide an "equilibrium," "the only antidote against rivalries" (323). The balance, however, here

[1] IX., 183, in his last period; but similarly in this period: "Emulation next to self-preservation will forever be the great spring of human actions, and the balance of a well-ordered government will alone be able to prevent that emulation from degenerating into dangerous ambition, irregular rivalries, destructive factions, wasting seditions, and bloody civil wars," vi., 279.

[2] VI., 219, *cf.* iv., 521, 556–7, 557–8, v., 29–30, 289, vi., 109, 125–6, 251, 263, 415, viii., 455, ix., 560; also iv., 410, from Machiavelli (he might have referred to Harrington, *Oceana*, 75–6, *cf.* 515). Not so in his early period, ix., 401, nor even in his last, ix., 636, x., 386.

[3] VI., 234, 248, 276, 284, viii., 560.

referred to, is not so much between different passions as
between the same passions in different classes of society
where they accompany the different interests of those
classes. At least Adams is not here definite, and does
not divide off the passions and array them against each
other, as Plato did[1]; and he treated, as we shall see, the
leaders of the lower classes as actuated by the same
passions that are manifested in the foremost men of the
upper classes.[2] We here approach the examination of
Adams's balance, and in doing so we touch the framework of his "science of government," which will be
found to be based on mechanical principles.

Power can be checked only by power.[3] Now, if there
be only two powers in opposition, it is against all
probability that these will be, or will remain for any
length of time, exactly equipoised. The one will at
some time be weaker, and then ineffectual as a check;
and the other will become unchecked. For the stronger
power, once in action, accumulates momentum, "like
the stone of Sisyphus" (iv. 521). A struggle between
two powers, says Adams, always "continues till one is
swallowed up and annihilated, and the other becomes
absolute master" (vi. 323). In other words, between
two powers there can never be any but an unstable

[1] Adams once wrote: "Men should endeavor at a balance of affec-
tions and appetites, under the monarchy of reason and conscience,
within, as well as at a balance of power without," iv., 407. Here he
bordered on Plato's treatment of politics, but only for a moment. He
had little respect for Plato, from whom, he said, he got nothing of importance, x., 103.

[2] So even, at times, of the classes themselves, once saying that "the
ruling passion of each was the same," v., 10.

[3] Montesquieu, *Esprit des Lois*, XI., iv., is quoted to this effect, iv.,
408. "Power must be opposed to power, and interest to interest," 557.
"Passions, interest, and power, which can be resisted only by passions,
interest, and power," 558.

equilibrium.[1] This he thinks true of bodies of men as well as of physical bodies. Of two assemblies, "one or the other will be most powerful, and whichever it is, will continually scramble till it gets the whole" (iv. 470). There is need, then, of a third power which can "preserve or restore the equilibrium," by throwing "weights into the lightest scale" (vi. 394). Here comes in the idea of a balance, for which are necessary, not two, but three factors,—the third, so to speak, as balancer. Thus he says, "there can be, in the nature of things, no balance without three powers" (iv. 354). With three powers, a stable equilibrium may be obtained by any one of them so acting as to balance the two others and correcting their deflections, or, as we shall later find him also maintaining, by any two combining against a third that has begun to be overbearing.

This idea he applies to governing powers. For a stable government there is need of three such balancing powers—or three orders, or three branches—"and no more" (ix. 556). "A balance can never be established between two orders in society, without a third to aid the weakest" (iv. 391, cf. ix. 570). What he wants, then, are "three different orders of men *in equilibrio*" (v. 10), "three orders forming a mutual balance" (v. 426), three orders or powers supplying as nothing else can (iv. 499) this "only natural" and "complete" "triple" or "tripartite" balance (iv. 347, vi. 108, 341, 128). These three are needed in the state in general (*cf.* iv. 440, 546), not merely in the government. They

---

[1] Adams did not use this phrase. But he used "equilibrium" alone frequently, and said of it: "When it is once widely departed from, the departure increases rapidly, till the whole is lost," vi., 399. Also he used "unstable" in connection with government, iv., 579.

must be in what Adams, forgetting the people, calls the sovereign power, the legislative, for this purpose being required the division into "three equiponderant, independent branches"; for "in this way, and in no other, can an equilibrium be formed."[1] But, for their natural introduction into the government, it is needed, or desired, that they should naturally exist in society. Adams now appears to have thought that he found such three orders of men in society ready to his hand. Here again, however, he will not prove clear or consistent.

CHAPTER VI

THE ORDERS AND CLASSES IN GOVERNMENT AND SOCIETY

IN his first period Adams insisted that all men are born equal, and was glad that in America there were no distinctions of rank. He still admits that men as men equally are men, and are equal morally, civilly, legally, —that they have equal duties and equal rights, and ought to be subject to equal laws[2] (or equally subject to the same laws). But he now dwells upon inequality. Inequalities he finds existing everywhere, and in all things. "Nature, which has established in the universe

---

[1] VI., 323.—This theory of the balance explains why Adams admitted only four kinds of government—the three simple and one mixed of all three. In idea we might form several more "mixtures of two ingredients only," v., 45. But these he conceived to be unstable and sure to run down into one of their simple elements. Even with all three in the mixture he thinks much care is needed to guard against its petering out.

[2] IV., 392, v., 453, 457, vi., 285–6, 458, ix., 570, i., 462.

a chain of being and universal order," he asserts in the
spirit of Leibnitz, "has ordained that no two objects
shall be perfectly alike, and no two creatures perfectly
equal" (vi. 285). So in all societies, even the most
democratic, in the meanest village, clan, or club (vi.
398), even in Massachusetts, "there are inequalities
which God and nature have planted there, and which
no human legislator ever can eradicate" (iv. 392).
These he analyzes into three kinds:—inequality of
wealth, inequality of birth, and inequality of merit.
Wealth, birth, and merit or talents, are causes of superiority.[1] The two former are no more matters of good
luck, than the last, since it is equally an accident to be
born with talents and genius as to be born from rich or
honored ancestors (vi. 396, cf. iv. 427). Inequality of
wealth cannot be prevented; for if properties were
distributed, they would soon be unequal again (vi. 89–
90, cf. 9). Birth is everywhere venerated: the children
of great men not only have better opportunities, but are
more respected (iv. 393, vi. 497), and in democracies
"the people, by their elections, will continue the government generally in the same families from generation to
generation" (124, cf. iv. 393). "Birth and fortune are
as much considered in simple democracies as in monarchies, and ought to be considered in some degree in
all states. Merit, it is true, ought to be preferred to
both; but, merit being equal, birth will generally determine the question in all popular governments; and
fortune, which is a worse criterion, oftener still" (vi.

[1] IV., 392–7, vi., 492. Merit is physical, moral, or intellectual,
cf. 491. In it education and learning are a principal feature, iv., 427, vi.,
185. Knowledge cannot be equally divided, any more than property,
517. Not a fifth, not a tenth, of the people can be regularly educated, 495.

105). These three qualities may be united in a very few individuals and magnify their power enormously (iv. 397, vi., 492). But, singly, each of them confers influence or weight upon its possessors.

Now, the possession of influence over others constitutes Adams's idea of aristocracy[1]; and as such influence arises naturally, he considers aristocracy to be natural. A natural aristocracy is an aristocracy of wealth, of birth, of merit,—singly, of two, or of all combined,— "the rich, the well-born, and the able."[2] Such a natural aristocracy, he maintains, exists everywhere, even where no aid comes from "artificial inequalities of condition, such as hereditary dignity, titles, magistracies, or legal distinctions," or from "established marks, as stars, garters, crosses, or ribbons" (iv. 392, cf. vi. 457); although even in America there are "distinctions established by law" between "laborers, yeomen, gentlemen, esquires, honorable gentlemen, and excellent gentlemen," differing principally from those elsewhere in not being hereditary.[3] With such natural aristocracy he always identifies the nobility, which he does

[1] VI., 504, which is a late writing. In the present period he did not define this term. It may be noticed that he makes little difference between *aristocrats* and *aristoi*. He thinks the latter always have influence, and therefore they come under his definition of the former.

[2] IV., 398, 399, 414, 415, 290; the rich, well-born, and well-educated, 583. Later, a curious variation (of *aristoi*) into "the rich, the beautiful, and the well-born," x., 64, and into "five pillars of aristocracy":"beauty wealth, birth, genius, and virtue," 65, cf. vi., 548.—The term "well-born" aroused much adverse criticism; and was animadverted on even in the conventions called for ratifying the Federal Constitution: see Elliot's *Debates*, iii., 266–7, 272, 295, iv., 311. The use of it by the opponents of the Constitution was referred to by Hamilton in *The Federalist*, Nos. 60 and 75. Cf. McMaster, *History of the People of the United States*, i., 469–71. For Adams's reply see vi., 420, and, later, 495, and his defense from Theognis, x., 58–9, vi., 498–9.

[3] V., 488, cf. vi., 123. "In America," he once said, "there are differ-

not consider of necessity hereditary, and which he asserts exists in every democracy (vi. 124), and which in Massachusetts he points out in certain old families, adding that "reproaches against the aristocratical part of mankind, a division which nature has made, and we cannot abolish, are neither pious nor benevolent" (417). Titles may be abolished, distinctions never (270). The artificial aristocracy may be destroyed, not the natural.

Thus there are orders or ranks in society, whether acknowledged or not. What is the number of these orders or ranks—or, more properly, classes (which term Adams seems to avoid)? Here Adams is not uniform. He divides society, and assemblies also, variously into two, into three, even into two different sets of three, and thereby all told into four, sorts, classes, orders, factions, parties. Indeed, as he spoke of a "chain of being," implying infinite gradations, among all created things, there is room for arbitrariness in the classification of such a series. The division into two is the general division already hinted at into superior and inferior, the upper and the lower classes, the latter "the common people,"—the aristocrats and the democrats, rich and poor, gentlemen and simplemen, learned and ignorant,

ent orders of *offices*, but none of *men*," iv., 380. This is an isolated passage. In the same work he spoke of our congressmen coming "from the natural and artificial aristocratical body in every State," 580. Later, he distinguished "natural aristocracy" as "those superiorities of influence in society which grow out of the constitution of human nature," and "artificial aristocracy" as "those inequalities of weight and superiorities of influence which are created and established by civil laws," vi., 451. But as he thought the members of the latter would still, by reason of their wealth and birth, even though unassisted by civic titles and dignities, be members of the former, he did not pay much regard to the distinction.

—the former few, the latter many; a division which he considered as old as creation, as extensive as the globe, as natural as the distinction between the sexes.[1] The two threefold divisions are, first, into the one, the few, and the many; and, second, into the upper, the middle, and the lower classes. Both of these are spoken of as natural divisions of society, and as constituting three natural orders of men.[2] They have in common the interposition of a middling term between an upper and smaller extreme on the one side and a lower and larger extreme on the other; but the upper in the first case is a topmost, higher than the upper in the second, which corresponds with the middling term in the first, while the lower in the second is a lowest (and largest, the most), beyond the lower in the first, which corresponds

[1] IV., 427, 539 (from Ferguson), vi., 180, ix., 570 (later, 217). "The two orders in the state," vi., 25. "The people, in all nations, are naturally divided into two sorts, the gentlemen and the simplemen," vi., 185. "The great and perpetual distinction in civilized societies, has been between the rich, who are few, and the poor, who are many," ix., 570. In vi., 185 and, later, 531, "the common people "are specified as laborers, mechanics, farmers, and the smaller merchants and shopkeepers. This class he once says comprises 99 per cent. of the population, 280. [Lassalle afterward reckoned it at 96 per cent., and drew a very different conclusion!] It is curious to note the contraposition of poor and vicious vs. rich and virtuous, 66, poor, idle, ignorant vs. rich, laborious, learned, 280, cf. 90 and 185. But he speaks of the middling people as the most industrious and frugal, v., 41.

[2] "Between the one, the few, and the many, or in other words, between the natural division of mankind in society," vi., 428. "A free people met together, as soon as they fall into any acts of civil society, do of themselves divide into three ranks" (the one, etc.), iv., 385; so again of an assembly, 399, and, later, of any body of men, everywhere, always, vi., 464. These three alluded to as the orders of men, iv., 440, vi., 25–6 (in the legislature as well).—"The three natural orders in society, the high, the middle, and the low," v., 90; similarly from Machiavelli, 183; (from Portenari, following Aristotle, he mentions a division into "the very rich, the very poor, and the middling sort," 458).

with the middling term in the second. So are produced
four parts, thus:—

| the one | the few | the many | (the most) |
| (the highest) | the high | the middle | the low |

This result may be viewed as reached through a
double dichotomy. First the whole society, the all, is
divided into the few and the many, the upper and the
lower classes; and then each of these is similarly divided,
the former yielding the one and the few, the latter the
many and the most; and finally the threefold division
is obtained by running together the few of the one set
and the many of the other and speaking of the most
simply as the many. Or, perhaps better, there are
two trichotomies after the first dichotomy. The first
dichotomy is a primary division of all society. Now, as
the few, the upper, are treated as aristocrats, that is, as
men of influence, partaking in the government, and the
lower are the men without influence, the men influenced
by the others, this is a division of society into the governing and the governed. Then each of these sections is
divided triply into a smallest, a middle, and a largest
part; but, the first section being small to begin with, its
smallest part reduces to a single individual; and here
we have the division into the one, the few, and the
many. In fact, this classification is employed by Adams
almost always in connection with the *government*,[1] and
is obviously the same with a division sometimes made
into king, nobles, and commons (iv. 296, 566). But
the moment the governed section is divided into an
upper, a middle, and a lower part (into the nobility, the
commons, and the artificers, as he once described "the

[1] IV., 381, 382, 440, 508, v., 10, vi., 168, 429; (so by Swift, quoted iv.,
384).

three natural divisions of *society*"[1]), the upper and
the middle, by the very fact of their being superior to
the lower, are raised into the ranks of the governing section,[2] where, however, they may not reach the ranks of
those actually engaged in the business of governing.
Those so engaged are viewed by Adams as properly
arranged in the three orders of the (single) king, the
(small)[3] senate, and the (large) house of representatives. The senate, or house of peers, *are* the few among
the governors, and *represent* the few among the governing and governed section; and the house of representatives *are* the many among the governors, and *represent*
the many among the governing and governed section;
but the king, while he *is* the one among the governors,
has no class to *represent*, unless it be some special adherents and partisans or "king's friends," who may be
drawn from any of the classes[4]; which makes a break
in the arrangement, that will cause trouble as we proceed. Under them all, at the bottom, are the most
numerous section or class of the wholly governed—the
plebeians, or rather "the populace, the rabble, the
canaille" (vi. 10), who are generally excluded even
from the franchise, or who, if admitted, cast their votes
under the guidance of others—the men without a will
of their own, along with whom were placed women and
children. The whole scheme may be exhibited as
follows:—

[1] V., 37–8, *cf.* 10 (from Nardi).

[2] Adams later wrote: "Every democracy and portion of democracy
has an aristocracy in it," vi., 516.

[3] At present in England, the House of Lords, if fully attended, is
larger than the House of Commons. But it was not so in Adams's day.
The American colonial councils had also been small bodies.

[4] For his own tenants, if he has any, now vote for the representatives
of their districts, like anybody else.

SOCIETY AT LARGE

Upper Classes		Lower Classes	
one	few	many	(most)
king	senate	representatives	
(highest)	high	middle	low
	nobles	commons	plebeians

Monarchy   *Aristocracy*   *Democracy*

Here the aristocracy is depicted as dividing the commons or the house of representatives with the democracy, because in Adams's plan, as we shall see, the nobles have votes for the representatives in the other chamber also, and in the English House of Commons, his model, peers' sons and relatives, and the gentry, who, though distinct from the peers, are really a part of the aristocracy, sit side by side with the popular leaders, with employers of laborers, distinguished from the laborers employed, who belong to the fourth class.

Thus in this part of his work, the very basis—the bedrock below the foundation—of his system, Adams's treatment of his subject is very unsatisfactory. He desiderates three orders in society, and at times affirms that he finds them; but he finds them differently, getting four in all, and then again contenting himself with two. One fault is an absence of the historical sense. Although running across them occasionally in his reviews of mediæval conditions (*e. g.* vi. 137), he makes no use of the three estates in France, Spain, and England,[1]

---

[1] The three estates existed in England, though the clergy was not so distinctly active there as elsewhere; but they taxed themselves till 1664, and met in Convocation (in two houses) till 1717: see Hallam, *Constitutional History of England*, ch. xvi. In ch. v. Archbishop Parker, under Queen Elizabeth, is quoted as speaking of laws "made and established

where the lower classes were excluded from representation, or of the four estates in Scandinavia and Russia, where the lowest, the hand-workers, the peasants, were admitted. These divisions of society included a distinction between the clergy and the nobility—a bifurcation of the upper classes which Adams never took into account. The distinction between the second and third estates was really between the nobility and the upper stratum of the cities, the leading burghers,—the distinction between aristocracy and plutocracy. Most defective was he in not making use of this distinction—between the land-holding descendants of warriors and the money-making upcomers from the populace—the former, with immobile property, patriotic and conservative, the latter, with mobile wealth, cosmopolitan and liberal (until they, too, acquire land and thus get what the English used to call "a stake in the country"). He met with the distinction in treating of the Italian republics, especially Florence and Siena, where after contentions between the nobility and the people, the latter led by the *popolo grasso* (the fat and rich), the victory of these was followed by contentions between them and the *popolo minuto* (the small and poor); and he had occasion to notice that the rule of the rich merchants was even more hateful to the rest of the people than that of the nobles had been.[1] In his own

by herself and her three estates"; and in the same connection Aylmer, afterward bishop, of "these three estates—the king or queen, which representeth the monarchy, the noblemen, which be the aristocracy, and the burgesses and knights, the democracy." The mistake made by the latter has often been repeated. But when the clergy sheltered themselves behind the king, the king, as far as he took upon himself to represent them, might be considered the head of one of the estates.

[1] V., 10, 41, 44, 234-5, etc.—Not that their rule is actually worse, but it is unmitigated. There has generally been a certain admiration for

country, too, toward the end of his life, he had occasion
to declaim against an "aristocracy," as he continued to
call it, "of land-jobbers and stock-jobbers," an "aristocracy of bank-paper."[1] He was himself by nature
much more of an aristocrat than a plutocrat—was fond
of honorific titles, and wished the prejudice for birth
to be used to counteract the prejudice for wealth (vi.
271, cf. iv. 395), and, like Washington, recommended
only gentlemen for official posts (iv. 583). But to make
this distinction did not fall in with his plan, and he
always entertained the absolutely false conception,
later avowed, that "property is aristocracy."[2] The
truth is, his classifications, in the chain of infinite
gradations, were always made for a purpose, to fit his
own needs. When he thought of contending classes, he
divided society into two, an upper and a lower, indiffer-
ent whether these two were ecclesiastics and aristocrats,
aristocrats and plutocrats, or plutocrats and democrats;
all which he reduced to a contest first between king and
aristocracy, and then between aristocracy and people
(iv. 285, cf. vi. 138). When he desired to provide an
arbiter between them, then he needed a three-sided
arrangement, so as to obtain a balance and an equilibrium, and he bethought him of the old threefold
divisions, and was not scrupulous how he took them.[3]

aristocrats, which has never existed for plutocrats. Plutocracy is essentially ugly. *Cf.* Cicero: "Nec ulla deformior species est civitatis, quam
illa in qua opulentissimi optimi putantur," *De Re Publica,* i., § 51.

[1] X., 70, in 1813; *cf.* vi., 530–1, in 1808.

[2] VI., 514.—Property is plutocracy. Yet it is permissible to say,
aristocracy is property. In an aristocratic state power confers wealth.
In a plutocratic state wealth confers power.

[3] So careless, indeed, was he, that he not only put both the threefold
divisions in the same paragraph, v., 10, but he even combined the twofold and one of the threefold divisions in the same sentence, vi., 50.

In the government proper, this third was a single individual. In society, then, where no class can be composed of only one person, he got this class by making it up of adherents of the one man, or partisans of monarchy. Here, as in the view of the contests, is an account of the division of society, and of government, not so much into orders and classes, as into parties.

With respect to political parties, enters again the same inconsistency. He represents the State, sometimes as naturally and always and only divided into two parties, and sometimes as naturally divided into three parties. In simple governments, in mixed governments, in general, he speaks of a necessary division into the two parties of aristocrats and democrats, rich and poor, gentlemen and simplemen.[1] He once even regretted the absence of "a third party," to act as umpire between them.[2] Elsewhere he has the three parties already provided, telling us that in certain former republics "there were parties,—a monarchical party, who desired to be governed by a king; . . . an aristocratical party, who wished to elect an oligarchy; and a democratical party, who were zealous for bringing all to a level,"[3] and also saying that "there can be no

---

[1] "We have all along contended, that a simple government . . . must of necessity divide into two parties" v., 10, cf. 331. The rich and the poor as such parties, vi., 280; the gentlemen and the simplemen as parties, v., 426, 473. Later: in America (under a mixed government) we have two parties, vi., 530; so long as inequalities exist (i. e., forever) "there will be an aristocratic and a democratical party in every country, especially in opulent commercial countries," 548, similarly 531, 547; he agreed with Jefferson that the two parties "belong to natural history," x., 52, like the sexes, ix., 217.

[2] VI., 430-1. Here, as in v., 79 and 115, what he desired is also described simply as "a third power."

[3] This of the Achaian cities, iv., 503; so in Florence, vi., 116-17; in Italy in general "there were in every city three factions at least," v.,

faction but of the one, the few, or the many" (vi. 181-2).
But all these statements are only about simple governments, and again he once expressed regret that in
certain cases there was no other, *i. e.*, a fourth, party,
"who thought of a mixture of all these three orders"
(iv. 503). And so of simple assemblies, though generally picturing them as divided into three parties (here,
too, doubly described as divisions of the one, the few,
and the many, and of the aristocrats, the men of middling rank and independent in their circumstances, and
the lower and most numerous class of dependents[1]),
he a couple of times described them as ultimately
divided into four parties, three of which are each for one
of the simple kinds of government and the fourth desirous of a mixed government, combining all the three
(586; vi. 272). Here, indeed, we have his complete
account of constitutional parties, corresponding to the
four conceivable kinds of government; but the constitution once settled, these must give way. There remain,
in his opinion, always two political parties, the aristocrats and the democrats, whose contentions he dreaded
(ix. 511), and between whom he desired, not really a
third party, but a third order or power, established in the
constitution of the government, the executive, as we
shall see, to mediate and to moderate. The first party,
of adherents of a simple monarchy, we shall find him
treating as imperfect advocates of such mediation,

289; in America under simple democracy "every town will have three
parties in it; some will be for making the moderator a king, others for
giving the whole government to the selectmen, and a third sort for
making and executing all laws . . . in town meeting," iv., 504.

[1] IV., 399, (*cf.* 385, from Swift); 414. In the last passage the third
class are represented as followers of the first; on 400 the third class are
followers of the second, really the same with the other first, and the
intervening class who neither follow nor have followers, are left out.

while the fourth are the only constitution-makers who successfully establish the conditions that produce it. We might wonder, however, if the three parties naturally exist in all states that have not a settled mixed government, why these do not supply the three elements of the balance Adams desired, and so lead to an equilibrium;—why should the world have waited all the ages for the English recently so to utilize them as to set them at balancing each other? Adams himself only wondered at this last. But he held that in the natural state the three parties did not balance each other because each strove to collect all power to itself and was unwilling to allow equal power to the others by recognizing their right to the negative (*cf.* iv. 503),—because, in short, the powers of each were ill-defined and not respected by the others (*cf.* 566, 578). In other words, he did not think the three natural parties or orders, struggling with each other, would balance, unless they agreed to some rules of the game, some conventional restrictions, some Queensbury regulations, to fight under. The working of the mechanical principles needs to be helped out by some artificial contrivance.

Thus, conceiving that he found "the three orders" "distinctly marked" in the primitive conditions of mankind (566), and being "convinced that three branches of power have an unalterable foundation in nature" and "exist in every society," he held "that if all of them are not acknowledged in any constitution of government, it will be found to be imperfect, unstable, and soon enslaved" (579). He advocated, therefore, that "the three natural orders in society" should all be "represented in the government, and constitutionally placed to watch each other" (v. 90), in order that, by making "legal" the distinctions which naturally arise between men and assigning "to each its share" (261), might be produced a "legal equilibrium."[1]

We, however, perceive that he found no such "three natural orders in society" "distinctly marked," and that the three he did point out he described differently; and we have caught a glimpse, which will grow clearer as we advance, of the fact that he made use of only the broad and indefinitely drawn distinction between two classes—the upper and the lower, the rich and the poor, the aristocrats and the democrats. Each of these, he maintains, must be represented in the government, and in addition they need another power "to hold the balance even between them" (vi. 65). The threefold division of society into the upper, the middle, and the lower, he did not introduce into the government; but, instead, after getting into the government the representatives of the upper and of the middle (to whom might or might not be attached the lower, or more or less of them), he added a third element of an entirely different character. His real desire was, then, to get into government a threefold division which is not found in nature, to set up artificially, and "scientifically," a third indi-

[1] V., 90. So he quotes Harrington's "Unless you share such orders of government as, like those of God in nature," etc., iv., 410 (from *Oceana*, p. 46). Similarly: "We see . . . that the triple balance is so established by Providence in the constitution of nature, that order without it can never be brought out of anarchy and confusion. The laws, therefore, should establish this equilibrium as the dictate of nature and the ordinance of Providence," vi., 341.—In view of his many appeals to authority, it is strange he never quoted Shakespeare's *Henry the Fifth:*—

"For government, though high and low and lower,
    Put into parts, doth keep in one consent,
    Congreeing in a full and natural close,
    Like music."   I., ii., 180–3.

Cf. Cicero, *De Re Publica*, ii., § 69 (in Augustine, *De Civitate Dei*, II., xxi.), which he did quote, iv., 295.

vidual power much more supernatural than natural,—a mediator, umpire, moderator, not provided by nature, between the two which, in his opinion, nature does provide. Thus even the sufficient materials for the balance are not obtained from nature. The element wanting, "the effectual control," must be created, must be "provided in the constitution" (vi. 398, *cf*. v. 68). Only under this view can the wonder be abated why the world has waited so long for the equilibrium, —and may even still continue as to whether we have yet got it. However this be, certain it is that what Adams desired was that instead of two unbalanced orders or parties there should be three powers pitted against one another in the government itself, checking one another, keeping an equilibrium by means of the balancing which is possible (and apparently, in his opinion, once established, everlastingly actual) where there are three independent and fairly equal rivals, any one of whom may uphold the weaker of the other two, any two of whom may combine against the strongest.

CHAPTER VII

CONTROL OF THE ARISTOCRATS IN MIXED GOVERNMENT

THE evils resulting from failure to establish the balance, are much dwelt upon by Adams. Such failure leaves unbalanced or simple governments. Government with all authority "collected into one center," according to Turgot's mistranslated phrase, or government in a single assembly, as Adams misinterpreted it, was the first object of Adams's attack. He frequently traces its inevitable deterioration.

At first a governing body of this sort behaves itself with moderation; then the great men, the aristocrats, most of whom have got into it,[1] will come to the fore and draw power to themselves; leading the people to victory over foreign foes, or fending off invasion, they will be looked up to with gratitude, and the people will acquiesce in their encroachments; gradually they will exempt themselves from burdens; they will lengthen the election periods, till their tenure becomes for life, then hereditary, and finally the assembly is closed except to those itself admits.[2] Thus is set up a simple aristocracy, which may last, if well regulated; but more likely will it divide into factions, following a few great families, becoming an oligarchy, and these will narrow down to two, and lastly one of these will subdue the other, and the end will be in simple monarchy.[3]

Or if perchance the people, by their superior numbers (*cf.* iv. 548), or taking advantage of the dissensions of the nobles, get the upper hand in the assembly and set up a simple democracy, they fall into all the excesses of that worst of all governments, as already described. They will plunder the rich and crush the aristocracy; but another set will gather wealth,[4] another aristocracy will arise (iv. 397), and the old will still exist (vi. 123)

[1] IV., 414; nineteen twentieths of them, composing an eighth to a third of the assembly, 399; *cf.* 587.

[2] IV., 586; example in Geneva, iv., 344. Remember a similar account in the first period, with references to Holland and the English Long Parliament.

[3] Pictured as taking place with greater or less rapidity, iv., 406, vi., 69, and, later, 457–8.

[4] So later, x., 268.

and, without its wealth, without its titles, will exert the influence of birth (*cf.* 270). The demon of inequality and distinction returning, the condition of the people will be sevenfold worse. By these orgies the people themselves are soon frightened,[1] and at last seek safety likewise in simple monarchy —"the eternal refuge of every ignorant people, harassed with democratical distractions or aristocratical encroachments."[2]

Thus simple monarchy is represented as the gulf into which simple democracy is sure, and simple aristocracy is likely, to be swallowed up. So strong he thinks this tendency among all men "towards a kingly power," that he once places "the whole art of government" "in combining the powers of society in such a manner, that it shall not prevail over the laws" (vi. 165). Even where simple aristocracy so ends, it is chiefly because the people unite upon some one aristocratic leader as their champion against the rest of the aristocracy. Or if a king or first magistrate already exists, he can defend himself against the aristocracy, who are as jealous of a superior as they are haughty toward inferiors, only by raising up the people, granting them privileges, calling them into his councils, making an alliance with them, and getting them to put in his hands a standing army for the purpose of protecting *them* against the aristocracy.[3] "It has been the common people, then,

---

[1] So, later, after the experience in France, vi., 477.

[2] IV., 347. Such the exit of almost all the Italian republics, v., 332. He predicted it of France in 1790, vi., 299, unless the other remedy, "a balanced constitution," were adopted, 393.

[3] IV., 355, 362. "Aristocracy is the natural enemy of monarchy; and monarchy and democracy are the natural allies against it," vi., 533 [1808].

and not the gentlemen, who have established simple monarchies all over the world."[1]

But the result of this alliance is that the king becomes the master of the people as well as of the aristocracy (vi. 533). And from the evils of this monarchic despotism the people can be freed again only with the help of the nobles, who, in defending their own rights and liberties, "have been obliged, in some degree, to defend those of the people, by making a common cause with them" (vi. 251), acting as their "able, independent ally" (iv. 463). Thus "the nobles have been essential parties in the preservation of liberty, whenever and wherever it has existed" (417). Then these, in turn, becoming unchecked, things have reverted to oligarchic despotism. Thus the ultimate alternative is always either a simple or absolute monarchy or a simple aristocracy or oligarchy (iv. 371, cf. vi. 273), more likely the former, both bad, that only slightly less so. Monarchic despotism is pictured as set up by the people alone, the oligarchic by the aristocracy alone. The former itself was resorted to as a refuge from the latter; but it turns out to be an unsafe one. The only effectual remedy is for the two classes together to set up one arbiter between them, a king or single executive, in a balanced government, a limited monarchy or a republic. "Let the rich and the poor," urges Adams, "unite in the bands of mutual affection, be mutually sensible of

---

[1] VI., 186. "It has ever been the people who have set up single despots in opposition to the body of the nobility," 125; similarly 120–1. But on 398 he once speaks of both the people and the leaders, wearied with worrying each other, as "setting up a master and a despot for a protector." The Mantuans, "strange to relate! adopted voluntarily an absolute monarchy," v., 484. Already in 1785 he wrote: "I think it has been the people themselves who have always created their own despots," ix., 542.

each other's ignorance, weakness, and error, and unite
in concerting measures for their mutual defense against
each other's vices and follies, by supporting an impartial
mediator."[1]

We have heard Adams assert that the great art of
government consists in regulating the mighty aristocratic passion, emulation, the love of distinction. On
the same line of thought, removed from the abstract to
the concrete, he treats the great problem of government
as being the control of the aristocrats themselves, in
whom that passion mostly manifests itself—the men
distinguished by birth, the wealthy, the superior gen-
iuses,—the eminent few. The *aristoi*, he later wrote,
"are the most difficult animals to manage of anything in
the whole theory and practice of government" (x. 51).
These, in spite of their small number, being augmented
by "their connections, dependents, adherents, shoe-
lickers, etc.," are generally an overmatch to all the
rest. More cunning than a king, more sagacious than
the people, with more art and union, they will generally
prevail.[2] The people, on the other hand, are supine
and humble[3]; preferring ease to liberty (vi. 418),
"they are as sure to throw away their liberties, as a
monarch or a senate untempered are to take them"[4];

---

[1] VI., 396; *cf.*, in a later writing, vii., 348 n.

[2] IV., 355, v., 9, ix., 570. In vi., 58, and, later, 530, he notices their
address in winning over bright young men.

[3] In his early period he wrote of the people being gentle and inclined
to overlook thousands of mistakes in the government, iv., 17.

[4] VI., 87-8. The humility of the people he sometimes treats as caus-
ing the pride of the aristocrats, iv., 419; and, again, he contrasts "the
fatal slumbers of the people, their invincible attachment to a few families,
and the cool, deliberate rage of these families . . . to grasp all authority
into their own hands," iv., 343. "The multitude are as servile as the
few . . . are aspiring; and, upon the whole, there is more superiority in

at first they willingly resign all power "into the hands
of those whom they think their natural superiors"
(vi. 336, *cf.* 345); then finding their trust betrayed,
driven into revolt, if successful, they are violent and
abusive in their turn[1]; but, insubordinate among themselves and inconstant in their unions, they can maintain
their independence upon the aristocrats only by giving
up their power, this time, into the hands of a single
champion.[2] The love of distinction and power on the
one side, and the willingness to grant it on the other;
the abuse of it that follows; the struggle then to resume
the power given away; the entrusting it again to a single
leader; his abuse of it in his turn; liberation from his
tyranny only with the aid of the aristocrats, and again
falling under their domination,—such are the evils he

the world given than assumed," 181, (this last already in the first period,
in 1776, in nearly identical words, ix., 404).

[1] "Mankind have, I agree, behaved too much like horses; been rude,
wild, and mad, until they were mastered, and then been too tame,
gentle, and dull. . . . When the many are masters, they are unruly,
and then the few are too tame, and afraid to speak out the truth. When
the few are masters, they are too severe, and then the many are too
servile," ix., 570. Later, he contrasts "the haughty, arrogant insolence
of aristocracy, and the feeble, timorous patience and humility of democracy," until the latter gets the upper hand, when it is bloody and cruel,
vi., 312 n.

[2] He quotes Swift: "The people are much more dexterous at pulling
down and setting up, than at preserving what is fixed; and they are not
fonder of seizing more than their own, than they are of delivering it up
again to the worst bidder, with their own into the bargain," iv., 388
(from *Contests and Dissentions in Athens and Rome*, ch. 3, *Works*, ed.
1766, vol. iii., p. 43). Under the oppression of the aristocrats the people
harbor "constant secret wishes" "to set up a king to defend them," vi.,
28. "The people in a simple democracy, collectively or by representation, are necessarily the most addicted to setting up individuals with
too much power," 125. "An unmixed, unbalanced people are never
satisfied till they make their idol a tyrant," 123–4. "They instantly give
away their liberties into the hands of grandees, or kings, idols of their
own creation," 64.

paints as besetting humanity until the English learnt
the secret of preserving their liberties without granting
a standing army to the king (iv. 382) and of terminat-
ing "the usual circle" of governments by mixing them
all into one system of mutual control.[1]

To these evils Adams considered mankind more exposed, if the people, or their representatives, and the
aristocrats are combined in one assembly; for there the
aristocracy collect in force and "overawe the people"
(vi. 37), and there "they will have much more power,
mixed with the representatives, than separated from
them" (iv. 445). To propose such an assembly,
therefore, is, "for the commoners, the most impolitic
imaginable"; "to the royal authority it is equally fatal":
"it is the highest flight of aristocracy" (vi. 300, *cf.* 58).
Then, should they be excluded altogether? This remedy the people have tried, and it has always proved
ineffectual. Neither temporary exclusion by rotation
and vacation, nor total exclusion by degradation and
disfranchisement of the nobility, nor even banishment
from the country, have ever availed. The few great
men still rule from the outside, even from abroad,
clandestinely by means of their adherents who are
elected, their tools in the assembly; forcibly, if necessary, by armed retainers.[2] Only one effectual remedy
remains,—and here we approach the kernel of Adams's
system, the great discovery ascribed to the English.
This is to segregate the aristocracy by putting them, at
least the most illustrious of them, together in one

[1] IV., 507–8. [So, of the ancients, Polybius, *Hist.*, vi., § 9, (quoted by
Adams, iv., 443, as also, 418, Machiavelli's copy). For an earlier
account of such revolutions, and of extreme polities going over into their
opposites, see Plato, *Republic*, viii., 563E–564A, and Cicero, *De Re
Publica*, i., § 68, (this not yet discovered in Adams's day).

[2] VI., 53, 68; v., 377–8; 24, 255, 411.

5

assembly, or senate,—in "a hole by themselves," he once phrases it (vi. 419),—where they are severed from their adherents, (he likens it to "an ostracism"), and where, nearly equal among themselves, the greatest of them "can govern few votes more than his own," so that the state may have "the benefit of their wisdom, without fear of their passions."[1] Then there are two assemblies, of the nobles and of the people.[2] But this is not yet enough, since they are still unbalanced, and the assembly of the grandees is likely to overcome the representatives and convert the government into an oligarchy, and finally, in all probability, into a monarchy, just the same as if they were together in one assembly (cf. iv. 336), though perhaps not so expeditiously. It is still necessary, he says, in that separate assembly "to tie their hands" (444). Or if the assembly of the people wins, it runs into all the excesses of simple democracy, until winding up in the rule of a single despot. What is wanted from the beginning is a place in the constitution also for this single despot, himself controlled by the two assemblies, and serving to arbitrate between them and to keep each from encroaching upon the other, his own interest lying always on the side of the weaker, for fear of the stronger.

Therefore there are three great principles in the science of government: first, the people or the multitude need a check, to keep them in their proper bounds; second, the nobles need a check, to bind them to their proper places; third, the single despot or first man in

---

[1] IV., 290-1, 398, 414, cf. v. 40.—Cf. Gibbon, who reported "a current bon mot" in Rome "that Julius Solon was banished into the Senate," Decline and Fall of the Roman Empire, ch. iv., n. 21.

[2] "The body of the people" in one, "the rich and illustrious in another assembly," v., 456.

the state needs a check, to prevent him from becoming too powerful (*cf.* vi. 418–20). The checks, however, are not additional powers, injecting three more elements into the system, but are provided by the very powers that need to be checked. They are to check one another mutually, especially by any two combining against the third. Thus, in place of the single alliances above represented as successively taking place between the three parties in unbalanced states, there are to exist simultaneously and perpetually three alliances: between the king and the nobles against the people, between the people and the king against the nobles, and between the nobles and the people against the king. But, as the nobles, or the few great men, are the most dangerous and the most likely to disturb the equilibrium and to subdue the others, we shall find Adams most insistently proclaiming that they need to be controlled by two masters, one above and one below—the monarch and the popular assembly,—this being the reason for isolating them in an assembly of their own. When so controlled, the superior few, the aristocracy, the natural or artificial nobility, we shall find him treating as becoming, instead of a curse, a blessing to society, like the passion of emulation with which their souls are filled; for they then become, he conceives, protectors of the people against the encroachments of the crown, and, in their superior wisdom, guardians of their own and the people's liberties.

Still, the safety of the people depends likewise upon their defending the king against the encroachments of the aristocracy; for aristocrats are the most inimical to kingship (iv. 361, 366, vi. 533), and when they can will always run it down as the hunter does a hare[1] and

---

[1] IV., 371; so already in his first period, ix., 506.

reduce it to a mere dogeship (iv. 355, 362, 475), a mere "head of wood,"[1] their first point being to make it elective (iv. 544)—from their own number, and then to strip it of power; or they prefer a foreigner, ever demanding equality among themselves, however covetous they be of superiority above others (v. 214); and after they have thus taken to themselves the executive power, pitted against the people alone, they have a good chance of establishing an oligarchy. They (the few) have a perpetual hankering to encroach upon both sides, upon the king (the one) above them, and upon the people (the many) below them.[2] Hence the need of the alliance between the king and the people, which can take only the two shapes of the people making the king sole master of all, losing their own liberty, or making him joint master with themselves and the aristocracy and bound by another alliance. Thus the only governments that have been able to subdue and tame the aristocracy are either simple monarchy or the mixed and balanced government (vi. 73, 393). But the former is little better than the disease of which it is the cure (cf. 397, 533). The latter alone is a free government. Therefore, he says, "an equal mixture of monarchy, aristocracy, and democracy, is the only free government which has been able to manage the greatest heroes and statesmen, the greatest individuals and families, or combination of them, so as to keep them always obedient to the laws" (124). Obviously it is better for the people to participate with the king in supervising the aristocracy, than to resign this job to him alone. Only, Adams insists, they must not think

---

[1] Added in his later period, vi., 534, ix., 634, from the Italian "testa di legno," x., 397.

[2] IV., 355, 379, 381, vi., 28, 125.

they can assume this job by themselves alone,—that
they can keep the aristocracy in order without the help
of a king or strong executive. In fact, he says, the old
adage, "No bishop, no king," should be changed into
"No king, no people."[1] Otherwise the aristocracy is
all, the people nothing. The people can exist in security
only with the aid of a king, either in a simple monarchy,
where they are not much more than nothing, or in a
limited monarchy or mixed republic, admitting also the
aristocracy, where they are one third of the state—
their proper portion (cf. v. 457). If they aim at more,
he maintains, they will lose even that much.[2] On the
other hand, the aristocracy also need such a royal power
"to appeal to against the madness of the people" (iv.
463). Properly understood, therefore, it is the interest
of both to set up and support the king or independent
executive power.

Let us linger a little over this conception of the
natural principles of good and bad government, partly
reviewing and partly amplifying; for there is so much
symmetry and simplicity in it, and it contains so much
promise, that we can almost wish it were true. Simple
government in a single assembly of all, or of the representatives of all, Adams thinks experience proves, will
divide between the aristocracy and the democracy, and
the one of these will subjugate the other, and either of

[1] IV., 371.—He might have quoted here the Cappadocians, who, when
the Romans offered them freedom, are reported to have denied "vivere
gentem sine rege posse," Justinus, xxxviii., § 2; cf. Strabo, xii. (p. 372).

[2] IV., 297, 488, cf. 548-9. It is the balance only that preserves the
democratical authority, 298. "Let the people take care of the balance
and especially their part of it. But the preservation of their peculiar
part of it will depend still upon the existence and independence of the
other two. The instant the other branches are destroyed, their own
branch, their own deputies, become their tyrants," 468; cf. vi. 399.

the ensuing conditions will constitute despotism, and
there is good chance that it will end in the tyranny of a
single ruler. For either the nobility will subjugate the
people, or the people the nobility. In the first case, the
nobility will either remain united, or they will divide.[1]
If they remain united, they will fasten upon the people
an aristocratic despotism, trampling all below them
into the dust. But the other alternative is the more
likely (*cf.* v. 258); for even the nobles are apt to fall
into factions, though not so fast as the people (vi. 59–
60), following different rival families, gradually narrowing down to a few, then to two, of whom the one will
espouse the cause of his class, the other that of the
people (38), and the one will finally overpower the other,
and whichever it be, the people will applaud, because
he puts a stop to the turbulence of the nobles. On the
other hand, if the democracy prevail, they are themselves sure to be still more violent, and to run into
anarchy; then the superior men will again come to the
top, rivalries will set in anew between them, and as
before one will become master, acclaimed by the people
as their deliverer. In all this the people are one cause
of the evil conditions, by their humility and setting up
of idols; and the aristocracy are another cause, by their
spirit of emulation and grasping at all power. The
latter are the original disturbers of the peace,[2] and all
effort should be directed at bridling them. In simple
aristocracy they have attempted to control themselves,
by rotation of offices, giving every one a turn at the top;
by blending chance with choice at the elections (iv.
381); by calling in a foreigner for chief magistrate

[1] IV., 406, 414–15, 466, 584–5, *cf.* ix., 564.
[2] Their rivalries can account for "every despotism and monarchy in
the four quarters of the globe," vi., 393.

(vi. 214); by instituting a strict inquisition into one
another's affairs, and then of their subjects, to guard
against any one getting ahead of the rest, especially
against his courting the people[1]; by granting to every
member of their own order an absolute veto upon all the
rest—"the most absurd institution that ever took place
among men"[2]: but generally in vain, as rivalries and
factions will break out and lead to final breakdown of
the system. In simple democracy, too, the people have
sought to protect themselves from the grandees, by
excluding them from office in rotation or entirely, or by
exiling them. But again to no purpose; for the great
men's influence rules from privacy, even from abroad,
or another set take their places,—

Naturam expellas furcâ, tamen usque recurret.[3]

The only proper way to treat them is to acknowledge
their superiority and assign them a distinct share in the
government of the whole, as one element in a mixed
government, taking care at the same time to provide
one more element in the person of a chief executive,
beside that of the people, thus, as Adams considers,
"giving the natural aristocracy in society its rational
and just weight" (iv. 463), and no more. Otherwise
the only method of repressing the aristocrats has been to
raise up a single tyrant, the people concentrating all
their power upon him, placing at his command a standing army, in return for his promised protection. But
then this king becomes a despot not only over the aristocracy, but over the people also; so that these two have
to unite against him, which sets the aristocracy up

[1] In Venice, iv., 354; in Carthage, 471; in general, 381, vi., 60; cf. 74.
[2] VI., 63, in Poland; in Carthage, modified, iv., 471.
[3] Horace, *Epist.*, I., x., 24; quoted in this connection, v., 151.

again, and so on almost without end, the pendulum being "forever on the swing" (285). Instead of a balance, each holding the others up, there is a knocking down of each in turn, till at last the king gets all the others under him. This remedy, therefore, though preferable to the anarchy of democracy, is but a trifle better than the despotism of aristocracy, itself being the despotism of a single ruler. The only true remedy, preservative of liberty, is the mixed government.

Now the people alone set up the monarchy to defend them against the oppression of the assembly or senate of the nobles, or against the turmoil of their own assembly, or against the rivalry of both; and this monarchy necessarily becomes an evil both to the aristocracy and to the people themselves. But the aristocrats brought this evil upon themselves by their ambition and perpetual opposition both to a limited yet powerful first magistrate and to the people. Even the successful establishment of an aristocratic or oligarchic government was inquisitorial and oppressive to themselves. Therefore it is to the interest both of the aristocracy and of the people to combine and set up an arbiter between them, endowing him with the proper amount of power for the purpose, who shall no more be master of the one than of the other, or of either only as he is master of the other and only as each of them is master of him and of each other.[1] What is attempted to be done naturally, but with combat and confusion, because without concert, should be successfully done with concert and with science. As in nature the two

[1] "Each of the three branches must be, in its turn, both master and servant, governing and being governed by turns," vi., 43. "Neither the poor nor the rich should ever be suffered to be [sole] masters," ix., 570.

classes of the people are set over against each other, and
from the upper classes emerges a single ruler, and then
this ruler and the people combine against the aristocracy,
or also at times the aristocracy and the people combine
against this ruler when he becomes too tyrannical, and
this ruler and the aristocracy combine to undo democracy when a simple democracy at times has come into
being; so these three classes (for the single man has his
adherents) should concertedly make this same arrangement in their constitution, to be amicably carried out
instead of by fighting, doing designedly what "nature
herself" has been "constantly calling out for" (vi. 39),
putting into execution the design of Providence, and
thereby accomplishing peacefully what even bloodshed
was not competent to perform, the establishment of a
permanent government.

II. THE PLAN OF GOVERNMENT

CHAPTER VIII

THE GENERAL STRUCTURE

W E are now prepared to examine the structure of government, according to Adams's plan. We have followed him through three stages in which he endeavored to prove "that there can be no government of laws without a balance, and that there can be no balance without three orders; and that even three orders can never balance each other, unless each in its department is independent and absolute" (iv. 548). The three orders in the government, he maintains, must be equally strong and equally independent.

To be equally strong, they must, in his opinion, each be armed with a full negative or veto upon the proposals of the others. "There can be no equal mixture," he assevers, "without a negative in each branch of the legislature" (447). These three vetoing powers he seems to regard as "the three checks, absolute and independent," needed for preserving the constitution (483),—needed for enabling each branch "to defend itself" from the encroachments of the others (296), and to "balance the other two" (503), the middling by this means helping the weakest against the inroads of the strongest. As already noticed, because such negatives

74

were generally supposed to belong to each of the
chambers wherever the bicameral system was introduced, he says little about them; but he dwells much on
the executive veto, which was not everywhere allowed,
or not to the full extent desired by him, being in all the
American States qualified and weakened. This veto—
absolute, remember—he considered indispensable for
preserving "the balance of power between the executive
and the legislative powers" (vi. 429), as "a constitutional instrument of self-defense" in the hands of the
executive magistrate, without which his executive
power would be "pared away" by the two other orders,
especially by the aristocratic[1]; furthermore, necessary
for enabling this magistrate to defend, not only himself,
but the judiciary (vi. 431), and also the people in their
contest with the aristocracy (iv. 398); in a monarchy,
moreover, essential, as otherwise the executive magistrate would not be a monarch[2]—and if the king of
England has no occasion to use it, the fact that he has
the power to use in case of need, tells.[3]

Then, the three branches must be independent of
each other. Here Adams dwells especially on the distinction between the executive and the legislative
powers: the executive power, he asserts, is no more
derived from the legislative than the legislative is
derived from the executive,—"both are derived from
the people" (vi. 172, cf. iv. 579). The one must
therefore not be appointed by the other: the senators

[1] V., 180, 67, iv., 579, (ix., 506, in his early period), cf. iv., 371.

[2] So, later, vi., 428, 429; but cf. iv., 371.

[3] VI., 654.—For our State governors he added an extra reason: that
they might defend themselves from the additional encroachment
threatened from the Federal Congress, iv., 580, as if the trespass of this
body, if happening, would be more upon the governors than upon the
State governments in general!

must not be chosen by the representatives, and the executive chief must not be chosen either by the senators or by the representatives or by both (as he himself had allowed in his first period); for if so chosen and appointed, there would not be the necessary independence of the powers (584); nay, more, as appointees are but tools in the hands of their appointers, the executive and legislative powers, all the three powers, would be "in essence but one power and in the same hands," and there would be no check, balance, or control (vi. 172-3, 176, 178),—in short, it would be a simple, not a mixed, government. The three powers must therefore be independently derived from the people, through different channels of choice, appointment, or institution, about which he is not precise except in the case of the representatives; the examination of which may therefore be postponed.

The three legislative powers being so independently constituted, Adams conceives that they will each watch and guard the other two. The three natural orders in society, the monarchical, the aristocratical, and the democratical, are, he says, thereby introduced into the government by "the judicious legislator," and "constitutionally placed to watch" and "control each other," and "stand the guardians of the laws."[1] Thereby, also, each will balance the two others (iv. 503, 557). The executive will balance the upper and the lower chambers, that is, the upper and the lower classes, the aristocracy and the democracy, especially preserving the people from the arrogance of the nobles; the senate will balance the king and the people or their representatives, especially preserving the people from the usurpations of the king and his favorites (or from the people's own

[1] IV., 462, vi., 10, v., 90, iv., 557.

tendency to set up a tyrant); and the commons, or the people's representatives, will balance the king and the senate, especially preserving the king from the jealousy of the aristocracy. Or again, any two powers, in this three-cornered arrangement, are to combine and guard against the encroachment of the third. The first magistrate and the house of representatives are to curb the senate or aristocracy; the aristocracy and the democracy, in the two chambers, are to restrain the executive or king; and this functionary and the senate are to control the representatives of the people.[1] They will do so because it is the interest of every two to keep the third from becoming too popular and powerful (vi. 127); while they have no interest, he maintains, to combine for overwhelming the third, since that would expose either, if weaker, to the further pretensions of the other, after destroying its natural ally in the third.[2]

[1] IV., 462, 463, vi., 57-8, cf. 159; in a particular instance, 92.

[2] He here supposes greater far-sightedness in the parts of the mixed government than in the separate simple governments, either because he thought the greater wisdom which presided at the formation of the mixture would continue, or because, the balance once set up, he thought the interests of the various parties in maintaining it would be more apparent. As an instance, we have seen how he seems to have considered that, in England, the combination of the two houses which overthrew Charles I., whereupon the one drove out the other, antedated the acquisition of such wisdom; although really the mixture then existed in fuller equality than at any time since. Yet his assignment of interests is faultless. James Mill subsequently asserted: "Any two of the parties, by combining, may swallow up the third. That such combination will take place, appears to be as certain as anything which depends upon human will; because there are strong motives in favor of it, and none that can be conceived in opposition to it," article *Government*, § 5, in Supplement to the *Encyclopædia Britannica*. Mill merely ignored the motives that had already been pointed out in opposition, and did not himself expound the motives for utterly swallowing up the third. Motives a-plenty of course there are for combining against the third when it is the strongest, but these motives cease as soon as it is reduced to the

In both these triple statements the first of the three operations is the one by Adams most insisted upon. The mediation of the senate between the executive and the lower branch, as "the two extreme branches of the legislature," was the reason originally assigned in his early period for dividing the assembly into two chambers (iv. 196). It is not now brought into notice except in a couple of allusions to the senate's function of checking the other two powers (572-3, vi. 118). The balancing of the popular branch between the two others, or its control of them, meets with barely more frequent special allusion.[1] The emphasis is constantly placed upon the executive magistrate being the third power needed for the balance between the two assemblies,[2] with function as mediator, arbitrator, arbiter, umpire, to mediate, intervene, interpose, and decide between the senate and the people, between the nobles and the commons, between the aristocracy and the democracy, between the rich and the poor, between the few and the many, in the two chambers,[3] and between two parties, as we shall later see,—impartial (vi. 396, *cf.* 541), made

---

weakest. Then new motives come into play, and the weaker of the two has an interest to depart from its combination with the other and to uphold the third and to combine with it. (*Cf.* Macaulay on *Mill's Essay on Government*, a little beyond the middle.) In this view, the equilibrium will never be much disturbed, a tendency always existing to restore it. This is what is meant by stable equilibrium. Thus, while between simple governments the swings may be wide and violent, in a mixed government, Adams maintains, there may be only slight oscillations, which of themselves settle back into rest. But all depends upon whether interests are, or need to be, so divided, and whether they will then be rightly recognized.

[1] V., 456, *cf.* vi., 118; elsewhere merely to its absence, iv., 355, 361, 573; but a good occasion even for such allusion is passed by in vi., 323.

[2] IV., 345, 470, v., 476, *cf.* ix., 566.

[3] IV., 440, v., 65 (*cf.* 45), vi., 420, (later, vii., 348 n.), vi., 280, 323.

so because his interest, for ultimate self-preservation, is to side with the weaker of the other two (v. 68, ix. 570, vi. 394), whichever it may be at the time being.

As for the combinations of the two powers to restrain the third, special mention is only occasionally made of the nobles and people controlling the executive (v. 290): of the executive and nobles controlling the people, rarely, if ever. Everywhere stress is laid upon the idea that it is the aristocracy which principally needs to be subdued by the other two. As, in the government, it occupies the middle position in a small senate, the pretty conceit was hatched that it needs to be guarded by two masters set to watch it, the one above, the other below, the one the king or single executive, the other the democratical or numerous assembly.[1] Otherwise, as we have already seen, the only remedy against the supremacy of the aristocracy is in a simple monarchy or tyranny, itself little better, as the people, the master below, is alone not strong enough to control them. Better, to repeat, for the people to remain one of the masters; but for this purpose it must retain the other master. And that other master must have power not only over the aristocracy, but over the people, to check both, and "to hold the balance even between them" (vi. 65). "The great desideratum in a government," says Adams, "is a distinct executive power, of sufficient strength and weight to compel both these parties [of rich and poor], in turn, to submit to the laws" (v. 473, cf. iv. 406); for "without an intermediate power, sufficiently elevated and independent to control each of the contending parties in its excesses, one or the other will forever tyrannize" (viii. 495–6).

[1] IV., 463, (cf. 354, 398, 414), vi., 39, 43, 73, 419, (cf. 94).

CHAPTER IX

THE EXECUTIVE

THE executive power, then, must be strong and efficient. "The executive power," says Adams, "is properly the government."[1] But "the sovereignty," he further says, "is in the parliament or legislative power; not in the king or executive."[2] And again, the legislative and executive powers being "naturally distinct," "the legislative power is naturally and necessarily sovereign and supreme over the executive; and, therefore, the latter must be made an essential branch of the former, even with a negative, or it will not be able to defend itself, but will be soon invaded, undermined, attacked, or in some way or other totally ruined and annihilated by the former."[3] This has very much the appearance of a contradiction and a *non sequitur* all in one sentence. The distinction between the executive and the legislative powers would seem to require that the executive should not be in the legislature,[4] nor a distinct branch of it, and should not participate in or interfere with its supremacy and sovereignty. Of course Adams's words above quoted are merely unprecise, and what he meant is that the sovereignty is not in the king alone nor in the parliament alone, in the narrow sense of this term, but in the parliament, in the wide sense, as composed of lords,

[1] IV., 581, *cf.* 584; "the essence of government," 585.

[2] V., 322; similarly 428, 431.

[3] IV., 579. Remember that in his early period the sole reason he assigned for the executive negative was to give power to the executive to preserve its own and the judiciary's independence: above, p. 9 n., *cf.* p. 75.

[4] Adams expressed satisfaction that in our States the "executive is excluded from the two legislative assemblies," iv., 492.

commons, and king.[1] But the king is then more powerful than either of the other branches of the legislative, since beside his legislative power, equal to theirs, he has the executive power in addition. If, indeed, the executive were entirely out of the legislative, there might be need of a check against the encroachment of the legislature upon the executive; but the balancer may be sought elsewhere, and be found in the judicial power; to which subject we shall revert when we come to examine Adams's account of that department.

Now, it is primarily the possession of the veto that constitutes the executive a branch of the legislative. Against the absolute veto, and proportionally against any modified veto, there are weighty objections. Against it may be urged, on the one hand, that it is unnecessary for defending the executive against encroachments, if there be a judiciary and a definite constitution; which, to repeat, is reserved for later discussion. Moreover, the same reasoning would equally well call for directly arming the judiciary with this weapon of self-defense,[2] especially as the judiciary was usually considered the weakest department.[3] On the other hand, that it exceeds its purpose, since it may be used against mere laws that are not encroachments, and thus enables the executive to block legislation desired by the people. Adams speaks of the case of a chief magistrate "wantonly" using his negative "for

[1] He would agree with Nevill, that "the sovereign power in England is in King, Lords, and Commons," *Plato Redivivus*, p. 109.

[2] As was actually proposed, in conjunction with the executive, and in a modified form, by the "Virginia plan," art. 8, in the Philadelphia Convention and urged by Madison: see Elliot's *Debates*, v., 128, 151–5, 164–6, 344–9, 428–9. *Cf.* also Jefferson, *Works*, ii., 329, 586.

[3] *E. g.* by Hamilton in *The Federalist*, No. 78, and *Works*, Lodge's ed., vii., 286. *Cf.* Jefferson, *Works*, vii., 322, 404.

6

other purposes," as one that "can rarely happen" (v.
181). He forgot that the wanton abuse of the negative
by Charles I. was a principal cause of the uprising
which forcibly unseated him and led for a time to
another system and eventually to the abolition of that
power in England.[1] There was also abundant experience of such abuse in our colonial governments.[2]
Continued experience since Adams's day only confirms,
what might have been anticipated, that the veto, instead of "rarely," is habitually used "for other purposes" than that of defending the executive, whether
"wantonly" or not being a matter of opinion, the fact
remaining that the judgment of one man is permitted to
overbear the judgment of two assemblies.[3] Further-

[1] This negative was an object of special aversion to Milton (see below);
and even the more moderate Nevill, who approved the negative of the
Lords, *Plato Redivivus*, pp. 132-3, 272-9, deprecated it, 128-32, and
would restrict it by committees appointed by Parliament, 256-60.

[2] In the Convention Franklin cited the misuse of the veto by the
Pennsylvania governors, Elliot's *Debates*, v., 152.

[3] When Jackson began to make a frequent use of the veto, some of his
opponents alleged it was intended only for constitutional objections.
But this appeared a "novelty" to the aged Madison, who wrote that,
beside serving as "a shield to the Executive department," "a primary
object of the prerogative most assuredly was that of a check to the instability in legislation," *Writings*, iv., 369. He had himself said in the
Convention: "The object of the revisionary power is twofold—first, to
defend the executive rights; secondly, to prevent popular or factious
injustice," Elliot's *Debates*, v., 538. He referred, in the later passage,
also to *The Federalist*, where in No. 73 (by Hamilton) the former was
called its "primary," and the latter its "secondary," purpose. Hamilton,
in fact, repeated that the President ought to veto any measure he thought
either unconstitutional or pernicious, *Works*, vi., 368, *cf*. iv., 297. In
the Convention, too, Gerry had confined its purpose to securing the
executive from legislative encroachment, Elliot's *Debates*, v., 345; but
this had immediately been denied by Mason, *ib.*, 347-8, and Gerry had
afterward spoken of the defense of the executive department as "the
primary object of the revisionary check," 537, leaving room for a secon-

more, this power may be used to support the executive magistrate in encroachments of his own,—and we have had experience of this also.[1]

But the greatest objection to the executive veto is the one above hinted, that it mixes the executive with the legislative, and thus violates the principle, laid down by Adams as fundamental, of the separation of the three departments of government.[2] This, indeed, is the great modern discovery which Adams has celebrated at the outset, and which really ought to undo the confusion anciently made. For the veto power in the hands of the executive chief is not a "noble invention," as we have seen Adams call it too, but had an ignoble origin in the days when to Augustus, already *princeps* and *imperator*, was further added the tribunitian power of negativing the acts of the Senate.[3] That tribunitian power had really represented the power of the plebs, and supplied the place of what in modern days is the

dary. Wilson even wished to give the negative likewise to the judiciary for both these purposes, *ib.*, 344.

[1] *E. g.* when Lincoln tried to put through a system of reconstruction on his own authority, he clearly invaded the authority of Congress and occupied the whole field of legislation; and when he vetoed the Congressional reconstruction bill, he used the veto power to uphold his own usurpation. As Johnson followed his example, most of the evils of the reconstruction period hailed from this faulty clause in our Constitution.

[2] This objection against assigning a veto to the executive does not appear to have been advanced in the Convention, but it was urged against the above-cited proposal to join the judiciary here with the executive; to which it was replied that the intention of the veto was precisely to keep the departments separate by enabling the executive and the judiciary to defend themselves, by Madison, Elliot's *Debates*, v., 347, *cf.* 164–5; by Morris, 348; *cf.* Wilson, 151.

[3] The tribunitian veto was originally the power of quashing a law already existing by *forbidding* the execution of it. But the exercise of this power gave importance to its non-exercise, so that, in the hands of the Emperors, the refraining from using it, that is, giving consent, came to be regarded as indispensable for the making of the law.

power of the lower house to negative the acts of the upper house; and when it was taken from the lower people's representatives, the tribunes, and conferred upon the executive chief, it was wholly misapplied, and was explainable only by regarding the executive chief also as the representative of the same people. Then, when it was later recovered by the people (or never wholly lost by the peoples of the north), to leave (or to place) it in the hands of the executive chief is both to undo and not to undo, and makes the mess of having two rival representatives of the people, both the lower house and the executive chief.[1] Seeking a precedent still earlier, one may reply that in primitive governments the king or chieftain always took part in the assemblies of the people. But this he did merely as one of the people himself. And so, when the people are excluded and only their representatives, chosen *ad hoc*, are admitted, the king too, or the executive chief, instituted for another purpose, ought to be excluded. The true theory is that the so-called first magistrate is the head of the department which is to administer and execute the laws made by the representatives of the people. If he does not like the laws he is ordered to enforce, he may resign. Being chosen for this purpose, he has no more to do with the making of the laws, than any other magistrate or citizen.[2] He may give advice,

[1] And perhaps the first instance of the triple negative was the atrocious bargain struck by the triumvirs, Cæsar, Pompey, and Crassus: "ne quid ageretur in republica, quod displicuisset ulli e tribus," Suetonius, *Julius*, c. 19.

[2] *Cf.* Milton: "If the king be only set up to execute the law, which is indeed the highest of his office, he ought no more to make or forbid the making of any law, agreed upon in parliament, than other inferior judges, who are his deputies," *Eikonoklastes*, ch. vi., § 104; "nor was he set over us to vie wisdom with his parliament, but to be guided by

like any other citizen; and if he is assigned a special
instrument for giving advice, in messages, this is because his position yields him special insight into the
working of the laws. His admixture into the legislative takes away from the persons chosen specially for
legislation, by making him share it with them, the
complete responsibility for legislation which should be
theirs. Adams himself later complained that in America
the President was "made to answer before the people,
not only for everything done by his ministers, but even
for all acts of the legislature" (ix. 270). He did not
reflect that this was because of the veto, even though
qualified, which our Constitution bestows upon the
President.[1] We shall see, too, presently, that Adams
wished the President to be impartial, or, as we say,
non-partisan. This, on the whole, is impossible; but
it is much less possible if he have a veto power, and less
and less so the greater that power. If that power were
absolute, all partisanship would revolve around the
President, as it tends to do even now. If he had none,
partisanship would be centered principally upon the
legislators, where it belongs; for partisanship relates to
the adoption of laws, not to their administration.

These strictures lead to two fundamental criticisms
of Adams's system. The one is that he desiderates
more power in the executive chief than is necessary for
the balance, or rather, that his treatment of the balance
itself is exaggerated. It is gratuitous to require that

---

them," ch. xi., § 182; "his reason" was not set "to be our sovereign
above law," but "his person" was set "over us in the sovereign execution of such laws as the parliament establish," § 184. *Cf.* §§ 97, 176,
and in ch. xxvii., §§ 348, 350, 352, 353, 359.

[1] Even this qualified veto enabled Van Buren to speak of "the executive" as "a component part of the legislative power," Richardson's
Messages and Papers of the Presidents, vol. iii., p. 536.

every one of three powers should in turn be the balancing power between the other two, and therefore that they must all three be equal. Adams himself, we have seen, laid more stress upon the executive chief balancing the other two powers. In fact, according to his own system, the only balance needed to be held even is that between the two great classes in society and their representatives in the government, which he regarded as the two great parties in politics,—the upper and the lower elements, the aristocrats and the democrats. All that is required for the executive chief, then, on Adams's own principles, is that he should have power sufficient for this purpose. This functionary is not one of three alternating powers: he is a special power, occupying a fixed position. The three-cornered arrangement need not be that of an equilateral triangle. An isosceles triangle with a small apex will do. For, according to the true theory of the mechanical balance, when only one of the three powers has the function of balancing the others, all that is necessary is that this balancing power should have force or weight greater, with a safe margin, than the difference ever likely to arise between the forces or weights that are to be balanced; for then the balancing power is strong enough to restore the equilibrium by adding its force or weight to that of the weaker or lighter. A power much inferior to the others, therefore, may act as balancer. A light stick may balance a heavy man. The so-called "king" on the seesaw may be a small boy, balancing two big boys. Then, too, the condition here supposed being obtained, it mathematically follows that each of the other two powers is similarly great enough to act as balancer in case of need, or to defend the weakest. Fault may further be found with a merely negative power like the veto, that it cannot serve this purpose of balancing, and that consequently, after all, sufficient power was not assigned even by Adams to the executive for holding the balance. But this is a bit of criticism that goes to the method of carrying out the idea; and it will call for our attention later. Here the criticism touches the idea itself. The true idea of the executive office, as already said, must be that it is to execute the laws. Even the function, then, of balancing between the two powers which make the laws would seem to be supererogatory to it, or wrongly placed in it. But, letting that pass, we find no need for so much as Adams asks. The balancing power does not have to equal the powers it balances. It does not, therefore, have to be introduced as one coördinate branch of the legislature.

The other fundamental criticism touches the converse of this introduction of the executive into the legislative, the exclusion of the legislature, in Adams's plan, from any interference with the executive, except only by impeachment for misbehavior. The two powers, he has said, are not derivative from each other, but both from the people, and therefore should be separate and independent. Although in the same breath violating this by introducing the executive into the legislative, he insists upon it, as we shall see, to keep the legislature out of the executive. Now, the principle itself is false, and the use of it made by Adams is exactly the reverse of the use that ought to be made of the true principle. The function of the executive department, to repeat, is to execute the will of the legislature, which expresses the will of the people; wherefore the executive power is distinctly derivative from the legislative power.[1] The separation of the two has a sufficient reason. It is to

[1] So Sherman in Elliot's *Debates*, v., 140, 142, *cf.* 147.

prevent temptation of abuse of power. If those who legislate also execute, or have subservient executors, they may legislate for their own special benefit, reaping the harvest through their own operations. Or, if those who execute also legislate, they may direct the laws against others, and exempt themselves and their own party. But if a separate department is to execute and in case of special and privileged legislation reap the harvest, the temptation is removed from the legislators and the opposite desire is substituted to keep the executors from acquiring any special benefit from the laws.[1] And as the legislators clothe others with the same authority over themselves as over the rest of the people, their own interest is identified with that of all, especially if they return among the people at the end of short terms, or are liable to do so. Here is a common-sense reason for the separation of the departments of government; for the judicial, which is similarly an offshoot from the executive, has its separation from the remainder of that department recommended by a prolongation of the same reasoning. It is the reason early adduced by Locke, and since by other expounders of the English Constitution.[2] It is especially forceful where the executive department is in the hands of a hereditary chief, who never returns into the body of the

[1] Now the only special beneficiaries of the laws will be those who pay for privileges ("protection," etc.) by bribery, either directly or by campaign funds and the like. But these are not the servants, they are the masters of the legislators, by right of purchase.

[2] Locke, *Of Civil Government*, § 143; Montesquieu, *Esprit des Lois*, XI., vi.; De Lolme, *Constitution of England*, II., x.; Paley (of the legislative and judicial characters), *Moral and Political Philosophy*, VI., viii.; *cf.* D. Stewart, *Political Economy*, ii., 366. Locke, of course, did not originate it. Before him the need of the separation was thus clearly explained, for instance, by Nedham, as quoted by Adams, vi., 170–1.

people and who never lives under the laws: it means that lawmaking must never be permitted to such an executive, but must be entrusted only to persons who do, or who will, live under the laws they make. But it has some force still even where the executive chief is in office only for a term; for that position already gives him quite enough power, without adding that of lawmaking, which might tempt him to make laws for the benefit he might derive from executing them; and conversely, the lawmakers have power enough in their department, and the added power of executing their own laws might put a similar temptation in their way. Now, this reason goes to prove, too, that it is the separation of the *departments* of government, and not, as Adams maintained, the additional separation of the *branches* of the legislature, that is the *sine qua non* of equal laws. It is entirely different from the fanciful reason added for the separation of the branches of the legislative, drawn from the idea, itself fanciful, that the two assemblies and the executive chief represent kinds of government that are mixed and need to be kept distinct in order to prevent the mixture from reducing to a uniform mass. Now, the true reason for separating the executive, and with it the judicial, departments from the legislative, allows recognition of the executive department being derivative from, and subordinate to, the legislative.[1] It therefore leaves some power of

[1] *Cf.* Milton once more: "In all wise nations the legislative power, and the judicial execution of that power, have been most commonly distinct, and in several hands; but yet the former supreme, the other subordinate," *Eikonoklastes*, ch. vi., § 104. And Nedham: "By the executive power we mean that power which is derived from the other [the legislative, which makes, alters, or repeals laws], and by their authority transferred into the hands of one person . . . or of many . . . for the administration of government in the execution of those laws. In the keeping of

control in the legislature over the executive officers; which, for instance, is the justification for the legislature's power of impeaching, left to it by Adams. But, while sanctioning this, it militates against the opposite view that the executive chief should have some control over the legislature. This is to be absolutely denied. Let the executive chief be appointed separately—by election of the people: that is a good means of insuring his independence, as far as independence is needed; but whatever connection is to be left between the two departments, the legislature has much better right to have a hand in the executive, than the executive to have a finger in the legislative. For the legislature ought to have some supervision over the officers entrusted with the enforcement of its laws; but the executive chief has nothing more to do with the legislature than, as above said, like any citizen, to give it information and advice. Sometimes, indeed, the executive chief may need, during a vacation of the legislature, to consult it, or to obtain its authorization for coping with unforeseen circumstances. Therefore he may need the power of summoning the legislature — a power which is really a confession of impotence. This power needs to exist somewhere, and has generally been left with the executive for convenience. It might just as well be assigned to a council, or to a standing committee of the legislature.

Adams, however, used his principle of the separateness of the executive from the legislative for a purpose to which it does not necessarily extend. Wishing them to be distinct and independent of each other, he main-

---

these two powers distinct, flowing in distinct channels, so that they may never meet in one, save upon some short, extraordinary occasion, consists the safety of a state," quoted by Adams, vi., 170.

tained that the executive must not be appointed by
the legislature, any more than the one chamber of the
legislature by the other. The reasons we have seen.
But, however good the separate derivation of the executive from the people has proved in practice, the separateness of the departments does not require it, since a
distinct and independent authority may very well be
set up by appointment of a body which in granting it
renounces it, or, better, which never had it, but only
the right to appoint its incumbent. Adams himself
distinguished the judicial authority from the two others,
and wished it to be equally independent; yet he allowed
the judges to be appointed by the executive magistrate.
Appointees—so ran the reason—are but tools of the
appointers. Then representatives would be but tools
of the people who elect and appoint them. Adams did
not so conceive the representative character (cf. vi.
400–1). And as he considered all the powers of government to be set up by the people, all would remain in the
hands of the people, and there would be no difference
between the mixed and the simple government of all.
Evidently the question depends on the amount of
authority that is handed over by the appointers to the
appointees and on the mode instituted of exercising it.
If the authority be complete for the purpose intended,
and if the terms of the appointment cannot be inter-
fered with or the authority withdrawn except at stated
periods or for definite abuse or delinquency, then the
appointees are not mere tools of the appointers. Adams
thought he made the appointed judges independent of
the appointing executive by making their tenure endure
during good behavior, with addition, probably, of assigning them fixed salaries, thus taking their removal
or loss of emolument out of the hands of their appointer

and making it subject only to successful impeachment.[1] In his early period he had similarly treated the executive chief also, with reference to the legislature. No reason is apparent for altering the position in the one case and not in the other, or for keeping it in one case only. It is a sound position, and may be kept in both. An executive appointed by the legislature may be rendered independent of the legislature in precisely the same way, and with equal efficiency. Even appointment for life is not necessary, as was recognized by Adams in his early period for the case of a State governor, appointment for a definite term being sufficient. Since Adams's day, and in our lifetime, in France the last has been done, and with success. Already in Adams's day the English had introduced another method in the case of what is really their executive chief, or nearly so, the prime minister, successfully rendering him equiponderant with the assembly which appoints him, by giving him power to dissolve that assembly and to appeal, between him and it, to the constituencies.[2] This is

[1] In the constitution of Massachusetts he had, we may remember, allowed even an easier removal—by the executive upon request of the two legislative assemblies, the English method; which, while making the judicial department dependent on the executive for its appointments, makes it independent of the executive alone for its removals, by requiring for these the concurrence of the executive and the legislature.

[2] Thus, while the assembly makes, only the people can unmake, this executive. The power of dissolving the legislature is allowed to such an appointed executive only for the purpose of rendering him independent of the power that created him. Where the executive already has an independent position, he ought not to have this power over the legislature. In the former case the appeal to the country is the main thing, and the executive jeopardizes his own position also. In the latter, the executive would have an unfair advantage, since his term is fixed. Here the legislature itself is the best judge of when its business is done, up to the end of its term of existence. Much evil resulted from the possession of this one-sided power by the colonial governors.

something Adams did not think of: he did not find it in the expositions he read of the English system, and he did not dig it out for himself. He simply refrained from looking for such means of rendering a legislatively appointed executive independent of the legislature, and asseverated a negative proposition through disinclination to seek its disproof, in spite of having, in his early period, been satisfied with an appointed executive whose independence was guarded by fixed tenure, fixed salary, and the veto power.[1]

Continuing on the institution of the executive power, Adams maintains that it must be confided to a single person. "I had almost ventured," he says, "to propose a third assembly for the executive power; but the unity, the secrecy, the despatch of one man has no equal; and the executive power should be watched by all men; the execution of the whole nation should be fixed upon one point, and the blame and censure, as well as the impeachments and vengeance for abuses of this power, should be directed solely to the ministers of one man."[2] These ministers, however, in conjunction with the chief magistrate, seem to form an assembly; but with the great difference from the other and from true assemblies, lending it more the nature of a council, that its members are all appointed and are removable by the chief who presides over them. Yet in England,—but less so in

[1] As for the case of the senate alone choosing the executive chief, where the senate represents the aristocracy, which arrangement Adams considered worse than a hereditary monarchy (as in Rome, iv., 544), we may very well agree with him; but here the evil comes from that magistrate being chosen by the aristocracy alone, not from his being appointed by a representative assembly.

[2] IV., 585–6. In his early period the need of "secrecy and despatch" had been adduced as a reason against assigning the executive power to a legislative assembly, 196, 206.

Adams's day, and not then recognized,—the Cabinet almost forms a true assembly, since it is almost independent of the King, who never presides at its meetings, and its members are almost equal to the Prime Minister, being collectively dependent upon the legislature.

It is noteworthy that the symmetry in the balance apparently set up by Adams is broken by this demand for an individual executive. He has told us there can be no balance between two *orders* without a third *order:* he now tells us there can be no balance between two *assemblies* without a third—what?—not assembly, but *power.*[1] To no purpose is it for him to say that "the body politic cannot subsist, any more than the animal body, without a head" (iv. 379); for each assembly has a head in its own president, and the executive assembly or council would have such a head too.[2] Concentration of responsibility is the great desideratum, and seems to be obtainable by such narrowing down to a president, in the true sense of the term. Unity would seem to be more jeopardized. Later, at the time of the French Directory, Adams wrote: "The worst evil that can happen in any government is a divided executive; and, as a plural executive must, from the nature of men, be forever divided, this is a demonstration that a plural executive is a great evil, and incompatible with liberty."[3]

[1] IV., 345, 470, v., 473, 476.—In his early period he had said there ought to be a mediator between the executive *magistrate* and the popular *assembly,* and this mediator ought to be another assembly. Why another *assembly?*

[2] In his early period, we may remember, he had been willing that the governor in the democratic States should be nothing more than the president of the council, iv., 197, 207, ix., 430.—Our term "President" was ill-chosen, except for the cabinet-meetings over which our executive chief presides. The term was inherited from the President of Congress, who was really and merely a presiding officer.

[3] VIII., 560, (1797). In 1809, looking back to this period, he wrote:

Yet that very Directory was one of the most energetic
executives known to history.

The doctrine of the necessity of a single executive
chief is not so sure as generally considered. The two
Kings of Sparta outlasted the other Greek single kings.
The two Roman Consuls remained at the head of the
state for as long a tract of time as did the Emperors that
succeeded them. And all through the dark and middle
ages two consuls (or alcaldes[1]) held the place of our
single mayors in French and Spanish municipalities.
The doubleness of the Roman consulship was designed
to prevent that institution from degenerating into a
tyranny; and in this respect it was eminently successful.
The Emperor did not develop from the Consul, but
from the general (*imperator*). When the Romans departed from their practice of annually rotating their
military commanders, and granted an army for five
years to Cæsar, then, as Cato foresaw, and not till then,
was the republic doomed. If in our country, the republic glides into a monarchy, it will be by means of our
single executive (and will be brought about by lengthening the term of office, or by repeated re-elections).

In England itself the executive power is divided
between the King and the Ministry, and as the latter
has become, in Bagehot's words, little else than a
committee of the House of Commons, it appears to be
divided between a hereditary monarch and an elective
legislative council. There the evil of want of unity in
the plural executive is guarded against by turning out
the whole, if its internal dissensions produce weakness
and loss of confidence; and this inevitable fate makes the

"I knew that in the nature of things an executive authority in five
persons could not last long in France or anywhere else," ix., 247.

[1] Annually elected by the regidors.

members hold together or purge their body of any element of discord. Of course, this method of securing solidarity cannot be employed if the several members all have indefeasible tenure of office during fixed periods. Either all, or all but one, must be easily removable. Such easy removability is obtainable where the executive body is appointed by the legislature, or where a ministry is so appointed to an independent first magistrate (as in England), or to one (as in France) with fixed tenure, whose authority, in either case, is so limited that he cannot alone be regarded as the executive head. The case, therefore, for the absolute unity of the executive power, all collected in one person, is by no means made out.

With respect to the ministry, it may be noticed that Adams always presupposes the English method of exempting the first magistrate from responsibility and holding only his ministers responsible, at the same time requiring that nothing can be done by him without their co-operation[1]; and with our system of making the executive chief himself responsible he later expressed dissatisfaction.[2] He even questioned whether it would not be desirable to require our "heads of departments" to be members of the legislature (ix. 272–3); which would literally put executive officers *in* the legislature, and, as in England, completely violate the separation which was his first principle. The reason he assigns is that "there they would be confronted in all things," whereas now "all is secrecy and darkness." The reason is a good one; but it is a good reason, then, for not completely severing the executive from the legis-

[1] VI., 62, 76, 105, 120, 127.
[2] IX., 269–70. Not so in his first period: he had then helped to introduce it.

lative powers. The objection to secrecy is peculiar, after this having been given as one of the prime requisites. On the other hand, the placing of all responsibility upon the ministers, requiring their signature for every executive act, would seem to do away with that unity and despatch, which had also been prime motives for instituting a single first magistrate. The ministers themselves, in Adams's plan, were to be responsible to the legislature only in the old English manner, which was already passing away, though still upheld by the Tories. The new system, already introduced by the Whigs, though not yet fully established, of finer responsibility by requiring the ministers at all times to be *personæ gratæ* to the legislature, and, too, to the lower, the supposedly democratical, branch of it, making them appointable only with its consent, and to be dismissed at its desire, at least after an appeal to the people,—this was never so much as noticed by Adams. Had he accepted it, it would have destroyed his system, since it makes the executive continually dependent on the legislative department, and even on only one of its two branches, except for the appeal to the people, and annihilates the balance, collecting all authority into one body, ultimately the people at the polls,—the very thing Adams was combating with all his might. He did, in fact, once touch upon the possibility of such a control over the executive by the legislature, but treated it as virtually reducing the government to that of the assembly, with all the attendant evils of the majority tyrannizing over the minority; and he later thought he found exemplification of this observation in the conduct of the French in the last days of Louis XVI. (vi. 335–6 and note). That such a system was actually maturing before his eyes in the model government of England, not one word!

7

As it is, in Adams's own plan, the ministerial, virtually the executive, responsibility to the legislature by impeachment was to be a check upon the executive power, in the hands of the legislature,—a check which called, for counterpoising, according to his principles, for another check upon the legislature, in the hands of the executive, as we shall see presently; for the executive veto is itself paired with the legislative veto upon the executive's projects. As a check, this ministerial liability to impeachment Adams considered sufficient protection against all abuse of the executive power. It, along with the representative's control over the public purse, he thought, would keep the executive power from ever being used for evil (v. 181, vi. 67, 127). To be sure, it may keep the executive magistrate from actual abuse, malfeasance, or misdemeanor; but it cannot restrain him from pursuing a policy not acceptable to the legislature, especially if he have also the veto power. Since Adams's day the want of any greater check than this has led to two revolutions in France and to much discontent elsewhere; while the new English system has worked smoothly and given entire satisfaction.

Concerning the functions of the executive magistrate, Adams wishes him to be "possessed of the whole executive power"[1]; and though this magistrate shares in the legislative power of the legislature, the legislature must be confined to legislation and be altogether excluded from sharing in the executive power.[2] But the

[1] V., 67, so iv., 398, 585, vi., 118; such is his conception of a king, "a first magistrate possessed exclusively of the executive power," iv., 371.

[2] This latter sharing he later reprobates as "mixing the legislative and executive powers together," vi., 466, i. e., as violating the principle of separation of the departments, although why it does so more than the former, is not easy to see. In his criticisms of our Federal Constitution

nature of the executive power Adams never analyzed or defined; and he simply accepted what was usually assigned to it in the practice of England and other countries. Thus, without any examination, he included in it the power (1) of pardoning, (2) of declaring war and making treaties, and (3) of appointing to all civil and military offices.

(1) In strict theory, the right of pardoning belongs only to the offended party. In civil actions only the winning suer can grant release. In criminal matters, however, the offended party has been transferred from the party actually injured, or from the friends of a person killed, to the state. By the social compact, the individual on entering upon citizenship delivers up to the state his right of self-defense, of vengeance, and consequently of pardon. In monarchic states, the king has usurped the position of representing the state in all things, and therefore has assumed this right. Then the conception has been variously amplified. As, in theology, sin is conceived to be an offense against the Supreme Law-Giver, who punishes or pardons at his pleasure; so, in jurisprudence, crime is conceived to be offense against the king as law-giver, an insolent breaking of his peace, even a direct injury by weakening his resources (murder, even suicide, depriving him of a subject). Therefore writs issue in his name only, he

he says, both: "The rational objection here is, not that the executive is blended with the legislature, but that it is not enough blended; that it is not incorporated with it, and made an essential part of it," by having the absolute veto instead of the limited, vi., 432; and, later: "The legislative and executive authorities are too much blended together. While the Senate of the United States have a negative on all appointments to office," etc., x., 397. The executive not enough in the legislative department; the legislative, or one branch of it, too much in the executive department—such the application of his principle to our Constitution!

alone prosecutes[1]: in the confused theory he is both prosecutor and judge. Hence that barbarous rule, now everywhere abrogated, that the prisoner charged with felony could not have counsel or produce witnesses, the king's dignity not suffering such opposition. Hence, too, the king's right, when he wins, to show clemency, if he pleases.[2]

This right, or power, of showing clemency is, however, a power also of dispensing with justice. Its possession by the executive chief is similar, in reference to the judiciary, to his power of the veto in reference to the legislature. In either case it is the power in one man to annul the judgment of others more numerous and wiser than he. And of the two, if we reflect that the judiciary is the scientific department of the government, we must conclude that to allow one man—perhaps born to the purple and raised in ignorance, or, perhaps again, taken out of the street—to pass, without examination if he chooses, upon the decisions of a highly technical body, is the more irrational of the two. Indeed, next to allowing one man to punish without the concurrence of judge and jury, most absurd is it to permit one man to free from punishment those whom jury and judge have convicted and sentenced. The pardoning power in the king was itself pardonable only in the rude times when punishments were themselves criminal enormities. It is the analog of the power of punishing without trial,

---

[1] Although in England, strangely, the prosecution was left to the afflicted individual.

[2] So Blackstone: "All affronts to that power, and breaches of those rights [delegated by the public to the one magistrate] are immediately offences against him. . . . Hence also arises another branch of the prerogative, that of pardoning offences; for it is reasonable that he only who is injured should have the power of forgiving," *Commentaries*, i., 268–9.

and was accorded to him only because that power was conceded to him. Both these functions were assigned to him on the blasphemous plea that he was a god, or the representative of God, on earth. When, in the course of enlightenment, the one was taken from him, the other was left to him only because of the false opinion (nowhere authenticated) that clemency is a specially divine attribute. To be sure, the process of convicting and sentencing was still for centuries rendered easy and capricious; and then it was not illogically counterbalanced by an easy and capricious method of pardoning. But now that conviction has been made difficult, the method of pardoning ought likewise to be made difficult. "Clemency," says Beccaria, "is the virtue of the legislator, and not of the executor of the laws."[1] To be more explicit, clemency is the virtue of the laws, both in their general statement, as made by the legislator, and in their application to particular instances, as made by the judiciary. Extenuating circumstances ought to be, and now are, taken into consideration by judge and jury. It is for these to season justice with mercy. The virtue of the execution of the laws is sureness,—and the surer the punishment, the milder it may be; but this is frustrated by leaving the power of pardoning to the good nature of one man.

Hence the example of the monarchic distribution of this power is of no value. In a republic the question

---

[1] *Dei Delitti e delle Pene,* § xx. Just before he remarked: " In proportion as punishments become milder, clemency and pardons become less necessary." Jefferson quoted these passages with approval, *Works,* ix., 263. And to the same effect, in the Massachusetts State (constitutional) convention of 1853, J. McK. Churchill said: "The exercise of the pardoning power is not so often necessary at the present time as it was when the criminal code was more severe," *Official Report,* vol. i., p. 967, and again to the same effect, p. 980.

need not even be, Who rightly represents the state in this matter? For foreign affairs the president may be permitted to fill this representative function. It does not follow that he must stand for the state in all things. If the power of pardoning belongs to the sovereign, for that very reason it does not belong to the executive chief, because he is not the sovereign. Nor is the legislature the sovereign. Sovereignty, in a republic, is nowhere in the government; it is in the people in their constitution-making and government-choosing capacity. They set up different departments in the government, to which they delegate various powers; and the question rightly is, To which department ought they to confide the power of pardoning? Evidently this is a judicial matter, being the reverse of sentencing. It ought therefore to belong to the judiciary,—that is, not necessarily to the same officers who are engaged with prosecution, but to an analogous set of officers, conducting themselves with similar formality, gravity, and impartiality; for as it is the function of the ordinary judiciary to take care that justice be done, so it is theirs to see to it both that injustice be not done and that justice be not undone. The constitution, then, ought to erect such a body or board; or, as it leaves the erection of minor courts to the legislative, so, under broad directions, it may leave to the legislative the erection of this court of pardons. There is no reason, even, except the trouble and expense, why a jury should not be summoned for pardoning as well as for convicting. The opinion of those who had to do with the original trial ought to be obtained. Certainly the parties injured ought to be heard, and not only the friends of the convict. As the executive chief has to sign warrants of execution, so he will still have to sign pardons, but only at the direction of this court. At most, the power may be left with him to summon such courts, or to bring cases before them. Here his concern in the matter should end: his business is to execute what he is ordered to do. The aim should everywhere be to make the courts of justice themselves so just, that their sentences shall not need revocation. Above all things, passion or emotion ought to be taken out of the affair. As the ordinary courts put reason in the place of anger, so these courts ought likewise to put reason in the place of pity.[1]

The subject, of course, is a complex one,[2] and should be decided in a practical way, rather than by pure theory, which here is somewhat abstruse. It is not

[1] "Always it [the exercise of the pardoning power] ought to be the work of mere reason," Rufus Choate, in the same convention, *Official Report*, vol. i., p. 968. It is regrettable that we have not, in this matter, borne out the words of Webster: our spirit of liberty "does not trust the amiable weaknesses of human nature," *Works*, vol. iv., p. 122. Instead, we have been exposed to such advice as this, spoken by an ex-Governor: "An Executive may err, it is true, in exercising this power of pardon; but if he errs in exercising that power, he has the sweet consolation of knowing that he is using that beautiful attribute—that sweet inspiration of the human heart, the most precious gift of Providence—mercy!" A. G. Curtin, *Debates of the Pennsylvania Constitutional Convention*, 1873, vol. ii., p. 370. It is overlooked that the commandment is to forgive *our* enemies, not those of persons committed to our protection. Shakespeare's words, so often quoted by advocates of indiscriminate pardoning, "the quality of mercy is not strained," etc., were addressed to the injured party. Speaking more generally, Shakespeare also says: "Nothing emboldens sin so much as mercy"; "Mercy but murders, pardoning them that kill"; "Sparing justice feeds iniquity"; "I show it [pity] most of all when I show justice." Godwin's words also should not be forgotten: "Clemency . . . can be nothing but the pitiable egotism of him who imagines he can do something better than justice," *Enquiry Concerning Political Justice*, B. VII., ch. ix.

[2] It really has three sections: of remitting punishment (when originally excessive); of pardoning proper (restoring to civil standing, after reformation); of restitution (when the conviction is subsequently shown to have been erroneous; for which the state itself ought to beg pardon).

surprising, then, that our American legislators have been
at a loss to do otherwise than follow the foreign model.
They have gone as far in improvements as their model
went, and have variously required the concurrence of
the council, where there was one (Massachusetts, New
Hampshire), or of a special council (Indiana, Florida,
Pennsylvania), or a board of pardons (Montana, South
Dakota, Idaho), and even of the senate (Rhode Island,
Texas). Adams himself led the way in requiring, in the
Massachusetts constitution, "the advice of council,"
and also the annulment of pardons before conviction
(iv. 248), which last has been followed by most of the
States. But his "advice of council" was itself an
executive operation, and vaguely restrictive of the
governor's action,[1] in no wise infringing the principle
of pardon being an executive function, which he got
from the practice of Europe. Yet a constitutional
theorizer like him might have been expected to make
some investigation into the subject; and his voice,
raised at the commencement, would have gone far to
set the States on the right track. Since then, the experience of over a hundred years leads to the conclusion
that the granting of this power to the governor even
when controlled by the slight restrictions in some
States imposed, and especially where not so controlled,
is liable to much abuse.[2] In the model constitution

---

[1] Later, when President, he pardoned Fries and his companions, ix.,
178–9, even against the advice of his Cabinet, 60–1, and always found
satisfaction in having done so, 270, x., 153–4.

[2] There have been constant complaints; and many reports of committees and commissioners have been drawn up on the subject. One
such, in Massachusetts, was copied by Beaumont and Tocqueville in
their *Système pénitentiaire aux États-Unis*, 1845, Appendix No. xiv.
Another, written by F. Lieber, deserves examination, and may be found
in his *On Civil Liberty and Self-Government*, Appendix ii. These quote

of England itself, this power hardly resides any more
in the King alone. The abuse of it by James II., which
was one of the chief causes of the revolt against him, is
there remembered.[1] For the power of pardoning is
really a power of dispensing with the laws. The execu-

M. Carey as stating that men have made a business of getting signatures
to petitions. Statistics showed that it was the worst criminals, with
longest sentences, who had the best chance at being pardoned. Recently (see newspapers of April 16, 1910) it was reported that the Governor of Tennessee in three years and two months of office issued 956
pardons (or one every day), letting loose upon the public 124 thieves and
162 murderers, among these a political friend who had slain a political
opponent. December 17, 1912, the Governor of Arkansas liberated 360
convicts, because they were worked in camps leased to contractors, according to a law which he had vainly tried to get rescinded,—i.e., he used
the pardoning power for a legislative purpose. The present Governor of
South Carolina seems to be doing his best to emulate both these records.
He is reported to have threatened in advance immediately to pardon
every one convicted on evidence supplied by a certain detective agency,
which had investigated his political activities. Under such circumstances
justice is a farce. And there may be such an outbreak of the crime
of pardoning at any time in any State that allows such a prerogative
to its governor. The day before Christmas, 1910, it was reported that
the Governor of Massachusetts pardoned a man who had pursued and
murdered his young wife for leaving him after learning that he was
already married to another woman. In the stern days of old, Adams
could not have anticipated such weakness. More recently a Governor
of New York pardoned a murderer after serving three years of a light
service of seventeen years, and refused to pardon a youth who had
committed some mysterious peccadilloes, to which he had been induced
to plead guilty, after serving five years of confinement, though he was
undergoing the monstrous sentence of imprisonment for thirty years.
At the farcical hearing of this case which took place in New York City,
February 20, 1912, the Commissioner is reported to have said: "He
[the Governor] has the absolute power of pardon of this man with or
without good cause." If the people have given such absolute power
to any one, it is time they should know it, that they may correct it.
At least, a governor should be impeachable if he pardons without good
cause, and also if he withholds pardon when there is good cause.

[1] In our country also, Johnson's use of the pardoning power, contrary
to the sense of the country, produced much irritation, and was a con-
tributory cause of his impeachment.

tive chief may thereby exculpate his subordinates for carrying out his unconstitutional or illegal orders or desires.[1] It has therefore necessarily been almost everywhere abridged in the executive. It ought to be entirely withdrawn from him; and he ought to be taken out of the judiciary department as well as out of the legislative department.

(2) Treaty-making is obviously a legislative act, since treaties are laws (and are so declared in our Constitution). Negotiation belongs to the executive, ratification to the legislature. The treaty-making power possessed by the king is a clear usurpation on the functions of the assembly. It was usurped in conjunction with other legislative powers, of which the king has, in many countries, again been stripped, though this one he has generally managed to retain, at least in form. So, too, in the case of the power of declaring war. This, in primitive times, was one of those important things about which the whole body of freemen, that is, the warriors, consulted.[2] It became a regal preroga-

[1] *Cf.* Mason: "I conceive that the President ought not to have the power of pardoning, because he may frequently pardon crimes which were advised by himself," Elliot's *Debates*, iii., 497; so again, i., 495. Hamilton would take away the power of pardoning cases of desertion, at least in time of war, *Works*, vi., 280.

[2] Tacitus, *Germania*, §§ 11, 13, of the Germans in general; which is confirmed by the practice found still many centuries later among the Franks, the Anglo-Saxons, the Danes, etc. So in early Rome itself, where the Senate was a sort of semi-executive, semi-legislative council and the assembly was the people convoked in the Campus Martius, the Senate proposed not only laws, but wars and treaties, and the people ratified or rejected: Polybius, vi., § 14; or as Livy frequently said, "senatus censuit, populus jussit," *e. g.*, xxxvii., 55. So also in some of the primitive conditions in America, the right of making peace and war (with the Indians especially) was accorded to the assembly in the first charter of East New Jersey in 1664, and was assumed in the Fundamental Constitutions of West New Jersey enacted in 1681 by the assembly

tive in the days of feudalism when the kings made war "at their own expense," going "to the field at the head of their own tenants."[1]

In abjectly following on these subjects degenerate European ideas (iv. 497, vi. 430, *cf.* v. 69), Adams threw away that great opportunity falling to the Americans of his day, of going back to first principles and being logical and consistent.[2] The Americans did

summoned under the incomplete Concessions of Penn and others (Grahame, *History*, vol. ii., 266, 290). And ratification by the legislature was required in the South Carolina constitutions of 1776 and 1778 (§§ 26 and 33 respectively).

[1] So Pulteney in Parliament 1738, claiming that "this favorite prerogative, this darling power," "may now be justly disputed," Cobbett's *Parliamentary History*, vol. x., col. 858.

[2] Blackstone wrote: "It is by the law of nations essential to the goodness of a league, that it be made by the sovereign power"; and, "It is held by all the writers on the law of nature and nations, that the right of making war, which by nature subsisted in every individual, is given up by all private persons that enter into society, and is vested in the sovereign power"; and, he added, "This right is given up, not only by individuals, but even by the entire body of the people, that are under the dominion of a sovereign," *Commentaries*, i., 257. But Blackstone had just before ascribed sovereignty to the king, *ib.*, 241. Adams, however, ascribed sovereignty to the legislative; therefore, for Adams, unlike Blackstone (and Hobbes, and other absolutists), the legislative should have the power of making war and peace and leagues or treaties. Even Blackstone himself was inconsistent, since he had started out by lodging the sovereignty in the King, Lords, and Commons collectively, *ib.*, 50–1. He here, then, has to speak of the sovereign power "*quoad hoc*" or "in this case" being vested in or transferred to the king or supreme magistrate, *ib.*, 257, 258, but without giving any reason whatever for the new location of the power in these cases. The true position was perceived by others in America. Thus in the Philadelphia Convention Wilson said that some of the English king's prerogatives were "of a legislative nature; amongst others, that of war and peace, etc. The only powers he considered strictly executive, were those of executing the laws, and appointing officers," Elliot's *Debates*, v., 141. Accordingly he moved to have the house of representatives participate in the making of treaties, 523, *cf.* i. 291. Hamilton considered this power "to form a

deprive the executive of all the regal perquisites and of
many of the royal prerogatives then thought inherent in
the crown, such as the powers of granting charters of
incorporation, establishing markets, regulating weights
and measures and the currency, etc., etc.[1] Adams
himself in his early period had advised divesting the
governors of "those badges of slavery called prerogatives" (iv. 196, 206). Surely, to be led to slaughter
without being consulted is such a badge of slavery! As
for the treaty-making power, he now rightly complained
of our Constitution for dividing it between the President and the Senate; but for a reason exactly opposite
to the true one. He said this should not be, because this
power belongs wholly to the executive function (vi.
433, 435, 436). The true reason is that this power
belongs wholly to the legislative function, and therefore
to the House of Representatives as well. But Adams
pays little attention to these subjects: he devotes
himself more to the last of the functions mentioned.

(3) The power of appointment he deems an execu-

---

distinct department, and to belong, properly, neither to the legislative
nor to the executive," *The Federalist*, No. 75 (followed by Story, *Commentaries*, § 1513); and so again in his *Camillus*, No. 36 (*Works*, v., 305).
But in his *Pacificus*, No. 1, he treated the power of making war and
peace and treaties as properly an executive function (*Works*, iv., 142,
145); and was combated by Madison in *Helvidius*, No. 1 (*Writings*, iv.,
612–16). Madison had in the Convention, agreed with Wilson on the
executive power: so reported by Rufus King, in C. R. King's *Life and
Correspondence of Rufus King*, i., 588. Later he well said: "The separation of the power of declaring war from that of conducting it, is wisely
contrived to exclude the danger of its being declared for the sake of its
being conducted," 494; similarly in Benton's *Abridgement of the Debates of Congress*, i., 516A, 650B.

[1] Bolingbroke wrote of "other powers and privileges, which we call
prerogatives," as "annexed" to "the executive power," *i. e.*, as distinct from it, *Remarks on the History of England*, Letter vii. (*Works*,
Philadelphia, 1841, i., 332).

tive function, and therefore wishes it to be entrusted wholly and solely to the executive magistrate, at most "assisted by a privy council of his own creation."[1] An old colonial contention he retains: "the executive *appoints*," he says, "and the legislative *pay*" (vi. 214). To prevent its abuse, he mentions the liability to impeachment for the use made of this power (212). Possibly he referred merely to treasonable or oppressive conduct of appointees countenanced by the ministry; but possibly, too, he had in mind the illegal appointments made by James II., which were among the causes of that king's expulsion. This implies that the legislative power can prescribe laws that must be observed by the executive, giving him a free hand only in the selection of individuals that fulfill certain qualifications for the respective posts. Beyond this, however, Adams desired no further legislative interference—and not always even so much. He disapproved even of "place bills," which forbid the appointment to offices of emolument of members of the legislature.[2] Especially was he vehement against the regulation in our Constitution which requires the presidential appointments to be submitted for confirmation to the Senate. Naturally, with the power of appointing and inducting into office he included the power of removal. Therefore when, on this *casus omissus* of our Constitution, as Vice-President

---

[1] VIII., 464; *cf*. vi., 435-6. The constitution of Massachusetts, drawn up by Adams in his early period, made the councillors appointees of the senators and representatives by joint ballot, and required the governor's appointments to be "by and with the advice and consent of the council" (iv., 253, 249). Adams later wrote of this as shackling the governor, and wished it to be abolished, vi., 465; *cf*., also, x., 397.

[2] IX., 484, later; *cf*. iii., 26 and ix., 397, from his early period, 1775, when he killed a suggestion of this sort by proposing another going too far.

he had by chance in the Senate the casting vote on the question whether the President could dismiss from office without the Senate's consent, he was prepared to decide it affirmatively,[1] probably more from his own views of propriety, than from a deductive interpretation of the instrument itself.

The independence of the executive, in this matter, especially on the senate (the representative body, in his opinion, of the aristocracy), was an essential part of his plan. That plan required, as we have seen, that the leaders of the aristocracy should be segregated in an assembly by themselves, and there have their hands tied. Chief means there to tie their hands was, first of all, "to keep all executive power entirely out of their hands as a body," and "to erect a first magistrate over them, invested with the whole executive authority"; and, furthermore, he now adds, "to make them dependent on that executive magistrate for all public executive employments" (iv. 398, *cf.* 414). He urged that "it is the true interest and best policy of the common people to take away from the body of the gentlemen all share in the distribution of offices and management of the executive power," "because if any body of gentlemen have the gift of offices, they will dispose of them among their own families, friends, and connections," whereas, if one man have this whole power, there thence "arises an inevitable jealousy between him and the gentlemen," which "forces him to become a father and protector of the common people," and "to promote from among them such as are capable of public employments; so that the road to preferment is open to the common

---

[1] I., 448–50, iii., 407–12. Maclay tells of his busying himself to persuade others, *Sketches of Debate in the First Senate of the United States*, p. 109.

people much more generally and equitably in such a government than in an aristocracy, or one in which the gentlemen have any share in appointments to office" (vi. 186–7).

However good the intention here be, the part of this scheme of arousing jealousy between the executive and the aristocracy which consists in making the senators dependent on the executive for public employment, is of a very dubious complexion. Later, against a proposed amendment to the Constitution forbidding the President to appoint to office the near relatives of Senators and Representatives, Adams maintained that the President "ought to have the whole nation before him," for his selection, "without being shackled by any check by law, constitution, or institution"; and added "without this unrestrained liberty, he is not a check upon the legislative power nor either branch of it" (ix. 634). This has but one meaning. It means that the executive must have a free hand to *influence*[1] the legislature by his appointments. It means that Adams approved the corrupt ministerial patronage which had in England grown into an immense power, taking the place of the vacated prerogatives of the Crown[2]; against which, while objecting to other defects in the English practise, he never uttered a word of protest or warning.[3] Here is the check, above referred to, that the

[1] Adams does not appear to have used this word in his writings, but no bones were made about it in the secret conclave of the Convention by Mercer, combating a proposition to render members of the legislature ineligible to office, Elliot's *Debates*, v., 421, 424.

[2] Thus Blackstone said that since 1688 the Crown had "gained almost as much in influence as it" had "apparently lost in prerogative," *Commentaries*, iv., 441.

[3] Except in his first period, iv., 54–5. Jefferson relates that at his table Hamilton praised the English government *with* all its corruption;

executive is to have upon the legislature, to counter-poise the check of impeachment which the legislature has upon the executive, and the check of withholding supplies.[1] If the executive disobeys the laws which they and he, or their predecessors, have passed, they may impeach him. If he will not carry out their policy, they may withhold supplies. On the other hand, if they will not grant him the powers or the measures he desires, or insist on things disagreeable to him, he will not make the appointments they seek; and opponents he may win over by promising to them personally or their relatives lucrative offices,—and if there are some sine-cures at his disposal, all the better. This means a dicker between the executive and the legislature, in which the counters are appointments and grants. Such a check upon the legislature, in the hands of the executive, instead of being to be constitutionally provided for, is an abuse which the constitution ought to be careful to guard against. As well allow the legislature the counter-check of bribing the executive to sign a bill by a bonus

Adams, *without*, *Works*, vii., 390, ix., 96, *cf.* vi., 95, 288, vii., 371.   Ames represents Adams as hating the British government "in everything but its theory," and as believing it corrupt, King's *Life and Correspondence*, iii., 305.   For a statement by Hamilton himself see Elliot's *Debates*, v., 229.   Hamilton refers to Hume; whose defense of the king's influence may be found in his essay on *The Independency of Parliament*.   The English were so used to this kind of corruption that Gibbon wrote of it, ironically to be sure, as "the most infallible symptom of constitutional liberty," *Decline and Fall*, ch. xxi., between notes 123 and 124; and again of its "gentle influence" in contrast with "the stern mandates of authority," ch. xxvi., between notes 13 and 14.

[1] In England this check, along with corruption at the polls, had grown so strong as to render the royal negative superfluous (*cf.* Franklin, Elliot's *Debates*, v., 152).   We shall find Adams complaining of electoral corruption.   He seems to have stopped there.   Indeed, the difference between him and Hamilton was that Hamilton would allow corruption of the legislature as well before as after election, Adams only after.

from the treasury or a raise of salary! All parties to
such dickering would deserve to be impeached, if only
there were other powers to do it. Yet, for the sake of
such abusive dickering, Adams wished the executive
chief to have the power of appointment completely,
and thought the depriving him of it, or the lessening it,
in the manner prescribed by our Constitution, would too
much weaken him especially over against the senate and
the class it represents.[1]

Another reason he urged in condemnation of this
feature in our Constitution was, that it would introduce
faction and party division within the Senate, in contending for offices (vi. 434-5). We shall see that Adams
wished, and but for this clause would have expected, to
keep party division out of each of the chambers, appor-
tioning it between them; but as we ourselves do not
expect, or even desire, such a state of things, this
reason is for us naught. Better is his argument that it
weakens executive responsibility, and by making the
Senators share with the President the guilt of bad
appointments, prevents them from criticizing and condemning when a mistake is discovered (vi. 433). From
the practical point of view, much can be said against
giving appointments to a legislature. In his early
democratical period Adams had been willing to have
even the military officers appointed by the assembly.
Experience in the Congress converted him from that
opinion (iv. 582-3).

Yet in strict theory it would seem that the legislative

---

[1] So a little later, Bayard (according to Gallatin, *Annals of Fifth
Congress*, col. 1138) lamented the weakness of our executive—its small
patronage and little opportunity for influencing the representatives;
and said that in England they would lop off the substance of the monarchy if only they got rid of their venal boroughs.

power ought to appoint the officials who are to execute its will. But there is a gradation of officials, executive officers having others under them to do their bidding, and these still others. It is, therefore, proper that the appointment of the lower officials should be delegated to those above them. Hence arises in the executive department the anomalous feature of one official appointing other officials—properly his own subordinates only. At the top comes the king, if there be one, or president, or whatever he may be called. To him, then, may be delegated the appointment of the higher officials, down as far as convenience may lead. But not necessarily are all the high officials to be handed over to him. Some may be reserved to the legislature, either to appoint directly, or to have a distinct voice in their confirmation. Moreover, all appointments by every official, it would seem, ought to be controlled by his superior; and the superior of the highest official is the legislature. Especially would this be necessary if the executive chief himself is not derivative from the legislature or subject to its control. Such is the arrangement in some of our State constitutions. In almost all, the executive chief is elected by the people, so as to be independent of the legislature. Few appointments are left to him, and these are generally subject to some control by the legislature—in fewer now than formerly through a council or committee. In the Federal Constitution the control is exercised by the Senate alone. Here the theory again is violated, as there is no good reason but convenience for confining the control to one of two "equal" branches. Our constitution-makers recognized that the House of Representatives would be too large a body to be entrusted with the annoying occupation of examining into appointments, and they

appear to have had some antipathy to a separate council, especially objecting to the expense it would entail.[1]
As the Senate at first consisted of less than twenty-six
members, and was hardly expected ever to reach a
much larger number, they appear to have thought it a
fit body to be employed also as a council.[2] A deter-
mining reason seems to have been one peculiar to our
circumstances. The new Federal government was an
object of dread to our forefathers, who looked upon it
almost as a foreign power, the successor of the government of England. As they had suffered before from

[1] Such a council, for this purpose, was proposed in the Convention by
Mason and Franklin, and advocated by Wilson, Dickinson, and Madison, but was rejected by eight States to three; see Elliot's *Debates*, v.,
522, 523, 525–6, *cf.* 570, i., 495. (For the error on 292 of assigning the motion to Madison, see Madison's *Writings*, iii., 176.) It was again urged in
the New York ratifying convention, by M. Smith, Elliott's *Debates*, ii.,
408. Unfortunately the report on this topic is meager. But see, further,
ib. iii., 494, 496, iv., 108–10, 117, 123, 128, 134. Also Mercer desired a
council, drawn from both houses, to direct the executive's influence
against the legislature, *ib.*, v., 421. And Jefferson objected to its absence, *Works*, ii., 317, 324; but later concurred (and agreed with Adams
that appointment to office is purely an executive function), *ib.*, vii., 12.
At the time there was an advisory council in every State except New
Jersey (and in New York its function went so far as to make appointments). In the unicameral States, in Georgia it was called the "executive council," and in Pennsylvania and Vermont it was conjoined with
the president or governor as part of the executive. In Connecticut and
Rhode Island it had no name, and its members were called "assistants."
In Delaware, New Jersey, and South Carolina the upper branch of the
legislature was named the "council," or the "legislative council," and
must not be confounded with the real council, severally called the "executive council," "privy council," or "council of state."

[2] Gorham, followed by Randolph, recommended the method finally
adopted, as a copy of the mode prescribed by the constitution of Massachusetts, Elliot's *Debates*, v., 328, 330, 350. This was incorrect, as the
Massachusetts mode was for the governor to nominate and appoint
"by and with the advice and consent of the council," not of the senate,
that constitution providing a council as a distinct body, elected out of
the senate.

appointments from abroad, they disliked the idea of this new strange government appointing officials within a State without the consent of the State. Then, when the Senate was instituted as a body within that government specially representing the States, it appeared appropriate to entrust to it the control over appointments. This is a feature in our system that cannot be used as a model for other governments; and even in our system the reason for it has long ceased to exist.[1]

In one point, however, Adams wished the executive power to be confined. Although the first magistrate must be the generalissimo of the military forces, Adams would have the people careful not to grant him a standing army to command in time of peace, or at least not a large one. The superfluousness of such an army in a mixed government or limited monarchy was one of his reasons for preferring that form to absolute monarchy (iv. 382). A navy, yes: an army, no (*cf.*, ix. 221). The militia may be relied upon, and should be kept up. The expenditure upon it being guarded by the representatives, its officers must be appointed by the executive.[2] He was right that a standing army is not necessary against internal enemies, such as a turbulent nobility, into whose hands it would most likely fall; while the need of it against the people is one of the evils of absolutism. But he rather unduly generalized the British exemption from external danger, which is owing to her

[1] Another operative motive may have been that pointed out by J. A. Smith, *The Spirit of American Government*, p. 142,—a desire on the part of the reactionary constitution-makers in 1787 to discard a check upon the President such as the earlier democratic constitution-makers had placed upon the governors in the executive councils.

[2] VI., 197, *cf.* iv., 359. So he had designed for the Massachusetts constitution of 1780, iv., 249.

peculiar isolation. We in America, however, share that peculiarity: we are practically an insular country, being a continental country, and may rely for protection from foreign aggression upon a navy,[1] which is little susceptible of being used against the liberties of the people.

CHAPTER X

THE SENATE

THE senate is described as "the reservoir of wisdom."[2] "Fast and tenacious of the maxims, customs, and laws of the nation," it is "the repository" of tradition, the controller both of king and people, "the patron and guardian of liberty" on occasions when "the giddy, thoughtless multitude, and even their representatives" would throw it away (vi. 152, 118, 92),—provided always it be "debarred from all executive power" (iv. 380), with which it has "nothing to do" (vi. 534, later). Especially is its purpose to be a barrier to protect the property of the rich from the envy of the poor (65, 118); for all property is "as sacred as the laws of God," that of the rich as much so as that of the poor,

---

[1] Cf. Madison in The Federalist, No. 41, and already Drayton, speech in the assembly of South Carolina, January 20, 1778 (Niles's Principles and Acts of the Revolution, p. 372), and R. H. Lee in a letter to Monroe, 1784 (Bancroft, History of the Constitution, i., 337–9). Similarly G. Morris, in Sparks's Morris, ii., 440. America like England in being free from attack by land, W. Winterbotham, Historical. . . View of the American United States, London, 1795, vol. iii., p. 337.

[2] IV., 320. So, in the first period, of the executive, ix., 506.

and libetry is in danger when the rights of the rich are insecure.[1]

It would seem, then, that the senate, consisting of the owners of the purses, ought to have the initiative and the principal say in the making of finance bills. The English Constitution gave the prerogative to the Commons, for the very reason that the Commons did not represent the poor, but the moneyed men, while the Lords represented the landed men.[2] But if Adams's scheme were carried out in the way we shall presently see him more fully describe it, his senate and house of representatives would be utterly dissimilar from the two English chambers, and it would be irrational to give the primary control of the purse-strings to the house representing the poor and comparatively moneyless and to give only the second say in the matter to the house of the rich and moneyed.[3] In that scheme the proper arrangement would be for bills principally affecting the liberty of the many to originate in the lower house, and for bills principally affecting the pockets of

---

[1] VI., 9, viii., 454; vi., 65, 89; cf. ix., 560. Yet he later treated property in land, like the tenure of office, as arising from the laws of society, vi., 473 (cf. Blackstone, *Commentaries*, i., 192), and as "the creature of convention, of social laws, and artificial order," x., 360.

[2] In England, remember, the land-tax has generally been levied on the tenant. Although it ultimately falls on the owner (a fact not at first known), this mode of collection makes the tenant the first to feel any change in its amount.

[3] Especially in a country, as in ours, where the land-tax is levied directly on the owner.—Parsons in *The Essex Result* would have had the lower house, representative of persons only, without property qualification, originate money-bills, on the strange ground that they would be less likely to be extravagant, Parsons's *Parsons*, 390-1. That house, however, was intended to represent the average wealth of the country, and the middle class were supposed to be more careful of their money than the very rich. It was overlooked that the poorest among them would be likely to be lavish with other people's money.

the few to originate in the upper. Each house would then, to be sure, have an absolute veto over the action of the other. This Adams, of course, admitted in the case of finance bills coming up to the senate from the representatives. He did not go so far as the English Constitution has gone—because he did not know it!—in withdrawing the veto (at least the absolute) upon finance bills, from the upper chamber. His senate was to have the absolute veto over everything passed by the other house. By this means it was to be the barrier to protect the interests of the propertied class.[1]

---

[1] Really, however, in our Constitution, as the Senate alone has to do with treaties and appointments, so the House alone ought to have to do with finance bills, which should go to the President with little or no meddling on the part of the Senate (which, in fact, has vitiated almost every tariff bill that has come before it). We escaped a worse fate only by an ace; for in the Convention the Senate came near receiving even the power of originating money bills, equally with the House (as in Connecticut where it was said to work well, Elliot's *Debates*, v., 189), Morris and Rutledge for instance thinking the Senate especially fit for this purpose, *ib.*, 394, 419. The Senate was deprived of origination by one of the compromises, to lessen the influence of the smaller States after granting them in that body equal votes with the larger, *ib.*, 274, 311, 394, 410, 418. It was given the right to make amendments, because of the danger of the House tacking other matters to money bills and so robbing the Senate of its amending right in those matters also (Randolph's method of preventing this being rejected as unworkable, *ib.*, 414–20). The example of South Carolina also had weight, where such a restriction (in §7 of the constitution of 1776 and in §16 of that of 1778, but without any definition, or provision against tacking) had led to evasion, *ib.*, 189, 419. Yet it would have required but little ingenuity to prevent tacking. Already the constitution of Maryland, 1776, contained a clear provision against it, in § 11; and soon that of Delaware, 1792, followed suit, in art. ii., sect. 14. The Constitution Act of the Commonwealth of Australia, 1900, accomplishes the purpose very simply in art. 55: "Laws imposing taxation shall deal only with the imposition of taxation, and any provision therein dealing with any other matter shall be of no effect."

The principal purpose of the senate, however, is, as
we have seen, to serve as a safety-valve for the superior
men dangerous to the state,—a hole wherein to ostra-
cize them. It is the place for segregating the natural
aristocracy among mankind, where, under two masters,
they are "the best men, citizens, magistrates, generals,
or other officers," "the guardians, ornaments, and
glory of the community"; for, destructive though they
be of the commonwealth and a curse to society if not
provided for, yet, if "judiciously managed in the constitution," they may be made a blessing, being, "like
fire, all-consuming masters, but good servants."[1]
"When a senate exists," says Adams, "the most
powerful man in the state may be safely admitted in
the house of representatives, because the people have
it in their power to remove him into the senate as soon
as his influence becomes dangerous"; and there he is
no longer so superior to the others, who even excel
him in some respects, and "has lost much of his influence with the people" (iv. 291). Would this simple
contrivance work? Would the people thus remove
their favorites? Adams evidently had in mind the
examples of Pulteney and Pitt.[2] Those popular men
lost influence with the people because they voluntarily
deserted the people. Suppose their entrance into the
upper house were forced: they would then not lose their
popularity. The entrance to the senate being voluntary, other popular leaders (Gladstone, for instance)
have been wise enough to keep out.[3] Leaders of the

[1] IV., 397, vi., 73, 395, and, later, 533.

[2] VI., 124, x., 13, 198; *cf.* iv., 290, note by Granville Sharp.

[3] Sometimes, too, the leaders of the aristocratic party have not been
wise enough thus to win an opponent when they could. In Massachusetts, it was one of the blunders of Governor Hutchinson not to

aristocracy (like Disraeli) have, of course, gained by
"promotion" to the peerage. The senate, says Adams,
is "eternally the very focus of ambition" (iv. 320, *cf.*
291). It is so chiefly because of its conferring greater
power. If instead it caused loss of power, it would be
avoided.[1]

But how does Adams conceive that the senate is to
be instituted? The same question should have been
asked in connection with the single executive magistrate; but Adams has united them, saying that they
must both together be either elective or hereditary,
since otherwise their mutual checks would not balance.[2]
We shall presently see that Adams wished the house of
representatives always to be elective. In regard to the
executive chief and the senators his attitude is different, and his language designedly less clear. Here occurs
the defect alluded to near the beginning, that Adams
did not devote attention to elucidate the subject of
representation. On the one hand, he treats all the
branches of the legislature as respectively representing
the three natural orders in society (v. 90), or at least,
more definitely, he makes out, as we shall have occasion
to notice more specially soon, that the two chambers

consent to the election of Hancock to the Council when he was vacillat-
ing in 1771, till it was too late and he refused it himself in 1772 and 1773
(see Wells's *Samuel Adams*, i., 398, 470–5, ii., 73).

[1] It is perhaps, in our country, from a half-conscious impression of
Senators being "shelved" that candidates for the presidency have so
rarely been drawn from their ranks. And this, too, is a reason why some
prominent American politicians have fought shy of the Senate. Yet in
the case of a certain perennial aspirant for the presidency it would have
been better both for his party and for the country, had his friends (and
his enemies) been able to immure him in the Senate a dozen years ago.
And now again a certain ex-President at large it would be well if his
native State could only incage therein.

[2] VI., 532, ix., 348 n. These passages are from the later period; but
they are borne out by his opinions in the present period, *cf.* ix., 566.

respectively represent the rich and the poor, the upper
and lower classes, the aristocracy and the democracy,
the few and the many. This scheme seems to require
that the single executive should represent a topmost
class of a single individual (which is an absurdity), or
at least a class of the very few—the very high, distinguished off from the high or upper. The executive
magistrate, however, is this topmost individual himself, and now, on the other hand, he is treated by Adams
as representing the whole nation. We might then
expect this symmetrical scheme: that the senate represents the upper classes, the house the lower classes,
and the executive both the classes, all the classes, the
whole people. But no, the scheme is now rather that
all the three branches of the legislative represent, each
of them, the whole nation, but each of them in a different way, or for a different purpose,—the first magistrate "for the management of the executive power,"
the representatives "as guardians of the public purse,"
the senate "for other purposes, namely, as a watch set
upon both the representative and the executive power,"
as "guardians of property against levellers," and as
guardians of liberty against the ambitious (vi. 117–18).
"The people," he maintains, "are the fountain and
original of the power of kings and lords, governors and
senates, as well as [of] the house of commons, or assembly of representatives. And if the people are
sufficiently enlightened to see all the dangers that
surround them, they will always be represented by a
distinct personage to manage the whole executive
power"; by "a distinct senate," for its purposes; and
by "a distinct house of representatives," for its.[1]

---

[1] VI., 118.—In England this was controverted doctrine. In the House
of Commons in 1693 Sir Edward Seymour opposed his colleagues, "that

And this is not only said once, but it is repeated in almost identical words even of the three departments of the government, taking in the judiciary. "The body of the people" is "the fountain and original of all power and authority, executive and judicial, as well as legislative; and the executive ought to be appointed by the people, in the formation of their constitution, as much as the legislative. The executive represents the majesty, persons, wills, and power of the people in the administration of government and dispensing of laws,[1] as the legislative does in making, altering, and repealing them. The executive represents the people for one purpose, as much as the legislative does for another." "The people are represented by every power and body in the state, and in every act they do. So the people are represented in courts of justice by the judges and juries," "as well as [by] members of the senate and the house" (171-2). All this may be true, in a way, of our government, where the offices are elective, and because they are elective; and it takes our state out of

---

represent the people," to "the lords, who only represent themselves," Cobbett's *Parliamentary History*, vol. v., col. 759. But others were willing, when the Lords were on their side, to accept them as representatives of the people, as was done, *e. g.*, in 1701 in a pamphlet entitled *Jura Populi Anglicani* (republished *ib.*, Appendix, col. 192) by a Whig tirading against a Tory House of Commons when the House of Lords was in the hands of Whigs. In 1770 Burke said: "The king is the representative of the people; so are the lords; so are the judges," *Works*, i., 492. But in 1784 Burke spoke of the members of the lower House as the "sole representatives" of the people; whereupon in the other House Lord Shelburne asseverated: "I say this House is equally the representatives of the people," *ib.*, ii., 544 and n. Also Chatham had said: "We are, equally with that House, intrusted with the people's rights," Speech, February 2, 1770. *Correspondence of William Pitt, Earl of Chatham*, London, 1837, vol. iii., p. 417 n., *cf.* p. 372 n.

[1] *Cf.* "the executive power, which represents the whole people in the execution of laws," vi., 197.

the category of the mixed, in which at least one element must be, or represent, the aristocracy in their own right. But Adams, besides failing to perceive this latter distinction, ignored the former, and looked upon all officials or rulers as representatives of all the people, even to the extent of taking the toleration of a government by an oppressed people for the consent of the governed. "Every government," says he, "despotism, monarchy, aristocracy, and every mixture, is created by the people, continued by their sovereign will, and represents their majesty, their august body. Resistance, therefore, to a despotism, or simple monarchy, or a mixed government, is as really treason against the majesty of the people, as when attempted against a simple or representative democracy."[1] Or still more explicitly, as he later avers, "all government, except the simplest and most perfect democracy," which hardly exists anywhere, "is representative government. The simplest despotism, monarchy, or aristocracy, and all the most complicated mixtures of them that ever existed or can be imagined, are mere representatives of the people, and can exist no longer than the people will to support them."[2]

[1] VI., 145–6. The last, of course, must be understood of resistance by an individual or a minority.

[2] VI., 469. And he converts Lafayette's saying, "For a nation to be free, it is only necessary that she wills it" (which hails from La Boëtie's *La Servitude volontaire, ou le contr'un*,—ed. of 1872, p. 9, *cf.* pp. 11, 13), into "For a nation to be slave, it is only necessary that she wills it," 474. But the nation would not be slave if she really wills (*i. e.*, desires) it, and if the tyrant represents her. This is absolutist doctrine, which Adams might have found in Hobbes ("quod volenti fit, injuria non est," *De Civitate*, c., 15) and in Pufendorf, whence the latter concluded that laws decreed by a king must be considered to have the implicit consent of the people, *De Jure Naturæ et Gentium*, I., vi., 13, VII., ii., 14, iv., 2. It does away with the need of any other representation, as was expressly

Now, it is evident that there is a great difference between such a kind of representation, little more than metaphorical, and that by officials chosen to their offices by the people, or appointed by others so chosen. It is plain, that the elected members of the lower house are, in common parlance, which Adams follows, distinctively called "representatives," those others not. But Adams runs the two together by holding that the original institution of an office by the people, "in the formation of their constitution," is sufficient. He exalts his early democracy[1] unto saying that "if the original and fountain of all power and government is in the people, as undoubtedly it is, the people have as clear a right to erect a simple monarchy, aristocracy," or an equal or any other mixture, if they judge it best, "as they have to erect a democracy,"—"as clear a right to appoint a first magistrate for life as for years, and for perpetuity in his descendants as for life."[2] He

---

enjoined by Hobbes, *De Civitate*, or *Leviathan*, chs. 18 and 19; although Pufendorf allowed that such other representation, under fundamental laws first agreed upon, would impair only the monarch's absoluteness, and not his supremacy, and found fault with Hobbes for not perceiving this distinction [without a difference], *De Jure*, etc., VII., vi., 10, 13. And since Adams's time, Austin has maintained that, though judges are subordinates, yet judge-made law, when permitted, is established by the state, *The Province of Jurisprudence Determined*, 1832, pp. 27–9. But somewhat similarly already Chatham had specified that to be, not so much law, as "an evidence of the law," the court's decision must be "submitted to, without reluctance, by the people," and be "unquestioned by the legislature (which is equivalent to a tacit confirmation)," Speech, January 9, 1770, *Correspondence*, iii., 382–3 n.

[1] *Cf.* iii., 16, iv., 17–18, 20, ix., 430, iv., 225.

[2] VI., 117. "The right of the people to confide their authority and majesty to one man, or a few men, can no more be doubted than to a larger number," 146. "The people, the nation, in whom all power resides originally, may delegate their power for one year or for ten years; for years, or for life; or may delegate it in fee simple or fee tail,

here invokes the democratical doctrine of the supremacy
and sovereignty of the people for the purpose of de-
throning democracy. It is like saying that a freeman
may sell himself into slavery, or that an omnipotent
power can annihilate itself. The people are so supreme
that they can do everything: therefore they can set up
a hereditary government. The Dutch, in fact, had but
recently done this very thing: only they had then ceased
to be a democracy,—had even ceased to be so long
before; and their case was hardly a happy precedent.
In acting thus, one generation seizes supremacy over
all succeeding generations, depriving them of choice in
their government. This is usurpation; and it is not
democratic doctrine. All true democrats restrict the
power of the people, considering many rights of men
inalienable and not transferable to their rulers. Their
own liberty is so treated by most; by all, that of their
posterity. Adams himself, in his democratic period,
spoke of "certain unalienable rights," and included the
right of the people to institute and to alter their government.[1] He still speaks of the right to the whole sovereignty being indivisible and inalienably inhering in
the people (iv. 308, vi. 469); though he has allowed the
people, in an equally mixed, even a free, state, to give
up two thirds of the actual sovereignty to the aristocracy and the king. He seems to mean that the people,
though possessing only one third of the actual sovereignty, still have the right to the whole if the others

if I may so express myself; or during good behavior, or at will, or till
further orders," 429.

[1] In the bill of rights of the Massachusetts constitution of 1780, iv.,
220, 225, where he adopted some popular clauses from the Virginia bill of
rights, which had been drawn up by Mason in 1776. The Virginia bill,
Sec. 3, admits the right of altering the government as residing in "a
majority of the people."

default in their duties. Thus he still concedes to the people the right of altering their government, if need be,—but now only by revolution.

To this effect he immediately qualifies the above statement. "When I say for perpetuity or for life, it is always meant to imply, that the same people have at all times a right to interpose, and to depose for malad-ministration—to appoint anew. No appointment of a king or senate, or any standing powər, can be, in the nature of things, for a longer period than *quam diu se bene gesserit*, the whole nation being judge. An appoint-ment for life or perpetuity can be no more than an appointment until further order; but further order can only be given by the nation" (vi. 117). But nowhere except in ancient Crete and mediæval Poland, had insurrection been recognized among the regular insti-tutions[1]; and nowhere does hereditary government provide any means for the nation to give such further order, which it is the distinguishing characteristic of elective government, of representative government proper, to provide. "It must be a great occasion," Adams continues, "which can induce a nation to take such a subject into consideration, and make a change." Precisely: in hereditary government no change can be made in the incumbent in the office but by changing the office itself, by upsetting the whole government, by revolution, which is almost synonymous with civil war. In representative government, not only the constitution

---

[1] But later the right of insurrection against a government that vio-lates the rights of the people was consecrated in the French constitution of 1793, art. 35. Compare also art. 68 of that of 1848. Long before, in England, a merely partial right of redressing grievances by distraining the king's possessions had been conceded to the committee of twenty-five barons, by Magna Charta, art. 61.

can be altered "on great occasions," but on ordinary occasions, at fixed periods, the incumbents can be and are changed without any trouble whatever. This, and not the amount of authority in the office, is the characteristic also of free government.[1] Moreover, the phrase "during good behavior" is a most deceptive misnomer. Life tenure, and *a fortiori* hereditary tenure, is not *quamdiu se bene gesserit*, but *quamdiu se non male* (or *pessime*) *gesserit*. There is a long interval between acting well and acting badly, between acting acceptably and acting intolerably. Government, the offices, must be instituted once for all; government, the incumbents, not. Our ancestors established a form of government for us, their descendants. But they established one which we may alter as peaceably as it was established, since no person and no class was endowed with a right and a power to negative our action. The people who sets up a hereditary government for its descendants confers such right and power to a person and to a class, and thus fastens upon its descendants a government which they cannot alter without the consent of those interested parties, except by force. As a matter of fact, no government that cannot be altered but with bloodshed has ever been inaugurated without bloodshed. Hereditary rights have always been usurped. The usurpers of course have had partisans among the people and the rest have acquiesced; but there is considerable difference between passive consent and active setting up for themselves: the people's usurpation over succeeding generations has always been compliance with the usurpation of their own despots. And the difference

---

[1] *Cf.* Livy: "Libertatis autem originem inde magis, quia annuum imperium consulare factum est, quam quod deminutum quicquam sit ex regia potestate, numeres," ii., § 1.

between the governments that result is still more pro-
found. A hereditary monarch ought, no doubt, to
represent the people; but in such a system there is
nothing to keep him to his duty but the distant fear
of an uprising. The people cannot tell him: 'If you do
not represent us as we wish you to do, we will choose
some one else in your place'; they can only say: 'We
will fight and try to drive you out'; to which he may
reply: 'I, too, at the head of my retainers will fight and
try to quell your rebellion.' In the seventeenth century, when the English Constitution more resembled
Adams's plan than it has ever done since, twice the
people so treated the King, and with success. Possibly,
Adams viewed those occurrences as the natural working
of his system, since they ended in the replacing of other
Kings. But the first led to the temporary establishment
of another kind of government, and the second to the
introduction, with a new line of Kings, of considerable
modifications in the character of the government. We
have, too, always been given to understand that the
design of instituting a properly mixed and balanced
government was, as he once expressed it, "to preserve
mankind from those horrible calamities which revolutions always bring with them" (iv. 509).

In the case of the senate, Adams says little about its
composition on the supposition of its being hereditary.
He always implies, of course, that it is not a closed
corporation into which no one may enter without the
permission of those already within. It is, indeed, his
desideratum that the popular and dangerous great men
should be injected into it. But how this operation is to
be performed, he does not say. Hume had suggested
an emendation of the British system by which the upper
house itself should, so to speak, pull such persons into it

9

by electing them, no one being allowed to refuse.[1] An objection is that probably the lords would seldom exercise this power. On the other hand, it would seem reasonable that the lower house, as most nearly representing the sovereignty of the nation, should have the right of raising its distinguished members into the nobility, thus getting rid of them and their descendants, and thrusting them into the upper house.[2] Between these opinions it might be hard to decide; and perhaps they might both merit adoption together. But on these and other plans Adams has not a word. For the beginning of a peerage here in America, he shows his view to be that this ought to be left to the people. The Order of the Cincinnati he criticized, not so much for setting up a hereditary nobility, as for doing so without consulting the people, or waiting for their consent (ix. 524, viii. 192–3, v. 488–9). He expected, as we shall see hereafter, that at some future date the American people would, in another constitutional convention, set up a peerage. As a people never establishes, but only sanctions masters already self-appointed, he in this expectation somewhat resembled Horace's rustic on the river's bank. But, however this be, he left it to the people to settle the system, and hardly so much as gave a hint himself, either because of its not being a pressing problem, or because he was satisfied with the English model, with the king or first magistrate as the fountain of honor (*cf.* vi. 256), and

---

[1] By this means "every turbulent leader in the House of Commons might be taken off, and connected by interest with House of Peers," *Idea of a Perfect Commonwealth.*

[2] A suggestion of this sort seems to have been made by Filangieri, *La Scienza della Legislazione,* 1780, I., xi. (ed. of 1826, vol. i., pp. 119–20). But his words are obscure.

was confident of its being followed. In so doing he left a lacuna in his "science of government"; but, as we shall see, avoided a dilemma.

CHAPTER XI

THE HOUSE OF REPRESENTATIVES

THE undemocratic doctrine of the omnipotence of the people, including the power to divest themselves of their power, passes even beyond Adams's intention, in that he not only limits it by the right of resuming it by force when abused, but further restricts it to two of the three branches of the legislative, and always urges that the people must reserve the third to themselves. The members of this third branch, the people, to be free—and he wished them to be free,— must hold elective, and, too, frequently elective. "There can be no free government," he says, "without a democratical branch in the constitution" (iv. 289). "Popular elections of one essential branch of the legislature, frequently repeated, are the only possible means of forming a free constitution"; "when popular elections are given up, liberty and free government must be given up" (466). Therefore a representative assembly must be "an integral," "an essential part of the sovereignty."[1] Such, we may remember, was his definition of free or republican government,

---

[1] V., 456, 457; cf. iv., 448, vi., 67; similarly, later, 478. All this, of course, is true, as far as it goes, but is so only because a hereditary senate and a hereditary king are *not* representatives of the people.

where the people retain "an essential share in the sovereignty."[1]

The people must retain such a share because they are "the best keepers of their own liberties, and the only keepers who can always be trusted," provided they be not the sole keepers (vi. 64, so 65, 66). Their representatives must form a distinct branch of the legislature, with a negative upon the others, "to be the guardians of the public purse, and to protect the people in their turn, against both kings and nobles" (118). For Adams, this is enough. He expresses contentment with "a constitution in which the people reserve to themselves the absolute control of their purses, one essential branch of the legislature, and the inquest of grievances and state crimes" (v. 290). "The people," he says, "have liberty to make use of that reason and understanding God hath given them, in choosing governors, and providing for their safety in government, where they annually choose all; nay, they have it even where the king and senate are hereditary, so long as they have the choice of an essential branch," since then "no law can be made, no money raised, not one step can be taken, without their concurrence," and not an act can be done by their ministers without liability to impeachment "if it is wrong."[2] "A representative assembly" is "the only instrument by which the body of the people can act" (v. 456, similarly 460). "The liberty of the people depends entirely on the constant and direct communication between them and the legis-

---

[1] See above, p. 27.
[2] VI., 119–20; similarly 67. He forgets pardons, treaties, and the excitation of war (for the purse-strings must be loosened if war be once brought upon the country); and he overlooks that impeachment would be futile, unless the lords convict.

lature, by means of their representatives" (iv. 468).
No other instrument is necessary.[1]

But why this distinction? The question may be
asked from the opposite sides. If hereditariness is good
in two cases, why not also in the third? If election is
good, and necessary, in the one case, why not also in the
two others? Adams's answer is that election in one
case is enough,—it is necessary in at least one branch,
even though it be not good there; but it is not necessary further, if it is not good in the other branches; now,
election is not good everywhere,—it has its evils: it is
subject to corruption,[2] to turbulence; and these evils
are the greater the more important the office, and
especially in the executive are they great, because here
foreign intrigue, he thought, would come in, as we shall
later have occasion to note. "Elections to offices which
are a great object of ambition," he wrote, "I look at
with terror" (viii. 465). Therefore, in the higher offices
the evils of election he believed would exceed the benefits of representation.[3] Rather than have the senators
chosen by the whole people, or by districts, he held
"the chance of having wisdom and integrity in a sena-
tor by hereditary descent would be far better."[4] But

[1] Montesquieu learned his English lesson a little more fully, saying of
the people, "Il ne doit entrer dans le gouvernement que pour choisir ses
représentants," *Esprit des Lois*, XI., vi.

[2] IV., 284, vi., 50–2. This was an early fear, ix., 435.

[3] The higher functions of the executive, exercised by an assembly,
would corrupt the assembly, iv., 290, vi., 64, *cf.* 172–3, ix., 302. Especially if this assembly be elective, the corrupting influence would
descend to the people, *cf.* vi., 66.

[4] VI., 249. He thus believed (even for state elections) in the shortest
of "short ballots." He would have been horrified at our ballots with a
score or so of offices to be filled and half a dozen candidates for each.
Never contemplating the possibility of such monstrosities he said little
about the objection to the elective system lying in the ignorance of the
electors.

why the necessarily small number of senators should not be elected by the aristocracy all told—the natural, or the artificial and hereditary,—he never considered. There is nothing in his principles opposing such election; in fact, his principles lead up to it. It is even partly sanctioned by his British model; for in the British House of Lords, when he wrote, the Scotch members were elective, and a little later also the Irish. It is sufficient that the hereditary principle (by primogeniture) should be in the aristocracy: it is not necessary that it should be in the members of the senate representing that aristocracy. It may be questioned, too, whether an assembly elected from the whole body of the aristocracy would not be stronger than one composed of a few great families, the individuals in which may be incompetents and idiots, and often are inexperienced youths.

As for the first magistrate, speaking of elective kings, that is, of such a magistrate with tenure for life, he said the experience of "Bohemia, Poland, Hungary, Sweden, etc.," "after long miseries, wars, and carnage," has always proved "chance to be better than choice, and hereditary princes preferable to elective ones" (vi. 121). This, however, proves nothing against first magistrates elected for short terms; and the shorter the term, the further removed are they from those proved evils. Adams's advocacy of life and hereditary tenure will be examined later: here are to be examined his objections to elections, even for short terms, which, not being clearly separated from objections to elections for long terms, can be gathered only from his general positions. First comes his fear of corruption,[1] intrigue, foreign

---

[1] "Disappointed candidates for popular elections are as often corrupted by their fall from power, as hereditary aristocracies by their continuance in it," vi., 75.

influence,—all consequences of long terms and excessive power (such as the absolute veto). An ambitious magistrate, elected for a short term, may abuse his power in order to seize and retain it.[1] Then we have seen that Adams wished the executive power to be acted upon by the interest of self-protection. A first magistrate may desire to uphold the power of his office, as also the greatness of his country, if he is to retain his position through life and leave it to his descendants; if he occupies it only temporarily, especially if he be not re-eligible, he has not so much interest: he is like a tenant on a short lease compared with the owner[2]: he may let his estate run down, and sell away the powers of the office, and even the interests of the people, for his own personal profit—to "make hay while the sun shines," as another expressed it.[3] As already men-

---

[1] Comparing temporary and permanent powers, though finding "little difference in effect" between them, the former, he says, "has often been the worst of the two, because it has often been sooner abused, and more grossly, in order to obtain its revival at the stated period"—the next election, vi., 73. But he cites no instances in a regularly constituted state.

[2] So Madison, *Writings*, i., 190; and Lacroix, *Review of Constitutions*, translated, London, 1792, vol. i., p. 312.

[3] Morris, Elliot's *Debates*, v., 325, *cf.* 334–5, 343, and in Sparks's *Life and Correspondence of Gouverneur Morris*, ii., 509. *Cf.*, also, Randolph, Elliot's *Debates*, iii., 485–6, and Henry, 388. Morris urged also that he might purposely sacrifice his executive rights to court popularity in the legislature, expecting to re-enter it and enjoy its greater power, *ib.*, v., 473; similarly Madison, *Writings*, i., 190, 345–6. On this account, it may be observed, the opinion was entertained that more power could safely be entrusted to a hereditary than to a temporary executive, *cf.* Henry, Elliot's *Debates*, iii., 202, Hamilton, *The Federalist*, No. 75, *cf.* No. 22, § 11 (followed by Story, *Commentaries*, § 1509), or to one for life than to one for a fixed term, Hamilton, Elliot's *Debates*, v., 204; and this consideration is assigned (by C. C. Pinckney) as the reason why the President needed to have the Senate associated with him in treaty-making, *ib.*, iv., 264. So, before, in Massachusetts in the controversy

tioned, and soon to be examined, Adams wished the
executive chief to be impartial between the two parties
severally placed in the senate and in the lower house.
Only a hereditary, non-elective magistrate can be such;
for, as his filial editor comments: "It is difficult to
suppose any president will be impartial between two
parties, to one of which he must owe his election."[1]
But the first is the great reason which preëmpts his
attention. Not only the senate, but especially the
chief magistrate is "an object of ambition and dispute"
(iv. 583). Division, faction, sedition, and rebellion
are the inevitable consequence of allowing it to be
striven for. Better, then, determine constitutionally
who is to be the first man (vi. 165, 181). Even the
second places, in the senate, are too important to be
left open to competition.[2] Only the minor powers of
the lower chamber, more burdensome than remunera-
tive, and ambitioned more for honor than for influence,
are, in his opinion, safely left open to election by the
people. Such is his general theory, admitting exception
in a people not highly developed.

with Burnett, the greater confidence in a hereditary than in a temporary
ruler was urged as a reason why the British Parliament might give a civil
list once for all to the King, but the colonial assembly should not give
a fixed salary to their temporary governors (Grahame, *History*, iii., 122).
The idea is to be found also in Montesquieu's *Grandeur et Décadence des
Romains*, ch. iv.

[1] VI., 534 n.,—especially if he must owe to it his re-election. Adams
himself, however, later wrote: "he [the President] must be the slave of
the party that brought him in," so long as he has not "unrestrained
liberty" in making appointments, ix., 634; and thereby implied that if
only he had such full "executive" power, he might be free from partisanship, even though elective.

[2] In general, the dissemination of knowledge makes it "the more indispensable that every man should know his place, and be made to keep
it," vi., 276.

The house of commons, as he liked to call the only legislative branch he left to be necessarily representative,[1] we have seen him describe as the only instrument by which the people in general can act, as providing the democratic element essential in free and republican government—and sufficiently providing it,—and as designed to protect the common people against both king and nobles, against both monarchy and aristocracy. Of course, the possession of the negative is understood (vi. 94): this branch must equal each of the others in power. Emphasis also is laid upon its being the great inquest, or impeaching body, of the nation (v. 290, vi. 118, 152). The people being possessed of these powers, we have seen that he expects no harm and much good from an independent monarchy and aristocracy.

Especially to the power of withholding supplies he attributed much restraining force (iv. 398, vi. 39). Against confining to this branch, as organized in Adams's scheme, the origination of finance bills, we have already brought a theoretical objection. But even without this confinement, the power of withholding supplies would still belong to this house, as it does to the other, too, in his system, through its possessing an absolute negative. The theory to which Adams himself adhered, is that the "government," or executive, and also the senators or lords through their general upper-handedness and closeness to the executive, desire for their projects contributions from the people, and that the power of "granting" or refusing these should

[1] "House of Representatives" is a misnomer in our constitutions, since this house, fortunately, is not the only representative branch of the legislature, the other being so too; and yet, unfortunately, in the Federal Government it is the only branch with direct representation.

be lodged with the representatives of the contributing people. This is a conception of things which once held, but which exists no longer. The power of withholding supplies was a great restraining force when the lower people, managing their local concerns in their communes or townships, were lorded over by an aristocratic race of conquerors; for when they became strong enough to win the power of withholding contributions, that is, of not being taxed without their own consent, and of granting contributions upon conditions bargained for, this was a great gain. Then the people, desiring certain laws protective of their liberties, obtained them from the lords and the king; and the lords and the king, desiring contributions needed for their enterprises, obtained them from the representatives of the people. Of course the commons, after putting in their petitions for laws, and coming to terms, consented to such laws as were loyally accorded them by the lords and the king; and the lords and the king, having made their demands for taxes, consented to those obtained from the commons without further ado, as they could not augment them without breach of the contract, and they had no motive to diminish them. Legislation, in the narrow sense of the word, and tax-levying went in opposite directions, like two articles exchanged.[1]

[1] From Edward III. on, laws were "declared to be made by the King at the request of the Commons, and by the assent of the Lords and Prelates," Hallam, *Middle Ages*, ch. viii., part 3. This practice continued till Henry VI., when the Commons began to introduce "complete statutes under the name of bills, instead of the old petitions," and it became "a constant principle that the King must admit or reject them without qualification," *ib.*, such qualification being sufficiently attended to by the Lords. Hallam remarks in a note: "Perhaps the triple division of our legislature may be dated from this innovation." But the bargaining continued for a couple of centuries. Laws, it may be seen,

Now, Adams drew up his plan of government as if such conditions still existed. But not only such conditions had ceased to exist at our Revolution,[1] when the foreign government was expelled (under which taxation by their own representatives in the colonial assemblies had been balanced with the regulation of trade by the British Parliament); but also they had ceased a century before among the English at theirs (when a foreign and consequently weak line of kings was introduced), and the English government no longer was conducted on that supposition, although some of the terms and forms belonging to the old system were still, *more Britannico*, observed. Towards the end of our war for independence in 1782, when Adams was in Paris and must have been well informed of what was going on in England, the Opposition in Parliament tried to apply this method of coercing the Ministry until their grievances were redressed; but without success: its obsoleteness under the altered conditions since 1688 was clearly pointed out to them.[2] For now the people are admitted into the administration, the government is theirs, not they the

were almost literally (in the modern meaning of the term) the bills which were rendered by the government, and which the people paid. Chatham was thinking of former times when he said in his oft-quoted speech on the Stamp Act: "Taxation is no part of the governing or legislative power. The taxes are a voluntary gift and grant of the Commons alone"; adding, "The distinction between legislation and taxation is essentially necessary to liberty," *Correspondence*, ii., 366 n., 367 n.

[1] In colonial days this right of withholding supplies had, for instance, been of service to the people of New York in their resistance to the despotism and malfeasance of Governor Cornbury (1702–8) by at last inducing the Queen to supersede him (Grahame, *History*, ii., 251–3). But if their representatives had had the power of auditing the governor's accounts (which they vainly demanded), the safeguard against executive misconduct would have been still stronger.

[2] Debate of November 30th. (*Annual Register*, xxv., 134–5.)

government's; and what was true when the people were one power and the rulers another, is not so when the rulers are merely the agents of the people. Now legislation comes from the people as well as from the lords, and tax-levying (and tax-paying) is just as much an affair of the upper classes as of the lower, and the former are, of right, no greater beneficiaries of the proceeds than the latter. To withhold supplies from the government would affect the people as much as the lords; for to stop the machinery of government would inflict intolerable injury upon everybody. Indeed, in such a case the lords or rich people could protect themselves much better than the commons or poor people; and so, if a bickering over supplies were to be re-instituted, as seems to have been desired by Adams, the aristocracy could hold out much longer than the democracy. The check which Adams thinks so important in the hands of the representatives is—and already in his day was— of no account whatever. This part of his theory—and unfortunately not this alone—was an anachronism.[1]

Continuing, he says that equal conditions will result— equal laws, the essentials of a free government, will be

[1] Even the House's right to refuse certain appropriations was denied by Adams's Federalist associates, as notably in the case of the appropriations required for putting into effect Jay's treaty, and again those needed to carry on the law establishing the mint, both in 1796. Since then in our country an attempt to coerce the executive by withholding supplies has once been made, under Hayes, and was a fiasco. A few years ago, the people of Porto Rico would have found their similar attempt a boomerang, had they been permitted to carry it out; and it is a pity they were not, as one's own experience is the best teacher. We may remember that in the disputes which preceded our Revolution, the American people tried to coerce the whole British people to repeal the Stamp Act and subsequent measures, by withholding commerce with them; and this conduct, though successful at first, ultimately was injurious by depleting stores before the outbreak of hostilities.

enacted,—because the representatives of the people,
being "the special guardians of equality, equity, and
liberty, for the people," will negative the special privileges always coveted by the upper classes (vi. 68, 67).
Here comes in his reason for dividing the legislature
into two chambers; for, in his opinion, the representatives of the people are more able to pass such negatives
in a separate assembly, where the traitors to the common people are likelier to be in a minority, than in a
single assembly, where, these being added to the aristocrats, the people's opponents would probably form a
majority, the aristocracy being always more united
than the democracy. For this purpose, however, not
only must the aristocratic leaders be segregated in the
upper chamber, but the aristocrats as a body ought to
be excluded from representation in the lower chamber,
that is, they ought to be neither electors of members nor
eligible as members. This would seem to be obvious;
yet it is nowhere noticed by Adams. Here, too, he is
never precise. He frequently says the lower house must
"fairly, fully, adequately," and "equally" represent
the people (iv. 398, 488, vi. 39); but in these statements he seems to refer to the whole people—"the
whole nation" and "all classes," as he once expresses
it (iv. 288),—including the upper as well as the lower.
It is treated as the democratical branch; and we have
seen that he defined democracy as the government, not
of the many, but of all. He approved the constitutions
of New York and North Carolina, in which a higher
property qualification was placed on the senatorial
franchise than on that of the so-called representatives.
This means that the richer people could vote for both
the chambers, and the common people only for one.
And this amounts to double influence of the upper

classes—the double influence which his model, the
English Constitution, then, and to some extent still,
accords to them.[1] That in the English government
the aristocratical ingredient far exceeds the democratical, he never allowed a hint to escape him. On the
contrary, he pronounced it an "equal mixture" (447),
thereby committing the most flagrant breach of faith,
since even in the lower house the upper and the middle
classes were in his day almost alone represented, the
lower classes obtaining representation only in a meager
pittance of districts.[2] Adams hinted at some correction
of this unfairness (cf. vi. 251 n., later), but he never
desired that the upper classes should be confined to
their own chamber. Apparently, then, only the leaders,
not the aristocratic class itself, were to be segregated.
Yet the cardinal principle in his theory, as expounded
in general terms, was always that the influence of the
two orders in society was to be constitutionally trans-
planted into the two branches of the legislature and
there made equal. To make the two branches equal,
but not to make them equally represent the two orders,
is not a thorough carrying out of the theory. Now, the
opportunity which the Americans then had in establishing new constitutions—and Adams's own opportunity as a legislator, as a modern Solon—was precisely
an opportunity to put into practice the entertained
principles, and to improve upon the English model
where it fell short of its supposed theory. Yet to take

---

[1] Or is it treble? seeing that they fill both halves of the upper chamber
and, say, one-half of the lower.

[2] Cf. Bentham: "If, instead of a House of Commons and a House of
Lords, there were two Houses of Lords and no House of Commons, the
ultimate effect would be just the same," *Book of Fallacies*, IV., iii.
(*Works*, ii., 445).

advantage of this opportunity, on this point, Adams unaccountably failed. Even the lower chamber was not to represent the whole of the lower classes; for he wished to exclude the lowest. He did not go so far as Aristotle and an Italian follower of his, Portenari, in excluding three out of seven classes of men,—excluding farmers, artificers, and merchants, admitting only warriors, rich men, priests, and jurists (v. 455-6, 459). To all these classes he wished to be given "the equal right of citizens, and their proper weight and influence in society" (457),—in their own branch, notice, not in the other. But he wanted a small property-qualification, to exclude even from that branch those who have "no will of their own." He had desired this even in his democratic days (*cf.* ix. 376); no wonder, then, that he does so still.[1]

---

[1] *Cf.* iv., 479 in the case of Athens. In the Massachusetts constitution, 243. In agreement with this line of thought, he was later cautious about naturalizing foreigners, *cf.* ix., 584. The exclusion of those "without a will of their own" was not only a Tory doctrine (as taught by Blackstone, *Commentaries*, i., 171, and previously by Swift, vol. iii., 280, x., 195, and by Montesquieu, *Esprit des Lois*, XI., vi.), but even Harrington, *Oceana*, etc., 83, 436-7, 531, 622, 623, and Sydney, *Discourses*, II., v., had excluded servants as not being free men—not "able to live of themselves," "not in their own power";—and contemporary with Adams, not only Parsons had excluded those who have not a will of their own, instancing minors, females, and slaves, *The Essex Result* (in Parsons's *Parsons*, 376), but such a true democrat as Franklin would have excluded all but land-owners, *Works*, iv., 221, 224; and so, too, Madison, Elliot's *Debates*, v., 387. Also Turgot and Condorcet would confine the suffrage to land-owners, on the plea that territory is essential to a state: see the latter's *Œuvres*, v., 255, xii., 16 (but Condorcet adopted universal suffrage in 1793, *ib.*, xviii., 227-32). This reason was later advanced also by Madison, *Writings*, iv., 24, 29, (Elliot's *Debates*, v., 581, 583). It is worth remarking that within a couple of centuries after the knights were first summoned to Parliament, not only the voters were, *e. g.*, "my Ladys servauntts tenaunts and wellwyllers," but even the nominees were "suche persones as longe unto him [the Duke of

On the other hand, he did admit five corrections of the English Constitution, lying "entirely in the house of commons" (iv. 468). For this branch he accepted American practices already introduced, most of them old English practices revived or never abandoned, in one case of doubtful advantage. He wished for (1) equal, or "proportional" electoral districts (iv. 468); he advised (2) confining representatives to residents of the districts[1]; and he still recommended (3) the payment of salaries to representatives as well as to all other officials (289–90, vi. 13–14, 83). The first and the third are rational; there is no good reason for the second. Indeed, if the electors' liberty of choosing whomsoever they will to represent them be restricted at all, it might seem better to forbid their selecting persons from their own districts. A person sent up by his neighbors is more likely to look upon himself as specially *their* protector than as collaborator for the interests of the whole country; and if the people must choose from elsewhere, they are more likely to call upon men of national reputation.[2] In the theory of government there is no reason for making any restriction in this matter, except expediency.[3]

Norfolk] and be of his mennyall servaunts," *Paston Letters*, iii., 52, i., 337 (Edinburgh, 1910). That state of the electorate enhanced the influence of the lords, and its curtailment was in the interest of the free men (till servants also became even freer than the knights who used to be servants of dukes).

[1] *Ib.* This had been the law in England since 1429, and though long in desuetude, had only recently been repealed in 1774. It had been law in Massachusetts by statute of 5 William and Mary.

[2] Adams himself raised objections against such confinement to districts in the case of senators, v., 250.

[3] To break down a bad custom, almost equal to a legal restriction, it might not be undesirable to enact a temporary legal restriction in the opposite direction.

Then, although nothing appears to be said on the subject in this period, but it crops out later, he still defends (4) the right of the people to instruct their representatives (ix. 605). This right, we may note, has nowadays been not so much abandoned as commuted; for our party platforms take the place of instructions. In Adams's day, in New England, the town-meetings drew up instructions after the elections. Now the politicians lay down platforms before the elections, promising certain courses of action, and the electors choose between the different assortments of measures offered. The representative is bound now as much as then, only in different ways—then by the electors' commandment, now by his accepted engagement. If the binding is not strong now, it probably was not stronger then. Whether Adams would prefer his own to this method, we cannot know. But Adams's position here for once, though little insisted on, was truly American, and entirely un-English in view of the practice of his day. It is democratic, while aristocratic was the English position of that day, which viewed the representative once elected as independent of the electors[1]—as a trustee[2] at a distance, or the guardian of an infant ward (his appointer and dismisser all the same!) not an agent in the presence of his principal,

[1] So avowed in Parliament in 1734 by the Attorney-General, Willes, Cobbett's *Parliamentary History*, vol. ix., col. 435, though it was then denounced by the opposition as new and monstrous, *ib.*, 437-8 (Plumer), 444-6 (Barnard), 455 (Wyndham), while Yonge defended it merely as meaning that they each represented the whole country and not his own particular district, *ib.*, 450. It was in full force when Brougham wrote: see his *Political Philosophy*, iii., 33.

[2] The representatives were so called by Shippen, Cobbett's *Parliamentary History*, vii., 317; Bolingbroke, *Works*, ii., 118; Burke, *Works*, i., 492.

who may interfere when he sees his confidence misused. The English people, of course, had originally had the practice of instructing their representatives, and the representatives had submitted to it: these had, in fact, at first been summoned for the express purpose of representing to the king the views, and expressing the will, not so much of themselves as of their senders. The usurpation of superiority by the representatives has since Adams's day even in England, yielding to the pressure of the English democrats (the Radicals), given way to the modern form of pre-election engagements.

Lastly, desiring the popular branch of the legislature to be a faithful portrait of the people, and therefore to be able to change with the popular changes, the principle of permanence being already guarded in the senate, Adams still desires (5) frequent elections (iv. 466, 468, v. 457). Here, too, during this period, he says nothing about their being annual; but later he repeats that early demand.[1] We must not be misled into thinking this an especially democratic position, when we consider the connection in which it occurs. Short terms weaken the incumbents in offices. Therefore to desire short terms in the popular offices and long terms in the higher offices, as Adams did, is to betray a peculiarly aristocratic spirit.[2] Democratic is it to shorten all terms, but if any are to be lengthened, it would be the lower.[3]

---

[1] VI., 468, in 1814. Yet in 1808 he condemned reducing the federal elections from biennial, 533.

[2] Short terms were not desired in England for the simple reason that the lower House was not democratic. When the aristocrats and plutocrats, especially the latter, once got themselves or their adherents into it, they wished to remain long unmolested.

[3] A combination of short and long terms is possible, and in the representatives might have some advantages. Let elections be annual, and

In the same spirit his early democratic demand for
rotation in office through forced vacations he now dis-
cards as "a violation of the rights of mankind," "an
abridgment of the rights both of electors and candidates," to which the people will not submit.[1] Yet it is
not apparent why a restriction in time is more an
abridgment of rights than a restriction in space—a
temporal more than a geographical. He adds, that it is
not necessary in a well-balanced government (vi. 188–
91). But neither is the other.[2] His position, however,
may be defended by balancing it with the right of
instruction, on the plea that where we have the one we
need not the other, and the combination of both is
supererogatory. The English publicists, while they
repudiated instruction of representatives in any form,
though not going so far as to require rotation, yet
expected it frequently to happen in practice, and put
their reliance, if not on its actuality, yet on its poten-
tiality. It is, they said, the return, or the possible
return, of the representative into private life, that will
effectually prevent his oppressing the people with
restrictive laws or burdening them with excessive taxes,

let every representative have the right to have his name head the official
ballot for two or three elections after his first. His party could not then
change him for three or four years, but every year he would be exposed
to being ousted by a candidate of the opposite party. The same system
is applicable to some other offices. With long terms, safety requires the
power of recall,—a remedy itself not free from evil.

[1] VI., 52–3, 48, 68; later x., 411, cf. 23. This forced rotation has,
however, been retained in a dozen or more of our States for sheriffs and
other county officers.

[2] Perhaps a combination of both would alleviate the harshness of each.
Let a person be prohibited from representing the same district for more
than three or four years together, and not be allowed again till after
serving one or more such periods of representation elsewhere. Then
both the district must rotate its representatives, and the representative,
if prominent enough to be able to do so, must rotate his district.

in general selling the liberties of the people, of whom he
and his children will be members.[1] Some of the
American revolutionists outside of New England, in
parts where instruction of representatives was not so
systematic, also made references to this source of
safety[2]; but it was especially the makers of the Federal
Constitution in 1787, who deprived the state legislatures of the power to instruct their delegates to Congress (in the Senate) and left no room for a power in
the people to instruct their representatives in the new
lower House,—especially these relied upon that English
doctrine,[3] thus putting their weight on thin ice. But
Adams, still upholding the right of instruction, thought
he did not need that other source of reliance, and said
little about it. Yet, of course, all precautions are
useful; and, of course again, the right of the whole

[1] Harrington, *Oceana*, etc., p. 543 (of governors in general); Sydney,
Discourses, III., xliii., xlv., xlvi.; Nedham (quoted by Adams, vi., 66,
127); Blackstone, *Commentaries*, i., 189; Price, *Additional Observations on
Civil Liberty*, p. 35; Godwin, *Political Justice*, V., xx.; Stewart, *Political
Economy*, ii., 427. *Cf.*, above, p. 88.—The principle was familiar to
the Romans: see Eutropius, I., ix. (or viii.)

[2] The Virginia Memorial and Remonstrance (this by Wythe), 1764,
in Wirt's *Patrick Henry*, Appendix pp. ii. and iv.; Henry, in his
Resolutions, 1765, *ib.*, p. 57; Dickinson, *Letters of a Farmer*, vii.; Fairfax
County Resolutions, 1774, drawn up by Mason (in Kate M. Rowland's
Life of George Mason, i., 419); Paine, *Common Sense*, i.; R. Morris,
Wharton's *Diplomatic Correspondence of the Revolution*, v., 642.

[3] Elliot's *Debates*, v., 369 (Mason, of the executive), ii., 87 and 88
(Bowdoin), 168 (Stillman), 288 (Livingston), 293 (Lansing), 310-11
(M. Smith), 495-6 (Wilson), iii., 17-18, 99 (Nicholas), 124 (Randolph),
417 (Corbin), 485 (Mason), 647 (Z. Johnson), iv., 57 (Johnston), 103
(Davie, of the executive); and in resolutions for amendments, i., 334,
iii., 658, iv., 243 (these copying the Virginia Bill of Rights, Sect. 6). So
also Hamilton, Madison, and Jay in *The Federalist*, Nos. 35 § 10, 57
§12, and 64 §13 respectively; N. Webster, *Collection of Essays*,
1790, pp. 51, 67, 69, 80, 143, 146; Story, *Commentaries*, § 557, 586,
620.

people to regulate the character of the representation is paramount.[1]

CHAPTER XII

THE TWO HOUSES AND THE EXECUTIVE

IN spite of occasionally treating the chambers individually, beside the executive, as representing the whole people and differing merely in the purpose of their representation, and in spite of practically giving double influence to the upper classes by having them represented in the lower chamber along with the lower classes and in the upper chamber exclusively, Adams emphatically maintains, in conformity with his fundamental principles, that the two chambers of the legislature respectively represent the two great orders or classes in society, which he also identifies with the two great parties in politics. In each chamber one social class is to be represented, and in each chamber the members are to belong to one political party. The senate is the representative assembly of the upper classes—of the nobles, the rich, the men of genius, the influential few: in it belongs the party of the aristocrats. The house is the representative assembly of the lower

[1] Nor did the result of the great democratic Middlesex election dispute in England over Wilkes's candidature contravene this principle. That result settled only a constitutional question *de facto*, not *de jure*. It settled only that the house of representatives could not, in the absence of a legal restriction, itself impose a restriction and exclude a representative constitutionally elected. In other words, to exclude Wilkes would have required Commons, Lords, and King: the Commons alone could not do it.

classes—of the common people, the poor, the stupid, the impressionable many: in it belongs the party of the democrats. And as a corollary to this division of the chambers between the two classes and the two parties, is the doctrine that the executive chief, the third power, the holder of the balance, the mediator, the umpire, must be impartial, and therefore must belong to neither of the two classes,[1] or must represent them both, must represent the whole people—be "national," as he later said[2]; therefore, again, must belong to neither party—must be, as we say, nonpartisan.

On this account, as already noted, Adams feared making the executive chief elective, since he would then be chosen by one party and would therefore be apt to side with only one party. On this account, also, he objected to our Constitution allowing the Senate to share in the appointing power, not only because he thought it would lead to the formation of two parties in that chamber and even in the other (vi. 434-5, viii. 464); but because, afterward, he attributed the partisanship of our Presidents to this senatorial interference (ix. 634, 397, cf. vi. 533-4). But only personal and temporary factions are formed in the squabbles over offices, not great and enduring parties, such as he has been dealing with. So it is difficult to see how the limitation of the President's "executive" power by the Senate can be a cause of his partisanship, especially as this is sufficiently accounted for not so much by his being elective as by his having the veto power, which brings him into the deliberative branch of the govern-

---

[1] What is necessary in order to permit this, we shall see later.

[2] X., 397. For this, we have already seen, he must be elective by all.

ment, the real seat of party division. A deliberating executive cannot help being partisan.[1]

However this be, it is Adams's scheme of government that not only the rivalries of the great few must be composed by segregating and weakening them in an assembly by themselves, but also that the rivalry between the great few and the leaders of the many, the contention between the different interests of the rich and the poor, must be rendered innocuous by being balanced. As, apart from simple monarchy, limited monarchy or mixed government is, in his opinion, the only possible means of regulating the rivalries between the nobles and of holding them in check, so it is the only possible means of regulating the rivalries between the two great parties of the nobles and the people and of preventing the one party from swallowing up the other (iv. 588, vi. 280–1, cf. 50). "All countries under the sun," says he, "must have parties. The great secret is to control them."[2]   The defect of other governments is that these "inveterate parties" are "not legally separated from each other, nor empowered to control each other" (v. 288). Some governments have been defective even with two assemblies, because they permitted the two parties to enter each.[3] "There will ever be a struggle between rich and poor"; "both rich and poor, then, must be made dependent" (vi. 68–9). The "controversy" and "rivalries" between the rich and the poor require that "these parties" shall "be repre-

[1] The nearest approach to non-partisanship possible is to make the executive bi-partisan, by means of an executive directory equally divided between the two parties. Such an executive has never proved satisfactory.

[2] IV., 587–8. Cf. "The essence of a free government consists in an effectual control of rivalries," vi., 280.

[3] Florence, v., 18; Padua, 476.

sented in the legislature, and must be balanced, or one will oppress the other.[1]   There will never probably be found any other mode of establishing such an equilibrium, than by constituting the representation of each an independent branch of the legislature, and an independent executive authority . . . to be a third branch and a mediator or an arbitrator between them. . . . The great art of lawgiving consists in balancing the poor against the rich in the legislature" (vi. 280).   The rich and the poor "should have equal power to defend themselves; and that their power may be always equal, there should be an independent mediator between them, always ready, always able, and always interested to assist the weakest."[2]   Neither the rich, represented in "an independent senate," nor the poor, represented in "a house of representatives of the people," "can be defended by their respective guardians in the constitution, without an executive power, vested with a negative, equal to either, to hold the balance even between them" (vi. 65).

These views he held to the end.   "Two such parties," he later wrote, "always will exist, as they always have existed, in all nations, especially in such as have property, and, most of all, in commercial countries [*cf.* 548]. Each of these parties must be represented in the legislature, and the two must be checks on each other.   But, without a mediator between them, they will oppose

---

[1] So in the later period: "The emulation between the rich and the poor among the people, should be made to check itself by balancing the two houses in the legislature, which represent these two classes of society," viii., 560.

[2] IX., 570.   *Cf.* his expression of desire for "giving all the executive power" to the first magistrate, and "dividing the sovereign legislature into two assemblies, giving to the nobles and people an equal share," v., 221.

each other in all things, and go to war till one subju-
gates the other. The executive authority is the only
mediator that can maintain peace between them"
(531). And once more: "Both [these parties] must be
represented in the legislature, and there must be a
mediator between them in the executive. This mediator must have power for the purpose. He must calm
and restrain the ardor of both, and be more impartial
between them than any President ever yet has been."[1]
Hence Adams desired the whole people to support the
Presidents "in their independence," and not to let
them be "shackled" by either "aristocratical or democratical manœuvres" (539–40, cf. ix. 302). For party
spirit is a monster, and "nothing but power lodged
somewhere in impartial hands can ever moderate,
soften, and control it" (541).

On this conception of the proper distribution of the
two parties and of the handling of them by an independent and impartial executive, it may be remarked,
first, that the scheme would not work as Adams imagines, and secondly, that an attempt to put it into
practice would lead to incalculable evil.

In the first place, even if Adams be granted all he
demands—a somehow independent executive, endowed
with the absolute veto, and free to make all appointments (including his ministers) without interference
from any other body not of his own creation;—still
the executive chief would be partisan, since his veto
power would draw him into the deliberative vortex

[1] VI., 533–4. In 1801 he criticized Jefferson's administration for
starting out too partisan, ix., 585. He would not except Washington's,
x., 23.—On the need of "an independent executive" as moderator, etc.,
between the two parties, vi., 32, later 532; "a third mediating power,"
340; a third power to balance them, v., 79, 115, 476 (balance by mediating), to control them, 68, 80, 473, cf. 488.

of the legislature: if hereditary, he would be more amenable, in the long run, to the influence of the aristocrats than to that of the despised democrats[1]; and if elective, he would be alternately partisan according to the party that brought him in.

And then, even if he should happen perchance to be impartial, he has never been endowed by Adams with sufficient power really to act the part of the mediator, arbiter, or umpire, as desired. This is important. Adams always treats the executive as having power to balance the two assemblies by joining his weight to one of them; which can only mean, so as to coerce the other. The executive, he reiterates, is to "interpose and decide" between them.[2] But he nowhere provides "power for the purpose"—and he has given other power to the assemblies that renders it unfeasible. We have frequently seen him invoke the absolute veto as supplying the requisite power for holding the balance. It is plain, however, that a mere negative power, where the other branches possess a similar negative power, can directly accomplish nothing. The only way to make sense out of those statements is through the syllogism:— the veto is necessary to defend the other powers of the executive; those other powers are necessary to enable the executive to hold the balance; therefore the veto is necessary for enabling the executive to hold the

[1] The party of the aristocrats have always and everywhere desired the ministry to be independent of control by parliament, renouncing their own control in the upper house in order to get rid of the control by the commons in the lower house. This is because they confide in their own courtly influence.

[2] IV., 440; "to decide between them," 462; to be appealed to "for decision," v., 10; to "decide when they cannot agree," vi., 65; by joining the side "nearest justice" "to decide the controversy and restore the peace," 203.

balance. But what are those other powers? The only
one bearing on this point, exerting influence upon both
houses, is the power of patronage by appointments.
Not only is this a corrupt and corrupting power, but it
would prove wholly insufficient for the purpose in cases
of serious antagonism between the assemblies or between the classes they represent. In England there was
still another, affecting the representatives alone, in the
executive's right to prorogue Parliament and dissolve
the lower House, thus threatening its members with
trouble and expense and possible exclusion at the next
election. But this, too, is of force only in minor matters,
and exercisable only once on any occasion; and, moreover, it was debarred in Adams's system through his
insistence upon annual elections.[1] Similarly in the
threefold balancing, in the combination of any two of
the three branches against the third, none of the combinations are of sufficient coercive force. The union of
the two chambers in impeachment can, properly at
least, be exercised only against actual misdemeanor on
the part of the executive. The withholding of supplies
we have seen to be a power obsolete. The union of the
king and the aristocracy can have no potency against
the democracy except through fraud and corruption,
let alone force, at the elections; which is in violation of
Adams's principles, and was not liked by him even in his
English model. The union of King and Commons has,
indeed, in the English Constitution, a powerful instrument against the House of Lords, which will be described presently. But Adams has never noticed it or
taken it into his scheme. His scheme gives the king and

---

[1] This mediative power possessed by the English executive, and its
absence from ours, was noticed in the Convention by Morris and Wilson,
Elliot's *Debates*, v., 284, 416.

commons no powers over the lords except the ineffective ones of withholding appointments and supplies. The cause of all the trouble is the absolute negative which Adams assigns equally to each of the three branches of the legislature. This leads to the second objection.

Such an absolute negative in each of the two chambers when each, as in our government, and in some of Adams's statements, represents the whole people, and each is renewed at frequent periods, so that in the language borrowed from Bodin only the government is mixed and the state is simple, or in the language of a later English publicist the checks are "imperfect," need do no insuperable harm. But if one of these chambers specially represents the upper classes of society, and the other alone represents the rest of the people, then the possession of an absolute negative by each is an entirely different affair; for then the state also is mixed, and the checks are perfect.[1] Then a

[1] On "imperfect" and "perfect" checks see Brougham, *Political Philosophy*, ii., 13–16; iii., 143–6, 156–8. In England, notice,—theoretically at least,—the negatives or checks, being between the classes, and at the roots, are deep; but in America, being in the governmental branches only, they are superficial. The separation not only of the branches, but of the roots, in the people, underlying the government, was taken by Brougham as essential to "mixed government," and he did not look upon any of the American governments as "mixed governments," *ib.*, i., 75, 89 (*cf.* 93), ii., 1, iii., 2, 105, 149. He here lacked precision through ignorance of Bodin's distinction. He should have called that separation essential for the "mixed state" and have denied that the American were "mixed states." Adams desired such mixed states here, but luckily succeeded in getting only "mixed governments." In England, of course, actually the fundamental mixture is no longer perfect because the fundamental separation no longer is so, and the people have indirect means of forcing through reformations. This was noticed by Condorcet, who considered the humiliating need of such measures a vice, and contrasted conditions in the United States where,

clash between the two sections may bring the government to a standstill, and an executive armed merely with an additional negative can effect nothing. Thus Adams's pretty three-cornered scheme of any two of the branches combining against abuses on the part of the third, where this already has the power, simply would not work, since, by giving to each an absolute negative, he has given it to that third and so deprived the two of power to dispossess the other of the abused power. His whole scheme of the balance falls to the ground, because each branch has power enough to prevent any balancing. The only good gained by the location of the negative in each of the three is the increased likelihood of barring a bad innovation: it may prevent not only any one, but any two of the three branches from encroaching and doing positive harm. But, on the other hand (and descending to particulars), suppose the representatives of the people have once been caught napping and an insidious measure passed that leads insensibly to greater and greater privileges of the few; suppose abuses have crept in little by little on the one side or the other, perhaps abetted by judge-made law; or suppose new conditions require new ordinances to preclude abuses; —then one of the parties may be interested to maintain the position thus subtly or naturally won, and its absolute negative enables it to do so: the other two may combine all they please, but in Adams's system they have no constitutional power to force through reform.[1]

he says, "this vice does not exist. Their legislative power is divided into several bodies, but into several bodies of the representatives of the people, who, in a manner more or less complex, more or less good, have the power of altering injurious laws," *Idées sur le Despotisme*, § 6 (*Œuvres*, xii., 210–11).

[1] As an instance of this may be cited the case of Brittany before the Revolution, where, as described by Condorcet in 1788, in their parlement

For this purpose the two ought to have a power of coercion over the third.   In Adams's system the trouble is caused by each of the equal branches having an undivided share in the whole legislative power. A better arrangement would be that which Adams himself pictured in the assembly of Arragon, where, he says, "if two estates agreed, it was a law" (vi. 137). So each of Adams's three branches ought to have only a divided third share of the legislative power.[1] Then

"nineteen-twentieths of the province have a third of the voices; where the body of the people have only representatives, and the nobles attend in person; where for what is decided by the plurality of the orders, the people find themselves in dependence upon those who are privileged, while the requirement of unanimity of the orders for other decisions renders indestructible all the abuses favorable to the privileged orders," one such being the principal impost, which made the poor pay sixteen times as much as the rich, the proceeds going partly in pensions to the nobles, etc., *Sentiments d'un républicain* (*Œuvres*, xii., 186). This is what the English government would have been like in Adams's day, had it really contained the three absolute negatives Adams supposed it to have—a condition which, because of this power in the privileged classes to obstruct reforms, Condorcet called "direct despotism," while he called "indirect despotism" the small representation of the people at large only in the lower house, *Idées sur le Despotisme*, § 3 (*Œuvres*, xii., 207–8). Earlier, however, the equality of the three branches had existed, and was the cause of most of the disorders of that period, till the Commons finally got rid of a great part of the incubus. The very supposition made in the text—of a suasible set of representatives once giving away (or rather selling) the liberties of the people,—with notice of the impossibility of recovering them by a better subsequent representation while that constitution lasted, was made in the House of Commons by Sir Charles Sedley in 1693, Cobbett's *Parliamentary History*, vol. v., cols. 757–8.

[1] This was claimed by a governor of New York (Fletcher, in 1693) when, reproving the assembly for rejecting an amendment of the council favored by himself, he declared: "You ought to consider that you have but a third share in the legislative power of the government; and ought not to take all upon you, nor be so peremptory. You ought to let the council have a share. . . . But you seem to take the whole power in your hands, and set up for everything" (Grahame, *History*, ii., 237).

any two by combining would form the majority and bear down the third: the two chambers, if agreeing, would not need the consent of the executive, and either of the chambers, with the executive, could dispense with the consent of the other chamber. This would amount to giving to the executive the casting vote when the two chambers disagree, and would constitute him the arbiter of their disputes, and leave him out when they agree. But then each of the three branches would lose its absolute veto, and Adams's distributed negative vanishes,—and the loss of it to the representatives of the people, where the other two branches represent upper classes, would be fraught with tremendous peril to liberty. In Adams's scheme, in default of the tribunitian power to stop the execution of an existing law (which might be represented now by a right of repeal in the lower house by itself), the only salvation from the risk of intrenched abuses would be in a constitutional provision making every law lapse after a fixed period (which ought to be short for a new law, until tested by experience, whereupon in reënactments its term might be extended). But no such provision was recommended by Adams.[1]

He made a mistake of fact, however, as the council constitutionally had exactly the same power. Adams himself once wrote of his scheme as if it were for the people to have "one third part of the legislature" (vi., 135). His words here merely lack precision.—*Cf.* Jefferson, in 1809, of a proposed Spanish constitution: "It has a feature which I like much; that which provides that when the three co-ordinate branches differ in their construction of the constitution, the opinion of two branches shall overrule the third," *Works*, v., 473.

[1] This feature, for another purpose (apparently to strike off obsolete laws), had in 1669 been introduced by Locke into his *Fundamental Constitutions of Carolina* (art. 79), fixing the period at a hundred years (perhaps in imitation of Solon, who set that period for his laws, according to Plutarch). Jefferson, on the principle (borrowed from Turgot, art. on

Now, such blocking of progress is more likely to come from the upper classes, the few, and not only from them but from the executive, the one, especially if hereditary, —and all the more from these two together. Therefore in England both of those branches of the legislature have been practically deprived of their absolute negative, which is preserved in full force only by the repre-

Fondements in the *Encyclopédie*) that "the earth belongs to the living," wished every law (also constitution, public debt, bequest, etc., but not the ownership of land itself!—to which the extension was later made by P. E. Dove, *Theory of Human Progression*, 1850; New York ed., pp. 301–3, 305, 306, 309) to be confined to the life of one generation, which he at first set at thirty-four years, *Works*, iii., 106, and then at nineteen, *ib.*, 108–9, vi., 137, vii., 15, *cf.* 311, 346, 359. The ill-fated Polish constitution of 1791 contained an article (6, end) requiring revision every twenty-five years (*Annual Register*, xxxiii., 181). The Plan of the Constitution presented to the National Convention in 1793 required a new convention after twenty years (Tit. ix., art. 4; in Condorcet's *Œuvres*, xviii., 356). The scheme, introduced into the constitutions of Iowa and New York in 1846, and adopted by Michigan, 1850, Ohio, 1851, Maryland, 1864, and Virginia, 1870, of submitting to the people every twenty years or so the question whether the constitution should be revised by a convention to be called for the purpose, is entirely contrary to Adams's principles. He put no clause on the subject in the Massachusetts constitution of 1780; and among the amendments passed by the convention in which he was a member in 1820 was one regulative only of "special and particular amendments." He would not jeopardize his great principles. Indeed, in a really, or fundamentally, balanced constitution any proposal of revision by the whole people would be dangerous, on account of the risk the upper classes would run of losing their privileges and their consequent resistance (*cf.* iv., 586–7; also Condorcet, *Œuvres*, xviii., 260–1). We shall find, however, that Adams approved the amendment clause in the Federal Constitution. This was because that Constitution did not come up to his standard, so he was glad it allowed itself to be improved. Similarly other "high-toned" Federalists (*e. g.* Morris, as we shall see) insisted upon this amendment clause, here agreeing with the Republicans or Democrats, but from different motives—the former desiring it for a particular purpose, the latter on a general principle. Had that Constitution been all that they wanted, the Federalists would not have cared for an amendment clause, or would have made it even more difficult than they did make it.

sentatives of the people (embracing both the upper and the lower classes[1]), in the single lower chamber. The King has lost it through having his Ministers held responsible not merely by impeachment but by the pleasure of the majority in the lower chamber. The upper chamber has resigned it, fundamentally no doubt from a sense of its own weakness over against the rest of the nation, but immediately from fear of the constitutional power acquired by the lower chamber, through its control of the Ministers, to exercise the royal prerogative of packing the upper chamber with new members in case of its stubborn refusal to yield.

Here is the instrument of coercion in the hands of the Commons and the King against the Lords above alluded to; and here is the lacuna often noticed in Adams's science of government. Supposing the upper chamber to be hereditary, he never tells us how it is to be renewed when old families die out, or in case of other reasons for additions,—how, for instance, the new great men or natural aristocrats are to be put into it, whether at the desire of the commons or at the will of the king, —by invitation, or by command. He does not insist that the peerage should be open. But if the peerage is open, and if the ministers come into the power of the lower chamber, then the creation of new peers may be used as a club to browbeat the house of lords at the instigation of the house of commons, and the house of lords no longer occupies that independent and equiponderant position demanded by Adams's theory. Adams's system was, in fact, not carried out in his day even in the theory of the English government, which from the beginning had left this door open, at least to

[1] The latter in theory at least, and since Adams's day continually more so in fact.

the King, if not yet fully to the Commons. On the other hand, if the peerage is to be closed, or no peers appointable save under narrow restrictions, as was once for party purposes proposed by the English Whigs and abandoned through Walpole's dissuasion,—if, in other words, the senate were given the independent and equiponderant position demanded by Adams's theory,—then, not only Adams's natural aristocracy would be replaced by a merely artificial aristocracy, but also the working of the system would be intolerable and might soon come to a deadlock. Even if the former of these evils were avoided, by making all individuals who attain certain positions or a certain degree of wealth enter the aristocratic class and then have a right to vote for members and to be eligible as members in the upper chamber, which is to be independent of any interference from king or commons, the latter evil would still be likely to ensue. The two classes in society, thus divided against each other, would be sure sometime to come into conflict, which the king would be helpless to decide and in which he probably would join the side that is the more favorable to an increase of his power, and from which, finally, there would be no escape but by the submission of one of the parties.

This is no idle fear. In fact, it is the very evil that Adams himself depicted so vividly throughout his historical reviews, and which made him sigh for a first magistrate with constitutional power (not an army) to decide between them, but sighed in vain. Indeed, he had an object-lesson before his eyes when he took his seat as presiding officer over the first United States Senate at New York in 1789; for the State of New York was there unrepresented, as it had also been unrepresented in the electoral college which chose him, because of a deadlock between its two chambers, the State senate, Federalist, and the assembly, Anti-federalist, not having come to terms on the method of electing to those national bodies, and there being no way to decide between them. New Hampshire also had come near being left out, for the same reason; only there the lower house had at last given in.[1] At the same time, across the ocean,—and all these events took place before Adams finished his writings of this period,— the French *tiers état* perceived the danger, and, to avoid it, compelled the other estates to join them in one assembly. Since Adams's time we have had more ample experience, through the coming into existence of more popular chambers.[2] Six years after his death England was saved from a riotous revolution only by the threat of the Commons, so to speak, to invade and, as the slogan then was, to "swamp" the House of Lords, thereby coercing them to pass the Reform Bill,

---

[1] And again in 1800, Pennsylvania had, by a similar yielding of the house only at the last moment, an equally narrow escape from losing her presidential electoral vote.

[2] In Adams's day English writers like Hallam expatiated on "the peculiar happiness" of their constitution, that few dissensions on any but inessential matters had arisen between the two houses of Parliament, *Constitutional History*, ch. xiii., pt. iii. Hallam, indeed, knew of no other government where "hereditary and democratical authority have been amalgamated . . . without continual dissatisfaction and reciprocal encroachments." The reason is the simple one that up till then the two houses had been homogeneous, not only the peers receiving newcomers from the Commons, but the House of Commons being composed of members from the same class as the peers, and under their thumbs, and not representing the democracy. Remember the quotation from Bentham above; later will be quoted a similar explanation from Ricardo. It was understood by Bancroft, *History of the Constitution*, ii., 329. For the change after 1832, see May, *Constitutional History of England*, vol. i., ch. 5.

not by any veto power lodged in an arbitrating executive, but by the menacing power of creating new peers; which power, we have just seen, has no place in Adams's scheme.[1] In the seventh decade of the nineteenth century the Prussian constitution very nearly resembled Adams's ideal. The hereditary King had the whole appointive power, even of the Ministers, who were responsible only by impeachment; the lower House, though elected with restricted suffrage, did not depart materially from what Adams considered a full and fair representation of the people (including the upper classes) —not so much so as did the English of his day; and each branch of the legislature was nominally endowed with an absolute negative. Even the standing army had been voted to the King by the people. In this alone did they depart from Adams's advice, constrained thereto by their situation. Then they began to act as if they were heeding him, and trouble began. The army the King and nobles wished to increase; the popular party, in majority in the lower House, refused. The "Crisis," as it came to be called, lasted over a year, and from it the only escape expected was by a *coup d'état*, had not the submissive German people at the next election yielded to their princes.[2]

[1] It may be said that the King put his weight in the one scale, and so carried out Adams's scheme. But he did not put his weight on the weaker side and restore an equilibrium: he put it on the side which at the moment was the stronger and confirmed its strength. He did not arbitrate, but was swept away by the current which overwhelmed the Lords, and was merely wise enough to yield.

[2] In Denmark, with a similar constitution, at the close of that century, the King and the upper chamber ruled the country for several years, against the opposition of the lower chamber, by taking advantage of a clause which impaired somewhat the latter chamber's control over the purse strings. But for this defect in the constitution serious trouble might have occurred there too. In Hungary, whose constitution most

Still more ample experience has been acquired far away in the southern seas in the states of Australia. In several of these the suffrage for the upper houses has been for about fifty years restricted by sundry property qualifications; and so many deadlocks took place between the two houses that various contrivances had to be introduced for unlocking them, all resulting in taking away from one or both of the houses its absolute negative. The property qualification has been omitted from the constitution of the federal government completed in the last year of the last century, but the method has been retained of deciding disputes between the two houses by referring the question to a new election by the people, with addition, if that be ineffectual, of combining the two houses into one, giving preponderance to the double numbers of the lower house.[1] Indeed, where the members of one of the houses have long terms, any new constitution would now be considered negligently defective that did not provide in some way for deadlocks.

In general, Adams's mistake, in his tripartite absolute negative, lay in dividing the sovereignty of the nation. He set three legislative negatives over against each other without giving even two of their possessors power by

closely resembles the English of the eighteenth century, when a deadlock over certain religious matters (civil marriage, etc.) was imminent between the two chambers in 1894, the union of the King with the Table of Deputies, by threatening to create new peers, induced the Table of Magnates finally to pass the bills it had rejected.

[1] This reduction of bicameralism to unicameralism, to dissolve the deadlocks of the former, was copied from Norway (where, also, the King's veto may be overridden by three successive legislatures). The new Australian scheme, *mutatis mutandis*, was inserted by the British government into the temporary constitutions conceded to the Transvaal and Orange River Colonies in 1906 and 1907.

combining to coerce the third, purposely making each of them invincible. The complete failure of his balance springs from his oversight of the nature of political checks. He wanted "three checks, absolute and independent" (iv. 483). But in government there should be only one absolute check, the possession of which constitutes the sovereign, which in a republic should be the whole nation. All other checks should be merely brakes or drags: they should retard, not stop. The legislature being divided into three branches, these should *not* be equal: the upper should rest upon the lower: there should be a gradual weakening as they rise from the base. The people are the ultimate sovereign. Next in potency come their immediate representatives in the lower branch of the legislature; then the senators; lastly, so far as *in* the legislative, and concerning legislation, the executive chief. Adams's peculiar error lay in placing the arbiter in exactly the wrong place: he placed it at the top: it should be at the bottom. The chief magistrate, be he president or king, cannot be the arbiter in government. He is one of the protagonists in the disputes within the government. The proper arbiter is the people at large. In the disputes of parties it is the people who hold the balance. It is they who throw their weight in the lighter scale when the stronger party becomes exalted and begins to usurp. It is they to whom the appeal should be made. In our governments the appeal is regularly made at short intervals. In the English system, and in those European governments which have adopted its methods, the appeal is made, regularly only at long intervals, but irregularly whenever the executive and legislative powers become discordant and neither is inclined to give in to the other: then they give way and bend to the decision of the people.[1]   The people, which comprises and encloses both the parties, is the only power that can arbitrate between them.   If it be objected that the people are the very ones who are divided into the two classes, or the two parties, it must be remembered that these are not hard and fast entities with a sharp line of demarcation between them, but that between them, especially between the parties, is a continual flux of persons in an indeterminate position. These incline to the one or to the other side as they think the parties approach toward or depart from the golden mean of justice.   They are the independents in politics, who are not hidebound to either of the two parties.   It is they who are the ultimate makeweight and arbiter.   Where this intermediate class does not exist, or where it does its work badly, there the cause of liberty and good government is hopeless, and no artificial king can take its place.   The evils which Adams deplored in past times came from the absence of such a class, not from the absence of a king. But, for the working of this check by the people, they must be represented all in one assembly, or in two assemblies either both springing from the whole people or the one representing a single class subordinate to the other representing the whole.

In our country, the election of all the three legislative branches ultimately by the people, makes the people the real absolute check.   Even if the three branches all had such absolute negatives as desired

[1] In the French constitution of 1791 the King had the veto (suspensive only, but for a considerable period), but not the right to dissolve the legislature and order a new election.   In the Belgian constitution of 1831, which still endures, the King has no veto, but he has the power of dissolution and appeal.   There can be no question which of these arrangements is the better.

by Adams, these would be but temporary negatives, all effaceable before the same master at a subsequent election.[1]   There is a tendency, however, already discernible, for the Senate to become more peculiarly the representative of the richer classes—a result reachable through the indirect mode of its election, in the hands of men who owe their own position to campaign funds contributed by the rich.   If this tendency ever reaches the extent desired by Adams, and if that body still retains its absolute and uncoercible negative, there will be trouble.   The end can be only one of three: either the same classes will acquire predominance in, or will impose upon, the other chamber also, which will spell plutocracy; or, to preserve democracy, the Senate must be restored to the whole people, by having its members elected by the people of the States; or, finally, it must be deprived of its equality with (and *a fortiori* of its superiority over) the House of Representatives. The last event would involve two mutually neutralizing alterations in the Constitution, of which the one would render up the Senate to a section of the people, and the other would strip it of its power.   This stripping might even be recommendable without that rendition.   But of this more anon.

[1] But to unlock deadlocks over measures of reapportionment of representation, the Virginia constitution of 1850 required immediate recourse to the referendum (Sect. 5).   This was because the reapportionment was needed for the next election itself.

CHAPTER XIII

THE JUDICIARY

IN Adams's scheme, then, the balance of the three legislative branches is a total failure. But despite his perfect satisfaction with it, he had another balance. The senate and the house of representatives he sometimes combined as two parts making up one legislature, which he contrasted, as the legislative department, with the executive department. Here are two separate powers, liable to contention, which must, according to his mechanical principle, be in unstable equilibrium unless they have a third power to balance them. This third power he finds in the judicial department. He thus has two entirely distinct balances,[1] perhaps being so well pleased with the balancing system that he thought the more the merrier.[2] The one now under consideration was, in fact, the first to make its appearance in his early period (iv. 186, in 1775). But, as we have seen, he then considered the judicial power not a strong enough mediator in a struggle between the other two, "because the legislature would undermine it"; wherefore he introduced the famous balance within the legislative (196, in 1776), though still allowing and desiring the judicial power to be "distinct from both the legislative and executive, and independent upon both, that so it may be a check upon both" (198). This is retained, then, as a secondary, subsidiary balance. And still in his last period he wrote of the judicial power

[1] The distinction is clearly recognized in vi., 429 and ix., 568, and also in 566 and, later, vi., 488.

[2] Later, vi., 467-8, he detected eight "balances" in our governmental system.

merely as "a salutary check" upon the others (vi. 488).

According to his principles, this balancing power also ought to be strong and independent, with equal authority as a representative of the people (for so we have seen him describe it). It should have a negative or veto, that is, should be able to undo illegal acts of administrators and to quash unconstitutional enactments of legislators. On these points Adams says little. Its independence upon the two other departments, as we have seen, he obtained in a different way from the independence of those departments upon each other. He made both judges and court officers appointees of the executive,[1] obtaining sufficient independence, presumably, by assigning them fixed salaries, and at all events making them removable only by impeachment.[2]

---

[1] Of course, in England and elsewhere the judges were appointed by the King because the judicial function was not separated from the executive, but "this authority," according to Blackstone, *Commentaries*, i., 266–7, "has immemorially been exercised by the King or his substitutes." So, in the Philadelphia Convention, Morris spoke of "the judiciary" being "part of the executive," Elliot's *Debates*, v., 429; and similarly Wilson, in the Pennsylvania ratifying convention, *ib.*, ii., 445. Such also was the opinion of Paine, *Rights of Man*, part ii., ch. iv. And since then James Mill has made the division thus: "The executive functions of government consist of two parts, the administrative and the judicial," art. *Government*, § 9. On the continent, Rayneval, for instance, treated the judicial power as "an emanation of the executive power," and concluded as a matter of course that "the appointment of the judges belongs to this latter power," adding that "this is the most important of its prerogatives," *Institutions du Droit de la Nature et des Gens*, I., xii., §§ 1, 5. Only on such a supposition is the appointment of judges by the executive justifiable; for, as we have seen, an executive officer has a right to appoint only his own subordinates.

[2] In England, as a matter of course, the judges had been removable by the King, at his pleasure, for the same reason that they were appointed by him. Now they can be removed by him only on request of the legislature. Naturally the desire to have the judges independent of the

The people, however, in most of our States have carried out this one of his principles further than he was willing to go with it himself, and have cut the Gordian knot by following the lead of Connecticut, under Jefferson's urging, and making many of the court officers and (beginning in Georgia) even the judges elective, with definite terms. The Justices of the United States Supreme Court might easily have been rendered independent of the President, even if popular elections were feared in this case, by having them appointed, for moderately long terms, in rotation, by the State governors with approval of the State senates.[1] Adams, however, preferred to follow the European mode of appointment (though not of removal), which is a relic from the mediæval times when the king himself was judge and the judges were merely his deputies. The appointment of the judiciary by the executive, though it may be historically explained, has no "scientific" principle in its support. The only argument for its continuance is convenience and the difficulty of finding any better mode.[2]

king's pleasure has always been strong with the lovers of liberty. The Dutch obtained it in their war of independence; the English not till 1688, and then imperfectly, and the King tried to retain control over the judiciary in the American colonies. In Massachusetts in 1773 there was a controversy on this subject, and Adams held that the King had this power, but wished it were not so, iii., 520 ff., cf. ii., 315–17.

[1] Unanimity in the decisions of the Supreme Court might then be required, as in other juries; for the prescription might be added that in case of disagreement the Justices should all be dismissed and replaced by new ones. Only the Chief Justice need be permanent, with the condition that he take no part in the verdicts.

[2] In our States perhaps a better way would be a combination of appointment and election. Let the governor a couple of months before the election nominate an official candidate. Then let other candidates be nominable by petitions signed by a certain (fairly high) number of voters. If the governor made a good nomination, probably no other

As for the judicial negative, Adams never alludes to
it. Apparently he did not perceive the important
function the judiciary was to exercise in recognizing the
Constitution as the supreme law made by the people
and therefore in withholding observance of laws passed
by representatives in contravention of it and of their
mandate—its function as guardian, or, to use Hamilton's
term, "bulwark," of the Constitution.[1] Consequently
the services of the judicial department in this "other
balance" are underestimated, and this balance sinks
into insignificance. In its case Adams does not pursue
the three-cornered system employed in the legislative
balance. He does not speak of the judiciary balancing
the legislature and the executive, or of the executive
balancing the judiciary and the legislature, or of the
legislature balancing the executive and the judiciary;
nor, again, of the combination of any two against the

candidate would be brought forward. If he made a bad one, there is a
remedy. Political parties should be forbidden to meddle in the matter.
Or see "a Scotch mode," humorously related by Franklin in Elliot's
Debates, v., 156.

[1] *The Federalist*, No. 78; or "fortress," according to G. Morris,
Sparks's *Morris*, iii., 401; "the keystone of the arch," according to C.
Pinckney, Elliot's *Debates*, iv., 258. Strictly speaking, if exercised
without bias (without employing lax or strict construction according
to party exigencies), this is not a negative upon the power of the legislature, but merely upon its abuse of its power. Our courts have, however,
been increasing a practice which really puts a negative upon the laws
constitutionally passed by the legislature. This is the practice of suspending sentence, which often amounts to suspending and nullifying
laws. It is an abuse of their own power, and is comparable with the
abuse of the pardoning power of the governors; and like that power, this
power itself ought to be curtailed. Of an opposite nature is the abuse
by the courts of their power of injunction, by which they introduce penalties of their own for acts, the penalties for which, if deserved at all, it
is the business of the legislature alone to prescribe. This power ought
to be brought under constitutional regulation, since the legislatures have
shirked touching it.

third. Instead, however, he once rather strangely adds the judiciary to the three legislative branches, getting every three to combine against the fourth in a four-cornered arrangement (vi. 209), entirely contrary to his usual scheme, which, for the balancing, requires three powers, "and no more."

Of this "other balance," then, Adams makes little use. The use of the judiciary he even avoids when he might, and ought, to have introduced it. Thus we have seen him leaving the trial of impeachments to the senate upon presentation by the lower house. Now, to impeach the executive is properly a legislative function, because the executive can be impeached only for disobeying the laws and instructions of the legislature, or of the constitution made by the people, whose substitute in the law-making capacity is the legislature. The legislature, representing the will of the people, is the offended party: it should be the plaintiff. If, therefore, the legislature consists of two chambers, both chambers should be the plaintiff. To make one of them the judge, is to make one of two offended partners the judge; which is contrary to the first principles of justice. Political offenses ought to be tried before the judiciary,—and military offenses too, except, of course, mere breaches of discipline that do not affect civilians. Thereby (which ought to have recommended it to Adams) would take place at least one of those combinations of two separate departments to restrain the third. That impeachments were to be tried by the Supreme Court, was the original intention of most of the plans submitted to the Philadelphia Convention, being in that of Virginia,[1] in that of New Jersey, and in Charles

---

[1] Art. 9, "impeachments of national officers" to be before "the national judiciary," which itself was to be "chosen by the national

Pinckney's. But as the appointment of the judges was afterward assigned to the President, the impropriety was pointed out of his being tried by his own appointees.[1] Yet a special court could easily have been constructed for the purpose,—made up, say, of a portion of the highest judges of all the States,[2] as indeed was suggested in the Philadelphia Convention.[3]

Here again Adams merely followed a European custom handed down from primitive times of almost undivided and unseparated political activities, and not sanctioned by his own political science thoroughly carried out. In England the impeachment of executive Ministers of the Crown is only in accordance with the fact, still remaining, that the Parliament is the highest court in the land—the "High Court of Parliament," as it is officially designated,—before which peers are brought to trial and certain appeals are carried. Primitive assemblies always had judicial power, along with the rest.[4] In Spain and Portugal the assembly receives its name from this function; and such, too, was the case in Adams's own colonial Massachusetts, the name being retained in its constitution of 1780,[5] and in two other New England States, Connecticut

legislature." Both these features were taken from the Virginia constitution of 1776 (cf. Madison, Writings, iv., 285).

[1] By Sherman, Elliot's Debates, v., 529.

[2] Leaving room for challenges by both sides.

[3] By Hamilton, Elliot's Debates, i., 180(v., 205), followed by Randolph, ib., v., 342. Hamilton later added the judges of the Supreme Court, ib., 588; and this full scheme was among the amendments recommended by the New York ratifying convention, ib., i., 331. Madison likewise would have preferred "the Supreme Court for the trial of impeachments; or, rather, a tribunal of which that should form part," ib., v., 528.

[4] See Tacitus, Germania, c. xii. Blackstone thence derives the English custom, Commentaries, iv., 260. Cf. Story, Commentaries, ; 742.

[5] And in Adams's own draft of it, iv., 230.

and New Hampshire. But this union of functions had to break down before the growing complexity of civilization, which in politics as in other fields of advanced activity demands division of labor; and when it was replaced by the principle of separation, why should this be applied incompletely? Why should some judicial functions still be left with the body of men chosen for their presumptive skill in legislation? Here, as in some other matters, American imitation has been left behind by the advance of the English model. For in England it is now only by a fiction that the House of Lords exercises any judicial functions, as these, since 1845, are left entirely to the few Law Lords, who, because of the small number (three) required for a quorum in that House, may act in the name of the whole body.[1]

On the whole, however, the subject of impeachment has been much overrated. Juridical trial for official delinquencies seems out of place. Ineptitude for office is different from criminality; and the dismissal from office, to which alone the former ought to lead, and to which it is now confined, is different from the punishment which ought to follow the latter. To dismiss, therefore, ought not to require formal trial. The requirement for such trial springs from the false idea

[1] In our Constitution the combination of making the Senate both judge of the President's actions and his council on appointments and co-legislator in treaty-making is peculiarly inappropriate, as was frequently pointed out in the ratifying conventions, Elliot's *Debates*, i., 379, 503, ii., 530, 531, iii., 220, iv., 117–18, 204, *cf.* 124–5 and ii., 477 (attempted defense, 534, 538, iii., 516, iv., 126–7, 265, and in *The Federalist*, No. 66). But this criticism does not attach to Adams as he did not wish the Senate to have those powers and advanced this very criticism, see above, p. 113. Already Parsons had seen the impropriety of making a senate advisory in appointments, if it is to try impeachments, *The Essex Result*, Parsons's *Parsons*, 387–8.

that incumbents have (or ought to be given) an estate in their office. All that should be guarded against is prejudicial dismissal through mere personal dislike or too hasty listening to charges. When there is criminality in office, of course juridical trial is necessary for the infliction of punishment. So in the case of officials whose terms are long or indefinite. There is difficulty only with regard to judges, who must be preserved at all hazard from dismissal for mere partisan reasons. Yet it is important there should be some means, not too difficult, of removing those who prove incompetent or corrupt, or who themselves behave like partisans. Impeachment is cumbrous, rarely resorted to, and more rarely carried to a satisfactory finish, especially in our country because of the extravagant requirement of a two-thirds majority. Our judges are left without fear, and are almost irresponsible. In England the judges as well as the executive chiefs are dismissable more easily than by impeachment. With us, in the case of the executive chief, short terms give opportunity of replacing a bad incumbent, and reliance is not placed on the clumsy contrivance of impeachment.[1] Had our presidential term been extended to seven years or longer, as was originally proposed, we should probably ere now have had many impeachment trials, with many convulsive spasms of the body politic, much pain, and little cure. Had the term been reduced to two years, we should probably not have so much as heard a threat of impeachment. As it is, our four-year term is so intermediate, and so near the ragged edge of being too long, that we have had in more than a century just

---

[1] On the connection between impeachment and long fixed terms *cf.* Morris, Elliot's *Debates*, v., 335, 339, 343, 361, and Rufus King, *ib.*, 342.

one unsuccessful impeachment and possibly one serious threat.[1]

In general, little attention is by Adams paid to the judiciary. In one passage, among the desiderata in his plan of a good government is mentioned the maintenance also of the jury-system. In the same passage, too, are included preservation of the *habeas corpus*, refusal of a standing army, and freedom of the press (iv. 382). But nowhere else in this period is there allusion to anything like a bill of rights. In a few other passages the participation of the people in the juries is set beside their participation in the legislative, as an essential feature in free government.[2] The institution of jurors, he says, "is that department which ought to belong to the people at large; they are the most competent for this; and the property, liberty, equality, and security of the citizens, all require that they alone should possess it" (iv. 483);—and he adds, "it is the unanimity of the jury that preserves the rights of mankind," wherefore judgment cannot properly be confided to a large assembly (583). In these passages he is arguing against the single-assembly system of government, or simple democracy, under which he seems to think that there would be no delegation of powers and that the jury-system could not exist—at least he excludes it from the form of government he was attacking (vi. 155); and he goes so far as to assert, that under such government even if the judges were given tenure during good behavior, this would not be respected, since they

---

[1] What is more needed in the Constitution is some definite determination of when a President is incapacitated, so that the Vice-President may take his place, and of when he becomes capable again, so that he may resume it, in case of illness or other failing, and recovery therefrom.

[2] VI., 69–70, 88, *cf.* 65–6, iv., 528. So in his early period, iii., 481–2.

12

could not be protected by the need of impeachment at the instigation of one assembly before another (200–1), as though other methods of impeachment, with "formal trial and full defense," if thought necessary, could not equally well be instituted.

Sheriffs, we have seen, he in his early period first wished to be elective; yet even in that period he allowed them to be appointed by the executive—but by an executive who was then an official elected at short intervals. Now he says little more about them. But we may infer that he would put sheriffs, justices of the peace, and all such minor officials, in the appointment of the executive. He wants this even of militia officers, complaining that some of them had in our States been made elective (iv. 359). If all these were appointees of an executive himself chosen frequently by the people, as in Adams's early plan, no great harm would ensue, and perhaps this would be best in the case of sheriffs. But Adams retained their appointment by the executive even when he advocated lengthening the term of this magistrate and finally making it for life, or hereditary, and no longer accountable to the people except by impeachment for positive abuses and by revolution for other misuses. He thus gradually took out of the hands of the people all those minor guards of liberty, small individually, but extensive and all-important in the aggregate. During his early period Adams no doubt heard of Wilkes, in London, when he was an elective alderman with magisterial powers, promising his constituents that he would commit to prison any officer of the Crown, or of Parliament, who attempted to arrest illegally or to impress any citizen, and remarking that he would not have been able to do this, had he been merely a justice of the peace appointed and re-

movable by a King's Lord-Lieutenant.[1] But instances
of this sort Adams forgot. Such officers, he held, are,
properly and "scientifically," appointees of the executive power. Therefore they should be appointees of
the first magistrate, whether this magistrate himself
be elective or hereditary. The total dissimilarity of
the two cases, in the science of government itself,
escaped his notice.

In Adams's science of government possibly the greatest defect is the underestimation of the importance of
the judicial department, and consequently of the balance in which it plays a part. The question may be
raised, Would not *this* balance between the three natural
departments be enough, without that other artificial
balance constructed inside the legislative department?
If the answer be affirmative, Adams's argument for
dividing the legislature, that is, for the bicameral system,
falls to the ground. Or if there is still need of a further
balance in that department, the three-cornered scheme
would require its division into three chambers,—of the
three estates, as in mediæval France, or to represent
the higher, the middle, and the lower classes, the very
wealthy, the well-to-do, and the poor (since there really
is no monarchical order, or one-man class, in the state);
for the executive would have to be entirely out of the
legislature, in order to take part in the more comprehensive balance of the departments, in which it is set
over against the legislative. Indeed, if, to employ the
favorite metaphor, the three orders in society, or the
three simple kinds of government, need to be represented
and joined in the mixed government, the present trial

[1] In the summer of 1776, reported in *Affaires de l'Angleterre et de
l'Amérique*, viii., 164-6. Adams himself made a contribution to this
journal, July 17, 1778, xi., 124-5.

provides as good a means as any. The executive department may be treated as having the nature of a monarchical power; the judicial, that of an aristocratic; the legislative, that of a democratic. In the executive, everything may hang from a single chief, himself, however, made responsible to the people (either directly, in elections, or indirectly, through the elective legislature). In the judicial, the judges ought to be men of distinction, comparatively few in number, equal among themselves, except for two or three stages or ranks, with authority, however, only to declare the law and impose the sentence, the verdict in criminal cases resting with the people (in juries). Here it would not be improper, if the judges are elected, that the suffrage should be restricted by a fairly high education qualification. In the legislative, the persons entrusted with the power of levying contributions upon, and making laws for, the whole people, should represent the whole people and be elected by them, without either educational or property qualification in the franchise, in firm reliance that the ignorant and the propertiless have little influence except when oppression excites their sluggish natures into opposition and when the justice of their cause awakens sympathy in members of the higher classes. Here the aristocratic element will exert influence proportional to its importance in the state, while, as we have seen, the democratic must also enter the other departments; which shows the futility of the metaphor about a mixture of simples. But in whatever way the three departments be constituted, between them is a balance ready to Adams's hand, which he neglected.

CHAPTER XIV

NEGLECT OF THE CONSTITUTION

A DAMS'S neglect of the departmental balance is connected with his neglect of another considerable subject in the science of government. This is no less a thing than the constitution itself—the constitution as a body of law enacted by the people in convention assembled, or voting upon a draft prepared by a convention, and repealable or alterable only in the same way, above and beyond the legislature, and therefore a norm for the judiciary superior to the laws enacted by the representatives. It is strange that neglect of the constitution should be made by Adams, who prided himself upon being one of the chief constitution-makers of our country; but such is the fact. In his writings during this period hardly a reference is made to the force of such a constitution. Toward the end of the first volume of the *Defense*, in one passage, he seems to think that for interpreting the constitution the convention itself must sit permanently, and that then, with this and the legislative assembly there will be two assemblies, which is what he contended for (iv. 585). That it would naturally fall to the judges to interpret the constitution, he says not a word. Soon after the institution of the new Federal Government he referred to the President, through his lack of the absolute veto, not having "equal power to defend himself, or the Constitution, or the judicial power, as the Senate and House have," especially not so much as the Senate has, which will therefore encroach and "swallow up the other two" (vi. 431). In other words, he thought that the balanced branches are necessary to sustain the constitution,[1] not that the constitution is a trunk strong enough to support them.

Similarly he once argued that where there is only one assembly, it would be no protection to the judiciary that this legislature should pass a law giving them tenure during good behavior, since the same or a later legislature might repeal that law (vi. 200). And so in general of any constitutional law, such as the Æmilian in Rome, limiting the duration of office, which might be set aside, in a "simple democracy," by a majority of the legislative assembly (189),—and of course more easily if this be single than if divided into three orders and the consent of all three be necessary. Here no mention is made of a constitution above the laws (as indeed in Rome there was none) giving the judges and other officials such tenure, not repealable by the legislative assembly. Of course, where the legislative is also, so to speak, a constitutive, the legislative is not bound by any constitution, and it may be better that such a legislative be a cumbrous body whose action may be easily impeded and checked when it would make a constitutional change, even though such checks and impediments may be injurious when applied also to merely legal matters. But when the legislative is one thing and the constitutive another, no reason is apparent why the limited legislative should be subject to the same checks needed for the unlimited constitutive-legislative, or rather, why there should be additional checks upon its legislative action when the constitution is already such a check.

Most of Adams's arguments against a single legislative assembly are explainable only on a similar dis-

[1] "Unless three powers have an absolute *veto*, or negative, to every law, the constitution can never be long preserved," iv. 483.

regard of a constitution, and are equally inept when the constitution is supplied. One passage is especially so. Arguing against a single assembly with all power "concentrated in it," he expressly excludes any "counterpoise, balance, or equilibrium," even any check on the part of the people, since "this idea supposes a balance," doing so because he conceives all these safeguards to be excluded by Turgot's position, to whose literal terms he now confines his argument; and he says of this assembly, "it is to make a constitution and laws by its own will, execute those laws at its own pleasure, and adjudge all controversies that arise concerning the meaning and application of them, at its own discretion," and he rightly implies that it will be tyrannical (iv. 400, *cf.* vi. 114). He later said his "whole" object was to combat that opinion of Turgot (486); but in the very passage in which he says this he shows that he had in mind also the single-chambered government of Pennsylvania — Franklin's system, Paine's system, the republican system, of which the extension he feared even to Massachusetts and from which he wished to defend his native State, notwithstanding that such governments are constitutionally established and thereby well checked.

His work, if confined to the exaggerated interpretation of Turgot's couple of sentences, which served as a model to nobody, would have been three volumes hurled at a man of straw. It was not intended for such a Quixotic emprise. In it Adams declared his design was "more extensive than barely to show the imperfection of M. Turgot's idea" (iv. 435). It was directed against the democratic principle of a unicameral legislature,—but, be it noted, in a republican and an American system, which included a constitution set up by the people and imposed upon the governors as a law of the government itself, and instituting other departments beside the legislative. For, of course, it was not aimed against any of the French unicameral governments, which did not exist when the *Defense* was written. And when he wrote his later works of this period, the Constituante purposed to be only a temporary body. This was, indeed, a government *in* a single assembly; but it proposed to establish a government *with* a single assembly—an entirely different thing. Governments thus constitutionally established with single assemblies existed only in three American States. Only once does Adams refer to and argue against such an establishment. This occurs on the last page of the first volume. And the argument is exactly on a line with the argument he has everywhere urged against a government composed of a first magistrate and a single assembly, but without a constitution, no allusion being made to a judiciary. It repeats mention of a strife immediately ensuing between the two powers, of the legislative leaders (*i. e.* the aristocrats) undermining the executive, or, if the people support the latter, of a civil war till one or the other (the aristocracy or the democracy) be subjugated.[1] Thus, where the constitution is once brought in, it is left out of sight.

In the democratic and American system, moreover, the executive and the judiciary were distinguished and variously separated from the single-chambered legislature.[2] Now, a government with its legislative

[1] IV., 587. Here is some reference to the State of Pennsylvania. As for the argument, compare with it vi., 335, where is no allusion to a constitution at all.

[2] *E. g.* the first article of the Georgia unicameral constitution of 1777 was taken word for word from the Virginia bicameral constitution of

department in one assembly and the other departments separate, is very different from a government with all the three departments collected in one assembly. Adams argued against the latter, and thought he disproved the former! For, although his purpose was not confined to merely disproving Turgot's misinterpreted position, his argument was. But, for his argument to have value, he ought to have directed it against a single assembly in which is lodged only, and not even wholly, the legislative function. This, however, he never did, not even in the futile passage to which attention has just been drawn. And so, in spite of all his long-winded tirades, he has given us not so much as a single argument really directed at the true question at issue.

As for Turgot's own words, it may be noted that they are perfectly compatible with the American system of collecting all authority in a single convention, or leaving it rather in the whole people, who adopt or reject the convention's proposals. Here, indeed, is the bicameral system in practical operation, the convention proposing and the people disposing. This was Turgot's own system; and it, and Condorcet's, as also Milton's and Hume's schemes, were with peculiar literalness carried out in the case of the United States Constitution, which was debated in a general convention and ratified in separate local conventions of the States.[1] When the State governments were formed by a convention drawing up

1776, and reads as follows: "The legislative, executive, and judiciary departments shall be separate and distinct, so that neither exercise the powers properly belonging to the other."

[1] And so, too, the Massachusetts constitution was ratified, not by a simple majority of the people of the State, but by a majority of the majorities in the "towns" (or townships), these being viewed as so many little republics leagued together.

a constitution and by this being adopted by a popular vote, the people at large is the popular assembly (assembling at the polls),[1] and the convention is its senate or council, its single representative body or committee.[2] Thus when Adams took part in the Massachusetts convention of 1779 and thanked God for affording "this people" an opportunity "of framing a new constitution of civil government for themselves and their posterity" (iv. 220), and when he again took part in the Massachusetts convention of 1820, he was merely acting under the very system against which he wrote three volumes of protest.[3]

Equally inept was his argument for that detail in a constitution which puts the executive chief into the legislative as a third branch thereof,—the executive

[1] "The people of a State," says Bryce, "when they so vote [on the draft of a constitution submitted to them,] act as a primary and constituent assembly, just as if they were all summoned to meet in one place like the folkmoots of our Teutonic forefathers. It is only their numbers that prevent them from so meeting in one place, and oblige the vote to be taken at a variety of polling places," *The American Commonwealth*, ch. xxxvii. (ed. of 1891, vol. i., p. 421).

[2] At first not all Americans understood the novel principle of the people extra-governmentally setting up their government. Some of the so-called constitutions (*e.g.* that of Virginia) were mere enactments of legislatures, and were repealable and amendable by their creators (who were also their creatures). Adams was among the first to avoid such inconsistent measures, although he had not occasion, like Jefferson (*Works*, viii., 363–7, ix., 252–3, 283, 290–1, iii., 202, vii., 344–5), to point out this defect, and hardly appears to have noticed it. In his *Autobiography* he represents himself as leading the way, in 1775, toward constitutional conventions and the submission of the result to the ratification of the people, iii., 18, 20. He never abandoned this position. But for such conventions he never proposed two chambers, nor for the ratification a concurrent vote of two or more classes of society.

[3] In iv., 586–7 he shows sign of fearing the single-chambered convention and the unbalanced influence therein of the aristocrats, except in the peculiar times "lately seen," when such conventions had been a necessity.

negative: that it is necessary to provide the first magistrate with a means of protecting his executive power from encroachment by the legislature. This argument is repeated even at the present day by careless writers on the science of government. It is overlooked that our constitutions themselves protect the authority they assign to the presidents or governors,—that encroachments upon it by the legislature would not be enforcible before the courts, and would be void of effect. These writers do not notice that because our constitutions by their very nature give such a negative to the judicial department, another negative, for the same purpose, is unnecessary.

This point of giving the executive chief a veto in order to protect his authority and dignity and his independence of the legislature, deserves some further attention. We have already seen that even if this magistrate were appointed by the legislature, his independence might be sufficiently guarded by constitutionally placing his salary beyond the reach of the legislature during his term of office. In reality it is this and the various items of authority or the general power of carrying out the laws and engagements and commanding the forces of the country, which the Constitution confers upon him, and not either the mode of raising him to office or his power over legislation, that give our President all his dignity and necessary strength. Of course, the veto function is in itself an additional power, and would be a tremendous one if it were absolute; but it might be left out altogether, without risk of losing or diminishing any of the other purely executive powers. Adams is mysteriously silent about the fixity of the governor's salary guaranteed by our constitutions. He seems to think that but for his veto power the legislature might starve the governor into subserviency. This silence is all the more surprising because just before the Revolution, in 1772, there had been in Massachusetts a recrudescence of the old controversy over this very matter. The Massachusetts "General Court" wished to keep the payment of the governor in its own hands. This was regarded as one of the mainstays of the freedom granted in the charter. To allow the payment of the governor to be settled by the Crown, a resolution of the House declared, would destroy "that mutual check and dependence which each branch of the legislature ought to have upon the others, and the balance of power which is essential to all free governments."[1] This was because the governor was appointed by the Crown, and would then be wholly dependent on it and independent of the people over whom he ruled. But when the governor is appointed or elected by the people, the case is different. Then he must receive his salary by their grant, and not by that of the legislature: his salary is a constitutional affair. This was generally recognized; and therein only have we an explanation of Adams's not dwelling upon it. But he had no right to drop it so completely out of sight as to overlook, if not to hide, this means of making the executive chief independent of the legislature and thereby dispensing with his veto.

And the same is the case, of course, with the judiciary. Their terms and salaries being fixed by the constitution,

---

[1] Reported in Wells's *Samuel Adams*, i., 480. *Cf.* Gordon, *History of the American Revolution*, i., Letter 5. For S. Adams's vigorous objections to the innovation see Wells, i., 371, 381, 408, 451. On this occasion J. Adams advised impeachment proceedings, which were begun in the assembly, but thrown out, as foreseen, yet had a moral effect. See his account in ii., 328-32 and x., 236-41. He mentions only judges; but the measure covered the Attorney-general, Judges, and Governor.

if the legislature should invade their authority and undermine their support, passing contrary laws, the judges would simply continue to make their decisions according to the old constitutional laws, ignoring, and thus negativing or vetoing the new unconstitutional laws. This judicial negative, supported by the constitution, supports the constitution: this judicial negative and the constitution together, support all the rest. The executive veto, for the purpose designed by Adams, is superfluous.

This power of the courts ought to have been foreseen before the establishment of the Federal Constitution, because this operation had already begun under the State constitutions. But there it was only in its infancy, and we need not be surprised that the feeble force of it was not yet fully recognized.[1] To-day inexcusable, the oversight was excusable then. And it was often made. Many of the members in the Convention at Philadelphia feared that the tendency of governments always is in this or in that direction, either toward all power in the legislature (especially in republics) or toward all power in the executive (at least in hereditary governments)[2]; and they wanted to guard against such encroachments in our government, the

[1] In fact, there had as yet been only a couple of instances of a State law being set aside—one in Rhode Island in 1786 and another the next year in North Carolina. Of these Adams in Europe may not have heard. But in the same year with the first, Jefferson in Virginia asserted that in the other States "the Judges would consider any law as void which was contrary to the [State] constitution," *Works*, ix., 290. Even in Virginia the Judges had made a claim to this power in 1782.

[2] For the former see Elliot's *Debates*, v., 327, 345 (Madison), 346, 429–30, 528 (Morris), *The Federalist*, Nos. 48, 49 (Madison), 71 (Hamilton), Madison, *Writings*, i., 478, *cf.* 475; for the latter, Elliot's *Debates*, 153 (Butler and Mason), 154 (Franklin), 186 (Randolph). For the qualifying terms above put in parentheses *cf.* Hamilton, *Works*, vii., 285.

ones by strengthening the executive and putting him beyond assault, the others by fortifying the legislature, all agreeing in looking upon the judiciary as (in all cases) the weakest of the departments,[1] of little efficiency to protect itself or the others, needing rather to be put under their common guardianship. For all this they relied on past experience of governments without constitutions, or of constitutions without an independent judiciary, where the judiciary was set up by one or both of the other departments themselves, and consequently was subservient to them; and they argued from them to a government with a constitution containing such an independent judiciary established by the instrument itself, not perceiving that however they might arrange the powers, provided they included such a judiciary, the constitution would fix those powers until the constitution itself was altered. Of course in the Convention it was expected and intended that the national judiciary should declare unconstitutional laws void, and this indeed was urged as a reason for not giving the national judiciary a prior negative upon bills passed by the national legislature[2] (as also for not giving the national legislature, or the Senate at least, a

[1] See above, p. 81.

[2] Elliot's *Debates*, v., 151 (Gerry and King), 346 (L. Martin), 347 (Mason), *cf.* 429 (Morris); but was disapproved by some, 429 (Mercer and Dickinson), or considered insufficient, 344 (Wilson). Madison also did not like it at first, preferring the other method, as noticed above, (p. 81 n.); but even in the Convention toward the end he appealed to it, *ib.*, 485, and later, while still remaining partial to the rejected method, *Writings*, iii., 56, he was reconciled to the one adopted, *ib.*, i., 554 (upon the first exercise of it in 1792). It was only incidentally, though very clearly, treated of in *The Federalist*, No. 78 (Hamilton); but it was relied on in the ratifying conventions, Elliot's *Debates*, ii., 196 (Ellsworth), 446 and 489 (Wilson), iii., 553 (Marshall), *cf.* 325 (at least in the States, Henry).

negative upon State laws[1]). Yet the oversight was unaccountably made of the fact that this judicial power of nullification would also defend the executive, as naturally a constitution will not be altered by constructive interpretation to the detriment either of the interpreting body or of its appointer. Since their day, in our Federal government, in spite of the President's limited veto and the not infrequent presence of sufficient majorities in the two chambers to override it, there has only once been the appearance of an encroachment of the legislature upon the executive, and that was in a matter where the Constitution is defectively silent[2]; and if the executive seems rather to encroach upon the legislature, this is due to the Constitution wrongly giving the President legislative functions. In our State governments there have been many re-arrangements, in general tending to weaken the legislatures and to strengthen the executives[3]; but these changes have everywhere been effected by the people altering the constitutions. There have been no overt encroachments by the departments within the governments, in violation of the constitutions.

[1] Elliot's *Debates*, v., 321–2 (Morris and Sherman). The rejected method, proposed in the "Virginia plan," art. 6, (at first adopted without debate, *ib.*, 127, 139, finally disposed of, 322), Madison also favored, *ib.*, 108, 171, 173, 251, 539, *Writings*, i., 285, 288. The control of the national judiciary over State laws he touched upon very gingerly in *The Federalist*, No. 39 near end; but later emphasized it, *Writings*, iv., 19, 49, 62–3, 76, 100, 208, 210–11, 222, 322–3.

[2] When Congress prevented Johnson from dismissing an objectionable Secretary.—Even the power of impeaching, in the legislature, has not led to any such result. This we have seen to be a defect. The prestige of the judiciary would have been enhanced, and its power in the balance strengthened, had it received this judicial function, rightfully belonging to it.

[3] See C. E. Merriam, *History of American Political Theories*, p. 183, *cf.* pp. 81, 109–10, 115.

On Adams's part, the neglect of the force of a constitution set up by the people may be explained by his absorption in contemplation of the excellences of the English system,—or of the English "constitution," which is merely the framework of the English government as it has made itself, not an instrument by which it was made. The English model was ever before his eyes. The essential difference between it and the new American system which he himself helped to establish, he did not recognize. He did not perceive that, while in England the King once had been, and the legislative then was, supreme and sovereign, so that in the former stage the legislature could not impeach their sovereign lord,[1] nor ever could the courts disregard a law passed by the sovereign legislative authority; in America the supreme and absolute sovereign, which has unlimited power, unchecked and uncheckable by court or king or legislature or previous constitution, is the people acting in its high legislative capacity in accepting or rejecting a constitution that has been prepared for its decision by a convention in a single chamber of members chosen by them for this special purpose; wherefore, once established, the constitution remains the expres-

---

[1] This, of course, was the source of the substituted practice of impeaching only the ministers (Blackstone, *Commentaries*, i., 242-3), which Adams wished to transplant bodily into our system, although he hardly ventured to bring over with it the idea of the first magistrate's sovereignty, which was its reason. Yet he inclined to import even that idea. In his early period he had spoken of rulers as "but the ministers of the people," iv., 15, *cf.* iii., 456-7. Even then he had in the Massachusetts bill of rights applied to all magistrates the term "agents" of the people, iv., 224, in place of "servants" in the Virginia bill of rights. But he now reprobates the practice of calling them by the latter term, vi., 14. (Perhaps he had just received a letter in which he read: the people of America "are content with their servants, and particularly with you": see Jefferson's *Works*, ii., 449.)

sion of the will even of succeeding generations as long as they leave it unaltered, the unlimited sovereign power meanwhile exerting itself constantly through the pressure of public opinion and periodically in appointing its agents, until again called into more direct activity to pass upon a new constitution or an amendment of the old or a construction of it, or to settle a dispute between its representatives in the government.[1] He did not recognize the full import of the fact that the legislative department instituted by a constitution is not a sovereign body, but that it has limited powers, and is only a restricted substitute for, and an instructed deputy of, the true sovereign, and, furthermore, is not supreme even over the other departments. His statement, therefore, was false, in this country, that the legislative is the supreme power in the state. He took this statement from English writers,[2] without noticing that it may be true in England and not be true here. That statement is true in England, because there the legislative is a perpetual constituent convention, with full authority to make constitutional as well as statute laws. In our country it is true of the ultimate legislature —the constitution-making, the fundamental-law-making people themselves. But in our country a distinction is drawn between two legislatives, and the statement is not true of the other, the ordinary, the annually

---

[1] Bryce strangely speaks, Rousseau-like, of there being "something unreal and artificial" in ascribing sovereignty to the American people, as it is "not a body habitually acting" and is "a body which is almost always in abeyance," *Studies in History and Jurisprudence*, American ed., pp. 539–40. Constitution-making or -altering is not the people's only function. And sovereignty may exist, though not acting.

[2] *E. g.*, Locke, *Of Civil Government*, §§ 132, 134, 149, 150, *cf.* 212; Blackstone, *Commentaries*, i., 46, 49; Paley, *Moral and Political Philosophy*, VI., vi.

13

sitting and biennially elected representative legislature. The power of this legislative in the making even of statute law the people have bounded, and have taken out of its hands entirely the enacting of constitutional law, and beside it have erected two other departments in many respects independent of it, and to these have given powers beyond its reach, and have made them co-ordinate with it, that is, no less and no more sovereign than it is, circumscribing to each a sphere of its own.[1] He failed to realize that above such limited sovereigns, which are no sovereigns at all, the constitution remains the symbol of the sovereignty of the people, and that the body of laws contained in it are primary and unrepealable by the executive and legislative departments, and are binding upon the judiciary, — a fact which, instead of weakening, strengthens this department over against the others, so that it may be equal to the task, not only of defending itself from encroachment, but of protecting each of the others from their mutual encroachments, if there be any attempts thereat,—in short, of performing its part in the balance and so of dispensing with the other balance within the legislative alone and with the executive negative there.[2]

[1] Not this essentially limited nature of an executive as of the other departments under an established constitution, but the fact that our Constitution "shackles" our Presidents by assigning them less authority than he thought proper, he later noticed as introducing a difference between the American and the English systems, preventing the American from coming "within the pale of the English system," as he had been accused of bringing it, vi., 463. Thus he continued wholly to miss the point.

[2] Adams remained in the position of Locke, who wrote: "The executive power, placed any where but in a person that has also a share in the legislature [and a veto there], is visibly subordinate and accountable to it, and may be at pleasure changed and displaced," *Of Civil Government*, § 152. Locke was speaking of a government not organized by a constitu-

On the other hand, even in the English system he overlooked the majesty of certain century-old laws won by insurrection and grown sacred and endowed, against the theory of the Parliament's supremacy, with almost constitutional force, being viewed (by some at least) as unrepealable by the Parliament, or repealable only after a special mandate from the people, or at the risk of a new insurrection in defense of them. He neglected there the influence of custom and tradition, and the conservatism of the people. And though he noticed that the people could not reform their government without the consent, or against the resistance, of the Lords and the King, yet he forgot Bolingbroke's assertion that "nothing can destroy the constitution of Britain, but the people of Britain."[1] For, after all, it is everywhere the people who, repressing their might, voluntarily submissive, permit the proudly styled sovereign bodies to exert their power, and thus really *give* them their power, or, as La Boëtie pointed out, allow it to them on sufferance.

This truth was received in dim perspective even by English upper-class publicists after the Revolution of 1688. Before that and during the prior Civil War the leaders of thought had clearly recognized it—always, of course, with some limitation of "the people" to men of some independence, who had a will of their own.

---

tion made by the people, and was excusable for ignoring what did not in his day exist, nor was then conceived of. But Adams ignored something which he himself had aided to bring forth. (And the same error was committed by Hamilton in *The Federalist*, No. 73.) Yet, later, just before deposing the presidency to Jefferson, on offering to Jay the position of Chief Justice, Adams wrote that "the firmest security we can have against the effects of visionary schemes or fluctuating theories, will be in a solid judiciary," ix., 91.

[1] *Dissertation upon Parties*, xvii. (*Works*, ii., 151.)

Their views, naturally, were not invented out of their own heads, but were taken from the great body of revolutionary doctrine which is handed on from one to another set of men aspiring to freedom, from antiquity down. To the English the transmitters were then more especially the Dutch[1]; but there had been English predecessors too. We need not, however, go further back. Among the English revolutionists, Milton offers a good specimen in his *Tenure of Kings*, in which the first principles are thus summarized: "The power of kings and magistrates" "was and is originally the people's, and by them conferred in trust only to be employed to the common peace and benefit; with liberty therefore and right remaining in them, to reassume it to themselves, if by kings or magistrates it be abused; or to dispose of it by any alteration, as they shall judge most conducing to the public good" (§ 20). But, the rest of the people not yet being ready to take up the reins of government, power fell into the hands of the army, composed of religious zealots, who thought themselves always in the right, and, fearing lest the populace hankered after the fleshpots permitted them by their former rulers, prescribed governments for them, without ever consulting them, until after a few years their yoke was thrown off and the old one put on again. This soon disappointed the people, and, because of the royal family's tincture of a foreign religion contracted abroad, offended even the aristocrats and ecclesiastics; and once more, revolutionary doctrines were broached. Then we meet with teachings resembling Milton's,

---

[1] Thus Hobbes spoke of many being content to see the late troubles and the change of government, "out of an imitation of the Low Countries"; though he ascribed greatest influence to the reading of Greek and Latin histories and "books of policy." *Leviathan*, ch. xxix.

weakly reproduced in Nedham's work (quoted by Adams, vi. 202), and strongly in the *Discourses Concerning Government* of Algernon Sydney, who asserted that God "hath granted to all a liberty of inventing such forms as please them best," and that "if the multitude do institute, the multitude may abrogate."[1] These also were written before the establishment of the government desired; but after the establishment of that government, the tone is changed: the establishment itself of the new government is still justified on the former principles, but its own possible abrogation is guarded against by limiting the application of those principles. The people are not to be allowed the right of instituting new governments at any time they may please, but only on certain very rare contingencies.

This change of tone is, to his credit, not so plainly discernible in Somers's *Vox Populi Vox Dei*, if indeed that political tract was written by Somers, in which the author, after speaking of men voluntarily uniting, mutually agreeing, and freely acting in the choice of the governors, goes on to say that what the people "by common consent have enacted only for the public safety, they may without any obstacle alter, when things require it, by the like common consent."[2] Possibly he saw the uselessness of forbidding the people

---

[1] I., vi.; *cf.* II., xxxii. and III. xxv.

[2] §§ 8, 9; *cf.* also §§ 7, 18, 31, 50, 65, 83. Published anonymously in 1709, this tract was republished in 1710 and thereafter frequently under the title *The Judgment of Whole Kingdoms*, etc. It is one of four whose ascription to Somers is doubtful. It seems to have been repudiated by the Whigs (certainly by Burke, who in his *Reflections on the Revolution in France* did "never desire to be thought a better Whig than Lord Somers"); and its reproductions were due to its popularity and the favor it met with among the reformers. For instance, it was frequently appealed to by the abolitionist and advocate of annual elections, Granville Sharp.

to do what they never will do—subvert a government that is good; and the folly of setting obstacles to their improving one that is bad. The transformation of the doctrine is especially manifest in Locke, who became the great authority of the Whigs. Locke in his treatise *Of Civil Liberty* (1690) acknowledged the supremacy of the people, latently, in his frequent mention of "the consent of the people" and "the right of appeal to heaven," and in the great passage where he admonishes that when the legislative by transgressing the "fundamental rule of society," and grasping at "absolute power," "by this breach of trust forfeit the power the people had put into their hands for quite contrary ends, and it devolves upon the people," these now are "absolved from any farther obedience" and have "the right to resume their original liberty" (§ 222); and explicitly he acknowledged it at the very end, where, after supposing the case of the reversion to the society of the supreme legislative power through such forfeiture, he speaks of the people having "a right to act as supreme, and continue the legislative in themselves, or erect a new form, or under the old form place it in new hands, as they think good."[1] But this is a qualified supremacy. "The community," he had previously asserted, "may be said in this respect

---

[1] § 243. Here he mentions also the case of the people having given only temporary power to their legislative, at the expiration of which the same reversion of supremacy and liberty occurs (and he speaks of an "original constitution" in §§ 153 and 156). He probably had in mind, as regards the legislature, the three-year period of the English House of Commons, once existent and then advocated (not anticipating the Parliament's extension of this to seven years in 1716); and in the executive, the fixed terms of the Roman Consuls and Dictators. But while his doctrine thus covered republicanism, it allowed also for the perpetual terms of the English King and Lords.

[of self-preservation] to be always the supreme power, but not as considered under any form of government, because this power of the people can never take place till the government be dissolved" (§ 149). Their power is intermittent and conditional. "*If* their former government be dissolved, they are at liberty to begin and erect another to themselves" (§ 185). "*When* the government is dissolved, the people are at liberty to provide for themselves, by erecting a new legislative, differing from the other, by the change of persons, or form, or both, as they shall find it most for their safety and good" (§ 220). But "when the legislative is once constituted," the people have "no power to act as long as the government stands" (§ 157). While the government stands, the legislative is "supreme," its power being "sacred and unalterable in the hands where the community has once placed it" (§ 134). Locke added also a third supreme something in the state; for he allowed that the single person who has "the supreme execution" may "in a tolerable sense be called supreme" (§ 151). Here he is at fault, since it is only as supreme law-giver that anyone is supreme or sovereign, the common definition of the latter being "whose will is law." The English King is still said by a legal fiction to be the maker of the laws, the Lords and Commons only consenting. By the same fiction he is still called sovereign, or supreme. But the other two supremes are inherent contradictions in the Whig position, due to its lying between two stools. In the mere literal and metaphorical sense of "highest," the governors (also literally and metaphorically the helmsmen, pilots, officers of the ship of state) may be allowed to be supreme or sovereign. But this is not the real sense in which these terms are usually taken: they mean "greatest," which is literally the meaning of "majesty"; and such is properly the people's power (who are the owners of the ship of state).[1] The people can place supreme or highest power over themselves in their rulers (*cf.* § 153); but the greatest, or fundamental power remains ultimately in themselves, even though they be not intelligent and united enough to wield it. Under an absolute government they do not wield it (whether they be competent or not): in a republic they do (also whether competent or not)—here the laws are their will (*cf.* § 214), and they are the sovereign. Locke and the Whigs advocated the former, with occasional and temporary recourse to the latter—much absolutism and little republicanism, or absolutism mitigated by republicanism (with risk of its some day leavening the whole).[2]

[1] So the Romans spoke of the "majestas populi." Their writers used distinctive terms. They mentioned rather the "auctoritas" of the Senate (because of its initiative in legislation), and the "imperium" of the Consuls, the executive. If they alluded to power in the magistrates, it was because to them "populus potestatem dedit." (So, for instance, Cicero, respectively, *De Re Publica*, ii., § 57, *Pro Rabirio*, § 3, *De Inventione Rhetorica*, ii., § 53.)

[2] Even on the continent, according to Pufendorf, some jurists had distinguished between "personal supremacy" and "real supremacy," and assigned the latter to the people. The authors referred to, however, (Hotman at least) do not appear to have used these terms, which are ascribed to them as expressive of their views. Pufendorf himself, from the side of the absolutists, condemned this leaving of any sovereignty to the people, *De Jure*, etc., VII., vi., 4, followed by Heineccius, *Elementa*, etc., II., vii., 130; and from the side of the Whigs, Burlamaqui, *Principes*, etc., vol. iv., pp. 101, 102. The chief argument for that distinction is said to have been, that the constituent is superior to the constituted; which would seem to be demonstrative; but it was met by very bad arguments (drawn from slavery) first used by Grotius, *De Jure Belli ac Pacis*, I., iii., 13, *cf.* 1; repeated by Pufendorf, *De Jure*, VII., vi., 6, but not by Burlamaqui. It was against such slovenliness that Rousseau protested, *Contrat Social*, I., iv. Already Bodin had dis-

But even this admission of occasional and temporary power in the people was too much for the Tories, and especially the latitude allowed the people of ever choosing whatever form of government they pleased. In this last point, at all events, they thought the Whigs went too far. The Revolution could be justified without danger of another, without it. Blackstone is their spokesman. He based the justification of the Revolution principally upon the "abdication" involved in the flight of James II., showing no squeamishness about profiting by the treasonable acts of those who drove him to it. This alone gave "the society at large" right to pass upon his title, but not to pass upon the office, since the King had only "endeavored," but had failed, to "subvert the constitution." In other words, only if the government subverts the constitution, are the people at liberty to revise the perverted constitution, apparently for restoring it to its former shape. Therefore he commended the statesmen of that day for only placing the old forms in new hands; and reprobated "the principles of Mr. Locke" for admitting the other alternative of a right to introduce new forms; which principles he later compared with those of "a Cade

tinguished between a "sovereign" simply so-called, who has power unlimited in extent and perpetual in time, and a "sovereign magistrate," whose power, unlimited in extent, but restricted in time, has been deputed to him by the real sovereign, *De la Republique*, I., viii. (p. 125, again pp. 408, 451). But instead of taking the people to be that perpetual sovereign, Bodin assumed it to be a "sovereign lord" (p. 328) in a line of kings, and never inquired how anyone could rightly attain to this position, merely accepting the doctrine of sovereignty by divine appointment, pp. 143, 152, 448, 986; which indeed is the only way an absolute sovereign can be set over a people. But the distinction drawn by Bodin was so essentially clear, that its proper application could not, in time, fail to be made. Hobbes adopted it (*Leviathan*, ch. xix.), and tried to base the sovereign lord upon the people (ch. xvii.), failing utterly.

and a Tyler." But all this subject was, from his point of view, so removed from any practical importance, that he declared "the reasons upon which those statesmen decided to be "matter of instructive amusement for us to contemplate, as a speculative point of history," and recommended care "not to carry this inquiry further than for instruction or amusement."[1]

On one important point we see the Whigs and Tories to be in unison: the people, during the continuance of the government, is not supreme, it is subject, the government is supreme—the government which makes laws and executes them. The difference is about the continuance of the government: the Tories say till it abdicates, or perverts its own nature; the Whigs, till it abandons its end, the good of the people, and forfeits its power through abuse.[2] But while neither of these contingencies occur, the government exists, and has an equal right to exist in the eyes of both, and the people have no right to alter it a jot—at least not without its own consent. During this continuance the blunt statement by Dr. Johnson is as true for the Whigs as for the Tories, that "there can be no limited govern-

[1] *Commentaries*, i., 211–14; iv., 434, *cf.* i., 162.

[2] Metaphorically there is this difference: the Tories make the sovereign or highest power on earth come down from above, delegated by God; the Whigs make it come up from below, erected by the people. The thoroughgoing Tories, the Catholic jurists, make it continually depend from the sky, and therefore allow one supposable case of forfeiture: when the sovereign turns from or disobeys God; of which the Pope is the earthly judge. The English Tories could not make this use of the principle, as they had no judge, and so left the government unattached above. On the other side, those who thoroughly raise up the government from and by the people, as we shall presently see, rest the government perpetually on the people; which the Whigs did not do, but left the government unsupported below. Thus to both Tories and Whigs the government had no visible attachment or prop.

ment," as in every society there must be "some power or other from which there is no appeal," which pervades the whole mass, which adjusts all subordination, and which, though not infallible, "is irresistible, for it can be resisted only by rebellion."[1] This unassailable power was taken as a matter of course to be the government, or in particular the legislative, which "enacts laws and repeals them," including the king as one of its branches, who in addition executes the laws he has contributed to enact.

It is noteworthy that among the functions of such an unlimited government Johnson included that of erecting or annulling judicatures. He does not say, of course, that this supreme power erects or annuls legislatures and executives; for, in his opinion, it *is* those things. Here again the Whigs and the Tories agreed. The supreme government, in the opinion of both, is the legislative, including the executive; apart, and subordinate, erected by it, stands the judicature. With regard to the supreme legislative, the two parties differed only in approaching it from opposite directions. The Tories would have liked, following their ancestors, to have placed it as much as possible in the King, or in the King and Lords; but the Whigs insisted, as a sop to the Cerberean monster—and it was one of their half measures—that the people should have a share in legislation, represented in the House of Commons; but in a House of Commons, remember, whose members were chosen by restricted suffrage, in pocket boroughs,

[1] *Taxation no Tyranny* (*Works*, ed. of 1824, viii., 168-9). Similarly another writer on the occasion of the Stamp Act, Allan Ramsay, *Thoughts on the Origin and Nature of Government*, 1769, pp. 15, 17, 28. Also Blackstone, *Commentaries*, i., 160, and Paley, *Moral and Political Philosophy*, VI., vi.

with bribery, intimidated by Lords, and which excluded, or would exclude, members it did not approve of (a Sydney, or a Wilkes). In accord on the Lords, the Tories had to accept this Commons, and the Whigs had to retain the King (whom they would use as a puppet). But both the Whigs and the Tories placed the supreme power in the Parliament, however composed.

This is important. It is still the legal principle in England. In legal phraseology, the members of Parliament (even of the House of Commons) do not *represent* the people of England, they *are* the people of England.[1] This has been declared by statute, which is unrepealed; and it is still entertained by British jurists.[2]

---

[1] For some strong expressions of this doctrine see Jephson, *The Platform*, i., 61, 80, 81, *cf.* 112–13. It led to the doctrine of the independence of Parliament (see above, p. 145), and to its resentment at petitions, Cobbett's *Parliamentary Debates*, vol. ix., col. 442. (*Cf.*, in colonial America, Winthrop, *History of New England from 1630 to 1649*, under date of May 22, 1639), and especially at other assemblages discussing public questions: see in Jephson's work *passim*, but particularly, i., 504–6, 584, ii., 11–12.

[2] So Bryce, *American Commonwealth*, ch. xxiii. (vol. i., p. 246), and *Studies in History and Jurisprudence*, p. 538 (against Austin, *Province of Jurisprudence*, p. 241, who there attempted to give a more "accurate" opinion than the legal one, yet everywhere else accepted the legal view, pp. 276, 280, 287, even of all government, p. 333, etc.).—A trace of this doctrine may be found even among our ancestors. In the Massachusetts ratifying convention J. C. Jones said: "The Federal representatives . . . will be the people," Elliot's *Debates*, ii., 29. And in the House of Representatives in 1798 S. W. Dana, of Connecticut, asserted that "the sovereignty of the country is vested by the Constitution in Congress," Benton's *Abridgment*, ii., 260A. But there, the year following, J. A. Bayard maintained that the judiciary was equally sovereign in its department, *ib.*, 369A; which, in a way, was also Jefferson's opinion, *Works*, iv., 68, and in Washington's *Writings*, x., 537, though he expressed his real view better in *Works*, iv., 302. Adams himself in 1809 referred back to the early Congress, in 1784, as "the then sovereign of our country," ix., 273.

The doctrine is ridiculous, because it is self-contradictory, declaring at once that a representative is the principal.[1] But it is the law all the same, and though a self-contradictory thing cannot exist, there is something in this law, or principle, that is not self-contradictory and that therefore can exist, and does exist; which is, that the English legislative is recognized as having all the power that the English people would otherwise have; and as a people can do anything it pleases with its own, so the English Parliament is recognized as being able to do anything it pleases with what belongs to the English people: in this field it was, and is, said to be "omnipotent,"[2] in spite of Magna Charta and other bills of rights, which, in theory, it can repeal. Such a Parliament once proclaimed the iniquitous dogma that it had the right "to bind the colonies and people of America in all cases whatsoever," and lost them in consequence. It did so, and in its own eyes had this right, only because the colonies in America

---

[1] The statute in question, 1 James II., c. 1, runs thus: "This high Court of Parliament, where all the whole body of the Realm and every particular member thereof, either in Person [*i. e.*, in the House of Lords, and the King himself] or by Representation (upon their own free elections) [*i. e.*, in the House of Commons], are by the Laws of this Realm deemed to be personally present." Thus by law those who are said to *be* present by representation are to be *deemed* present in person! And if the members, at least in one branch, who made this legal definition, were at the time representatives, did their declaration make them principals? or did it compose a legal fiction? Notice that the English people, the principals, have never made this law or declaration. Yet they have acquiesced. More fully explained, the point is this:—There is no distinction between principal and agent, *qua* agent, over against third parties; but in relation to each other there is a great and important distinction between them. Now, in governmental matters, the Tories and Whigs denied or overlooked the distinction in the latter case, to do so making use of its absence in the former case.

[2] Blackstone, *Commentaries*, i., 161.

were considered to belong to England. And in its own eyes, too, the people of America had no more reason to object than had the people of England, because it had the same right over the people of England, with the little difference, then small indeed, that the people of England, a few of them, had the right of electing some members to one branch of it, which none of the Americans had. In fact as well as in fiction, the English people were subjects, not only of their own representatives, but of the Lords and of the King, who were not their representatives. The English people were not supreme even in theory.[1]

The Tories, of course, would never admit anything else. They inherited the doctrine which led the origin of government directly up to God. The Whigs did not deny this, but, taking *vox populi* for *vox dei*, when driven to bay, they had to admit, with Locke,[2] that the people "did, and nobody else can, set up" the authority of government. Only they confined themselves to admitting it: they did not make a point of it. They perverted it also. We might have expected that they would have admitted that the people erect the legislative and the executive in the same way as these were allowed to have erected the judicature. But no: the Whigs drew a distinction, and while the judicature is merely commissioned and the terms of the commissions may be altered at the pleasure of the grantors, at least for new incumbents, the Whigs invoked a convenient

[1] Rousseau merely paraphrased Locke when he said the English people were free only during elections, *Contrat Social*, III., xv. *Cf.* Price, *On Civil Liberty*, p. 9. He went even too far. At those moments the English people were free, or sovereign, in respect to or over only one branch of three in their supreme legislative, or sovereign only in conjunction with two other powers. (*Cf.* Austin, *Province of Jurisprudence*, 239, stating the common view.)   [2] *Of Civil Government*, § 227.

theory, to the effect that at least the line of executive chiefs, forming the nucleus of the legislative, and being the creator of the Lords, was instituted by an original compact between it and the people, and consequently the terms of the compact, which provide for perpetuity, cannot be altered by the people without the consent of the other party and his advisers (in the legislative), unless upon his abdication, or the failure of the line, or else only for forfeiture through not himself abiding by the terms, one of which is to observe the laws already made and to act for the common welfare.[1] The strict Tories, of course, would have nothing to do with a contract.[2] The King is *jure divino*, and cannot be dis-

---

[1] The theory of an original contract between King and people, shortly before denounced as a republican chimera (Hallam, *Constitutional History*, ch. xiv., near end), was, in the Convention, January–February, 1689, treated as new (Cobbett's *Parliamentary History*, vol. v., col. 76 by Clarendon), the only authority cited for it being Hooker (*ib.*, col. 79 by Treby), yet it was there by the Commons put into the resolution declaring James's "abdication," and was accepted by the Lords in a close vote (*ib.*, cols. 50, 59). It is omitted in Locke's treatise, but, having been brought forward again at the trial of Sacheverell, it was insisted upon in Somers's (?) *Vox Populi*, §§ 3, 4, 5, 43, 44, 62, 65, 143. Burke, in his later writings, drew out the inference of the people being bound by the contract, almost to the Tory position of passive obedience, not only for the French, *Reflections on the Revolution in France* (*Works*, vol. iii., p. 250), but also for the English, there (pp. 250, 258) and especially in *Appeal from the New to the Old Whigs*, (*ib.*, vol. iv., pp. 133, 135, 162, 167; here quoting the old Whigs at the Sacheverell trial, pp. 122, 124, 125, 127). This contract theory is treated as a Whig doctrine by Macaulay, *History of England*, ch. x.

[2] But some of the Tories had been persuaded to vote with the Whigs for the resolution affirming this theory, and William and Mary were plainly set up upon it. Therefore it was employed by such discreet Tories as Bolingbroke, *Dissertation upon Parties*, ix. (*Works*, ii., 85), and Blackstone, *Commentaries*, i., 245. Other Tories were inclined to revert to the doctrines of Filmer's *Patriarcha*. A specimen may be recommended in an exiled American loyalist, Jonathan Boucher, whose *View of the*

missed at all.   Only if he abdicates, can another be chosen to his place, the same divine institution of kingship being retained.   But while the King neither abdicates nor forfeits, the Tories and the Whigs agreed in denying any right to the people to do anything in the matter.

The Tory doctrine being put out of court, the fine-spun Whig theory could easily be met, not only by denying the validity of any such perpetual terms of the contract, if ever made, or the fact of their ever having been made, but also by adducing another theory equally fine and much more rational.   This is the theory of a social rather than a civil compact—of the formation of society, prior to that of the *civitas* or state, by men coming together, combining their forces, compacting with one another to observe their mutual rights, and erecting over themselves a government to protect these. The office-holders in such a government the people appoint or elect, and contract with only on strict and limited terms—if swearing allegiance to them, yet binding them by oath.   Them the people, retaining the sovereignty in their own hands, commission, exactly as a sovereign king (in the absolutist theory) commissions, or ought to commission, his ministers, with power to discharge, whenever occasion requires, or their short terms expire, not only for downright misconduct, but for negligence or incompetence or difference of policy. To them the people delegate all the power and authority they—representatives as well as magistrates—can legally exercise, and, while thus granting away coercion over themselves, reserve to themselves all the rights they do not wish to see infringed.

Cause and Consequences of the American Revolution was published in London, 1797.   (It is reviewed by Merriam, *op. cit.*, pp. 63–9.)

Such a theory had been advanced in earlier revolutionary periods—by Milton for instance.[1] Another

[1] The social contract theory in *Tenure of Kings*, § 9 (the other theory of a covenant between king and people, but without the item of perpetuity, *ib.*, § 37, and in *Mode of Establishing a Free Commonwealth*, § 2). Power and authority the people communicated to kings and magistrates "not to be their lords and masters," "but to be their deputies and commissioners," exercising "intrusted power," *Tenure of Kings*, § 10. The reservation of rights was clearly made in *The Agreement of the People*, drawn up by the Council of Officers, October, 1647, and intended for submission, but never submitted, to the people; in which, art. 4, the power of the successive Representatives [the Parliaments] is said to be "inferior only to theirs who choose them," and which, prescribing how far this power extends, ends with "and, generally, to whatsoever is not expressly and impliedly reserved by the represented to themselves," one of the reservations being liberty of conscience. (This paper is reprinted in Gardiner's *History of the Great Civil War*, London, 1893, vol. iii., p. 393. Gardiner remarks that this "was the first example of that system which now universally prevails in the State Governments of the American Republic," p. 387. Say rather the "suggestion," as it was not then carried out. An amplified version of the *Agreement*, containing the same reservations, was published December, 1648, *ib.*, iv., 267, 276–7, 295–6, reprinted in the same author's *Constitutional Documents of the Puritan Revolution*, 270–82.) Milton also would stand on this reservation in his *Divisions of the Commonwealth*. And Sydney wrote, in a general way, that nations "give so much [power] as they think consistent with their own good, and reserve the rest to themselves, or to such other officers as they please to establish," *Discourses*, III., xxi., *cf.* xliv. Even the Whig Somers (?) wrote: "What he [the magistrate] cannot derive from some concession of the society, must be acknowledged to remain still vested in the people, as their reserved privilege and right," *Vox Populi Vox Dei*, § 3, and similarly § 6; and still more remarkably, the Tory Bolingbroke (in opposition) wrote of the king having "a right to no more than is intrusted to him by the constitution," and of the people really having an indefeasible right "to that part which they have reserved," *Idea of a Patriot King* (*Works*, ii., 393). But these two post-revolutionary politicians did not make this reservation in the case of the legislature, because, as we have seen, the legislature was then identified with the people and clothed with all the authority of the people. On the other hand, the social contract theory was used by Hobbes, but most unsuccessfully, as the basis of his doctrine of absolute power in either king or assembly, *Leviathan*, ch. xvii. Locke also used only this theory,

revolutionary period was now coming on, and it re-appeared. In an isolated instance in France it was brilliantly worked over by Rousseau, in his *Contrat Social* (1762), to whom, as a Genevan, it came naturally. But in a strong-willed people, "guided," as Milton said,[1] "by the very principles of nature" in them, theory was not needed to arouse and to justify, but only to direct and to cap, resistance to oppression and advocacy of reform; and in England, where a Tory King had come to the throne, another body of men, another party almost—it afterward became one, with the appellation of "Radicals,"—sprang into being during the troubles which were stirred up soon after those excited in America by the Stamp Act, these also provoked by similarly high-handed measures on the part of the government at home. They all sympathized with the Americans in the struggle for their rights as men and as Englishmen. One of their coryphœuses, Cartwright, had been in America; and another, Paine, went there. Among their leading lights were Priestley and Price. Also Franklin joined them during his third stay in England. They did not borrow from Rousseau, or draw out the theory so minutely as he did; but they emphasized the admission of popular sovereignty which had been made by the Whigs and which the Whigs wished to suppress, and they rejected the Whig doctrine of kingship by perpetual contract, and instead accepted the doctrine of kingship by commission. The supremacy of the people they extended even over Parliament, denying its omnipotence,[2] maintaining

Of Civil Government, §§ 95, 97, and left his perpetual government un-supported. Absolutists like Pufendorf (*De Jure*, VII., ii., 7–8) have not hesitated to employ both. [1] *Tenure of Kings*, § 21.

[2] Price: "All delegated power must be subordinate and limited. If

that the fundamental or consitutional laws, especially
the charters or bills of rights, which had been frequently
confirmed, were not repealable by Parliament except
after appeal to the people,[1] on whose will the continuance of the government depends, and who can change
it as they please.[2] And yet they showed timidity in
being content with having the people possess only a
share in the legislative.[3] Their teachings had little
influence in their own country at the time; but, aided
by the long "inning" of the Tories, when the danger
from French Jacobinism and Imperialism was over, they
at last converted the Whigs into Liberals.

It was in America, where social and economic condi-

---

omnipotence can, with any sense, be ascribed to a legislature, it must be
lodged where all legislative authority originates; that is, in the People.
For their sakes government is instituted; and theirs is the only real
omnipotence," *On Civil Liberty*, p. 11.

[1] So Granville Sharp, *Declaration of the People's Natural Right to a
Share in the Legislature*, 2d ed., 1775, pp. 17, 169–70, 234–8, on the
principle "eodem modo quo quid constituitur, eodem modo dissolvitur,"
ib., pp. 201–4, and *The Legal Means of Political Reformation*, pp. 92–3.
The successors of the Tories, the Conservatives, are now holding, as their
last intrenchment, that whatever they disapprove (in the House of
Lords), the House of Commons cannot alter without such an appeal
to the country.

[2] Price: "Government is an institution for the benefit of the people
governed, which they have power to model as they please," *On Civil
Liberty*, p. 10.—This doctrine, repeated in 1789, was the occasion, and
butt, of Burke's *Reflections on the Revolution in France* (see *Works*, iii.,
244, 251). It was again denounced by him as a principle which "con-
founds, in a manner equally mischievous and stupid, the origin of a
government from the people with its continuance in their hands,"
Observations on the Conduct of the Minority (*Works*, v. 45). This, of
course, was common doctrine in America. "The people," said Madison,
"were the fountain of power. They could alter constitutions as they
pleased," Elliot's *Debates*, v., 500; *cf.* Benton's *Abridgment* i., 141A–B,
and Gerry, *ib.*, 142B. Jefferson called it "the catholic principle of
republicanism," *Works*, ix., 129–30, *cf.* iii., 500, 521.

[3] See above, note on p. 28.

tions were favorable, that such doctrines met with the widest recognition, not coming from France, but from the earlier English tradition[1]: indeed, those doctrines had here never been in abeyance; and they were carried further, and what is more, were now first put into practice.[2]   Beside repudiating the Tory principles, and beside uncovering the Whig kernel from its shell, as the English Radicals had done in theory, the Americans extended the idea of an agent commissioned by the people from the executive also to the judicature, and with regard to the legislative, instead of rearing representative plenipotentiaries, they realized the Radical ideal by actually restricting the whole body of legislators to limited, even to enumerated powers.   Actually there is no unlimited government: intolerable misconduct is not necessary before changes can be made: in-

---

[1] Probably a score of persons in America had read Milton or Sydney, and a hundred Locke, to one who had heard of Rousseau. Montesquieu was known chiefly because of his admiration of the English constitution. Rousseau's ideas later acquired force in France because of the corroboration they received from America. "This war," wrote Brissot de Warville in 1787, of our revolutionary struggle, "has occasioned [in Europe, and particularly in France] the discussion of many points important for the public welfare—the discussion of the social contract, of civil liberty," etc., *De la France et des États-Unis*, p. xxx.

[2] *Cf.* Madison, *Writings*, iv., 58.—Even before putting it into practice in their own governments, the Americans, like (and even before) the English Radicals, claimed that it was the principle of the English government,—that even there the constitution underlay not only the executive, but also the legislative (which still was metaphorically called "supreme," though in reality inconsistently).   This is first found expressed in official letters of the Massachusetts legislature in January and February, 1768, which were written by S. Adams: see Wells's *S. Adams*, i., 153–4, 159, 160, 163, 164, 166, and Pitkin's *History of the United States*, i., 458.   This subject had been started by the Stamp Act in 1765, which was in a general way called "unconstitutional," and appeal was made, by Otis and others, to Lord Coke (Bancroft, *History of the United States*, v., 291).

cumbents in office may be dismissed periodically at
such short intervals that the people need not wish to do
it oftener; and their commissions may be altered at any
time the people desire, improvements by amendment
being a regular procedure. The legislative part of the
government cannot even in theory repeal the bill of
rights: only the people is the unlimited power, from
which is no appeal, and which cannot be resisted without
rebellion (of a part against the nearly whole, instead
of the nearly whole against a part). The people erects
its government, every part of its government, the legislative and the executive as well as the judiciary, and
the judiciary as well as those, not allowing any of the
great departments of government to erect another
except by its express permission and under its direction;
and it by no means grants to them, or to any of them,
all its unlimited power, but it reserves much to itself;
and the judgment as to when the legislative or executive
overstep their commissions and act voidly, it leaves to
the judiciary. Herein is originality in both theory and
practice, where Rousseau and the English Radicals
knew nothing of the principle of the judiciary's delegated supremacy in the judicial field,[1] and the English
statesmen, after their Revolution, led by the Whigs,
when they made their judicature "independent," as
they said, made it independent of the executive only,
not of the legislative,[2] and it still is in England depen-

[1] *Cf.* Milton, quoted above, p. 89 n. Of course Locke knew it not:
cf. Of Civil Government, §§ 240, 242.

[2] *Cf. Wealth of Nations*, Book V., ch. i., part 2 end, where Adam Smith
demands that the judicial should be rendered independent of the executive power, but says not a word about its relation to the legislative.
Similarly Blackstone enumerates the independence of the salaries of the
judges among the curtailments of the power of the Crown, *Commentaries*,
i., 336; in a dispute between a society and its magistrates vested with

dent upon the only legislative there existing, and cannot disregard anything that legislative enacts; while with us the judicature is as independent of the representative legislative as it is of the commissioned executive (except in permitted details, and for punition), and it is dependent solely on the people, who instituted them all.[1] Here the people's law is the constitution, which is constructive of the government,[2] delegative of authority to all its parts, and restrictive of the extent of that authority in each case. Here the people make laws for their government before they allow their government to make laws for them; and the constitution is the people's collective law over the government, whose laws are over the individuals among the people.[3]

authority from itself, he knows "no other tribunal to resort to" but "the voice of the society itself," p. 212; and he asserts that if any branch had a right to animadvert upon another (though here he refers only to the king and the houses of the legislature), "that branch, or branches, in which this jurisdiction resided, would be completely sovereign," p. 244.

[1] Cf. the fifth article of the Massachusetts bill of rights (drawn up by Adams, iv., 224): "All power residing originally in the people, and being derived from them, the several magistrates and officers of government, vested with authority, *whether legislative, executive, or judicial,* are their substitutes and agents, and are at all times accountable to them."

[2] Gerry: "The constitution is the great law of the people, who are themselves the sovereign legislature," Benton's *Abridgment*, i., 301B. J. Q. Adams: "The constitution is the organic law or commission of the government," in Clay's *Correspondence*, 312.

[3] Here is carried out of the government, what Aristotle (*Polit.*, III. x. (xv.), 10) said of the king, in relation to the people; for here the people is greater than the government, and the government is greater than any and many individuals. Already in the Federal Convention Rufus King said that "in the establishment of societies, the constitution was, to the legislature, what the laws were to individuals," Elliot's *Debates*, v., 269, (so, later, Calhoun, *Works*, vi., 228–9.) Hamilton: "the constitution is the creation of the people; . . . the legislature, a creature of the constitution," *Works*, iii., 495, cf. 492; cf. Page, Benton's *Abridgment*, i., 325. And these principles of the sovereignty of the people, the creature-

And here the courts must observe the people's law before they act upon the government's laws.[1]

This, in distinction from Whig doctrine, is democratic or, better said, republican doctrine. As the Tories, out of power after the peace of Utrecht, taught almost Whig doctrine, so now the Whigs, out of power in their turn since the accession of George III., bordered on, and even passed the borders of, Radical teaching,[2] and the American revolutionists called themselves Whigs, although English Whiggism was something in reality very different, and American Whiggism was at first

ship of the legislature, etc., were well expounded by Madison in the Virginia Proceedings of 1799, *Writings*, iv., 520, 542-3, 543, and were later constantly expatiated upon by him: *ib.*, iii., 491, 663, iv., 139 (467), 184, 249, 319, 385. They were taken to Europe by Paine in his *Rights of Man*, Part I., and Part II., ch. iv.

[1] Bryce in his *American Commonwealth*, ch. xxiii., has shown that the judiciary's overriding the legislature's law where there is a higher law in the constitution, is a natural consequence of "the ordinary principles of the law of agency" (i., 241). But in England the application of this principle to Parliament, or to the legislative in any country, by treating it as a mere agent, was never so much as thought of; and even in America the theory was hardly evolved before the practice was begun. After that, in England it was well explained by Austin, *Province of Jurisprudence*, 243-4.

[2] At this period even Burke went with the Radicals (see especially *Thoughts on the Cause of the Present Discontents*, *Works*, i., 492, where he makes even the King and the Lords representatives and trustees of the people); but at the period of the French Revolution he abandoned Fox and the rest, and denounced them as New Whigs, himself claiming to remain an Old Whig. Really there was a split, and Burke went more toward the Tory position and Fox more toward the Radical, Fox emphasizing the people's sovereignty more than the early (at least post-Revolutionary) Whigs had done, and Burke wishing to suppress it more than even they had done. Now, like Blackstone, Burke denied Locke's principles, but without citing his venerated name, *Appeal from the New to the Old Whigs*, *Works*, iv., 133, *cf.* 170; again comparing them with those of Cade, Ball, etc., 177-82. He would admit the people to be "the natural control on authority" exercized by others, but for them "to exercize and to control together" he found contradictory, 164.

genuine Radicalism. Yet the "long train of abuses," evincing that the English government was grasping at absolute power over "the lives, liberty, and estates" of an unrepresented people, justified the Americans in "an appeal to heaven" even on Whig principles; and in some of the colonies the people were justified in setting up new governments even on Tory principles, since the governors had fled and thus "abdicated."[1] But it was the pre-Revolutionary Whig doctrines, those at least of a Sydney, which the Whigs afterward placed in the background, that the Americans again brought forward, and kept in the foreground, and passed beyond, the state of society not permitting a halt at the Whig station. Radical doctrine was taught by the leaders of the American Revolution—Samuel Adams,[2] Franklin, Jefferson, Madison, and many others; and was adopted and carried through by the American people, after first throwing off the yoke of foreign domination. Here for the first time revolutionary doctrine was put into

[1] This term, and some of Locke's very words (*Of Civil Liberty*, §§ 222, 225), Jefferson purposely put in the *Declaration of Independence*. Here the "abdication" is applied directly to George III. So the precedent of 1688 had been insisted upon by Judge Drayton in his *Charge* to the Grand Jury at Charleston in April, 1776 (Niles's *Principles and Acts of the Revolution*, pp. 330–2).

[2] Samuel Adams acknowledged the sovereignty of the people (Wells's *S. Adams*, iii., 308, 324, 345, 347), though he also, carelessly, used Locke's doctrine of the "supremacy" of the legislative (*ib.*, i., 430); and he early maintained that the legislative cannot alter or contravene the constitution (*ib.*, 417) even in England (see above, note on p. 212). For this last, although he had American fact before his eyes, he appealed (*ib.*, 455), for the general principle, to Vattel (*Droit des Gens*, I., § 34; which had been translated in 1760). But Vattel knew no better than his compatriot Rousseau, that it is for the judiciary to decide disputed points of the constitution, but left the decision to "the nation" (§ 36). So, even in our country, at about that time, in 1765, it was the legislature of Rhode Island which nullified the Stamp Act.

practice, and so the need of any new revolution done away with for all time—to the extent at least that the doctrine has been realized.[1] "Happy for us," wrote Jefferson in 1787, "that when we find our constitutions defective and insufficient to secure the happiness of our people, we can assemble with all the coolness of philosophers, and set it to rights, while every other nation on earth must have recourse to arms to amend or restore their constitutions."[2] All previous revolutions in modern Europe had failed. The Dutch burghers freed themselves from Philip only with the aid of the country nobility, and submitted to the rule of one of them. The English popular "Rebellion" ended in military despotism, and the subsequent "Revolution" was under the leadership of nobles who tightly curbed it. Only a

[1] Locke claimed for Whig doctrine that it was "the best fence against rebellion, and the probablest means to hinder it," *Of Civil Liberty*, § 226. Much more is this true of republican doctrine. Erskine wrote: "The only remedy against mobs is to extend to the multitude the full privileges of a people"; but explained it by adding: "When the people themselves actually choose the popular branch of the legislature, that forms the controul upon the other part of it, which are, for the wisest purposes, put out of their own choice by other modifications, and where that choice is made for a very limited season, upon what principle can rebellion exist against such a Parliament, and who, in God's name, are to be the rebels?" *View of the War with France*, Philadelphia reprint, 1797, p. 68. Much more is this the case where, for still wiser purposes, the other parts are likewise entrusted to the choice of the people.

[2] *Works*, ii., 264, cf. 429; ("a philosophic revolution" he also called that of the French in 1790, *ib*., iii., 134). *Cf*., of our change of government, also C. Pinckney, Elliot's *Debates*, iv., 331, Pendleton, *ib*., iii., 293, Humphreys, *Miscellaneous Works*, New York, 1790, p. 339, and Washington, *Writings*, ix., 401, cf. xii., 222. But L. Martin did not advance to this new position, and retained Locke's doctrine that after once establishing their government the people have no right again to exercise that power till the government's dissolution, Elliot's *Debates*, i., 387–8, cf. v., 218. Even Jefferson had once rested in that position, in 1774: see his *Works*, i., 138.

few mountain nooks, as in Switzerland, whose inhabitants quickly drove out their foreign oppressors, and some marshes along the Baltic preserved primitive democracy. But nowhere yet had republicanism, once lost, been restored. In America it was set up almost at once upon the mere declaration of independence, without awaiting the successful outcome of the war to maintain it. At first there was not full agreement on the principles of constitution-making. Most of the original State constitutions were made by special conventions chosen for the purpose. In a few States the existing legislative converted the old charters into constitutions, in Connecticut declaring it "under the sole authority of the people." This was done in New Hampshire at first, but conventions were soon summoned, which, after many amendments had been suggested, made the constitution of 1784. In Massachusetts the people rejected a constitution drafted by the legislature in 1778, and compelled a convention to be called, whose draft of the constitution was in 1780 accepted by the towns. On this was modeled the procedure in making the Federal Constitution. The change of having the ratification performed by a majority vote of the people at large, was introduced in the new States, where local sentiment was weak; and, adopted by the old, has become the prevailing method. But even where the conventions made the constitutions without any further ratification, as those conventions were chosen for this express purpose, their acts were regarded as the people's.[1]

[1] In the Pennsylvania ratifying convention Wilson pointed out that "In our [State] governments, the supreme, absolute, and uncontrollable power *remains* in the people. As our constitutions are superior to our legislatures, so the people are superior to our constitutions," Elliot's

There had, of course, been precedents, mostly well known; for revolutionists are archæologists. Antiquity furnished many instances of constitution-making, though with considerable differences in method and result.[1] In England there had been several "con-

Debates, ii., 432; similarly 456. The people "never part with the whole [of their original power]; and they retain the right of recalling what they part with," *ib.*, 437. "The sovereignty resides," not in the State governments, but "in the people; they have not parted with it; they have only dispensed such portions of power as were conceived necessary for the public welfare," *ib.*, 443; similarly 456–8, 502. Milton had said, of the legislative assembly: "In this grand council must the sovereignty, not transferred, but delegated only, and as it were deposited, reside," *Mode of Establishing a Free Commonwealth*, § 16; but more correctly, of magistrates, that their power is "nothing else but what is only derivative, transferred, and committed to them in trust for the people to the common good of all, in whom the power yet *remains* fundamentally, and cannot be taken from them, without a violation of their natural birthright," *Tenure of Kings*, § 12. But here Milton was declaring what ought to be, in a state still ideal: Wilson was describing what was already the real condition in the American States, inscribed and prescribed in the constitutions of many of them, notably in those of his own State and of its offspring Delaware. See also the Massachusetts Proclamation of 1776 (Force's *Archives*, IV., S., iv. 834). But in May, 1776, Wilson had been in Milton's position, and called it "a maxim, that all government originates from the people" (reported by Adams, ii., 490). —This doctrine, we may note, is fuller than Mason's statement, that with the people "all power remains that has not been given up in the constitutions derived from them," Elliot's *Debates*, v., 352. *Cf.* Sydney and Somers quoted above, p. 209 n.

[1] The Greeks generally entrusted the drafting of constitutions not to many men meeting in convention, but to one man (Lycurgus, Zaleucus, Solon, etc.), and the Romans to a committee of three or of ten. Their drafts, adopted by the people, generally contained not only the frame of the government, but also ordinary laws (comparable with our bills of rights, only positive instead of negative). But all laws being enacted by the referendum, no distinction was possible between the constitutions and ordinary laws (though many expedients were resorted to for rendering the former less easily repealable than the latter). Of course only where the legislature is confined or representative, can *its* laws be distinguished from the *people's*. Hence there is partial, though not complete, truth (except as to modern times) in the statements made by

ventions," and under Cromwell an *Instrument of Government* or written constitution; but the two had never been combined: the conventions had never drawn up constitutions, and Cromwell's constitution was neither enacted by a convention nor submitted to the people.[1] The clearest precedents were supplied at home, as the colonies had been governed by legislatures with powers prescribed in charters, and the legislatures' transgressions had been denied by the courts, at all events on appeal to the Privy Council in England or to the House of Lords in its capacity as highest court.[2] These charters had been granted by the King of England, to whom alone the people owned allegiance;

Jay in 1777 (*Correspondence*, i., 161) and by D. Ramsay in 1778 (Niles's *Principles and Acts*, etc., 379 A), that the American people were the first deliberately to choose their forms of government and to agree upon constitutions; as again, in 1788, by the constitution-makers, priding themselves on the novelty of their procedure: in Elliot's *Debates*, ii., 200 (Huntingdon), 209 (R. Livingston), 422 (Wilson), iii., 616–17 (Madison), iv., 313 (J. Lincoln), 331 (C. Pinckney); *cf.* also Jefferson, *Works*, ii., 429.

[1] This *Instrument* contained a proviso that bills, to become laws, must "contain nothing in them contrary to these presents." But as it was a mere decree made by a Council of Officers, the only legislature that sat under it did not submit to its restrictions, nor was there an independent judiciary with power to disregard laws violating this proviso. So, previously, in 1369, in one of the many confirmations of the Great Charter, it was declared: "If any statute be made to the contrary, that shall be holden for none" (42 Edward III., c. 1); which also was never observed.

[2] Instances had been known of the people of a colony actually being protected from their own legislature by appeal to England, as in the case of a law against dissenters enacted in Carolina in 1704, in spite of the dissenters being in the majority; whose appeal to the House of Lords led to the quashing of the law as exceeding the charter powers of the (proprietary) government, Grahame, *History*, ii., 145–6. Already in 1768 W. S. Johnson of Connecticut, later a member of the Federal Convention, claimed that colonial laws contravening the British could be declared void only by "a court of law having jurisdiction of the matter," according to Bancroft, *History*, vi., 115.

but on declaring independence from him, the people became his inheritors, and owned allegiance only to themselves, and the people's sovereignty was substituted for the King's sovereignty.[1]   And they maintained their sovereignty in the only way they well could, by special conventions of elected delegates, later held in leash by the referendum; and they perpetuated it by the constitutions thus set up.[2]

In all these new constitutions, if not explicitly, at least implicitly, was accepted the principle that they could be amended by a process not very dissimilar from that by which they were originated.   Only in the later Constitution of the United States, produced at a moment of reaction,[3] was a clause inserted so strictly

[1] This is plainly stated in the Connecticut declaration above cited. *Cf.* Bryce: "So long as the colony remained under the British Crown, the superior authority, which could amend or remake the frame of government was the British Crown or Parliament.   When the connection with Britain was severed, that authority passed over, not to the State legislature, which remained limited, as it always had been, but to the people of the now independent commonwealth, whose will speaks through what is now the State Constitution, just as the will of the Crown or of Parliament had spoken through the charters of 1628 and 1691," *American Commonwealth*, ch. xxxii., vol. i., p. 415.   Simple as this looks, it was in the modern world a new thing.   When the Dutch renounced Philip, the sovereignty fell to the Estates-General, who gave it away. And in England, on the deposition of Charles, the sovereignty was retained by the Parliament.   Even in America at first there was some wavering toward the idea of the Congress being the king, as by S. McMasters of Delaware in 1775 (Niles's *Principles and Acts*, etc., 242 A).

[2] That the Americans gave the first example of constituent conventions, *cf.* Condorcet, *Œuvres*, xii., 175, xiii., 158.   That their example would be followed in France was expected in 1788 by Madison, *Writings*, i., 435, and the fact later stated, *ib.*, iv., 467.   *Cf.* Jefferson, *Works*, ii., 429, 435, iii., 12.

[3] As an example of the then reactionary rejection of the early Whig and present Radical principles and return to later degenerate Whig doctrine, may be cited Rush's *Address to the American People* in 1787, recommending revision of the Confederation, in which like Burke (above

regulating amendments as to render them almost impossible, a small minority of politicians or of the people being permitted to obstruct reforms desired by a considerable majority. A pretext for this, probably, was the idea of the Federal Constitution being a compact between the States, although, in all strictness, compacts need, for sanctioning any alterations, the consent of all the parties thereto.[1] But the form which the Constitution took was of a national government set up by the peoples of the States, and welding these peoples into one people for certain purposes, though leaving them distinct for others.[2] This one people, therefore, ought to have the same power of amending their constitution as have the peoples of the States in amending theirs.[3] Thus the Federal Constitution

p. 211 n.) and even before Burke, he denied that "the sovereign and all other power is seated *in* the people," though admitting that it "is derived *from* the people," and, accepting what Rousseau had denounced in the English system (above p. 206 n.), maintained that "the people possess it [all power] only on the days of their elections. After this, it is the property of their rulers; nor can they exercise it or resume it, unless it be abused" (Niles's *Principles and Acts*, etc., 234–5). All this notwithstanding that only eleven years before, in the Virginia Bill of Rights, sect. 2 (then followed by Adams, iv., 224), Mason had logically put the derivation of all power from the people as consequent upon its being vested in the people.

[1] As in the Articles of Confederation, and in the Dutch Act of Union.

[2] *Cf.* Jefferson, *Works* (i., 531, ii., 217, 249, 250), v., 570, vii., 296, and Madison, *Writings*, iv., 75, 85, 96, 293, 320.

[3] It is this single clause (art. 5) in our written Federal Constitution which has misled Bryce, in his *Studies in History and Jurisprudence*, Essay iii., to distinguish written constitutions made by a people as "rigid" and unwritten ones as "flexible," whereas it is the former that in reality are flexible, when properly made, being amendable by the people at large, and the latter, which grew up from the days when the ecclesiastical and warrior classes and the chief of all, the king, were independent self-sufficient powers in the state, cannot now be changed by the whole people except with the consent of such classes and of the king. The German and Japanese written constitutions are very similar

alone failed to put into practice the revolution-breaking revolutionary doctrine which Jefferson inserted in the *Declaration of Independence*, that "whenever any form of government becomes destructive" of the ends for which governments were "instituted among men," "it is the right of the people," yea, "it is their duty," "to alter or to abolish it, and to institute new govern-

to the English unwritten constitution as it existed in the seventeenth century (which is called "flexible," p. 190), and very different from the United States written constitution and the English unwritten constitution of to-day. The English constitution of to-day could easily be written out, only that many of its clauses would be vague and unprecise; but the amendment clause would run thus: "This constitution can be amended by Parliament in the same manner as any law is enacted." As Parliament consists of Commons, Lords, and King, the latter may be counted upon to resist amendments that adversely affect them. Facts, too, show that since 1789 the English constitution has been altered perhaps as frequently in appearance as our Federal Constitution, but by no means so frequently as many of our State constitutions (and if these have been mostly patched in minor matters, they allow themselves to be altered with equal ease in fundamentals). Yet in reality our Federal Constitution does not suffer in the comparison. The greatest alteration in the English constitution was the redistribution of seats and extension of the suffrage made by the Reform Act of 1832, supplemented by two or three later acts; but our Federal Constitution contains a clause which automatically redistributes seats every ten years, and apart from the great change in citizenship made in 1868, the suffrage for the representatives has been altered every time a State has changed its suffrage, which has been done not infrequently. All Bryce's argument for the superiority of flexible over rigid constitutions, is an argument for making the method of amending written constitutions easy. The lax construction-treatment of our Federal Constitution is a direct result of its rigid amendment clause, one fault producing another. Here, as Bryce says, "flexibility" is "supplied from the minds of the Judges" (p. 197); which is a great abuse. It is a pity our constitution-makers did not invent the system later adopted in Switzerland and copied in the Australian Commonwealth, which requires constitutional amendments, after being sanctioned by the federal legislature, to be presented first to the state legislatures and then to the people, only a simple majority being necessary in each case. This favors both the small and the large states, as a majority of the former with a minority

ment, laying its foundation on such principles and organizing its powers in such forms, as to them shall seem most likely to effect their safety and happiness," in confidence, based on "all experience," that "prudence will dictate that governments long-established should not be changed for light and transient causes," yet affording opportunity for changing them for serious and permanent reasons.[1]

Among the reactionaries of this brief period unfortunately John Adams was one of the leaders, as he had in the early period been among the leaders of the democratic tendency. In that earlier period he had stood shoulder to shoulder with his kinsman Samuel Adams, and with Jefferson and the others. Now he abandoned them. After his stay in Europe he came back from his embassy to England antagonistic to the Radicals there, and infected with Whiggism—another instance of the melancholy spectacle, not uncommon, of a Sydney before turning into a Locke after success. And like

of population, or a majority of the latter with a minority of states may stop proposals injurious to their respective interests, while other proposals that really are improvements have a fair chance of getting through. It would have been eminently in the spirit of compromise which reigned in the Convention, and would probably have been adopted if it had been thought of (though Madison came near to it, Elliot's *Debates*, v., 499, supported by Wilson, 500; cf. *The Federalist*, No. 62, sect. 3; and long before, in another connection, Sherman, reported by Adams, ii., 499). Is it too late? Almost any improvement in our Constitution (except by the dangerous method of construction, almost wholly and solely aristocratic, or in our case plutocratic) is impossible, except after long delay, until this amendment clause itself is amended.

[1] But for this mistake in our Federal Constitution, it is possible the Civil War might have been averted, since an amendment regulating and gradually suppressing slavery might then have had a chance of passing: cf. Bryce, *op. cit.*, p. 190. Possibly also the mistake of permitting the protection of special privileges in high tariffs might have been rectified, which would have smoothed the way to allay the irritation between the two sections.

the Whigs he tried, having used the people, to shove them into the background—as yet not quite so far, perhaps, as the Whigs, since he still had use for them. He still allows that the *right* to the sovereignty resides inalienably in the people[1]; but the sovereignty itself may be divided, and when the people have once used their right to share it with the aristocracy and with a line of kings, they will give up the right to resume it except by revolution. Hence he had little further use for the people's law, the constitution, embracing as it does the people's inherent power of revising and altering it to all perpetuity[2]: that also, after its general outlines as plotted in his theory had once been established, had to be ignored as much as possible, and the government alone had to run of its own force, its equilibrating system being relied on to prevent any upsetting. But the government, he held with the English lawyers, is the legislative (composed of king or governor and two chambers); and the balances had to be poised between these—that is, within the legislative.[3] The

[1] See above, p. 131.

[2] As inserted by himself, in his first period, in the Massachusetts constitution of 1780, iv., 225, following that of Virginia, which latter, sect. 3, placed it inalienably in "a majority of the community."

[3] Obviously Adams desired the negative in each of the three branches of the legislative for exercise not only against ordinary legislation, but against constitutional alteration. For an Anglicanized constitution of this sort, it is evident, as is quoted from him in the first note in this chapter, that a veto in each branch is necessary for its preservation; since a people, possessed of the distinction between primary constitutional law and representative legislation, would not permit the continuance of such a constitution. This should be remembered by those who honestly advocate the negative in each of the branches of the legislative merely for ordinary legislation. Its usefulness in this field Adams did not think much of (at least in the case of the executive negative); nor need we.

judiciary stood apart, and was of little importance in the affair.

Still, the Constitution—the fundamental law, possible only because our ancestors did not have separate orders, and written because it was new and all new laws are now written in civilized states—exists. It is the instrument attesting the people's act. It frees them from the need of continual surveillance, which, in fact, is left to the judiciary as the custodian of the people's reserved rights. That the Americans, in setting up their governments under government-binding laws of their own, and retaining the amendment of these in their own hands, were perfecting the science of government left imperfect by the English, Adams refused to see; nor could he foresee that in so doing they were setting an example to be, after many failures, more or less perfectly followed by the rest of Europe.[1]

[1] Perfectly, of course, only where the constitutions have been set up by the peoples themselves. Elsewhere the constitutions are nothing but charters, like our colonial charters, granted to the people by the kings. But even so they are, in some countries, regarded as irrevocable without the concurrence of both parties, and consequently without the consent of the people. This, we may notice, is the utmost concession from the Tory position, and approaches, from the opposite side, the Whig position: the Tories conceding that the king cannot alter the constitutions without the people's consent, and the Whigs maintaining that the people cannot alter the constitutions without the king's (or the lords') consent. If the Whigs have sometimes allowed the people alone (especially the lords) to do so on occasions of royal misbehavior justifying revolution, the Tories have not hesitated, even more frequently, to urge the king alone to do so on occasions of popular misbehavior which, they thought, disengaged the king. The last occurrence of the latter sort took place in Portugal a few years ago; and it cost the King his life.

III. SOURCES AND ORIGINALITY OF ADAMS'S DOCTRINES

CHAPTER XV

CONTEMPORARY EXPOSITORS OF THE ENGLISH CONSTITUTION, AND UNNOTICED CHANGES

ADAMS laid no claim to originality. He expressly (though, as just shown, wrongly) asserted that "America has made no discoveries of principles that have not been long known,"[1]— that, in fact, no "general principles" remain to be discovered.[2] In his opinion, all the true principles had already been reduced to practice in England. The English Constitution, therefore, he especially admired, along with its "miniature" copies in the American colonies, which, with their governors and councils or upper chambers independent of the people, were closer copies than the subsequent more popular governments of the States. Still, the dissimilarity of the social conditions, especially at the North, had prevented even the colonial governments from becoming perfect imitations. In his early studies Adams no doubt had heard of, and perhaps now grieved over, the little incident near the beginning of Massachusetts history, in 1634–6, when an unsuccessful

[1] VI., 477, in 1814.   [2] IX., 188, in 1798, and x., 45–6, in 1813.

attempt was made to introduce bodily a missing branch of the English social and political system. Then certain "persons of quality," dissatisfied at home, offered to come out to the infant colony and take up large estates of land, provided they and their descendants were permitted, as "hereditary gentlemen," to sit in their own right as an upper house of legislation, while all "freeholders" were represented by deputies in a lower; which proposal was rejected, not from any opposition to aristocracy itself, but because the then ruling theocrats wished to confine the government to church members and dignitaries, objecting alike to the hereditary feature in the aristocratic plan and to the universality in its democratic part.[1]

Yet even in Massachusetts, as in the other colonies, with the lapse of time had sprung up a more or less cohering class of influential men—clergy, lawyers, officeholders, landowners, merchants,—who sought for special recognition in the management of affairs, and by getting on the governors' councils had succeeded in bringing into existence distant imitations of the English type of society and government, and naturally desired their own department to be continued. Adams, who aspired to be and became one of them, in his first period hoped our people would be wise enough, in setting up State governments, to "preserve the English Constitution in its spirit and substance, as far as the circumstances of this country required and would admit," omitting only the hereditary features (iii. 17–18), which had never existed here and which this country would not tolerate.[2] These departures from

---

[1] Hildreth, *History of the United States*, i., 217, 234.
[2] III., 20. In his last period he said that the non-hereditary features of our government were borrowed "from our colonial constitutions,"

the model he in that period approved; in the present period, although still recognizing the necessity of the departure, he rather regrets this necessity, and looks forward to a time when the model may be more fully copied. Meanwhile he applauds the Americans for "imitating it as far as they have" (iv. 358), and exults at the thought that our constitutions may bear comparison with the English (382); which he sometimes ventures to assert (380), and even to hope that several of them "will prove themselves improvements" (440). The praises of the English Constitution he constantly sings. It is "the only scientific government" (vi. 118, *cf.* 44), "the most stupendous fabric of human invention" (iv. 358), "the most perfect model that has yet been discovered or invented by human genius and experience,"—in one word, "a masterpiece."[1]

But it was not the English government as actually existing he thus praised. It was the theory of the English Constitution[2]—and the theory of it as then understood.[3] The English government was in a stage of

vi., 528; that even the independent executive, senatorial, and representative system was adopted in the States of Massachusetts, New York, and Maryland, not from "an affected imitation of the English government, so much as an attachment to their old colonial forms," 487. He had said the same, to be sure, in this second period, iv., 300; but he then also spoke of the Americans having taken the English Constitution "for their model," 556.   [1] IX., 622, in 1809.

[2] IV., 358, 440, 556. The only falling short in the practice that he condemned was in the House of Commons, iv., 468, *cf.* 358, vi., 119,— *i. e.* the inequality and other defects in the representation, his correction of which has been noticed (above pp. 144-6). The corruption at the elections was an evil which it was one of the merits of the English system to render innocuous. The corrupting influence of patronage was part of the system itself, to counterpoise the otherwise excessive power of the Commons.

[3] A good outline account of that theory was given by Walpole in 1734 thus: "Ours is a mixt government, and the perfection of our constitu-

transition. What it has since become, was already foreshadowed, but not yet recognized by the theoretical expounders. These gave rather the theory of the English government as it had been, by no means what it was becoming, and not even what it had already become.[1]

The first great expounder for Adams had been Bolingbroke.[2] From him probably Adams early got the idea of "the balance" of the three "parts" of government, and their "independency on one another"[3]; and learnt the scheme of any two of them "uniting their strength" to keep the third from abusing its

tion consists in this, that the monarchical, aristocratical, and democratical forms of government are mixt and interwoven in ours, so as to give all the advantages of each, without subjecting us to the dangers and inconveniencies of either," Cobbett's *Parliamentary History*, vol. ix., col. 473. And similarly Jenkinson (Lord Liverpool) in 1793 spoke of the blessings of the mixed form of government, "where the faults of each [of the simple forms] might correct the faults of the others," Hansard's *Parliamentary History*, vol. xxx., col. 820. But all the while the democratic part, in the House of Commons, was very ill represented. Still Walpole was so pleased with the balance, that the reduction of the terms from seven to three years, making the members more dependent on their constituents, he believed would throw so much power into the hands of the people "as would destroy that equal mixture, which is the beauty of our constitution," Cobbett's *History* as before, cols. 474–5.

[1] The prerogatives of the Crown had fallen into abeyance under the first two Georges. George III. restored them, and at the same time lent greater authority to Parliament, which he dominated. They were lost again during the imbecility of his old age, passing to his Ministers, and through them to the House of Commons. The Lords were willing to have power center there because of their own influence there. Later, when reform measures put an end to corruption and broadened and equalized the franchise, both the monarchical and the aristocratical departments found themselves stranded.

[2] In 1813 Adams wrote that he had read Bolingbroke more than five times, beginning more than fifty years before, x., 82, *cf.* i., 43–4.

[3] *Remarks on the History of England, Works*, i., 306–7, 331, 333, *Dissertation upon Parties, ib.*, ii., 114.

power or usurping more,[1] even of any one having
weight to retard the mischief of the two others combining in usurpation or abuse[2]; and consequently
imbibed the belief in the superiority and greater permanency of the mixed form of government, and the
absurdity of the simple forms, which establish the very
arbitrariness which men in submitting to any government seek to avoid, absolute monarchy being tyranny,
absolute democracy tyranny and anarchy both, while
aristocracy, though a mean, is on a ridge and must
slide down, into tyranny if the few are united, and if
disunited, into turbulency as great as in the most tumultuous democracy.[3] From him, in particular, may
have been acquired the fear and admiration of the
few great men, who may be devastating instruments
of divine vengeance or guardian angels of the good of
mankind,[4] and the delight in them, in a limited monarchy, as having interest for their own salvation to
defend the people against the king, and as forming a
"middle order" of "mediators between the other two."[5]
Bolingbroke's idea of the "patriot" and non-partisan
king[6] likewise seems to have had influence; from which
Adams ought to have been saved by the fact that the
son of Bolingbroke's disciple, the very King against
whom he fought, was a Tory of the deepest partisan
dye.

---

[1] *Ib.*, i., 332; this is called their "constitutional dependency," 333,
ii., 114.   [2] *Ib.*, i., 332, *cf.* ii., 148.

[3] *Ib.*, ii., 119–20. The English Constitution the most durable, 115;
those of Rome and France defective in having only two of the three
forms, Rome wanting the monarchical, and France the democratical,
132.

[4] *Letter on the Spirit of Patriotism, ib.*, ii., 352, 354, (quoted by Adams,
iv., 413–14).   [5] *Ib.*, ii., 130–2; 118–19, 130.

[6] *The Idea of a Patriot King*, ib., ii., 401 ff.

Then came Blackstone and De Lolme. Blackstone
spoke also of the legislature being "intrusted to three
distinct powers, entirely independent of each other,"
either of which if attempting any inconvenience, "will
be withstood by one of the other two," since each
is "armed with a negative power sufficient to repel any
innovation which it shall think inexpedient or dangerous"[1]; and of "the true excellence of the English
government" consisting herein, "that all the parts of
it form a mutual check upon each other," the people
upon the nobility, the nobility upon the people, the
king upon both, and both upon the king, every branch
supporting and being supported, regulating and being
regulated, and "mutually" keeping "each other from
exceeding their proper limits";—"like three distinct
powers in mechanics," he added, "jointly" impelling
"the machine of government in a direction different
from what either, acting by itself, would have done;
but at the same time in a direction partaking of each,
and formed out of all"[2];—in which comparison he employed the mechanical principle of the parallelogram of
forces,[3] instead of that of stable equilibrium.

But especially De Lolme was it whom Adams in this
period relied upon,—De Lolme, whom he ranked with
Montesquieu,[4] the Genevan whose book he pronounced

[1] *Commentaries*, i., 50–1.

[2] *Ib.*, i., 154–5. *Cf.* also 240, where he says the prerogative of the
Crown, when properly counterpoised, "invigorates the whole machine."

[3] This has since been used by Brougham, *Political Philosophy*, ii., 12,
cf. 44. *Cf.* Russell, *English Government and Constitution*, p. 89.

[4] VI., 119.—Montesquieu himself need not be reviewed in this connection, as he merely gave an epitome of what he found in earlier English writers, chiefly Locke. It may only be mentioned that he was the
recognized authority for the *separation* of the departments: see *The
Federalist*, No. 47. Of course the *division* of these departments dates
back to Aristotle, *Polit.*, IV., xi. (xiv.), 1.

"a more intelligible explanation" of the English Constitution than any composed by an Englishman,[1] and "the
best defense of the political balance of the three powers
that ever was written."[2]   In his work Adams found
emphasis laid upon the need, on the one hand, of a
single chief magistrate, clothed with the full executive
authority, one of whose services to the state is rendered
by his preëmpting the first place and so keeping others
from aspiring to it and contending with one another
for it[3]; and on the other, upon the need of the people
retaining in the hands of their representatives the right
of granting or withholding supplies[4]; and in between
them, upon the need of a settled place for the privileged
classes of the lords, "a kind of ostracism,"[5] where they
shall possess clearly ascertained distinctions and preclude others from hopes of usurping them,[6] and where
a great popular leader arriving loses his influence,
coming among his equals in dignity, erewhile his superiors, "who are firmly resolved that after having been
the leading man in the House of Commons, he shall not
be the first in theirs."[7]   Here, too, Adams may have
come across the precept, Unite the executive power,
and divide the legislative,[8] which he himself likewise
recommends (v. 316, *cf.* 221).

Now, De Lolme had given a masterly idealization of
the English system as it had been. He expounded it as
though the King were still the sole executive chief,
invested with the absolute veto, and as though the
Lords still actively possessed such a negative.   The

[1] VI., 396. Similar praise had been expressed by Bentham, *Fragment on Government*, iii., § 21 (*Works*, i., 282).

[2] IV., 358. De Lolme is quoted, 409, referred to, 443.

[3] *The Constitution of England*, 3d ed., 1781, pp. 387, 428; 196, 204,
206-7.   [4] *Ib.*, 420, 451-2.   [5] *Ib.*, 210.

[6] *Ib.*, 429-30.   [7] *Ib.*, 210; 207-12.   [8] *Ib.*, 222, *cf.* 392.

Ministry he hardly noticed. That these had become a part of the executive department responsible and accounting to the Commons, that the executive power, instead of being united in a single person, was divided between the King and a committee of the House,—all this De Lolme did not perceive; nor did Adams either. Adams had no inkling of the invading supremacy of the single House of Commons, and of the almost complete dependence on it of the executive, and of the subordinate position taken by the House of Lords, the King entirely renouncing his veto, at least in ordinary legislation, and being well on the road of reduction to a "Doge of Venice" and a wooden figurehead, and the veto of the Lords becoming nothing more than timidly suspensive, except on matters of vital importance to themselves.

Similar ignorance was shared by most of the other constitution-making Americans; for De Lolme and Blackstone were authorities also to them.[1] Nothing shows better the influence of one little bubble upon the course of events. Blackstone was a Tory, and did not care to discover and disclose the incoming changes; and, too, he was more concerned with the laws than with the Constitution. But De Lolme, as a professed republican, might have been expected to trace out the republicanization of the Constitution he was analyzing. Had he done so—had he been clever enough to unravel the true theory of the English Constitution as it was then developing—had he anticipated Bagehot by beginning his treatise with an account of the Cabinet;

---

[1] In the debate in Congress over Jay's Treaty, in 1796, J. Holland pointed out that we were imitating the English theory, and not the English practice, Benton's *Abridgment*, i., 661 B. This seems to be one of the first belated intimations of that fact.

Adams and other Americans would have had their eyes opened to a different system, would probably have advocated adoption of some of the new evolvements, and would possibly have produced some variations in our State constitutions and in our Federal Constitution, in a direction less inclined toward monarchy and aristocracy (or rather plutocracy).[1]

Adams, it may be further noted, seems never to have recognized the development of the English Constitution even as it came to be more widely proclaimed in England during the thirty-five years he survived after writing his works on government.[2] Shortly after Adams's presidency, Dugald Stewart delivered a course of lectures in which, while praising the mixed form of government for its balance, in a manner very similar to Adams's, and the English Constitution for

---

[1] For instance, they must have given less power to the Senate, the power of which, as it exists, is the insuperable barrier to the introduction of the cabinet system, and renders out of place the fitful demands that our Heads of Departments should have seats in Congress. The cabinet system was evolved in England *pari passu* with the effacement of the House of Lords. In some European countries, notably in France subsequently to 1870, the pretensions of the Senate to share in the control of the Ministers have caused much confusion. In Germany, on the contrary, a strong Bundesrath has quenched the aspirations of the Reichstag; while in Austria the authority of the Emperor steers the Ministry between the almost equally powerful chambers. The fact is, the Cabinet really is the upper chamber, and where it is powerful, it cramps the room for any other. The Australians seem not to have perceived this, and are experimenting with a responsible cabinet and two equal houses. The Canadians were wiser, and weakened their Senate, as have done also the framers of the constitution for the South African Union.

[2] Even before, Junius had complained both of the House of Commons and of the House of Lords for not "preserving the due balance of the constitution," and regretted that "King, Lords, and Commons, which should for ever stand clear of each other, were . . . melted down into one common mass of power," Bohn's ed., vol. ii., pp. 362-3.

affording "the first instance in the history of mankind in which the theory delineated by the ancient philosophers has been realized with success,"[1] pointed out that the actual Constitution of England differed from the theory in that now "the whole practical efficiency" of the government "is either centered" in "or operates by the intermediation" of the House of Commons; but that still the theory was respected in that "the three powers" are "blended together in the composition" of that House, "an assembly which is no longer [sic] composed of men whose habits and connections can be supposed to attach them exclusively to the people, but of men, some of whom, from their situation, may be presumed to lean to the regal part of a government, others to the aristocratical; while, on important questions, the majority may be expected to maintain the interests of the community at large"[2]; so that there,

[1] *Lectures on Political Economy*, ii., 417. Here and 418–19 Stewart approves that "a senate possessing no share of the executive power" should be checked, "on the one hand," by "a single magistrate possessing the sole executive power, to prevent the competitions and rivalships among the order of nobility," and, "on the other," by "a popular assembly, to secure the enactment of equal laws." On the threefold working of the balance, any two preventing the third from encroaching, *ib.*, 430–1. His resemblances to Adams probably came from drinking at the same source, especially De Lolme. Other instances showing this, *e. g. ib.* 425, 427.

[2] This is putting it mildly. We have seen Bentham's statement of the case. Ricardo, remarking that the House of Lords seldom opposed the House of Commons, said this was unnecessary, "for the House of Commons is not appointed by the people, but by the Peers and the wealthy aristocracy of the country"; and the only check he found was in "the good sense and information of the people themselves, operating through the means of a free press," *Works*, McCulloch's ed., 551, 552. (The last check also noticed by Mackintosh, *Works*, Cabinet ed., iii., 155, and by Canning, who seems to have been satisfied with it as sufficient, Speech, August 30, 1822, in *Select Speeches*, Philadelphia, 1835, p. 523.) So late as 1867 A. Todd in his work *On Parliamentary Govern-*

the king and the aristocracy having "parliamentary
weight" as well as the people, "the three powers may
balance each other, and may produce the happy result
aimed at in the theory of our constitution, in a way"—
observe this addition—"still more advantageous than
if it were exactly realized, by saving the machine of
government from those violent shocks it must occasionally suffer if king, lords, and commons were openly and
avowedly to draw, in any instance, in different directions."[1]   In other words, all the benefits attributed to
mixed government might be, and were supposed in
England actually to be, obtained by a government with
all power concentrated in a single assembly, provided
that a new balance, replacing or buttressing the old,
were there established between the three powers by
taking care to have them all represented.

A few years later, and not long before Adams's
death, the newly named party of Radicals began to
make an impression on British politics. This, under the
leadership of Bentham, was composed of agitators and
theorists, who sympathized with the people. They
little appreciated the beauties of their "matchless
constitution," as the poet Thomson had called it[2]—
a phrase Bentham never wearied of ridiculing;—and

ment in England wrote of "the growth of a system by which each of the
three co-equal elements of the Crown, the aristocracy, and the commonalty, . . . has been effectually, if not formally, incorporated into
the Commons' House of Parliament,"— the first by the Ministry's
control of Treasury seats, the second by those of the peers who controlled
"in their own behalf" many small boroughs and by all who could exercise influence over their tenants at elections, 2d ed., 1887, i., 9–10, *cf.* 12;
and he quoted a computation "that in 1865 the thirty-one great governing families of England supplied 'one clear fourth of the English House
of Commons,'" *ib.*, 13 .

[1] Stewart's *Political Economy*, ii., 443–50.

[2] *Liberty*, IV., 815, *cf.* 689, and *Castle of Indolence*, II., xxiv.

cared not at all for mixed government, the system of
balances, and the house of peers.[1] The house of rep-

[1] Bentham had begun to find fault with the mixture in 1776 in his
Fragment on Government, ch. iii., and carried on the criticism of it and
the "balance of power" (against this urging that a machine, when the
forces in it balance, is at rest; an objection which Montesquieu had
answered in advance, *Esprit des Lois*, xi., 6) in his *Plan of Parliamentary
Reform*, Introduction, iv. (1817), and his *Constitutional Code*, I., ix.
(1827). (*Cf.* Lowndes: "Too many checks in a political machine must
produce the same mischief as in a mechanical one—that of throwing all
into confusion," Elliot's *Debates*, iv., 309.) Likewise opposed to two
chambers were Godwin, *Political Justice*, V., xxi., *cf.* VI., vii.; and
Bentham's disciple and coadjutor, James Mill, in the article on *Government*, § 5 (*cf.* above, note on p. 77). In the *Constitutional Code*,
I., xvi., § 1, Bentham condemned the "two-house system" (and here,
§ 6, wished the single legislative body to be "omnicompetent"), as also
in his *Essay on Political Tactics*, i., § 5; and advised the Spaniards and
the French not to reinstitute the house of peers, in the first of *Three
Tracts on Spanish and Portuguese Affairs* (1820, here comparing that
house to the Trojan horse), and in his address *To his Fellow-citizens of
France* (1830, this in reply to a question put to him by Lafayette).— To
Bentham has been ascribed the term "bicameral," as by Lieber, *On
Civil Liberty*, 1853, p. 157 (3d ed., p. 193); followed by Creasy, *Rise and
Progress of the English Constitution*, 3d ed., 1856, New York ed., p. 178,
and in the 1865 ed. of *Webster's Dictionary* (whence copied in Murray's
New Dictionary). But this does not seem to be so correct as Woolsey's
assignment of it to Lieber himself, *Political Science and the State*, ii., 302.
Along with "unicameral," which he used in the same work on the next
page, Lieber probably imported it from Europe. The English did not
use the term "chamber," but "house" (see Bentham, *Works*, iv., 438 B).
Bentham employed that term in his address to the French, and there also
adopted "second chamber" for the upper house, "because such appears
to me to be the practice"—apparently in France (*ib.*, 421 note). Yet in
France "second chamber" is also used of the house of representatives
and "first chamber" of the house of peers or senate, as by Demombynes,
Les Constitutions européennes, passim. The senate is officially called
"the first branch of the legislature" in the Massachusetts constitution
of 1780 (Adams's *Works*, iv., 235) and the New Hampshire constitutions
of 1784 and 1792 (sec. 28), and "the first chamber" (and the other
"the second") in the constitution of the Netherlands, 1815, arts. 80,
81, etc. There is, of course, nothing to determine which is first or second.
Parsons in *The Essex Result* treated the representatives as the first body
and the senate as the second, Parsons's *Parsons*, pp. 390, 391. In the

resentatives they wished to be really representative, and therefore to be open to the votes of even the lower classes, who at that time were excluded from the polls except in a half-dozen constituencies. Their demand for universal suffrage was scouted by the Tories, and refused by the Whigs. Then one of the favorite arguments urged, not only by the Tories, but by the Whigs, for instance by Mackintosh, whose political philosophy, very much after the manner of Adams's, had moved up from a first to a second phase,[1] was that as the

Federal Convention the House of Representatives was spoken of as "the first branch" apparently for no better reason than that it happened to be placed first in the draft (Elliot's *Debates*, v., 129, 135, etc.). Similarly in Cromwell's last Parliament, 1657, the new upper chamber was referred to as "the other house," the House of Lords having been abolished for several years, and this being now introduced as "another house . . . in imitation of the House of Lords," Cobbett's *Parliamentary History*, vol. iii., cols. 1506, 1518. Perhaps it is more democratic to deal with the representatives of the people first, and more aristocratic to begin with the lords or senators. At any rate, to the terms "upper" and "lower" applied to the houses, Franklin objected as a sign of a disposition "to commence an aristocracy," *Works*, v., 169, *cf.* i., 409. Yet Mason would have employed them in the Virginia constitution (see his draft in Rives's *Madison*, ii., Appendix C); and Jefferson did not hesitate to speak of the Representatives as "the lower House," *e. g. Works*, iv., 241, 244. These terms are appropriate enough wherever it is generally considered a promotion to pass from the one to the other; and there has never been any confusion in the use of them.

[1] Mackintosh also had begun as a democrat, and in his *Vindiciæ Galliæ*, 1791, had argued for "radical reform" in general, *Works*, iii., 53, and in particular for universal and equal representation, 106–8, 153, and for a single legislative assembly, 121–3. He then wrote: "It is perhaps susceptible of proof, that these governments of balance and control never existed but in the vision of theorists," 122, and similarly 155. Later, he maintained exactly the opposite opinion, and after praising "the distribution of political authority" among different bodies corresponding to the classes of society, "each interested to guard their own order from oppression by the rest, each also interested to prevent any of the others from seizing on exclusive, and therefore despotic power," asserted that "the simple governments are mere creatures of imagination of theorists,"

lowest classes are the most numerous, "the whole political power of the state would be thrown into" their
hands,[1] and the government become a "pure democracy."[2] The existence of the King and Lords as checks,
outside the House of Commons, was passed over; the
whole power of the state was viewed as collected into
that one chamber.

Thus the English Constitution—Adams's model for
all the world, the only one ever existing in Europe that
he considered an "equal mixture" (iv. 447), nicely
poised between the three branches each with its negative—was expounded after all, even in his lifetime, by its
own statesmen, as a government predominantly in one
assembly, and only saved from being what he called a
"simple democracy" by having restricted and irregular
suffrage (the sole feature in it that he condemned),
haphazardly upgrown, which, in "rotten boroughs,"
preserved and reserved some seats for the upper classes,

that no such "detestable" absolutely unbalanced governments ever
existed, but that as governments "approach more nearly to that unmixed and uncontrolled simplicity they become despotic, and as they
recede farther from" it "they become free," *On the Study of the Law of
Nature and Nations*, 1799, *ib.*, i., 378, 379. Therefore he now repudiated
uniform representation, *On the Right of Parliamentary Representation*,
1818, *ib.*, iii., 212, and called universal suffrage "more mischievous than
any other uniform right," *ib.*, 214–15.

[1] Mackintosh, *ib.*, iii., 218–19. He now agreed with Adams, saying,
"Wherever property is not allowed great weight in a free state, it will
destroy property," 223; but differed in that he placed reliance upon its
being represented in the same chamber with the people.

[2] Canning, Speech, March 18, 1820, *Select Speeches*, p. 509. Canning
also said: "I cannot conceive a Constitution of which one-third part
shall be an assembly delegated by the people, . . . which must not in
a few days' sitting sweep away every other branch of the Constitution
that might attempt to oppose or control it," 510, and set up "a republic," 524, *cf.* 343-4. The new balance within the one branch of the
legislative is thus regarded as essential. The influence of the French
Revolution, leading to hasty induction, is perceptible.

and mixed the aristocrats with the popular representatives (the great object of his aversion), and was con-
veniently supposed to do so equally.[1] Even that
barrier has since been broken down and the popular
flood let in, and now, after this "political revolution,"[2]
Britain is, according to those theorists, a "simple
democracy," saved only by some retarding but not
checking drags in its upper parts[3]; and this unbalanced

[1] Canning: "The balance is now, perhaps, as nearly poised as human
wisdom can adjust it. I fear to touch that balance, the disturbance of
which must bring confusion on the nation," *Select Speeches*, 514. T. E.
Kebbel: "It was only by means of the nomination system that the aristocratic, plutocratic, and democratic elements, which were intended to
be mingled in equal degrees in it, could be made to work harmoniously
together," *History of Toryism*, London, 1886, pp. 204–5.

[2] It is so-called, for instance, by Kebbel, who says of the Reform Act
(what is applicable only to it along with the subsequent Acts extending
the franchise): "The Act of 1832 was not a reform of the old Constitution, but the creation of a new one," *op. cit.*, 206, 224. This Tory writer
also maintains that between 1688 and 1832 no one element—either
Crown, aristocracy, or people—could be predicted to come off successfully in any contest [although the aristocracy always did], but before
1688 the Crown would have won [although it did not], and after 1832
the people; wherefore in that intervening period existed "a really mixed
government," 224—mixed in the House of Commons, remember.

[3] Even after the first opening of the flood-gates in 1832, but before the
complete extension of the suffrage Earl Grey wrote: "For this great
happiness [of public liberty], I believe that we are indebted to the peculiar character of our system of representation, which has admitted the
democratic element into the House of Commons without allowing it to
become predominant. . . . [That this House has not become tyrannical
is] to be accounted for only by the circumstance that our system of
representation has always given an ascendancy in the House of Commons
to the upper classes of society, who have felt that they could not hope
to retain the great power there placed in their hands, unless they exercised it in a spirit of moderation and of respect for the rights of others.
If the House of Commons had been so constituted as to render it the
mere organ of the popular will, this motive to moderation in the exercise of its powers would have been wanting," *Parliamentary Government
considered with reference to a Reform of Parliament*, London, 1858, pp.
67–8.

system, in spite of its imperfection, still endures.[1] Adams's theory, the older one, and the newer one of Dugald Stewart and others, were serviceable as alternatives: *either* the balance between the branches, *or* the balance within the single all-sustaining trunk.[2] The older balance had departed in Adams's day, and the newer one had alone been relied on. This, too, has gone, and the older one has only of late been partially restored.[3]

[1] Blackstone prophesied that "if ever it should happen that the independence of any of the three [branches] should be lost, or that it should become subservient to the views of either of the other two, there would soon be an end of the constitution," *Commentaries*, i., 51; and De Lolme, that "the English government will be no more, either when the Crown shall have become independent of the nation for its supplies, or when representatives of the people shall begin to share in the executive authority," *Constitution of England*, II., xviii., end. *Cf.* also Lord Cavendish, in *Annual Register*, xx., 43 B. It may be reasonably supposed that Adams shared these views. And they were true: *that* constitution did come to an end; but its place was taken by a better one.

[2] This alternative was erected into a principle by the German publicist Rohmer, expressing it thus: *either* an upper chamber (confined to the aristocracy of birth and by service, with full negative), and then the broadest franchise for the popular chamber; *or* no upper chamber (or an imbecile one), and then close restriction of the people's representation, *Der vierte Stand und die Monarchie*, 1848, in *Fr. Rohmer's Wissenschaft und Leben*, iv., 522. Rohmer preferred the former, Adams considered it essential. It is instructive to compare their reasons, which are exactly opposite. As a conservative, Rohmer wished the aristocracy to be carefully guarded and hedged in by constitutional provisions against the invading power of the people. Having been a democrat, Adams wished the people to have a means of preserving themselves from the encroachments of the aristocracy. Rohmer feared the people; Adams, the aristocracy. Rohmer wished the power of the people to be recognized, but to be limited; Adams wished the same of the power of the aristocracy.—It may be added that an alternative similar to Rohmer's was entertained by Calhoun, *Disquisition on Government*, Columbia, 1851 (also as vol. i. of *Works*), pp. 45-6.

[3] According to Gladstone, at the time of the Reform Act it was expected the House of Lords would have to resume its function of passing adverse judgments, *Gleanings*, i., 77. As a matter of fact, in the lower

Meanwhile the new condition was welcomed even by admirers of balanced government, on the ground, as explained by Mill, that there are certain contrivances for "the distribution of strength in the most popular branch of the governing body" by which "a balance of forces might most advantageously be established there."[1]   How Adams would have stood aghast, had he lived long enough to read Bagehot's declarations that "the efficient secret of the English Constitution may be described as the close union, the nearly complete fusion, of the executive and legislative powers"; that "it is a remarkable peculiarity, a capital excellence of the British Constitution, that it contains a sort of upper House which is not of equal authority to the lower House, yet still has some authority"; and that "the English is the type of *simple* constitutions, in which the ultimate power upon all questions is in the hands of the same persons"![2]   The irony of correction could not further go.

House the two parties are still pretty evenly matched, frequently alternating, and as the Lords are always overwhelmingly Conservative, if they had so much as a suspensive veto (forcing a dissolution and an appeal to the constituents), the balance would be uneven; which is what the Liberals recently objected to, when the prophecy referred to by Gladstone was fulfilled.   Adams's system would be fair (*i. e.* an "equal mixture") only if the Commons were guaranteed to be always Liberal (*e. g.* by disfranchising the upper classes); although there would be considerable alleviation if the Lords' veto merely compelled a *referendum* to the people (including the upper classes) of the single question at issue.

[1] J. S. Mill, *Considerations on Representative Government*, 1861, p. 235, *cf.* 129, 133 ff. (the allusion is especially to various schemes for the representation of minorities).   "I set little value," Mill says, "on any check which a Second Chamber can apply to a democracy otherwise unchecked; and I am inclined to think that if all other constitutional questions are rightly decided, it is of comparatively little importance whether the Parliament consists of two chambers, or only of one," 231.

[2] *The English Constitution*, 1866, in *Works*, Hartford ed., iv., 59 (*cf.* 77); 129-30; 235 (similarly 230).   Comparing it with the American

Yet, although the drift of the British Constitution be-
lied his theory, and he prudently shut his eyes to it,
the course of events in France confirmed his faith by
carrying out the predictions he made in accordance with
his principles.   The anarchy of the simple democracy
with all power in a single assembly (the Convention)—
the dissensions and evanescence of a government with
a plural executive (the Directory)—and the sinking of
such defective systems in a despotism (the Empire):—
these he later noticed, and found consolation in taking
them for proofs of his doctrines.[1]

CHAPTER XVI

EARLIER SPECULATIVE AUTHORITIES, AND ADAMS'S DEVELOPMENT

NOT only the expounders of the English Constitution did Adams follow.   He had studied the
republican theorizers of the seventeenth century, and
they had made a great impression upon him in his first
and revolutionary period.   In the present period he retained much respect for only one of them.

By Harrington, himself considerable of an aristocrat,

(modeled upon it! *cf. ib.*, 97–8), he says: "The English Constitution is
framed on the principle of choosing a single sovereign authority and
making it good: the American, upon the principle of having many
sovereign authorities and hoping that their multitude may atone for
their inferiority," 236.

[1] *E. g.* vi., 252 n., 273 n., 299 n., 300 n., 393 n., 394 n., 485.   Canning,
however, we have seen, and other English Tories took the French
example as confirmatory of the need of restricting the representation in
the lower house.

Adams had early been indoctrinated with views about a "natural aristocracy," or nobility of wise men, who, when well regulated by the constitution, and kept under, but given an opening in the elective senate, become an "ornament" of the state and indispensable for its welfare, serving as "guides" to the "natural democracy."[1] From the *Oceana* also he must have learned of the "immortality" of an "equal commonwealth,"[2] consisting of "three orders," only two of which, however, were treated as natural in society, the third being the factitious one of executive magistrates, created in the government[3]; and there he read of the tendency of single assemblies to split into the two orders of the deliberating few and the listening many,[4] whence had been deduced the necessity of separating them into two assemblies, the one to represent the wisdom of the commonwealth, as its council, to debate and to propose, the other to represent the interest of the commonwealth, as its general assembly, not to debate, but to resolve by adopting or rejecting; which had been advocated also on the pleasant conceit of two girls with a cake to share between them, who find the task best performed if the one divides and the other chooses;[5]—all which Adams quotes and appropriates for his two utterly

---

[1] *Oceana*, etc., 47, 134; 272; 42, 56, 135, 231; 253.

[2] *Ib.*, 100, 161, *cf.*, 53–4, 539; 54–5, 259, 394–5.

[3] *Ib.*, 48, 55, 58, 160, 259, etc.

[4] *Ib.*, 47, 253. Since, and independently, H. Carnot has borne witness to this, saying that in a large assembly "the major part play the rôle of jurymen: they judge by yes or no if what the *élite* propose is good or bad" (quoted from V. Pierre's *Histoire de la République de 1848*, p. 98; *cf.* J. S. Mill, *Dissertations and Discussions*, Boston, 1865, vol. iii., p. 36).

[5] *Oceana*, 46–8; similarly 252–3. Note the pregnant words: "The wisdom of the few may be the light of mankind; but the interest of the few is not the profit of mankind," 48.

different chambers (iv. 410–13, *cf.* 440, 585). Harrington, of course, had taken these two bodies, with their peculiar correlative functions, from the Roman Senate and Comitia and the systems of some other ancient republics.[1] Such two bodies, so functioning, had once been contemplated for use on this side the Atlantic in the Carolinas, and actually had an ephemeral existence in Pennsylvania.[2] Probably through Harrington's influence had furthermore come into American politics the use of the ballot, which he got from Venice,[3] and, if not the principle of rotation and compulsory vacations of representatives and magistrates, for which he assigns no authority,[4] yet the other rotation of the members of the council or senate by a third part being elected every year for three years[5] or the like, which he may

[1] *Ib.*, 51, etc. *Cf.* Thucydides, vi., § 39.

[2] They were embodied by Locke in his unapplied *Carolina Constitutions*, art. 51, and by Penn in his *Frames of Government* of 1682, art. 16, and of 1683, art. 15, which were superseded in 1696.—It may be added that, probably not from Harrington, but from his Roman model, this division of functions, between the Tribunate and the Legislative Body, was adopted in the French constitution of 1799, arts. 28, 34, and continued, with some modifications, in Napoleon's of 1804, arts. 82–3, 96–7.

[3] *Oceana*, 55, 111, etc. This also was used by Locke in his *Constitutions*, art. 32, and by Penn in his *Frames*, art. 20 and art. 18 respectively. But already in 1638–9 Connecticut in its *Fundamental Orders*, art. 2, had improved upon the ballot proper (a ball, still used in social clubs) by the voting paper, borrowing it from its use in church elections.

[4] *Oceana*, 54, 303, 394, etc. It was not Harrington's own invention, as it had been employed in Genoa for the Doge and the "governors" in the Signiory, and but recently adopted in the Connecticut *Fundamental Orders*, art. 4, for the Governor. For the occasional retention, in some of our States, of this rotation, the object of which was to exercise many citizens in office and to have many ex-officials among the public, see above, pp. 147–8.

[5] *Oceana*, 98–9, including the representatives in the popular assembly —so again, 439, 622–3; also in the case of the councils and other elective bodies, 124–5.

have taken from the Venetian Senate or the Dutch Provincial Estates.[1]

The author who appears to have influenced Adams most in his second period, was far away from a republican, being the turncoat Swift. From Swift's satirical *Discourse of the Contests and Dissentions between the Nobles and Commons in Athens and Rome* he quotes long passages, and remarks that, but for the style, they might be taken for his own (iv. 388–9). Swift, indeed, had written of a single assembly "naturally" dividing into *three* parts (of the one, the few, and the many),[2] and of a balance between them; and had developed the idea of the balance as supposing "three things," to wit: the holding hand and the two scales. "The balance," he wrote, "must be held by a third hand, who is to deal the remaining power with the utmost exactness into the several scales." But he added a truth which we have criticized Adams for neglecting: "it is not necessary, that the power should be equally divided between these three; for the balance may be held by the weakest, who, by his address and conduct, removing from either scale, and adding of his own, may keep the scales duly poised"[3]; and again, though not so clearly, in another

---

[1] *Cf. ib.*, 43, 98–9, 139, 394, 439. Harrington was one of the founders of the Rota Club in 1659, which practiced these measures, *ib.*, p. xxix. (*Cf.* the Tribunal of the Rota in the Papal and several other Italian states.) This rotation was borrowed by Penn in his *Frames* of 1682, art. 3 (with vacations also, art. 4), and of 1683, art. 2 (vacations, art. 3), and was restored in the Pennsylvania constitution of 1776 for the council (with vacations), art. 19 (and vacations for the delegates to Congress, art. 11), and simultaneously in the Delaware constitution of 1776, art. 4, as already in the Virginia constitution of 1776, and afterward in the New York constitution of 1777, art. 11, and the South Carolina constitution of 1778 (with vacations), art. 9.

[2] Swift's *Discourse*, ch. i., *Works*, vol. iii., p. 10 (quoted by Adams, iv., 383).   [3] *Ib.*, iii., 17 (quoted by Adams, iv., 387).

work, alleging "that in such a government as this [the English], where the prince holds the balance between two great powers, the nobility and the people, it is the very nature of his office to remove from one scale into the other, or sometimes put his own weight in the lightest, so as to bring both to an equilibrium."[1] Also— here setting the example to Bolingbroke—he wished the king to be non-partisan,[2] at least between the two real parties; yet excused him for siding with the one "national party," if the other (Swift's adversaries, of course) had degenerated (in his opinion) into a mere faction.[3]

Swift's influence is discernible further in that pessimism which is so conspicuous in Adams's present period—in his remarks upon the endless exorbitancy of the passions,[4] and the possession by assemblies of every "folly, infirmity, and vice, to which a single person is subjected."[5] The optimism of Harrington and other republicans in thinking that evils may be dispelled, he abandoned: he thought now only of taking human

---

[1] *History of the Four Last Years of the Queen*, B. i., *Works*, xv., 68–9.

[2] *Sentiments of a Church of England Man*, Sect. ii., near end, *Works*, iii., 97–8.

[3] *The Examiner*, No. xxxv., *Works*, viii., 197–8.—Some suggestions may also have come to Adams from Paley's *Principles of Moral and Political Philosophy*, which was published just before Adams began to write, and, being immensely popular, could hardly have escaped his notice, although he never alludes to it. (It was taken as an authority, on "the intermixture of which all actual governments are composed," by C. Pinckney, Elliot's *Debates*, iv., 328.) Therein, VI., vii., is an account of the "balance of interest," in which every two of the branches are described as combining against the third that may be encroaching. On this point Paley has since Adams's day been followed by Brougham, *Political Philosophy*, iii., 160.

[4] Swift, *Discourse*, ch. i., *Works*, iii., 19; quoted by Adams, iv., 387, 408; adopted, 406.

[5] Swift, *Discourse*, ch. iv., *Works*, iii., 53; quoted by Adams, iv., 388.

nature as it is (vi. 115) and of curing bad effects by regulating their conditions.[1]

Yet from Harrington he had probably got the first hint of the idea of the balance; and from him he took a doctrine frequently enunciated, that dominion follows property.[2] But Harrington had used this principle in a way much better than Adams did. Harrington maintained that for a settled state the form of the government must be adapted to the economic condition of the people:—if all property, or the largest portion of it (two thirds or more), is in the hands of one man, the government must be monarchical; if in the hands of a few, aristocratical; if distributed among the people at large, democratical.[3] The "balance of dominion" itself must be in a balance with the balance of property: the superstructure must be according to the foundation.[4] And not only this, but when the superstructure is once erected upon its proper foundation, the foundation itself must be fixed, or else the superstructure will topple.[5] Hence there must be an agrarian law, which in a monarchy will preserve the property all in the hands of the king, by the doctrine of his sole proprietorship; which in an aristocracy will keep property in a few heads of families, by primogeniture and entail;

---

[1] Cf. De Lolme's praise of the English Constitution, because "it has taken mankind as they are, and has not endeavored to prevent every thing, but to regulate every thing," Constitution of England, near end.

[2] Harrington's Oceana, 39, 70, 72, etc., meaning mostly land, 243-7. Adams looked upon this as an "infallible maxim in politics," ix., 376, in 1776; and, applying it to America, iv., 359, he called it "a noble discovery," 428, and Harrington "the Newton in politics," vi., 506, in 1814. But it had been held before, according to Nevill, Plato Redivivus, Preface to the second edition; and there is a hint of it in Aristotle, Polit., IV., ix. (xi.), 8, and x. (xi.), 2-4.

[3] Oceana, 39-40, 290, 381, 387, 494, 498, 621-2.

[4] Ib., 73, 391.   [5] Ib., 73, cf. 105-6.

which in a democracy will cause dissipation by division among children, and prevent accumulation beyond a moderate standard by forbidding inheritance and even purchase of land beyond a certain value.[1] Harrington himself preferred the last, and thinking his country had already reached this stage, wished to keep it there by limiting the amount of land purchasable or inheritable.[2] Adams, however, although *his* country began at this stage, not only despaired of keeping it there, but now actually had no desire that it should stay there. He now had a fondness for only one form of government: limited monarchy he considered the best of republican governments (iv. 558). He wished all governments to be reduced to that,—and if the condition of the people does not admit of it, he virtually said *tant pis!* and hoped that in time it would become fit for it. Instead of looking upon the English Constitution as an alleviation of the evils of gross inequality both of wealth and of education, he looked upon it as a perfect whole, to be imitated in its foundation as well as in its superstructure.

Not always had he held this opinion. In his first period he had followed Harrington more closely. He had then written, in 1776: "The only possible way of preserving the balance of power on the side of equal liberty and public virtue, is to make the acquisition of land easy to every member of society; to make a division of the land into small quantities, so that the multitude may be possessed of landed estates. If the multitude is possessed of the balance of real estate, the multitude will have the balance of power, and in that case the multitude will take care of the liberty, virtue, and

<hr />

[1] *Ib.*, 40, 54, 392, 456–7.   [2] *Ib.*, 102, 303, 435, 456.

interest of the multitude, in all acts of government"
(ix. 376–7). This passage sets off by contrast a deterioration in his second period. Throughout this period
in his denunciation of pure democracy he treats the
rule of an ignorant and propertiless populace, such as
a little later at times during the French Revolution
committed havoc in Paris and the provinces, which we
have seen him take for confirmation of his doctrine, as
proof simply of the evil of this form of government, not
distinguishing between that mob government, or ochlarchy, and the democracy of a people fit for it—of a
people possessing property and education. According
to Harrington, all government is violent and of short
duration whose superstructure is not adjusted to the
foundation, or whose foundation is in an unsettled
condition intermediate or transient between two
clearly defined ones.[1] Evidently the badness of such
misfits proves nothing against a form of government
where the foundation is prepared for the superstructure.

An equally mixed government may be the proper and
a good government in countries where the land is nearly
equally divided between the one, the few, and the
many, each of these having about a third of it—perhaps
the king a little less and the people somewhat more.[2]

[1] *Oceana*, 40, 388, 498, 621.

[2] For this government, notice, the king must have an exceedingly
large domain of his own: he must be, not *primus inter pares* of landed
aristocrats (though they would like to consider him such), but so far
and away ahead of all the others as to stand by himself, if not equaling
in power all the nobles together, yet, agreeably to the dictum of Fortescue (*The Difference between Absolute and Limited Monarchy*, edited by
J. Fortescue-Aland, 1714, p. 58), excelling any two of the greatest of
them. Such was the case in England when the King really had an equal
share in the government with the other classes, and with the cessation
of it he lost his authority. Here is a requirement which Adams always
overlooked. He did not recognize that without it the executive chief,

And this triply mixed government is unquestionably better than a monocratic government, where the king owns nearly all, or say nearly two thirds, of the land and the freemen are in a minority compared with his dependents. It also may be better than an aristocratic government, where the land is nearly all in the hands of the few (at least two thirds of it, they having the king's share too), for the reason that such a division of the land, though not so bad as that in the monocracy, is worse than that appropriate for the mixed government, since the excluded people are more courted and better cared for, if the power of the few is offset and balanced by that of the one, than if the few form a clique having undisputed sway. But the conclusion does not follow that the triply mixed government, in a mixed and tri-cratic *state* (to use the distinction obtained from Bodin) is better than demarchic or popular government in a country where the people at large have most of the land, divided with fair approach to equality—where, in fact, the conditions are democratic. To prove superiority of the mixed government, it must be proved that its accompanying unequal division of land is better, eco-nomically, socially, morally, than the nearly equal division. This Adams never so much as undertook to show. He was satisfied with merely pointing out cases of violent and short-lived governments conducted by so-called democracies where the division of land was not suited for this form of government, and which therefore deserve rather to be classed as ochlarchies.[1] Of course, to prove the triply mixed government to be superior to

whether hereditary or not, could not stand outside the two classes, or even outside the two parties.

[1] Note that since his time the land in France has become more evenly distributed, and now a democratic republic is firmly established there.

ochlarchy, is not to prove it to be superior to democracy
(in the sense of republic, embracing the whole people).
The failure here of Adams's argumentation is of the
same nature as his failure to prove the superiority of the
bicameral over the unicameral system where there is a
constitution established by the people. In each case he
thought he proved what he wanted by proving something else.

Mixed government, then, being his ideal, within this
alone he developed the idea of another balance, different
from Harrington's. This other balance he also found in
his teachers, even in Harrington himself,—in Sydney, in
Swift, in Bolingbroke, in many others. But none had
developed it to the full extent it was capable of.[1] Some
had set up only two powers to balance each other[2];
which would obviously be unstable. Swift, to be sure,
had pointed out the need of a third power to hold the
balance even; but he had placed this third balancing
power chiefly in one hand only, the king's, and the two
others he kept mostly in the position of balanced
parties. So other writers had treated of the king
balancing the nobles and the people, or these balancing
the king[3]; and again others—and these the most—of the
nobility balancing and mediating between the king
and the people[4]; and one at least, a lawyer, had as-

[1] It was only indefinitely referred to by Ferguson, *Essay on the History of Civil Society*, 3d ed., 1768, p. 273; and in America by J. Otis and
S. Adams in 1768 and 1772, (quoted x., 372, vi., 277).

[2] So Harrington, senate and people, as oligarchy and democracy,
Oceana, 446; but again, in an aristocracy, he wrote of the nobles needing
a prince as moderator, to keep the potent among them from aspiring
to absolute monarchy, they balancing him, and he them, *ib.*, 498.

[3] Gibbon, *Decline and Fall of the Roman Empire*, ch. iii., opening.

[4] Lord Say: "they have been at the beam keeping both scales, king
and people, in an even posture," *apud* Firth, *Last Years of the Protectorate*,
ii., 13; Sydney, *Discourses*, 384, *cf.* 419, 420, (indefinitely 379, 446, 447);

cribed the position of "mediator between the prince and the people" to the Lord Chief Justice,[1] while another, a historian, had portrayed the people coming up as an intermediate power to balance the king and the nobles,[2] though not till our time did anyone assert this as descriptive of existing conditions.[3] Blackstone, as we have seen, had even generalized the working of all the three powers into a scheme of mutual action and reaction, like the composition of forces in mechanics.[4]

It was reserved for Adams to elaborate this three-cornered scheme into a hard and fast system in which each power is to play the part of mediator and balancer with almost complete indifference (though not wholly so, as he sometimes inclined, with Swift, to allot this

Bolingbroke, already cited; Burlamaqui, *Principes*, vol. iv., p. 126; Rousseau, of the English nobility, *Nouvelle Héloïse*, I., lxii.; Governor Bernard in 1764 (quoted by Adams in his early period, with disapproval of setting up nobles for this purpose, iv., 26-7, but himself for this purpose then wishing to institute a legislative council, see above, p. 9); Chatham, speeches in the House of Lords, see *Correspondence*, iii., 385, 418 ("the constitutional barrier between the extremes of liberty and prerogative"), iv., 478. The theory of this balance is the oldest of all; for it was hinted at by Aristotle, *Polit.*, IV., ix. (xi.) (quoted by Adams, v., 458-9), and expressed by Cicero, *De Re Publica*, i., § 52; whence it was adopted by Hotman, *Franco-Gallia*, c. 12 (vol. iii., col. 40 B).

[1] Fortescue-Aland in the Dedication of his edition of Fortescue. *Cf.* Hamilton's treatment of the courts as "designed to be an intermediate body between the people and the legislature," *The Federalist*, No. 78.

[2] Robertson, *Charles V.*, 1769, ed. Glasgow 1817, vol. i., pp. 20, 44.

[3] Bryce: "This kind of government [the English system of Cabinet Government] rests on a balance of three authorities, the Executive, the Legislature, and the People, the people being a sort of arbiter between Ministry and Parliament," *Studies*, 429.

[4] Burlamaqui also wrote of Lycurgus casting the three kinds of government into one so as to serve as counter-weights to one another, *Principes*, vol. iv., p. 193. But the idea of balancing, as of a ship, belongs to Polybius, VI., x. (quoted by Adams, iv., 436).

office chiefly to the king), and for this purpose he assigned to each and all of them perfect equality of power—that is, of legislative power, as the additional executive power he consigned solely to the king. Herein lay Adams's originality—the originality of working over an old careless and semi-figurative (and already moribund) doctrine into a completely systematized and literal scheme, thereby bringing to view its initial inaccuracy and laying bare its inward defects, unwittingly performing the part of an embalmer, who, in attempting to make eternal, kills deader than ever.[1]

[1] The subsequent history of the general scheme, especially in America, will be given later. Confining ourselves here merely to the balance, we may note that occasional repetitions and resuscitations have occurred, mostly of the mere metaphor, gradually becoming rarer. Thus of the king Coleridge wrote as "the beam of the constitutional scales," *Church and State*, 1830, p. 28. On the senate or council, Burke wrote of its "holding a sort of middle place" between the people or their representatives and the executive, *Reflections on the Revolution in France, Works*, iii., 496. So also Fox, to be quoted later. And more particularly of the English House of Lords, C. Pinckney, Henry, and Monroe, Elliot's *Debates*, v., 235, iii., 164, 218-19, respectively. Similarly Calhoun, adding that the Lords are conservative and "in favor of preserving the equilibrium," because they are so privileged that their condition cannot but be "made worse by the triumph of either of the conflicting estates over the other," *Disquisition on Government*, 103. The United States Senate Story called "the real balance-wheel, which adjusts and regulates" the movements of the system, *Commentaries*, § 700. And in France Thiers, who wished to take the "mixed government" of England as model, *Discours parlementaires*, i., 154, treated the second chamber as "the equilibrating body" between the crown and the country, 171, indispensable as "intermediary between royalty and democracy," 158 (at the same time treating the king as useful to impede usurpations by great men, 173, *cf.* 156, 183, 188, 189). Prince Napoleon: "Liberty cannot exist without intermediate bodies—centers of resistance—between the throne and the people, breakwaters for the throne and bulwarks for the people," in Senior's *Conversations during the Second Empire*, ii., 24. D. Stewart's account of the aristocracy being checked on opposite sides has been cited, as also Brougham's balancing of any two against the third (following Paley). Rohmer wrote of the

And now this triple balance became Adams's idol. "I am in the habit of balancing everything," he once playfully wrote.[1] Unfortunately he paid no heed to Condorcet's warning that "there is a great difference between seeking the means for most advantageously combining three powers already subsisting, and seeking to establish similar powers, in a country where they do not exist, in order to have the pleasure of setting them against one another."[2] The play of balancing became to him grim earnest. For the balance equal orders in the government were needed; and for equal orders in the government, equal classes in society. The mixture was not to be merely in the government, but in the state also: what Bodin would not allow, Adams would

---

king's function being, not as counterpoise to the people (this belonging to the house of lords), but as mediator, *Der Vierte Stand*, etc., in his *Wissenschaft und Leben*, iv., 523; and also of the nobility as standing between the king and the people, and of a twofold check, of the nobility and people upon the king, and of the king and nobility upon the people, *Lehre von der politischen Parteien*, § 142, *ib.*, 243. (He, too, desired equiponderance of the "estates," *Der Vierte Stand*, *ib.*, 524. But his three "estates," or orders, were king, nobles, and rich burghers. He wanted the king to be the special spokesman and guardian of the fourth estate, the poor, *ib.*, 528–9.) And Parieu wrote of the superiority, over two, of three equilibrating powers, of which any two can always unite against the third, *Principes de la Science politique*, 1870, p. 187.

[1] IX., 558, in 1789; and again the next year: "You see I still hold fast my scales, and weigh everything in them," 570.—Maclay reports a conversation after adjournment of the Senate, May 1, 1789: "He got upon the subject of checks to Government and the balances of power. His tale was long—he seemed to expect some answer. I caught at the last word, and said, undoubtedly, without a balance there could be no equilibrium, and so I left him hanging in geometry," *Sketches*, 22.

[2] *Lettres d'un Bourgeois*, *Œuvres*, xii., 120. Condorcet adds: "Because one has been able to make a machine run well by establishing a sort of equilibrium between forces that tend to destroy it, the conclusion need not be drawn that it is necessary to subject a machine one is about to create, to the action of these contrary forces."

bring about. Thus for his best government inequality in the conditions of the people at large was necessary. Advocacy of a theory naturally leads to the desire for its prerequisites. Republicans who profit by Harrington's principle, consider that the condition of the people where property is well divided is the best; they consequently hold that democratical government is the best, not in itself, but as the form that suits the best condition of the people—if not necessarily simple democracy, yet the mixed government in which democracy prevails. Harrington, indeed, wanted an aristocracy of men of leisure, but he wished them to be overbalanced by the rest.[1] Republicans therefore ought to bend their energies to obtain this condition, and to prevent its deteriorating into a condition of unequal distribution, fit for aristocratic or monarchical governments, or for mixtures in which these forms prevail and predominate.[2] But Adams said, the exactly evenly mixed government is the best; which amounts to saying that the democratical element should be subordinate; and therefore he wanted the condition of the people to be suitable for this status of their power. He recognized what Mill later said, that "an aristocratic House is only powerful in an aristocratic state of society"[3]; and he wanted an aristocratic state of society—and even went too far, never assigning a sufficient domain to the

---

[1] *Oceana*, 134-5, *cf.* 72, 84. Harrington desired the people to possess about two thirds, 498, or even three quarters, 387, of the land, the aristocracy only a third or a quarter.

[2] *Cf.* J. G. Baldwin: "A constitution is made for a people, not a people for a constitution; and the folly and futility of building up a class of people in order to get up a constitution properly balanced, are so manifest, that it would seem to strike the plainest apprehension," *Party Leaders*, New York, 1855, p. 76—of Hamilton, but still more appropriate of Adams. [3] *Representative Government*, 233-4.

executive chief or king, to counterpoise the aristocracy, so that his government, adapting itself to his state, would inevitably have degenerated into an aristarchy, like England in his day.

At all events, he did not mind the oncoming of the aristocratic condition: he did not mind inequality, paying but scant attention even to the preservation of a middle class (*cf.* iv. 363, v. 459); he did not mind luxury; he would not waste effort in trying to prevent the intrusion of corruption, which he regarded as unavoidable. "The problem ought to be," he said, "to find a form of government best calculated to prevent the bad effects and corruption of luxury, when in the ordinary course of things, it must be expected to come in."[1] He therefore made no provision against the rich few acquiring all the land and overbalancing the many. Agrarian laws he contemned[2]: he would leave the distribution of property to take its own course, and derided Jefferson's plan of dividing intestate estates as insufficient for the purpose for which it was designed (x. 103), —which is only too true[3]; and with other suggested

---

[1] VI., 94.—In a little skit on *Parties* written by Madison in 1792 there is an obvious hit at Adams. Madison concludes: "From the expediency, in politics, of making natural parties mutual checks on each other, to infer the propriety of creating artificial parties in order to form them into mutual checks, is not less absurd than it would be in ethics to say that new vices ought to be promoted, where they would counteract each other, because this use may be made of existing vices," *Writings*, iv., 469. (*Cf.* 483 on this being effected by "a mysterious operation," which he represents as advocated by an "Anti-Republican.")

[2] *Cf.* iv., 540 (of the Gracchi). "Do you suppose Americans would make or submit to a law to limit to a small number, or to any number, the acres of land which a man might possess?" vi., 21–2.

[3] But his editor and descendant thought it sufficient, iv., 359–60 n. *Cf.* C. Pinckney, Elliot's *Debates*, v., 233, 235, iv., 320–1, and Lee, *ib.*, iii., 185; also Webster, *Works*, i., 35–6.

remedies he later showed impatience, such as alienation of land and inhibitions upon monopolies, sophisticating against the former that it only transfers from one to another, and against the latter that in our free country there were as many monopolies as elsewhere (vi. 507–10). For all the evils of a highly complex and corrupt civilization he had in reserve one full and sufficient remedy in his threefold balance of an equally mixed government (96)— on the model of the English! Like one possessed of a panacea, he feared no disease.[1] And his cure-all, always stable, was of a nature to preserve itself. He would therefore do nothing further to guard the mixture when he once got it.

Such, be it remembered, is his frame of mind in his second period, which began in the fall of 1786. It was not so in his first period, during the stress of the Revolution, when he sided rather with the democrats, following Harrington rather closely, as we have just seen, and, as we saw before, combating "the barons of the south" who wished to introduce into our governments some of the aristocratic concoctions he is now himself prescribing. So late as February, 1786, he wrote: "It has ever been my hobby-horse to see rising in America an empire of liberty, and a prospect of two or three hundred millions of freemen, without one noble or one king among them. You say"—he was addressing a German count—"it is impossible. If I should agree with you in this, I would still say, let us try the experiment, and preserve our equality as long as we can" (ix. 546).

---

[1] For this reason he did not agree with Jefferson, who in his *Notes on Virginia* had written: "The time to guard against corruption and tyranny, is before they shall have gotten hold of us. It is better to keep the wolf out of the fold, than to trust to drawing his teeth and talons after he shall have entered," *Works*, viii., 363.

About the same time he mentioned his having half a mind to devote the next ten years of his life to writing a book upon the subject of nobility, wishing to inquire into the practice of all nations "to see how far the division of mankind into patricians and plebeians, nobles and simples, is necessary and inevitable, and how far it is not. Nature," he added, "has not made this discrimination. Art has done it. Art may then prevent it. Would it do good or evil to prevent it? I believe good."[1] Then in the late summer and fall of that year occurred the so-called Shays's rebellion in Massachusetts, reports of which, probably distorted, reached him in Europe.[2] He now made no allowance for the unsettled condition of the country after a desolating civil war and during the affliction of a depreciated and fluctuating and therefore at times appreciating currency.[3] He gave way to the belief that the American people were showing themselves no less violent than the *mobile vulgus* had elsewhere generally shown itself.[4] What had been written by Europeans in denunciation of democracy under an ignorant and propertiless lower class, he applied to democracy in a people with a propertied and educated lower class. And now his second

[1] VIII., 370. For this project *cf.* 431. It was abandoned, 435, or rather replaced by the books extolling aristocracy as the unpreventable product of nature.

[2] One of the demands of the insurgents, it may be noted, was the abolition of the senate, Bancroft, *History of the Constitution*, ii., 395.

[3] This last he did notice in the summer of 1787 (when the Convention was sitting) as paramount to any "defects in their [the Americans'] constitution or confederation," viii., 447.

[4] Indeed, the first germ of Adams's distrust of the people may be traced back to an incident which occurred eleven years before in the camp before Boston, when a debtor expressed satisfaction at the closing of the courts. See ii., 420.

period comes in with a rush.[1] His new science of government, in which democracy is reduced to one third, and that occupying the third place, is fully developed in the first volume of his *Defense*, written in the last three months of the same year, and published early in 1787. Yet it was not till the third volume of that work, published in 1788, that his hints at monarchy and hereditary aristocracy became unmistakably plain and emphatic. The *Discourses on Davila*, which appeared serially in 1790, and which he says may be called the fourth volume of the *Defense* (x. 96), was the culmination; following which, after an interval, came a gradually louder-sounding palinode.

[1] For the influence of Shays's rebellion, see i., 432, ix., 551, 552 (*cf.* 623), x., 53. *Cf.* Jefferson: "Mr. Adams had originally been a republican. The glare of royalty and nobility, during his mission to England, had made him believe their fascination a necessary ingredient in government; and Shays's rebellion, not sufficiently understood where he then was, seemed to prove that the absence of want and oppression was not a sufficient guarantee of order," *Works*, ix., 97.

IV. ATTITUDE TOWARD THE AMERICAN GOVERNMENTS

CHAPTER XVII

CRITICISM OF THE FEDERAL CONSTITUTION

WE must now turn to this aspect of Adams's second period—his attitude toward the governments of the several American States and the government of the United States. His *Defense of the Constitutions* was written entirely with a view to defending the constitutional systems inaugurated in the States, particularly his own constitution of Massachusetts and those which resembled it,[1] in the matter of the two divisions, of the whole government into three departments, and of the legislative department into three branches (viii. 458, ix. 572–3), against the unicameral and "simple democracy" system embodied in the constitution of Pennsylvania, falsely (he said) ascribed to Franklin, but really due to Matlack, Cannon, Young, and Paine,[2] and in

---

[1] VI., 463, 465, 486, ix., 623–4, x., 413.

[2] II., 507–8, iii., 220, ix., 622–3. But he ascribed the French single assembly to Franklin's authority, vi., 394 n. As for the Pennsylvania single assembly, that was really due to Penn, who put it (with an executive council) in his last constitutions, in 1696 and 1701; and, being approved, it was continued in the State constitution of 1776. This, according to Graydon, "was understood to have been principally the work of Mr. George Bryan, in conjunction with a Mr. Cannon, a school-

reply to the admirers of this system in France—Turgot,
La Rochefoucauld, and Condorcet, even Lafayette,
but especially the first.[1] It had little to do with the
constitution of the Confederation, to which he made
only a couple of allusions,[2] and nothing at all with the
then forming Constitution of the United States, of
which he later said: "I scarcely knew that such a thing
was in contemplation till I received it at the moment
my third volume was about to issue from the press,"
and when "I had hardly time to annex it at the end."[3]
With the State governments themselves he was not
altogether satisfied, so far as they fell short of his un-
compromising scheme and lost the balance, privately
complaining of them with bitterness,[4] but in the published work only incidentally confessing his mortifica-
tion at their omission to give the absolute negative and
full appointing power to the governors (iv. 358–9).

In the passages in that work referring to the Confederation he expressed satisfaction even with its unicameral feature, "because Congress is not a legislative
assembly, nor a representative assembly, but only a
diplomatic assembly," and because "a single council
has been found to answer the purpose of confederacies

master," *Memoirs*, ed. of 1846, pp. 285–6. Condorcet, in his *Éloge de
Franklin*, said that Franklin's voice alone decided the adoption of a
single chamber, *Œuvres*, iv., 133.

[1] IX., 623–4, x., 53; vi., 252, 486, viii., 448, 558, ix., 572–3, *cf.* vi., 403,
470, x., 256. In England also, he mentions the writings of Paine, Mrs.
Macauley, and Burgh, as works whose bad influence he wished to stem,
ix., 558–9.

[2] Only one he says in x., 413, referring to iv., 579–80; but there is
another in vi., 219–20.

[3] IX., 624, referring to vi., 219–20. Not so x., 54, in 1813, when he
forgetfully said it was written "to support and strengthen the Constitution of the United States."

[4] In viii., 458, Oct., 1787; ix., 560, Aug., 1789.

very well"; for here the States, controlling their deputies, are "the checks" and are "able to form an effectual balance."[1] More power in Congress over foreign affairs, with full authority to make commercial treaties, and at home ability to secure a revenue for fulfilling engagements by common imposts, to protect the fisheries in the north and the navigation of the Mississippi in the south, and to preserve the Union,—these he had enumerated in his official correspondence as desirable objects[2]; but he elsewhere expressed himself with hesitation about extending the powers of Congress.[3] He himself had no time to engage upon "the vast subject of confederations"[4]; but he recommended this labor to others, and applauded the American people for being cautious (iv. 580–1). His ideas were, then, confined to the mere strengthening of the confederation.[5] A consolidated government he never

[1] IV., 579–80; but without *three* powers! "effectual" possibly, but how *stable*? and if effectual, why not likewise the control of districts that instruct their representatives? (The States had the right of recalling their deputies: then why not give that right to the districts?) It may be noted that later (in 1805) Adams remarked of the Confederation that "all the powers of government, legislative, executive, and judiciary were at that time collected in one center, and that center was the Congress," iii., 87; *cf.* ix., 273 quoted above p. 204 n. When he wrote this, he must have disapproved of the Congress, although he did not do so "at that time" itself.—To Jefferson's objection that Congress was not a diplomatic assembly, but legislative, even executive, and almost judiciary too, viii., 433, he replied without insisting on the point, 435, March, 1787, but repeated the assertion, vi., 219. His opinion was at the time shared by Randolph, Elliot's *Debates*, v., 198; Livingston, *ib.*, ii., 215; Knox, Bancroft, *History of the Constitution*, i., 412; and Morris, to be quoted later.

[2] VIII., 107–8 (1783); 241–2, 243–4, 282–3 (1785); 439 (1787).

[3] IX., 526 (1784); iv., 580.   [4] VIII., 448 (Aug., 1787).

[5] To this point Jay took exception, in letters thanking Adams for the present of his book, *Correspondence and Public Papers*, iii., 247, 249. Adams replied (from London, Sept., 1787) that if he ever wrote "on

would have approved (x. 413). He did not contemplate a United States Senate, or expect that others would introduce it (vi. 465). The idea of compounding the federal and national elements and of using them to balance each other, was not conceived by him; and to this partial consolidation, such as was effected in the United States Constitution, he contributed nothing— except, as he alleged, the model in the constitution of Massachusetts.[1]

But when the new Constitution was framed and submitted to the judgment of the people, although he found some difficulty in reconciling himself to it,[2] he advised its adoption,[3] approving it on the whole because it carried out to some extent his principles.[4] Rather curiously, the passage of Gladstone's so fondly quoted by American worshippers of the Constitution was anticipated by this lukewarm supporter, in both its parts. That passage extolls both the British and American Constitutions in one breath, for opposite reasons. It reads: "As the British Constitution is the most subtle organism which has proceeded from the

the great subject of our confederation," he would do so less hastily, but would only aspire to be one of the "under-workmen" to the "heroes, sages, and demigods" at Philadelphia, *ib.*, 254 (Adams's *Works*, viii., 452).

[1] VI., 458.—In the Convention his satisfaction with a single chamber for confederacies was appealed to as an argument against the introduction of the second chamber in the new constitution, by Luther Martin, Elliot's *Debates*, i., 453, (also in his *Letter*, *ib.*, 359). And views similar to his on this subject without mention of him, were expressed by Sherman, arguing for Lansing's motion, *ib.*, v., 218. In the ratifying convention of his own State Gore classed "Dr. Adams" with Montesquieu as an admirer of the British Constitution, *ib.*, ii., 17.

[2] VIII., 464 (Dec. 6, 1787).

[3] VIII., 467 (Dec. 16, 1787); 476 (Feb., 1888).

[4] IX., 559 (May, 1789); so, later, in his inaugural address in 1797, ix., 106.

womb and the long gestation of progressive history, so
the American Constitution is, so far as I can see, the
most wonderful work ever struck off at a given time by
the brain and purpose of man."[1]   Adams's unqualified
praise of the English Constitution we have already seen.
He also said: "The English Constitution is the result
of the most mature deliberation on universal history
and philosophy" (iv. 556).   On the American, the
passage added at the end of the third volume of the
Defense, when he had barely had time to read it, runs
thus: "The deliberate union of so great and various a
people in such a plan, is, without all partiality and
prejudice, if not the greatest exertion of human understanding, the greatest single effort of national deliberation that the world has ever seen."[2]   But Adams does
not commend the new project without immediately
looking ahead to its amendment.   The passage continues: "That it may be improved is not to be doubted,
and provision is made for that purpose in the report
itself.   A people who could conceive, and can adopt it,
we need not fear will be able to amend it, when, by
experience, its inconveniences and imperfections shall
be seen and felt."[3]   He referred, however, not to the

---

[1] *Gleanings,* i., 212; from the *North American Review,* Sept., 1878.

[2] VI., 220. Knox could hardly have seen this, but drew from an
informant lately returned from England, when he wrote to Washington,
May 25, 1788: "Mr. John Adams, who probably has arrived in Massachusetts, is exceedingly pleased with it, and thinks it the first production
ever offered to the human race," in Bancroft's *History of the Constitution,*
ii., 469.

[3] *Loc. cit.* Also in his official letter recommending it, written about
the same time, he noticed its not being satisfactory to everybody, and
adverted to the provision contained in it "for corrections and amendments, as they may be found necessary," viii., 467. And similarly in
Davila praise is immediately followed by suggestion of the need of
alteration, vi., 269–70 and 276–7. Here, indeed, it is called "a promis-

democratic amendments which were soon carried through, but to amendments of a monarchical and aristocratical nature, for which he did not meet with the support he expected, even from "the enlightened part of the communities."[1]

With the Federal Constitution Adams found fault on three different lines. In the first place, at the commencement, he had little faith in that composite feature which has been considered its main excellence,—the composition of national and federal elements, which we owe mainly to the Virginia statesmen (and among them perhaps most to Jefferson, Randolph, and Madison). "Our new government," Adams wrote about a year after being inducted into the office of Vice-President, "is an attempt to divide a sovereignty; a fresh essay at *imperium in imperio*. It cannot, therefore, be expected to be very stable or very firm. It will prevent us for a time from drawing our swords upon each other, and when it will do that no longer, we must call a new convention to reform it."[2] Although he was attracted to the so-called Federalist party (really the nationalist) by a common dread of the supremacy of democracy,[3] he

ing essay towards a well-ordered government," 276. Jay had already expressed to him a hope "that experience and the good sense of the people will correct what may prove to be inexpedient in it, *Correspondence*, etc., iii., 258.   [1] IX., 559 (May, 1789).

[2] IX., 564 (April, 1790). Within another year he was still more despondent, and compared the national government to "a frail edifice" which thirteen Samsons would easily pull down, 573.—Yet this "attempt to divide a sovereignty" was in reality a new kind of "mixed government," providing, in a new balance of powers, a new check which ought to have been welcome to Adams. It was often so treated by Madison (perhaps with the affection of a father): see his *Writings*, iv., 473, iii., 507, iv., 139, 327, 424, *cf.* 141–2. Only here was no third power to hold the balance.

[3] Jefferson describes him as having been "taken up by the monarchical federalists in his absence," and upon his return, deceived by them as

was really a States'-rights man (a true federalist). In
his opinion, the revolution had not only made the
colonies independent of England, but had made them
into states independent of one another.[1] For their
common concerns he had desired merely a confederation, and complained of the old one only for its want of
powers adequate to its purpose. He devoted most of
his attention to forming the State governments, and
placed his chief reliance upon them (*cf.* iv. 580, ix.
553). The new Constitution he called "our national
compact" (147). His fear, however, of its dissoluble-
ness from the doubleness of its make-up, he expressed
only in private.

Treating the new government as a national government, and confining his criticism to this side of its
double character, he, in the second place, found fault
with it for allowing the Senate a share in the executive
functions, and in depriving the President of the absolute
veto.[2] The great powers assigned to the President

to the sentiments of the people, *Works*, ix., 97. They took him up
because of the change in his views. "Mr. Adams," wrote Sedgwick to
Hamilton, "was formerly infinitely more democratic than at present,"
i. e. is at present infinitely less democratic than formerly, in J. C.
Hamilton's ed. of Hamilton's *Works*, i., 482. His writings were praised
by Cabot, Gibbs's *Administrations*, ii., 370, by Ames, *ib.*, 368, and by
King, who flattered him by calling his book "the best work that has
been written upon the intricate subject of government," *Life and
Correspondence*, ii., 527.—How similar to Adams's opinions were those
of many of the Federalists may be seen in Jefferson's account of the
latter in 1804, *Works*, iv., 563.   [1] IX., 387, 391, x., 95, *cf.* i., 210.

[2] The partial veto he thought no President would venture to use, vi.,
432. More probably, however, its partiality has made it be used more
frequently than otherwise. Adams never exercised it himself. Later
in life he still regretted that the absolute veto had not been adopted
in the Massachusetts constitution of 1780; for then he believed it would
probably have been adopted in that of the United States: see Quincy's
Quincy, 141.

make ours a monarchical republic; but it is not enough so (*cf.* vi. 430, 470). As is well known, Adams advocated pomp and high-sounding titles,—"decent and moderate titles," he said he wanted, but considered "Your Excellency" too mean for the President,—and entertained ideas about a "civil list" for the President's household, with a number of "chamberlains, aides-de-camp, secretaries, masters of ceremonies, etc."[1] At all events, he urged granting a goodly salary, to support the dignity of the country "in the eyes of all nations" (vi. 540).

What Adams desired, was not so much the "energetic government" advocated by Washington and Hamilton, as a strong executive in "a well-ordered, a well-balanced, a judiciously-limited government" (viii. 495). Our government is not properly balanced. The executive power is too weak; the Senate, or aristocratical branch, is too strong; only the democratical branch in the House of Representatives, he later says, is as it should be (vi. 466), although he would prefer annual to biennial elections (468). He feared, therefore, that in our government the aristocratical power would "swallow up the other two" (431). We have seen that this was a

[1] VIII., 492-3 (May, 1789), 512-13 (1792), *cf,* vi., 242-4, 270. Even in his early period he had introduced honorary titles and ranks of precedence in the Massachusetts constitution of 1780—one of only three American constitutions that have contained such tomfoolery. Georgia had led in 1777, and New Hampshire followed in 1784.—In his *Sketches* the democratic Maclay, who disliked Adams, p. 58, often made fun of his "nobilimania," as he called it, 265,—"his supreme delight in etiquette," 59; his harping on "his favorite topic of titles," 41, *cf.* 9, 93, "dignities, distinctions, titles, etc." being "his hobby-horse," 131; and his fondness for British precedents, 20-1.—*Cf.* George III.'s comments, reported by Rufus King, *Life and Correspondence*, iii., 549-50.—On leaving office he told Jefferson he would be "as faithful a subject as any you will have," Jefferson's *Works*, v., 560.

general fear of his, when the aristocratical branch has a
share in the executive power.[1] "You," he wrote
to Jefferson, "are apprehensive of monarchy, I, of
aristocracy."[2] The legislative and executive authorities are both too much and not enough blended together (x. 397, vi. 432, cf. 466). The Senate must be
weakened by depriving it of its "executive" power over
appointments and treaty-making,[3] also by enlarging its
numbers (532, cf. 471). The President must be un-
shackled (vii. 348 n., cf. vi. 466), and be given legislative power in the absolute veto, along with full power
over appointments, treaty-making, and war-declaring
(430-1). Here Adams called for immediate amendments. At first, in consideration of "the present state
of society and manners in America, with a people living
chiefly by agriculture, in small numbers, sprinkled over
large tracts of land," he admitted that the people could
"live and increase under almost any kind of government, or without any government at all"; and then he
wished for these amendments only because of the "great
importance to begin well," since present "misarrange-
ments" would have "great, extensive, and distant
consequences," affecting "the happiness of a hundred
millions of inhabitants at a time, in a period not very
distant" (iv. 587). But soon his solicitude turned into
apprehension of impending danger. He feared that but
for such amendments, even in our then simple population, the ill-balanced government, with its unequal
distribution of powers, would before long lead to anarchy, and the Constitution be subverted (vi. 431, 432).
These fears never left him, and he continued to insist

---

[1] As especially in iv., 379-80.   [2] VIII., 464, Dec., 1787.

[3] VI., 531, 534. These and some of the other references are from the
last period; but on these matters his opinions underwent no change.

upon such amendments as necessary for rendering our Constitution durable, even in his last period,[1] when, as we shall see, he withdrew his third criticism.

This third criticism consisted in warnings against a certain element in our Constitution—and not only in the Federal, but in the State constitutions as well,—which, though possibly harmless in the days of American simplicity, would eventually, he thought, with the growth of the country in wealth and luxury, lead to intolerable evils; and he expected that these would then evoke desire for new amendments of a nature which he did not enlarge upon, but which he drew with hints gradually rising to the clearest declarations.

[1] VI., 531, 534, 461, 471, cf. ix., 302.—It is interesting to note that without the presidential office being thus strengthened, the encroachments actually made in our Constitution, mostly at a point sanctioned by it, and for a time tolerated by the people, have come from the Presidents, showing that the danger of subversion, if any, comes from their already having too much power. Even before Jackson's administration, in 1828, Pitkin wrote: "From the manner in which this power [of removal] has been exercized, it has given a tone and character to the executive branch of the government, not contemplated, it is believed, by the framers of the constitution. . . . It has greatly increased the influence and patronage of the president, and in no small degree made him the center, around which the other branches of the government revolve," *Political and Civil History of the United States*, ii., 330. And six years later Webster made his comparison of the President to "a Briareus," who "sits in the center of our system, and with his hundred hands touches every thing, moves every thing, controls every thing," *Works*, iv., 137, cf. ii., 84. How different is this central position from Adams's avowed predilection for the President's occupancy of one of the three corners of the government! (And yet Adams himself, in one passage, vi., 256, apparently following Blackstone, *Commentaries*, i., 252, placed the President at the center, or rather at the apex of a cone.) Still later, came Lincoln's encroachments, under cover of alleged war powers. And in our own day a President has made appointments alone, has tried to make a treaty alone, and has virtually declared war alone.

CHAPTER XVIII

HIS MONARCHISM

THE greatest evils Adams dreaded in our State governments, and all the more in the newly framed federal government, were evils connected with elections to high offices, those objects "of ambition and dispute," his "terror" at which we have already noticed.[1] Sometimes he was "apprehensive of foreign interference, intrigue, and influence," the danger of which renews "as often as elections happen" (viii. 464); and he called "the pestilence of foreign influence" "the angel of destruction to elective governments" (ix. 109). But in general, whether stirred up from abroad, or indulged in by domestic factions, it was "corruption at elections" that he held to be "the great enemy of freedom" (iv. 284). Already in 1776, hating a corrupted "popular government" worse than despotism, he feared "we shall find that popular elections are not oftener determined upon pure principles of merit, virtue, and public spirit than the nominations of a Court" (ix. 435); and in 1790 he owned "that awful experience has concurred with reading and reflection, to convince me that Americans are more rapidly disposed to corruption in elections than I thought they were fourteen years ago" (566).

The executive chief and the senators, we have seen him assert,[2] must be either elective together, or hereditary together. Now, in the first volume of his *Defense*, writing of our State governments, he says that in accordance with Harrington's principle, because of the extensive distribution of "the agrarian," which requires

[1] Above, p. 133. [2] Above, p. 121.

the sovereignty to reside in the whole body of the people and renders a hereditary king and nobles impossible, it is proper that the executive magistrate and the senators have been made elective. "In the present state of society," he adds, "and with the present manners, this may be done, not only without inconvenience, but greatly for the happiness and prosperity of the country. In future ages, if the present States become great nations, rich, powerful, and luxurious, as well as numerous, their own feelings and good sense will dictate to them what to do; they may make transitions to a nearer resemblance to the British Constitution,[1] by a fresh convention, without the smallest interruption to liberty. But this will never become necessary, until great quantities of property shall get into few hands" (iv. 359). This passage occurs after one praising the theory of the English Constitution; and again after praising that theory, and also again alluding to Harrington's principle, Adams wrote of the American people, "in the present stage of society among them," when they are "so circumstanced as to be able to bear annual elections" of the first magistrate and senate, as having ventured on "this improvement," "sensible, however, of the danger, and knowing perfectly well a remedy, in case their elections should become turbulent"; of which, "at present," he added, "there is no appearance."[2]

Then in the third volume, which he himself characterized as "the boldest and freest, and most likely to be unpopular" (ix. 556), occur several passages augmenting the disparagement of popular elections. "It is still

[1] Rather, on the whole, to the present German and Japanese constitutions!

[2] IV., 556. It is curious that an "improvement" should be "remedied" by going back to that on which it was an improvement.

problematical," he there wrote, whether annual elections "will be the grand preservative against corruption, or the grand inlet to it. The elections of governors and senators are so guarded, that there is room to hope; but, if we recollect the experience of past ages and other nations, there are grounds to fear. The experiment is made, and will have fair play. If corruption breaks in, a remedy must be provided; and what that remedy must be, is well enough known to every man who thinks" (vi. 25). Again: "In what manner annual elections of governors and senators will operate, remains to be ascertained. It should always be remembered, that this is not the first experiment that was ever made in the world of elections to great offices of state; how they have hitherto operated in every great nation, and what has been their end, is very well known. Mankind have universally discovered that chance was preferable to a corrupt choice, and have trusted Providence rather than themselves. First magistrates and senators had better be made hereditary at once, than that the people should be universally debauched and bribed, go to loggerheads, and fly to arms regularly every year. Thank Heaven! Americans understand calling conventions; and if the time should come, as it is very possible it may, when hereditary descent shall become a less evil than annual fraud and violence, such a convention may still prevent the first magistrate from becoming absolute as well as hereditary" (57). "This hazardous experiment," he reverts to saying, the Americans "have tried, and, if elections are soberly made, it may answer very well; but if parties, factions, drunkenness, bribes, armies, and delirium come in, as they always have done sooner or later, to embroil and decide every thing, the people must again have recourse to conventions and find a remedy. Neither philosophy nor policy has yet discovered any other cure, than by prolonging the duration of the first magistrate and senators. The evil may be lessened and postponed, by elections for longer periods of years, till they become for life; and if this is not found an adequate remedy, there will remain no other but to make them hereditary" (66–7). Once more: "If it should be found that annual elections of governors and senators cannot be supported without introducing venality and convulsions, as is very possible, the people will consult the dignity of their nature better by appointing a standing executive and senate, than by insisting on elections, or at least by prolonging the duration of those high trusts, and making elections less frequent."[1]

Language could not be plainer. Adams was willing to put up with the experiment of popular elections for the two upper branches, now, as a necessity. But confidently expecting its failure, he looked forward to a time when it would no longer be a necessity and might

[1] VI., 116. Similarly: "Standing powers have been instituted to avoid greater evils,—corruption, sedition, war, and bloodshed, in elections; it is the people's business, therefore, to find out some method of avoiding them, without standing powers. The Americans flatter themselves they have hit upon it; and no doubt they have for a time, perhaps a long one; but this remains to be proved by experience," 118. "It is impossible to say, until it is fairly tried, whether it [the institution of an hereditary first magistrate] would not be better than annual elections by the people; or whether elections for more years, or for life, would not be better still," 122.—In 1798 Jefferson reported a conversation, in which Adams said: "No republic can ever be of any duration without a senate, and a senate deeply and strongly rooted, strong enough to bear up against all popular storms and passions. The only fault in the constitution of our Senate is, that their term of office is not durable enough. Hitherto they have done well, but probably they will be forced to give way in time," *Works*, iv., 215; more fully in the *Anas*, ix., 189–90.

be corrected ere its breakdown into despotism. For it, too, he had but one alternative—to make those offices first for life, and at last hereditary. This is in agreement with his preference for the well-balanced monocratic, aristocratic, and democratic state of things above the solely democratic or republican. However good the republican state of things might be in itself, he looked upon it as frail and bound to become corrupt. Rather than attempt to preserve the health of a community so organized, he would prepare for the oncoming disease, and would even welcome it because he considered the later condition of inoculated immuneness the greatest good.[1]

But to avoid corruption at the election of the first magistrate (for there need be none at the election of senators if their power were properly curtailed), we know of a preventive, applicable at the beginning without waiting for the corrupting process and the ingrowth of unequal conditions. The preventive in question is the plan of making the first magistrate elective or appointive by the popularly elected representatives. This, to be sure, Adams had already argued against, but with insufficient reason, as we have seen.[2] Not

---

[1] The opinion of Governor Bernard, utterly reprobated in his early period (when, too, in 1778, he had laughed at the suggestion of an American peerage, iii., 177–8), he did not consider as yet correct, but expected it before long to be, viz. that "although America is not now (and probably will not be for many years to come) ripe enough for a hereditary nobility, yet it is now capable of a nobility for life" (quoted, iv., 27). The idea that America was gradually becoming fit for a great blessing (that of having a constituted aristocracy and consequently the possibility of perfectly working the balance) was precisely Adams's present opinion.

[2] Above, pp. 91–3. He now refers to it only in this passage: "A hereditary first magistrate at once would, perhaps, be preferable to elections by legislative representatives," vi., 122. He preferred that

entering again into that question, we may go deeper, and simply deny the premises upon which the present argument is based.

Adams asserts, as we have seen, that ours is not the first experiment with elections to the "great offices of state." In a private letter of the same time he repeats: "Experiments of this kind have been so often tried, and so universally found productive of horrors, that there is great reason to dread them" (viii. 465). We, on the contrary, with perfect assurance, may simply assert that ours *is* the first experiment of the sort, and that no previous experience has gone against it. Ours is the first experiment with periodic elections of a chief magistrate and of senators, in addition to representa-

the president or governor should be "appointed" by "the people at large," iv., 584, that is, by direct election, or at least, as he later said, the presidential electors "ought to be chosen by the people at large," ix., 302, which seems to mean that they ought to be elected by simple plurality throughout the whole country.—It may be noted that since Adams's day J. S. Mill also disliked the popular election of the first magistrate, but as a remedy advocated that "the chief magistrate should be appointed avowedly, as the chief minister in a constitutional monarchy is virtually, by the representative body," *Representative Government*, 250; *cf. Dissertations*, iii., 78. And the French republic is now organized in this way, French experience having shown that a popularly elected first magistrate, being regarded as preëminently *the* representative of the whole people—at the head, too, of a large standing army—was always too strong for the legislature, whose members were only representatives, individually, of fractions of the people. It may be remembered that in our country Jackson set up the pretension to be such "a direct representative of the American people" (Richardson's *Messages and Papers of the Presidents*, iii., 90, *cf.* ii., 648), although here our system of indirect election enabled Calhoun to retort that "he never received a vote from the American people," *Works*, ii., 417; and also, luckily, he had no imposing standing army under his command. Yet Jackson had with him the authority of Hamilton, Elliot's *Debates*, ii., 253, and Wilson, *ib.*, 505, *cf.* 448 ("the man of the people"), in the ratifying conventions; and in Congress in 1796, of T. Bradbury, Benton's *Abridgment*, i., 666B, and W. Smith, *Annals of 4th Congress*, col.

tives. There have been, and still are, small primitive states—some of the cantons of Switzerland are examples —where the head men and other officers were elected annually, but where there were no representatives nor senators, although there were councillors, the assembly being primary. And so far as the experience of those peoples can be invoked, it was favorable for the success of our experiment. No experience had cast doubt upon the likelihood of its success, for want of any previous experiment with its peculiar features. Adams's own historical review of the causes of the decay of republics, always found the trouble in the ill-balanced arrangement of the powers and the confusion of the departments, never in the elective feature of the higher offices, except only in certain countries where those elections were entirely different from ours. The "long miseries, wars, and carnage," which we have seen him cite,[1] in "Bohemia,

442; and, too, of Story, *Commentaries*, § 882. Also that the governor was to be the representative of the whole people, was declared in the Address to their Constituents, of the Massachusetts convention after drafting the constitution of 1780, written by Samuel Adams (Wells' *S. Adams*, iii., 94, 95). It would, of course, be more correct to say that the governor or president, the executive chief, is not a representative of the people at all, but their commissioned officer. Election is not sufficient to make a representative, else our village constables would be representatives. The essential quality that constitutes a representative is his taking the place of the people he represents, and doing for them what they ought really to do for themselves, but do not merely because they are too numerous and too busy. But the executive chief does work which the people cannot do for themselves, and which they must hire some one, or a few, to do for them. Executive officers or magistrates are properly viewed, not as representatives, but as functionaries. At best, the executive chief may represent the state in intercourse with other states; but never does he represent the people of the state. All this, of course, is said of him *qua* executive. So far as, possessing a veto, he is made a member of the legislative, he may be said to be the representative of the whole people *quoad hoc*.   [1] Above, p. 134.

Poland, Hungary, Sweden, etc.," as proving "chance to be better than choice, and hereditary princes preferable to elective ones," are the only instances he adduces, and they are not to the point. In those countries the elections were not of the senators and of the executive chief for fixed periods and ultimately by the people, but they were by the hereditary senators or nobles, of the king for life, "with very inadequate methods," he acknowledges, "of collecting the votes of the people," though he should have said there were none. "The Americans," he adds, "have hoped that these circumstances might be arranged so as to justify one more experiment of elective executives, as well as senates and representatives" (vi. 121). This new arrangement ought to have shown him that the American experiment did not fall under the disproof furnished by past experience of other arrangements. His desire, therefore, for bridging the intervening period of miseries while the American experiment was disproving itself, by lengthening the terms of offices, was a prodigious blunder, since in so doing the Americans would be resorting to the very feature in the past experiments which caused their failure. His argument that because elections to high offices are an evil, "the less frequently they happen, the less danger" (viii. 464), is specious, but false. It flies in the face of his own principle. His principle is that the greater the office, the greater the inducement to corruption at elections. But the longer the term of office, the greater the office; therefore, the longer the term of office, the greater the inducement to corruption at elections.[1] Contrariwise, the shorter the term of office, the less inducement to corruption at elections.

[1] For instance, to double the length of the term, doubles both the importance of the office and the dis-chance of anyone being elected to it,

Therefore to render elections to high offices innocuous, the only possible way is that of making the terms short —preferably annual, as Adams himself had in his democratic days desired.[1] Lengthening the terms of our governors and state senators, and *a fortiori* of our President and federal Senators, already on the edge

and thus renders it four times more covetable, but as happening only half as often, on the whole twice as harmful.

[1] All this was understood and expounded by the advocates of the Triennial and the opponents of the Septennial Bills in England in 1693, 1716, and 1734: see Cobbett's *Parliamentary History*, vols. v., cols 760, 762, vii., 304, 306-7, 335, 355, ix., 404, 427-31 (by Wynn, that the lesser sum offerable for shorter terms may cut off so many bribe-takers, as to make any bribery useless), 448, 449, 458, 459-63 (by Wyndham, as by Wynn), 469-70 (by Pulteney, who extended the argument to indefinitely long terms, saying "as good an argument may be drawn against electing any new parliament at all; so that I do not know but I may see a proposition made for continuing our seats in this House [of Commons] for life; and after that it may be thought proper to make a law for transmitting them to our heirs"). In the last year the position was tamely disputed, *ib.*, 415-16, 435, 451-2. In America, Hamilton (who in the Convention had remarked that "frequency of elections tended to make the people listless," Elliot's *Debates*, v., 226; *cf.* Jenifer already, *ib.*, 183) later, in 1803, said that considerations like the above reconciled him to short terms, *Works*, viii., 607-8. Jefferson (including rotation): "Experience says, they [elections] must be rendered less interesting by a necessity of change. No foreign power, nor domestic party, will waste their blood and money to elect a person, who must go out at the end of a short period," *Works*, ii., 330. But Adams deliberately shut his eyes to these reasons, which of course are not confined to the terms of "representatives." Of the Roman Senate, after the expulsion of the Kings, he says: "It was not its *permanency*, but its *omnipotence*, its being *unlimited*, *unbalanced*, *uncontrolled*, that occasioned the abuse; and this is precisely what we contend for, that power is always abused when unlimited and unbalanced, whether it be permanent or temporary," vi., 72-3. He fails to see that a body of men, however great the power entrusted to it, is not uncontrolled if it be subject to renewal by election at short intervals. And the same, of course, is true in the case of a single man. We have already seen Livy's testimony to the Roman view on this subject.

of being too long,[1] instead of alleviating the transition
to hereditary tenure, would merely hasten the end by
rendering the transition unendurable.[2]

In 1790, in the *Discourses on Davila*, dealing mostly
with the federal government, it may be said that
Adams almost went wild in praise of inequality and of
emulation, in exaltation of aristocracy, and in declaim-
ing against factions or parties, which, he once says, in
presidential elections, would divide the nation "into
two nations" (vi. 254). These *Discourses* appeared
currently in the newspapers, and aroused so much
hostility that the publication was discontinued. He

[1] Indeed the wonder evoked by the success of our experiment, is not
properly that we have got along with elective first magistrates and
senators, but that we have got along with these officers elected for such
long terms.

[2] Already in 1787, unlike Jefferson, Adams preferred that the President should be "chosen again and again as long as he lives," viii., 464.
And still in 1815 he did not approve the practice, introduced by "Washington and Jefferson," and on the point of being followed by Madison,
of the President retiring after eight years, x., 181.—We have recently
been taught by the Italian historian Ferrero, in his *The Greatness and
Decline of Rome*, American ed., vol. iv., p. 134, that the change of the
Roman government in 27 B.C. when much power was heaped upon
Augustus and he was made "princeps" for ten years, this title did not
then mean what is now meant in Europe by "prince," but what is
meant in America by "president." But in Rome the "president" soon
became the "prince" proper. And so we may believe that, the process
already having begun of deferring all sorts of authority to the President,
if the presidential term of office be extended, or the incumbents frequently re-elected, the American "president" will approach more and
more to the European "prince." Concurrently with this will go an
increase of his salary (and this word itself will be disused)—probably it
will be effected through perquisites, which have already been begun in
traveling allowances and the use of a war vessel as a yacht. As for the
governors, it is pleasant to think that annual elections have continued
in Adams's own State for a hundred and thirty years without any sign
of a desire to change. Possibly the small importance attached to state-
hood has contributed somewhat to this result.

now seems to have come to his senses somewhat. He
stood on the defensive. Even while composing the
Discourses, he privately defended himself from one
charge, but repeated the substantial part that gave
offense. "I deny," he wrote, "an attachment to
monarchy, and I deny that I have changed my principles since 1776," though claiming progress through increased experience and reflection." I am," he resumed,
"a mortal and irreconcilable enemy to monarchy," by
which he evidently meant simple or absolute monarchy.
"I am no friend to hereditary limited monarchy in
America," knowing it to be "unattainable and impracticable"; nor, he declared, would he "scarcely be for it,
if it were." "I am," he continued, "for having all
three branches elected at stated periods, and these
elections, I hope, will continue until the people shall be
convinced that fortune, providence, or chance, call it
which you will, is better than election. If the time
should come when corruption shall be added to intrigue
and manœuvre in elections, and produce civil war,
then, in my opinion, chance will be better than choice
for all but the House of Representatives" (ix. 566).
A year later he wrote to Jefferson: "If you suppose
that I have, or ever had, a design or desire of attempting to introduce a government of King, Lords, and
Commons, or in other words, an hereditary executive,
or an hereditary senate, either into the government of
the United States or that of any individual State, you
are wholly mistaken. There is not a thought expressed
or intimated in any public writing or private letter, and
I may safely challenge all mankind to produce such
a passage, and quote the chapter and verse."[1] True, he

[1] VIII., 507. Many years afterward, in 1813, again to Jefferson: "I
will forfeit my life, if you can find one sentiment in my Defense of the

never advocated the immediate introduction of monarchy and hereditary aristocracy into America, or against the will of the people. He was no Tory, no dreamy supporter of the Bishop of Osnaburg. The fact remains, however, that he had looked forward to it with pleasurable contemplation, that his spirit leaned toward it. He characterized limited monarchies as "the best species" of republican governments (iv. 558). He despaired, if the defective balance of the Senate, left uncorrected, should destroy the present form of our government, of introducing in its place a "better limited-monarchy" (vi. 434). In his reviews of past history he always reprobated the substitution of a democratical republic for an absolute monarchy, wishing that instead it had been amended into a limited monarchy.[1] And he fell into the habit of using "king," and even "crown," for "executive magistrate."[2] Even for America he was a determined advocate of the elective principle only in the case of the house of representatives. In the other two branches he admitted the coming necessity of the hereditary principle, and recommended its adoption when the proper time should arrive. Had he lived till the advent of that time, or had that time arrived during his life, he would have advocated its actual adoption. Had the monarchists at any time had a chance of success, he must have ranged himself on their side, in advocacy of

Constitutions, or the Discourses on Davila, which, by a fair construction, can favor the introduction of hereditary monarchy or aristocracy into America," x., 54.

[1] In Rome the happiest period was under the Kings, vi., 73; the Romans did not well in overthrowing the monarchy, they ought to have limited it, 60, or later have restored it limited, iv., 533. So of the Florentines, v., 68, *cf.* 23. Such advice he gave to the French, vi., 252.

[2] *E. g.* iv., 371; 398; later commented on, vi., 492.

the cause. It was, therefore, by no means an unjustifiable use of language for his opponents to class him as a monarchist.

The wonder is, that a man with his alien views,[1] and so bold in expressing them, could ever have reached the Presidency in a democratic nation.[2] He had, however, for several years kept silence on the subject. In his inaugural address he reassured the people that he had never objected to the Constitution on account of the executive and Senate not being more permanent, asserting with perfect truth that he had never "entertained a thought of promoting any alteration in it, but such as the people themselves, in the course of their experience, should see and feel to be necessary or expedient, and by their representatives in Congress and the state legislatures, according to the Constitution itself, adopt and ordain" (ix. 106–7). Thus his fundamental constitutional democracy, of the people being the source of all government, stood him in good stead, while he kept from view the right he accorded them of erecting hereditary rulers for all future generations.[3]

We must remember, too, that Adams was not the only one who held views with a monarchical tendency.

[1] To which a patriotic American might have applied this passage from the Roman Cicero, when it was brought to light: "Facile patior non esse nos *transmarinis* nec *importatis* artibus eruditos, sed genuinis domesticisque virtutibus," *De Re Publica*, ii., § 29.

[2] Only a year before, at Lexington, an effigy of Jay was guillotined from whose neck was suspended a copy of Adams's *Defense of the Constitutions:* J. C. Hamilton's *History of the Republic*, vi., 197.

[3] But in the same address he could not refrain from again hinting at his favorite idea, warning the people that if elections become corrupt and fall under foreign influence, then "candid men will acknowledge, that, in such cases, choice would have little advantage to boast of over lot or chance," ix., 108.

In their private correspondence, or behind the closed
doors of the conventions, Jay, Hamilton, Gouverneur
Morris, and less-known leaders, such as Read and
McClurg, had recommended immediate introduction
of life tenure (or during good behavior) for the presidency and senatorship, with absolute veto in the hands
of the executive magistrate.[1] Hamilton, who condemned Adams's writings for their indiscretion, and
boasted of not publishing his own want of faith in the
new government and admiration for the British form
"in Dan and Bersheba,"[2] in the Convention had given
his "sentiments of the best form of government—not as
a thing attainable by us, but as a model which we ought
to approach as near as possible," praising the British
Constitution as the "best form"[3] or as "the best model
the world ever produced,"[4] and proposing an extremely
centralized scheme, which was "toned as high as
possible"[5] and went as far "in order to attain stability
and permanency," that is, in the direction of monarchy
and aristocracy, "as republican principles will admit"[6]
—keeping within them by making the standing executive and senate elective and impeachable,[7]—and which
he thought the people, though then too prejudiced to

[1] Jay, (but with definite term for the "governor-general"), in a letter
to Washington, Jan., 1787, *Correspondence*, iii., 227. Hamilton, *Works*,
i., 358, Elliot's *Debates*, i., 179, 422-3, (v., 203, 205). Morris: senate
for life, *ib.*, v., 271 (i., 475), president during good behavior, v., 325,
absolute veto, 429. Read: senators to be appointed by the executive
during good behavior, *ib.*, 167, 242 (i., 448), approves Hamilton's plan,
v., 256 (i., 461). McClurg: executive during good behavior, *ib.*, v., 325,
327. Even Rufus King did not mind this, *ib.*, 342.

[2] According to Jefferson, *Works*, ix., 99-100.

[3] In the brief of his speech, *Works*, i., 357.

[4] In the speech as reported, Elliot's *Debates*, i., 421, *cf.* v., 202, 203.

[5] Elliot's *Debates*, v., 244.   [6] *Ib.*, v., 203, *cf.* i., 422.

[7] *Ib.*, v., 204, i., 422, and later, *Works*, viii., 607, *cf.* vi., 329.

accept it, might before long (especially in the event of a war[1]) desire, in view of the great progress already made and still going on "in the public mind," the people already showing signs of beginning to be "tired of an excess of democracy."[2] He there had "acknowledged himself not to think favorably of republican government" and to dislike the plan then under way of adoption, which was too democratic for him, being "but pork still, with a little change of sauce," but which, nevertheless, he intended to support "as better than nothing,"[3]—which, in fact, he did advocate in the New York ratifying convention and in *The Federalist* (with arguments like those of a lawyer pleading a case he does not believe in[4]), but for which after its adoption he

[1] *Cf.* Morris's account, Sparks's *Morris*, iii., 217, 261.

[2] Elliot's *Debates*, v., 204 (*cf.* 202); i., 423.

[3] *Ib.*, v., 244; i., 423 (*cf.* v., 206 n.); v., 517.

[4] Often inconsistently with his first position. In the constitutional Convention he had said the central power would either swallow up the State powers or be swallowed up by them, since "two sovereignties cannot coëxist within the same limits," Elliot's *Debates*, v., 202. In the New York ratifying convention he praised the balance between the national and State governments, *ib.*, ii., 257–8, and declared sophistical the proposition "that two supreme powers cannot act together," each in a distinct field, 355–6, *cf.* 362. Here he shows conversion to a truer position, probably under the influence of Madison (see *The Federalist*, Nos. 39 and 46). But he behaved differently on another point. In the constitutional Convention he had not actually proposed, yet had recommended, abolition of the State governments, Elliot's *Debates*, v., 202, 212, *cf.* 220 (and his plan practically did do that in its articles 10 and 11, *ib.*, i., 180, and art. viii. of the fuller draft, *ib.*, v., 589); but when in the ratifying convention Lansing referred to his argument, he vehemently contradicted the charge of inconsistency, and a dispute ensued which lasted the rest of that day and much of the next, *ib.*, ii., 376.—Even his admirer Story wrote of one of Hamilton's arguments in *The Federalist* (No. 84): "It is rather the argument of an able advocate, than the reasoning of a constitutional statesman," *Commentaries*, § 1857. Also Maine noticed the captiousness of some of his arguments, *Popular Government*, p. 212. And Jefferson felt that the author did

showed little respect both in the free way he construed
and violated it in public and in the contemptuous
language he used of it in private.[1] This same Hamilton
afterwards, in 1792, publicly denied having in the
Convention opposed the Constitution as too republican,
or having "advocated the British monarchy as the
perfect standard to be approached as nearly as the
people could be made to bear,"[2] and after his views
in the Convention were published by Callender[3] in
1798, quibbled that the condition "during good behavior," with liability to impeachment, gave to the
offices "a responsible and temporary or defeasible
tenure," and again asserted a falsehood in declaring
that his final plan, the draft of which he had given to
Madison, had assigned to the office of President a
duration "no greater than for three years,"[4] the pub-

not always concur in the opinions he was defending; but without distinguishing between Hamilton and Madison, *Works*, ii., 506 (quoted
by Madison, *Writings*, iv., 314).

[1] To his friend Morris he wrote of the Constitution as "a frail and
worthless fabric," *Works*, J. C. Hamilton's ed., vi., 529–30, again "so
frail a system," 536. (*Cf.* Jefferson's report of his calling it "a shilly
shally thing, of mere milk and water . . . only good as a step to something better," *Works*, ix., 122, *cf.* 167, vi., 95, vii., 390.) Morris, who
wrote of himself that "in adopting a republican form of government,
I not only took it as a man does his wife, for better for worse, but what
few men do with their wives, I took it knowing all its bad qualities,"
Sparks's *Morris*, iii., 181 (*cf.* Elliot's *Debates*, v., 556), also wrote of
Hamilton that he "detested" democracy as leading to despotism,
"hated republican government," confounding it with democracy and
believing it "radically defective," and "disliked" the Constitution,
because of its republicanism; but that "he heartily assented" to it
"because he considered it as a bond, which might hold us together for
some time," Sparks's *Morris*, 260, 261.

[2] *Works*, Lodge's ed., vi., 328–9.

[3] In *Sketches of the History of the United States*, 83–7.

[4] In the *Letter* to Pickering, 1803, *Works*, Lodge's ed., viii., 608. For
Madison's reference to this, see his *Writings*, iv., 177. Possibly reliance

lication of the draft since showing that this was the tenure assigned to the representatives, and that to the President and Senators it still assigned tenure during good behavior.[1] In short, as Adams's son afterward remarked of these men, "like the priests of Egypt, they had a revelation for the multitude, and a secret for the initiated."[2]

Suggestions of this double dealing could not help leaking out and arousing suspicions. Probably, the comparison of such secretiveness and prevarication with the frankness and honesty of Adams, contributed to recommend him to the people at large.[3] They

on this or similar statements was what induced Marshall to write that Hamilton "is understood to have avowed opinions in the convention favorable to a system in which the executive and senate, though elective, were to be rather more permanent than they were rendered in that which was actually proposed," and to add in a foot-note that "it has been published by the enemies of Mr. Hamilton that he was in favor of a president and senate who should hold their offices during good behavior," as though this were a calumny! *Life of Washington*, v., 353.

[1] Elliot's *Debates*, v., 205, 585, 587.—Fenno's paper, *The Gazette of the United States*, was Hamilton's unavowed mouthpiece. Therein were published, anonymously, opinions outstripping Adams's. Thus in one number (March, 1790): "Take away thrones and crowns from among men and there will soon be an end of all dominion and justice. . . . The people of the United States may probably be induced to regard and obey the laws without requiring the experiment of courts and titled monarchs. In proportion as we become populous and wealthy must the tone of the government be strengthened" (quoted from S. E. Forman's *Political Activities of Philip Freneau*, 42–3).

[2] J. Q. Adams's *Review of the Works of Fisher Ames*, Boston, 1809, Preface, p. 6 (reprinted from *The Boston Patriot*).

[3] Added, of course, to his previous services, and to the opinion that it was now, after Virginia's, the turn of Massachusetts.—In 1792 Madison told Washington that for his successor Adams's "monarchical views, which he had not concealed," put him out of the question, but that Jay would be "extremely dissatisfactory on several accounts," one being that "by many he was believed to entertain the same obnoxious principles with Mr. Adams, and at the same time would be less open,

distrusted those others: they knew not what under-
hand machinations they might be contriving, to circum-
vent the popular will, and to bring in a different kind
of government against the popular desire. But Adams
they knew would fight in the open, and they expected
he would rely solely on the weapon of persuasion,
though in this respect he disappointed them by his
support of the Alien and Sedition Acts. In his mouth
at least, the pledge given in his inaugural address "to
support the Constitution of the United States"—
"until it shall be altered by the judgments and the
wishes of the people, expressed in the mode prescribed
in it" (ix. 109, 110)—had a religious meaning. The
fact of his election, however, proves that the American
people, formed in colonies from a monarchical parent
state, were not yet so thoroughly democratic as they
later became. But they were already in the process,
and, during a brief period of reaction after the French
republican excesses, Adams got his one election in the
nick of time. Then he was swept aside into private
life, to mourn over the transitoriness of personal greatness, and yet himself, almost alone among the revolutionary heroes, in fulfillment of his own theory of natural
aristocracy by birth, to found a family that should
continue high in the councils of his country.

and therefore more successful in propagating them," *Writings*, i., 558–9.
Then, however, Jefferson wrote: "The strength of his [Adams's] personal worth and his services will, I think, prevail over the demerit of
his political creed," *Works*, iii., 494. *Cf*. Ford's ed., v., 362, where
Adams seems to be the person referred to as "the honestest man of the
party."

19

THE THIRD PERIOD

CHAPTER XIX

RECONCILEMENT WITH REPUBLICANISM

NOW gradually came in, in Adams's long career, a third period,—a period of calm and contentment. He grows more reconciled with our State and Federal governments as they are. He becomes convinced that after all they are more permanent than he had anticipated. Experience has confirmed them. "Say, if you will," he wrote in 1808, "that in such an empire as the British, it is necessary that the executive and the senate should be hereditary, because elections to these powers would totally corrupt the nation, produce a civil war, and raise a military despotism at the first trial. But, in an experiment of twenty years, we have not yet found such dangers among us" (vi. 529). He now speaks of the two hereditary branches as poisons, to be used as antidotes for each other. "A proper equilibrium may be formed between elective branches as well and perhaps better than between hereditary ones. And our American balance has succeeded hitherto as well as that in England, and much better than that in Holland. May it long endure!"[1] "There never has been a system of hereditary nobility rationally digested

[1] VII., 348 n., in 1809.

290

in any nation. That in England has been accidentally brought the nearest to a rational theory."[1] He returns to his early democraticalness. "I know of nothing more desirable in society than the abolition of all hereditary distinctions. . . . There is nothing more irrational, absurd, or ridiculous, in the sight of philosophy than the idea of hereditary kings and nobles. . . . A government, a mixed government, may be so organized, I hope, as to preserve the liberty, equality, and fraternity of the people without any hereditary ingredient in its composition. Our nation has attempted it, and if any people can accomplish it, it must be this; and may God Almighty prosper and bless them!"[2] Not only officially in 1800 he expressed desire that our present Constitution should be delivered "unimpaired to a free, prosperous, happy, and grateful posterity" (ix. 148), but he undertook to defend it from amendment in 1808,[3] and privately in 1819 and 1824 "devoutly" repeated "with Father Paul, '*Esto perpetua.*'"[4]

[1] VI., 300 n., in 1813. He here adds, most astonishingly: "Nature produces nobilities in all nations, but those very nobilities will never suffer themselves to be disciplined or modified or methodized but by despots."

[2] X., 268, in 1817. He here even admits some doubt as to the theoretical impropriety of universal suffrage, having acquired some confidence in the people. "I believe with you," he wrote to Rush in 1808, "'a republican government,' while the people have the virtues, talents, and love of country necessary to support it, 'the best possible government to promote the interest, dignity, and happiness of man,' " ix., 602. The danger of foreign influence at the elections of Presidents, to which he still admits "our form of government, inestimable as it is, exposes us more than any other," he now thinks can be averted by "our inflexible neutrality," 277.

[3] In a *Review* of Hillhouse's propositions, only published in his *Works*, vi., 527–50.

[4] X., 386, 413. The allusion seems to be a reminiscence of Blackstone, *Commentaries*, i., 145, which has again been echoed by Story, *Commen-*

Meanwhile he renewed his friendship with Jefferson, and tried to belittle the differences of political opinion between them[1]; while his son, carefully trained in politics under his eye, joined the Republicans.

Yet he still sticks to his guns, theoretically.[2] Our governments are good and lasting, because they are aristocratical, and monarchical,[3]—they do satisfy his theory. He so defines aristocracy as to include everything but the lowest stratum of society. "The moment you give knowledge to a democrat," he now says, "you make him an aristocrat" (vi. 516). An "aristocrat" is "every man who can command or influence two votes; one beside his own."[4] By "democrats" he means "exclusively those who are simple units, who have but one vote in society" (515, cf. 511)—who simply belong

---

taries, § 516. But it had been used, of the Massachusetts constitution, by Parsons in *The Essex Result*, Parsons' *Parsons*, 364, and, of "the New Sovereign Republic of America," by Th. Pownall, *Memorial to the Sovereigns of America*, London, 1783, p. 52. Blackstone himself probably got it from Johnson's *Father Paul Sarpi*, in his *Lives of Sundry Eminent Persons*.

[1] Of course, the differences were deep. Adams was conservative, dreading innovations, cf. ix., 379, 410 (in 1776), vi., 489, and "the spirit of leveling," ix., 393; he preferred an excess of confidence to an excess of diffidence toward rulers, 404, cf. 542, vi., 181, and tyranny to anarchy, vi., 151; and in 1801 he did not like the prospect of Jefferson's "tempestuous sea of liberty," ix., 98. (Yet in his first period he had quoted with approval "a saying of Macchiavel," that "while the mass of the people is not corrupted, tumults do no hurt," iv., 57.) They "agreed perfectly that the many should have a full, fair, and perfect representation," 464; but Jefferson wished them to be represented in all the departments and branches; Adams, in only one branch. Jefferson wished the executive and the senate to be dependent upon the people; Adams, to be independent, and placed his reliance on their neutralizing each other by their equal strength.

[2] Especially in his *Letters* to John Taylor, 1814, only published in his *Works*, vi., 447–521.   [3] *Cf.* vi., 471–2, 530–1; 470.

[4] VI., 456; similarly 451, 457, 462.

to the *demos* and have no *kratos* at all! Therefore
demagogues and popular orators—John Cade and
Wat Tyler, Callender and Paine, Shays and Fries—are
aristocrats: "mobs never follow any but aristocrats"
(508). Literally, then, "democracy" is more than ever
identified with ochlocracy; but in its usual acceptance,
it is exalted into aristocracy, so that his words are
equivocal when he ecstatically proclaims that "democracy must be respected; democracy must be honored;
democracy must be cherished; democracy must be an
essential, an integral part of the sovereignty, and *have
a control over the whole government*" (477-8). Every
government, we have seen him assert, except simple
democracy (which does not exist) is representative
government (469). He further says: Every representative government is an aristocracy; and he finds "a
contradiction in terms" between representation and
democracy (462). He thus dispenses with the hereditary feature. In his middle period itself he had occasionally said—and wrongly, as we have seen—that it
matters little whether the powers that are or are not
properly balanced be temporary, permanent, or hereditary, the essential feature, which gives the name to
the government, being the location and the amount of
power, not its duration.[1] He now emphasizes this.
"Hereditary powers," he says, "and peculiar privileges
enter in no degree into the definition of aristocracy"
(vi. 529). Authority in one man, "as long as it lasts,
may be called a monarchical authority with great
propriety, by any man who is not afraid of a popular
clamor."[2] In his middle period that indifference to

---

[1] VI., 429; *cf.* 73 already cited, also the definition of "king" merely as
"a first magistrate possessed exclusively of the executive power," iv., 371

[2] VI., 473,—or who is not afraid of committing a solecism. All

the duration of the power had rather taken the form: Why not, then, have long terms—for life—hereditary? He now denies that. "I had nothing to do with the ecclesiastical establishment in England. . . . Nor had I anything to do with the hereditary quality, superadded to the monarchical and aristocratical powers in England. . . . It is true that, in my apology [the *Defense*], I expressed in strong terms my admiration of the English constitution; but I meant no more of it than was to the purpose of my argument; that is, the division and union of powers in our American constitutions, which were, indeed, so far, imitations of it. My argument had no more to do with hereditary descent than it had with the Church or the Bank of England" (489). Unfortunately he had, unnecessarily to be sure, gone out of his way to mean more of it than was required for his defense of the American constitutions— to include that very hereditary quality as a model for our future revisions.[1] However, he has now discarded

authority in one man is monarchical authority. Some authority in one man is not monarchical authority. Even all executive power in one man is not such. All legislative power (meaning also the primary) is, because it includes all the rest. Every officer in a government has some authority. "Regal" and "monarchical" are not synonymous. If the term "monarch" is, through force of habit, conventionally applied to limited kings whose predecessors may have had some right to it, there is no reason why it should be transferred to a new line of limited presidents. "Limited monarchy," is really a contradiction in terms. "Limited kingdom" would be more proper.

[1] Some time now he intercalated in his *Diary:* "It appeared to me then, as it has done ever since, that there is a state of society in which a republican government is the best, and in America, the only one which ought to be adopted or thought of, because the morals of the people, and the circumstances of the country, not only can bear it, but require it. But, to several of the great nations of Europe, kings appeared to me to be as necessary as any government at all," iii., 154. He forgot he had looked ahead and advised preparing for the day, which he would wel-

that superadded quality as foreign alike to his subject and to America.

The beauty of this last period may be well brought out by contrasting it with the course of another representative Federalist. Hamilton, after vainly striving to stir up civil and foreign war, and becoming Adams's arch-enemy, was early killed in a duel. There remained for a while, as most eloquent among his followers, Fisher Ames.

From Massachusetts, and so Adams's own "countryman," Fisher Ames in 1798 defended "president Adams's book,"[1] and afterwards continued to vent Adams's opinions, without further acknowledgment. He, too, held that British freedom and security arose "from the distinct existence and political power of three orders"; that all enduring governments are mixed governments, and all simple governments are despotisms,[2] and that of all simple governments pure democracy (or "mobocracy") is the worst—an "illuminated hell," "a Briareus," "a Cerberus,"—but the least durable, and if there be a worse, "the certain forerunner of that," being ordained by its nature to pass into military despotism.[3] In our country he recognized the need of a large democratic ingredient and the impossibility of voluntarily setting up a mixed monarchy, and considered the Constitution "as good, or very nearly as good, as our country could bear"; but, himself turned out of office with his party, on the one hand

come, when conditions in America would be like those in Europe and require the same kind of government.

[1] Ames's *Works*, Boston, 1809, p. 95.   [2] *Ib.*, 475; 382.

[3] *Ib.*, 96, 382, 400, 419, 432. No democracy is free, 213; a government by popular passions, 200; never failing to excite, never restraining, the passions, 432; destructive of morals, 415, *cf.* 179; the rule of the French Kings was never so bad, 243–4.

alleging that the Federalists were "essentially democratic," that they had never thought of introducing
mixed monarchy,[1] and that if this government ever
should fall, they would seek to replace it with "a new
republican system,"[2] and on the other hand assimilating
with French Jacobins the Jeffersonian Republicans,[3]
who, while falsely accusing their opponents of desire
for mixed monarchy, themselves aimed at introducing
pure democracy, he feared that these would destroy our
government and lead to the substitution of an absolute
monarchy, though without the name, rendering the
British system forever impossible, this revolution pro-
ceeding "in exactly the same way, but not with so
rapid a pace, as that of France."[4]

While the scholarch was sinking back into peace with
the Republicans, it is amusing to see this bumptious
scholar, most scurrilous of "respectable" writers, firing
at them his borrowed, but overheated, shot.

[1] *Ib.*, 383. *Cf.* Marshall, in the Virginia ratifying convention: "We
idolize democracy. . . . We prefer this system [the proposed govern-
ment] to any monarchy. . . . We admire it because we consider it a
well-regulated democracy"—regulated, remember, by the aristocracy,
Elliot's *Debates*, iii., 222.   [2] Ames's *Works*, 227.

[3] Fire-eating like salamanders, poison-sucking like toads, venomous
like serpents, *ib.*, 98. Their managers however, despisers of democracy,
225; "noble lords of Virginia and the South," who, like the senators of
Venice, are for rotation in office, to divide power among themselves,
"in the genuine spirit of an oligarchy," 487.

[4] *Ib.*, 424–9, 437.

CHAPTER XX

HIS TYPICAL SCHEME OF GOVERNMENT

WHAT, then, was Adams's theory of government during this last period? He did not rewrite it: he had retired. But we may attempt to reconstruct it; and this reconstruction will supply an opportunity further to test the value of his theorizing.

The typical scheme of government deducible from Adams's surviving principles would be something like this:—Divide all society into two classes. In the upper put all men possessing a certain amount of property, all educated men (who have, say, received a university degree), all men who have distinguished themselves in any notable manner. It may be thought that, to carry out Adams's idea of aristocracy by birth, all the descendants of such persons would have to be included. Here, however, Adams was never clear; for he did not disclose his opinions concerning primogeniture or other kinds of heritage, although he probably inclined to the former (cf. iv. 577). If all descendants of all who once belong to the upper class were left in it, unless positively disqualified by proved misdemeanor or squalid poverty, the class might grow to a size that would defeat its object; for nobility is weakened by dilution. But to confine it to eldest sons would be no better, unless property were also confined to eldest sons, and then the membership in this class would follow, as at first, the ownership of property. It would seem, then, necessarily to be confined to property and merit, birth following property. As Adams himself said, "birth and wealth are commonly so entangled together" as to be with difficulty separated for comparison (vi. 505). And when the class is thus confined, there would be no need to confine descent of wealth to eldest sons: it may be allowed to take its course. This class, then, should have the right to vote for representatives in the senate. Beside them, all the rest of the male grown-up population should have the right to vote for representatives in the lower house. Moreover, eligibility in the senate should be confined to members of the first class (it might even be confined to an inner circle, of the very wealthy or wise); and eligibility to the lower house, to members of the other class.[1]

Here arises a question which Adams left unmooted. Should members of the upper class be allowed to vote for members of the lower house? In his model, England, this is the case; for, although the actual peers are not voters nor eligible for the House of Commons, yet that part of society whose interest the peers represent in the government, the upper class, containing many nobles too, though not peers, and the so-called gentry, do vote in common with the lower class, and are equally eligible to the latter's House.[2] Adams probably in-

---

[1] Something like this state of things would be brought about, if the scheme were to be carried through of remodeling the British House of Lords by reducing its members to a small number of peers to be elected by the whole body of peers or barons. In this case, it would be a pity to miss the opportunity of trying, in this comparatively small electorate, Hare's plan of proportional representation, which was advocated by Mill, and which is the most perfect, theoretically, that has ever been suggested, having against it only its impracticability in a multitudinous electorate.

[2] This is so much in accordance with British tradition and sentiment that it seems to be included in most schemes of reform like the one referred to in the preceding note. Thus W. C. Macpherson expressly adopts the position that peers who are not elected to their own House shall be eligible to the other, *The Baronage and the Senate*, London, 1893, p. 340. Similarly Lecky, *Democracy and Liberty*, New York ed., 1896, vol. i., p. 462.

tended the same for America; for, as we have seen, he implied that the lower chamber should represent the whole people. But this violates the theoretical scheme, as Adams himself so frequently stated it, of separating the two classes and giving each "equal power to defend themselves" (ix. 570) in a chamber specially representing each. Keeping him strictly to this symmetrical arrangement, we must require that members of the upper class be excluded from voting with, and from representing, the lower class. This would mean that *ipso facto* upon acquiring the requisite property qualification for membership in the upper class, every individual must pass into it from the lower,—that he cannot be excluded by the members above, nor held back by the members below, nor follow his own inclination, except by disposing of his property. By this means, too, a member of the upper class could descend to the lower, unless he were authoritatively distinguished; for distinction once recognized cannot be cast aside, except by forfeiture through misconduct. By merit a man might rise from the lower to the upper class only by some public action recognizing it—of what nature, it would be difficult to prescribe, although it would be something of the legion-of-honor sort.

Wealth, however, would in this scheme be the distinguishing mark of the upper side. Instead of being aristocratic, this scheme would be plutocratic, contrary to Adams's own desire; for he complained that unless birth gives power, the only distinction left would be wealth, and this, unchecked, would lead to venality and corruption (*cf.* vi. 271). But he would have difficulty to point out a case in which birth regularly counted unless accompanied by wealth, where the result has been good; for nothing has been more dispiriting, and nothing more absurd, than a poverty-stricken peerage—a set of privileged beggars. In England itself no one is raised to the peerage unless sufficiently wealthy, as is said, to support the dignity.

In regard to the total exclusion of the upper class from the lower house, we may remark that this, instead of weakening, would really strengthen the position of that class in their own upper house. When they have a share also in the lower house, the very unfairness (not to speak of the superfluousness) of their double position leads to its own undoing; for the people will always claim, and the lordlings may finally admit, that as they are already represented in the lower house (especially if they be predominant there), their will need not be again attended to as expressed in another house. But if the upper class have no share in the lower house, not to heed their representatives in their own house would entirely exclude them from a share in affairs of state, and this they would never submit to, nor would the people demand. It is not believable that the British House of Lords would have sunk to its present position of inferiority, if the class it represents had not already in the lower house the power they desired. In fact, this class recently sought to regain some of the lost position for the upper House only because their power in the lower was no longer satisfactory.

Lastly, as to the chief executive magistrate, this officer ought to be elected either by the two chambers together or by the whole people. In the former case, the members of the chambers, if voting jointly instead of concurrently, must bear some determinate proportion to each other, according either to the numbers of the two classes, or to their total wealth, or to a medium between both; or be simply equal. In either case, this magistrate might be supposed—not rightly, indeed, to represent the whole people, yet—to have been chosen to look after the interests of the whole people, and therefore be expected to be impartial.

As for duration of offices, there is nothing in this plan itself to determine it. Each class might be left to regulate the period of its own representatives. The upper class would probably grant a longer lease, since their smaller numbers give them closer intercourse with and stronger control over their representatives. But both classes together would have to decide upon that of the executive. Of this officer the tenure ought to be affected by the powers accorded him, or conversely. If he be elected annually, there might be no harm in entrusting to him an absolute veto, as Adams laid down in his early plan (iv. 197, 207). But if he be elected for a longer period, the longer it is, the more intolerable such a power would become. The veto power, in fact, should be curtailed the more, the longer the tenure granted. If for life, or hereditary, there should be no veto at all, or a very atrophied one, as in England.

In regard to the negative of the two houses upon each other, it would seem that, unless all new laws are constitutionally of short duration, one of the houses would have to be limited in some way, or be required to yield on some occasions (say on all repeals within a few years after the enactment), or after a certain length of resistance, if the executive chief is on the side of the other. Otherwise one class in the state would be able to block progress or retain a gradually or clandestinely acquired privilege. Merely to give the executive magistrate another negative, would only add to the power of blockade, not to the power of breaking through; while little dependence could be placed upon his influence through patronage, the recognized exercise of which only leads to corruption and increase of abuse. Either this magistrate must be given a power of coercion, in conjunction with either of the chambers, a casting vote in favor of one of them, or one of the chambers must have such power over both the other branches. In the latter case, the government would be plutocratic or democratic according to the chamber which has this power. In the former case, the arbiter, elected by both classes, it would at first glance seem, might join the one at one time and the other at another. But both classes would strive against this yielding to the other, and would try to get one of its own members into the office, pledged to side with it always; and the one which first succeeded might fasten its grip upon the power perpetually, remodeling or construing the constitution, if there is one, in its own behoof; for under such a government there would be no appeal to the legislative power of the whole people at once, and even the judiciary could not preserve observance of the original plan, as they would come from one of the classes. Thus this scheme of government is merely a pitting of plutocracy against democracy, with the sure supremacy of one in sight.

Should we, then, make a more evenly three-sided balance, between three classes? Little would be gained, if the third be made merely by another artificial line drawn in the same material, dividing the whole into the very rich, the well-off or middling, and the poor; as the two former would run together against the third. The truth is, past societies have been divided into other classes than those with which Adams dealt and which were ready to his hand. They have developed at times the ecclesiastical, the warrior, and the moneyed classes, distinguished from the remainder, the hand-laborers.

When these distinctions have broken down, and the two former been swallowed up by the third, or where the two former have not grown up and the only distinction evolved is that between the rich and the poor, the three-fold mixed government possible in the former societies is no longer or not yet possible or desirable. Here the alternative is only between plutocracy and democracy, or between either plutocracy or democracy in a narrow sense as the rule of the lower class alone, more distinctively called ochlocracy, and democracy in a wide sense as a government that tries to make no distinction of classes—pantocracy, as it would be more properly called, the true republic. And the last, though imperfectly, was established in our country in approximate agreement with the social and economic conditions of the people; and for its continuance depends upon the continuance of those conditions, that is, upon the non-existence or abeyance of a perceptible distinction between the classes, being doomed in time to give way to plutocracy if the plutocratic element be permitted to increase indefinitely and outweigh the democratic. Adams's scheme, of combining plutocracy and democracy by first separating them and then balancing them by means of an artificial arbiter, is unworkable and worthless.

CHAPTER XXI

SIMILAR VIEWS SINCE HELD BY OTHERS

THIS scheme has not been confined to Adams, or else there would be little utility in examining it so fully. Adams's merit lies in his carrying out logically to the bitter end, laying bare its faultiness, a scheme which others often fall into partially, attracted by a glamour of symmetry, and not going deep enough to disclose its defects, yet far enough to err and to mislead. In Adams it reached its climax, and thereafter its decline was steady.

Even in England Adams's interpretation of the American constitutions seems to have made some impression; for considerations like his were urged in Parliament by Fox in the famous debate over the constitution to be prepared for Canada, the so-called Quebec Bill of 1791. There Fox, entering into a declaration of his political opinions, said he looked upon the aristocracy as "the proper poise of the constitution, the balance that equalized and meliorated the powers of the two other extremes and gave firmness and stability to the whole"; and for that colony he wished to establish an elective council with a higher property qualification both for the electors and the elected than in the case of

the other house, "after the model of the American
constitutions, where the three powers of monarchy,
aristocracy, and democracy, were judiciously blended,
although under different names."[1]   But naturally
Adams's influence was greater and earlier felt in his own
country.

Views similar to his, if not directly borrowed from
his book, which had just been published and quickly
ran through several editions, were frequently presented
in the Convention which in the summer of 1787 framed
our national Constitution.[2]   There, after Randolph,
the proposer of the scheme under discussion, had stated
that the object of the senate was to check and control
the follies of democracy in the other branch,[3] Hamilton
protested against setting a democratic senate to check
a democratic house, and a democratic chief magistrate
to check both.[4]   He declared that society naturally
divides itself into two political divisions—of the few and

[1] Speech of May 11th (*Annual Register*, xxxiii., 134).   On the same
occasion Burke denied that aristocracy can be founded solely on property,
and objected to this proposal as belonging to "a democratical constitution" (*ib.*, 135).   It was, of course, a mixture of a plutocratic and a
democratic constitution.   Political nomenclature will be incomplete
so long as the terms "plutocracy" and "plutocratic" are tabooed.

[2] In the midst of it, June, 1787, Madison wrote from Philadelphia:
"Mr. Adams' book . . . has excited a good deal of attention.   An
edition has come out here, and another is in the press at N. York.
It will probably be much read, . . . and contribute . . . to revive the
predilections of this country for the British Constitution.   Men of
learning find nothing new in it; men of taste many things to criticize;
and men without either, not a few things which they will not understand.
. . .   The book also has merit, and I wish many of the remarks in it
which are unfriendly to republicanism may not receive fresh weight
from the operations of our governments," *Writings*, i., 332.

[3] Elliot's *Debates*, v., 138, 186.

[4] Brief of his speech, *Works*, Lodge's ed., i., 359; *cf.* also Elliot's
Debates, ii., 317.

20

the many, the learned and the ignorant, creditors
and debtors, on the one side "the rich and well-born"
and "the mass of the people" on the other,[1] as inequality of property, which will exist as long as liberty lasts,
constitutes "the great and fundamental distinction of
society"[2]; and he maintained that each of these classes,
if alone dominant, would tyrannize over the other.[3]
Hence his plan, resembling Adams's ideal in all but its
consolidating feature,[4] and based on the same model, the
British:—the separation of the classes in two chambers,
the one immediately derived from the people with
"frequent" (but only triennial) elections, on a broad
basis of suffrage, to act as their representatives,[5] the
other the place for the rich to have their "distinct"
share in the government, holding office "for life, or at
least during good behavior," and over them both an
executive chief, whose office ought to be hereditary,

---

[1] *Works*, i., 359, 357, Elliot's *Debates*, i., 421–2 (v., 202–3), ii., 257.
But he eschewed the word "aristocracy," affecting not to know what was
meant thereby (probably considering the use of it one of Adams's in-
discretions), *ib.*, 256. (So in the New York ratifying convention, where
the idea was introduced by Melancthon Smith, 246–7, with reference to
Adams, 281, and was likewise rejected by Livingston, who said, "we are
all equally aristocrats," because "offices, emoluments, honors, are open
to all," 278, and even anticipated Adams in reducing all others to the
good-for-nothings, 277. For references to "the well-born," see above
p. 47 n.)   [2] Elliot's *Debates*, v., 244.   [3] *Ib.*, 203.

[4] That is, Hamilton applied to the whole country the scheme which
Adams applied to each State. His plan reduced the States to mere
provinces or satrapies. It is given in Elliot's *Debates*, i., 179 (*cf.* 423),
and v., 205; a later, longer, and modified draft, 584–90.

[5] In the plan adopted he reminded Sherman that this branch "was so
formed as to render it particularly the guardians of the poorer orders of
citizens," *ib.*, 244, implying that that amount of democracy ought to
satisfy them. The government of Connecticut, democratic in all its
branches, he urged, had been successful only because it had been controlled from above by the British government and confined to very
simple local affairs.

but at least must be for life, and with the absolute veto
—all forming a government which we have seen him
pronounce "republican" because of the elective features in it, and which, furthermore, he did not consider
"monarchical," because this term contains no reference to "the duration of power."[1] "The best writers
on government," he said in the New York ratifying
convention, without citing any, "have held that representatives should be compounded of persons and property"[2]; and he wished the two chambers to be aimed
respectively at "safety for the people, and energy in
the administration," and to be endowed, the one "with
sensibility," the other "with knowledge and firmness,"
so that "through the opposition and mutual control of
these bodies, the government will reach, in its operations, the perfect balance between liberty and power."[3]
It looks as if Hamilton must have read Adams's first
volume, and have borrowed from it.[4]

[1] *Ib.*, 204. The reasons he assigns for desiring long terms in the two
upper branches, while not going the full length with, diverge but slightly
from, Adams's. He desired them in order to differentiate those branches
from the representatives and give greater stability to the senate and
greater power and interest to the executive, as well as to guard against
foreign influence, *ib.*, i., 422, ii., 301–2, 305. Of the rich and permanent
senators he says: "they will check the unsteadiness" of the popular
branch, "and, as they cannot receive any advantage by a change, they
therefore will ever maintain good government," *ib.*, i., 422 (similarly of
the British House of Lords, that "most noble institution," *ib.*, v., 203);
which amounts to saying: Give the upper class all they desire, and they
will rule well because they cannot get more!—as though bad government consists only in encroaching and grasping at more power, and not
at all in badly using the power already possessed. (Compare Calhoun's
statement, previously quoted, which expresses the idea Hamilton probably had in mind.)   [2] *Ib.*, ii., 237.   [3] *Ib.*, 316.

[4] Adams himself claimed to have influenced the writing of *The Federalist*, iii., 23.—In the New York convention, it may be noticed that, on
the opposite side, M. Smith used some of Adams's ideas to combat the
Constitution, on the ground that the democratic element was not

Such borrowing almost reaches demonstration at least in the case of Gouverneur Morris, whose opinions, both in the Convention and in his writings, follow those of Adams too closely to be accidental. "One interest," also he asserts, "must be opposed to another interest. Vices, as they exist, must be turned against each other." "The rich," as they always have done, will "strive to establish their dominion, and enslave the rest"; and if mixed with the poor, will set up an oligarchy, probably ending in despotism. "The proper security against them" is to "gratify them" and "to form them into a separate interest," in an "aristocratic body," which "should be as independent, and as firm, as the democratic"; and to make it so, "it should be for life," which will also provide the element of permanency, for, "having distinct privileges," this "order of men" "will feel a constant and regular desire to prevent innovations and change"; and they should receive no pay, so as either to be made desirous of office or to be confined to rich men, of whom alone this "branch ought to consist." This body, "he hoped," would "do wrong," "constantly" opposing "the popular will" and "constantly laboring to oppress," so that, being regarded by the people as "the common enemy," it "may unite

sufficiently provided for in the House of Representatives, where, on account of the small membership (only sixty-five at first), it was likely to be crowded out by the "natural aristocracy," or that the legislative powers should be further limited in proportion to this smallness and failure to be "a true picture of the people," *ib.*, ii., 245–9, 281; while, in Virginia, others opposed the Constitution as containing no "real checks" like the English, but only "ideal," *i. e.* delusive ones—Henry, *ib.*, iii., 54, 59, 164–6, 325, 387–8 (evidently following either De Lolme or Adams, see especially 164), Monroe, 219, Grayson, 280, 421,—the last even preferring to it, next to continuance of the Confederation, a system with a president and senate for life and a triennial house of representatives (like Hamilton's), 279, *cf.* 283–4.

them into a steady and constant support of the rights of mankind" and save them "from their most dangerous enemy . . . themselves." It is not wise "to put all these enemies in one body" with the people and there "suffer them to elude the vigilance of observation, by dressing in the popular garb." "By combining, and setting apart, the aristocratic interest, the popular interest will be combined against it. There will be a mutual check and mutual security." "The two forces will then control each other."[1] "The executive magistrate should be the guardian of the people . . . against the great and the wealthy," and therefore (if not hereditary) "he ought to be elected by the people at large—by the freeholders of the country."[2] If he be a hereditary king, there should be opposed to him "the resistance of a hereditary senate, whose members should possess great landed property"; which body itself, to prevent it from becoming oppressive, needs to be checked by the king "on the one hand and by representatives of the people on the other."[3] In our Constitution he desired the executive magistrate should appoint

[1] Elliot's *Debates*, v., 271–2 (i., 475–6), Sparks's *Morris*, ii., 466–7, 470, 475, *cf.* iii., 379, also Madison's account of him, *ib.*, i., 284 (or Elliot's, *Debates*, i., 507).

[2] Elliot's *Debates*, v., 334; 322, 335. Appointment of him by the legislature, the worst, *ib.*, 361, 366. Morris did not mind an admixture of lot, *ib.*, 366.

[3] Sparks's *Morris*, ii., 509, i., 376, *cf.* 350. He was, he told Lafayette, "opposed to democracy from regard to liberty," *ib.*, i., 314, *cf.* 315. And, differing with Jefferson, he thought "distinctions of order" ought not to be annihilated, *ib.*, 313. The French king should have the absolute veto, *ib.*, ii., 496, *cf.* 70–1, iii., 482, and the whole executive power, including war-declaring, treaty-making, and all appointments, *ib.*, ii., 501–2, *cf.* 73. He endeavored to show some French deputies "the absurdity of their suspensive veto and the probable tyranny of their single chamber," *ib.*, i., 323.

the Senators,[1] and that such appointments should be used as "loaves and fishes" wherewith to "bribe the demagogues"—and in the "captivating prospect" of becoming Senators for life he saw "a noble bait" for inducing the popular leaders to accept the new Constitution.[2] The Constitution finally adopted, which he himself wrote out in its finished form,[3] he advocated as a whole, considering it not so bad as the old (in which the Congress he regarded as composed of ambassadors[4]). He had done his best to make it good, and left it "with those who should come after us to take counsel from experience, and exercise prudently the power of amendment, which we had provided"; but refused to collaborate with Hamilton in writing *The Federalist.*[5] Associating much with the nobility abroad, he later became mostly aristocratic[6] in his sympathies. Adams sincerely wished the rich and the poor to balance each other, trying to provide a balancer for the purpose. These men made use of his views to prevent the poor from overbalancing the rich and thereby to give the rich a chance ultimately to overbalance the poor.[7]

In the Convention also lesser lights borrowed from

[1] He here adopted one feature, in default of the principal, in the composition of the English House of Lords, and thus came nearer even than Adams to the common model. *Cf.* Wilson in the Pennsylvania ratifying convention, Elliot's *Debates,* ii., 479.

[2] Elliot's *Debates,* v., 272 (i., 476).

[3] Sparks's *Morris,* iii., 323, *cf.* i., 284. He was on the Committee of Revision, Elliot's *Debates,* i., 295.   [4] Elliot's *Debates,* i., 476.

[5] Sparks's *Morris,* iii., 339, *cf.* 181 already quoted. But at one time he was opposed to making amendments, *ib.,* 174.

[6] In the strict sense of the term, *ib.,* iii., 172, 218, 238.

[7] Morris wished the suffrage for the representatives to be confined to freeholders, ostensibly to prevent rich "aristocrats" from getting undue influence by buying the votes of the populace, Elliot's *Debates,* v., 385, 386, *cf.* Sparks's *Morris,* iii., 172; but really to protect the landed aristocracy against the commercial plutocrats and democrats.

Adams's candle. Baldwin, of Georgia, a State in which
Adams claimed to have had some influence, said that
"the second branch" (the Senate) "ought to be the
representation of property, and that, in forming it,
therefore, some reference ought to be had to the relative
wealth of their constituents, and to the principles"
(put into it by Adams) "on which the senate of Massachusetts was constituted," where "the first branch
represents the people, and the second its property."[1]
Butler "urged that the second branch ought to represent the States according to their property."[2] Davie
"seemed to think that wealth or property ought to be
represented in the second chamber; and numbers in the
first branch."[3] Charles Cotesworth Pinckney "proposed that no salary should be allowed" to the Senators; for, "as this (the senatorial) branch was meant to
represent the wealth of the country, it ought to be
composed of persons of wealth, and if no allowance was
to be made, the wealthy alone would undertake the
service."[4] Mercer wished the contention to be, not
"between the aristocracy and the people," but "between the aristocracy and the executive,"[5]—a diversion
which was one of Adams's objects. And in the Virginia
ratifying convention Stephen pressed the familiar doctrine: "In all safe and free governments, there ought to
be a judicious mixture in the three different kinds of
government. This government is a compound of those
different kinds. But," he added, "the democratic kind
predominates, as it ought to."[6]

[1] Elliot's *Debates*, v., 260–1, i., 465.   [2] *Ib.*, v., 275–6.

[3] *Ib.*, 281.

[4] *Ib.*, 246. *Cf.* Morris above. Even Mason recommended a property
qualification for Senators, *ib.*, 247.

[5] *Ib.*, 421.   [6] *Ib.*, iii., 643.

These opinions, however, did not prevail in the Convention,—at least, it was not deemed advisable to make them apparent; and the Senate was organized ostensibly on another principle, though still with intent to represent a different interest from that represented by the other chamber. The scheme of avowedly dividing the two chambers between the rich and the poor, with a strong executive balance, was despaired of by Dickinson, who admired a limited monarchy as "one of the best governments in the world," but admitted that this "form, the most perfect, perhaps, in itself," was "unattainable" here, because of our lack of a class of nobles.[1] It was opposed by Charles Pinckney, despite a similar admiration for "the constitution of Great Britain," likewise as being inapplicable to our conditions, in view of the great equality of circumstances among our people and its likelihood of long continuance because of the laws against primogeniture and because of the vast extent of unoccupied territory.[2] The Convention, he said, "will not, surely, then, attempt to form a government consisting of three branches, two of which shall have nothing to represent."[3]

[1] *Ib.*, v., 148. Yet even he, later, repeating his "warm eulogiums of the British constitution," wished the Senate to be assimilated "as nearly as may be to the House of Lords," *ib.*, 163. "Wealth, family, or talents," should be the recommendation of its members, and if "the families and wealth of the aristocracy" could be combined, there would be established "a balance against and a check of the democracy," King's *Life and Correspondence*, i., 595-6. But the only means he had of approximating to this desideratum was by making the Senators elective by the State legislatures. It may be added, however, that in the very first Congress a member of the other house, Vining, expressed his apprehension that this result was to be attained—that "we may have there men whose wealth has created them the influence necessary to get in," Benton's *Abridgment*, i., 124 B. [2] Elliot's *Debates*, v., 234-8, *cf.* iv., 320-1.

[3] *Ib.*, v., 237. His own plan had been to have the Senators chosen by the Delegates, *ib.*, 129. But the Convention did do in a way what he

It was combated by Edmund Randolph, on account of the dissensions it would inevitably produce, instances of which, under a similar constitution, had occurred in Maryland.[1] And it was denounced by Franklin, a little later upon a like proposition being made for altering the constitution of Pennsylvania, out of principle, as he did not see how a minority could have a right to check a majority, especially as the property they are to represent is "a creature of society," and not assimilable to the property which merchants put into a joint-stock company, which they have gained and which is protected independently of that company.[2]

In his *Notes on Virginia*, published in 1785, Jefferson had found fault with the constitution of his State for making the Senate "too homogeneous with the house of delegates," averring that "the purpose of establishing different houses of legislation is to introduce the influence of different interests or different principles,"

reprehended, and in the ratifying convention of his State (South Carolina) he defended its scheme, asserting that "the purpose of establishing different houses of legislation was to introduce the influence of different interests and principles"—namely, of the people and of the States, *ib.*, iv., 257 (but we have seen them to be of an entirely different kind. *Cf.* the earlier words of Jefferson to be quoted presently, and their connection). Pinckney there further dilated on the merit of the new government as "a mixed system, possessing all the virtues and benefits, and avoiding all the dangers and inconveniences, of the three simple forms," 326; and he gave Paley's enumeration of them, 328-9.   [1] *Ib.*, v., 272.

[2] Franklin's *Works*, v., 167-9. His disapproval of the two chambers in the Federal Government, *ib.*, x., 345, 361 n. (For the principle about property being a "creature of society," see also *ib.*, ii., 479, x., 45-6.) In the Federal Convention the only vote against two branches in the national legislature was given by Pennsylvania, "probably from complaisance to Dr. Franklin, who was understood to be partial to a single house of legislation," Elliot's *Debates*, v., 135.—There, too, it may be added, Ellsworth apparently had Adams in mind when he remarked, "As to balances, where nothing can be balanced, it is a perfect Utopian scheme," *ib.*, i., 446.

citing both the English Constitution as relying "on the House of Commons for honesty and the Lords for wisdom," and certain American constitutions as providing representation of persons and of property, and desiring some such "complication of principles" in compensation for "the evils which may be produced by their dissensions."[1] While always maintaining the need of two chambers in some form or other, for the purpose of slowness and deliberation,[2] Jefferson later disavowed Adams's system of separating "the pseudo-aristoi" in a chamber by themselves, thinking it unnecessary for the protection of property, and fearing that "to give them power in order to prevent them from doing mischief, is arming them for it, and increasing instead of remedying the evil."[3] Finally, in 1823 and '24, he condemned making any of the legislators "the representatives of property instead of persons," and suggested that all representatives should be chosen together, and then divided by lot into two chambers, with frequent reshuffling, even weekly.[4]

On the other hand, Madison was infected with ideas similar to Adams's. Even before Adams's work appeared, he suggested the scheme of narrowing the suffrage in the one branch of the legislature and of enlarging it in the other, as "a good middle course"

[1] Jefferson's *Works*, viii., 361.   [2] *Cf. ib.*, ii., 333, iii., 136.
[3] Letter to Adams, Oct., 1813, *ib.*, vi., 223-4.
[4] *Ib.*, vii., 357, 321, and Ford's ed., vi., 520 n. Without the reshuffling, and only for debate, such a division by lot had been proposed in 1792 and 1805 by Paine, *Rights of Man*, Pt. II., ch. iv., and *To the Citizens of Pennsylvania, on the Proposal for calling a Convention;* and a similar scheme had actually been put into practice in Norway, by the constitution of 1814, still retained, where the newly elected representatives choose one fourth of their number to form the upper chamber, and upon disagreement reunite into one chamber, where a two-thirds vote is required to pass the matter in dispute.

between universal and restricted suffrage.[1] But this
was merely a compromise in a "delicate" subject,
where he could not make up his mind to adopt either
extreme. In the Federal Convention he even suggested,
but did not propose, another compromising scheme,
which would proportion the representation in the first
house to the free population and in the second to the
total population, so that the former should satisfy those
who believed in excluding slaves from counting as
persons, and the latter those who demanded their in-
clusion; by which arrangement, he added, "the southern scale would have the advantage in one House, and
the northern in the other."[2] At all events, he there
declared the Senate to have "for one of its primary
objects, the guardianship of property," and advocated
its being "so constituted as to protect the minority of
the opulent against the majority," at least by assigning
long terms to its members.[3] But during his association
with Jefferson he broke loose from Adams's views,[4] and

---

[1] *Writings*, i., 181, 187–8 (in 1785).　[2] Elliot's *Debates*, v., 265, 290.
[3] *Ib.*, v., 290, and i., 450, respectively, *cf.* in King's *Life and Correspond-
ence*, i., 596. With the last *cf.* Adam Smith: "Civil government . . .
is in reality instituted for the defense of the rich against the poor,"
Wealth of Nations, Book v., ch. i., pt. 2, (a Whig sentiment, *cf.* Locke,
Of Civil Government, § 85, but by him qualified, §§ 123, 173). So G.
Morris and Rutledge, property the main object of society, Elliot's
Debates, v., 279 (also in King's *Life and Correspondence*, i., 613).—In
The Federalist, after giving the democratic definition of "republic" in
Nos. 10, 14, and 37, Madison suddenly in No. 39 sprang on his unsus-
pecting readers this: "a government which derives all its powers directly
or indirectly from the great body of the people, and is administered by
persons holding their offices during pleasure, for a limited period, or
during good behavior." The gist of this definition lies in the words
"or indirectly" and "or during good behavior," *i. e.* for life. This
stops just short of no elections and hereditariness, and it betrays the
influence of his collaborator, Hamilton.

[4] We have seen his neutral opinion of Adams's book at its appearance (above, p. 305 n). In 1791 he wrote of it as "a mock defense of

dropped reference to the scheme of diverse representation,[1] only to take it up again after Jefferson's death, in senile meditation. In a paper written in 1829 he reviews certain methods of dealing with the suffrage, two of which are these:—"confining the right of suffrage for one branch to the holders of property, and for the other branch to those without property," and confining the right of electing one branch of the legislature to freeholders, and admitting all others to a common right with holders of property in electing the other branch." The first is what we have seen was really demanded by Adams's principles, the second what Adams himself permitted. Madison recognizes that the latter gives the holders of property a twofold share of the representation, but sees some justification for this in the fact that they have their own persons to protect as well as their property, whereas the rest have only their personal rights at stake; and he seems to prefer it to the former, as that might lead to dissensions. Further than this, however, Madison does not give a decision, asserting only that universal suffrage for both branches is preferable to a confinement of the entire right of suffrage to the property-holders, since in the one case those who have the greater interest are deprived of only half of it,

the Republican Constitutions of his country," under cover of which Adams had "attacked them with all the force he possessed," and was still doing so in "his anti-republican discourses" (*On Davila*), *Writings*, i., 536. Further on Adams's "monarchical principles," *ib.*, 558, 572. See also above, p. 258 n.

[1] Thus in a letter to Cartwright in 1824, against that Radical's advocacy of a single chamber, he urged, beside the argument from experience, the need of a second branch "consisting of fewer and riper members," for correcting the errors due to the ignorance, passion, or precipitancy of the other, and spoke of this as increasing the probability "that the will and interest of *their common constituents* will be duly pursued," *ib.*, iii., 355–6, (*cf.* 41–2).

but in the other, those with the lesser interest are deprived of the whole.[1]

Although Adams's method of dividing the legislature was not carried out in the Federal government, it had been, in a partial way, anticipated in the constitutions of North Carolina and New York, adopted in 1776 and 1778 respectively, during Adams's early democratic period, when indeed, as he claimed, his early democratic ideas had had influence in those States, yet this feature had not then been recommended by him. Both those constitutions assigned a higher property-qualification for voting for senators than for voting for members of the other house.[2] The North Carolina constitution remained unchanged in this respect till 1854; the New York constitution was altered in 1821. In the convention which reframed the latter constitution, the Federalists were mostly for retaining the old difference, but the Republicans succeeded in reducing the franchise to a low qualification the same for all. Hammond in

---

[1] *Ib.*, iv., 21–7 (Elliot's *Debates*, v., 580–2); cf. *Writings*, iv., 2–3. In all this Madison had been anticipated long before by Parsons in *The Essex Result*. There Parsons maintained that for laws affecting only persons, the consent of the majority of members is needed; if they affect only property, the consent of those who hold a majority of the property is enough; if they affect both, the consent of both these majorities is necessary: if the latter is not obtained, the security of property vanishes. The property-holder is affected both as to his person and his property, the propertiless only as to his person: hence the majority of the members should include those who possess a major part of the property. Parsons's *Parsons*, 371, 372, partly repeated 375, cf. 376, 392.—By both Parsons and Madison the nice little oversight is made that the propertiless are, at least in their potential property, affected by laws concerning property, since by such laws their acquisition of property may be rendered more or less difficult.

[2] In the Massachusetts constitution of 1780, remember, Adams had introduced a gradation of property-qualification only for eligibility to the three branches of the legislature.

his *Political History of New York* reports the speeches of two former Federalists, Judge Spencer and Chancellor Kent, both of whom wished the senate to be guardians of property, especially of the landed interest, while they conceded extensive suffrage to the assembly as the democratic branch more emphatically charged with the protection and promotion of personal rights. It is indicative of the unpopularity of Adams's extreme statement of this doctrine that neither made reference to him, but the former appealed to the authority of Hamilton, in a number (the 62d) of *The Federalist* which is disputed and probably was written by Madison and of Jefferson, in the *Notes on Virginia*, already retracted.[1]

Likewise without any mention of Adams's name, his views were almost travestied by Noah Webster in an open letter to his more famous namesake, published in 1837. Here is to be seen the same disparagement of virtue in the people as insufficient to insure good government[2]; the same admiration of the English government, and, in addition, of the contemporary French government, under Louis Philippe; which two governments he

---

[1] *Political History of New York*, ii., 23–39. Hammond himself thought the danger to republics comes from a union of the extreme rich and the extreme poor, and placed salvation in a strong middle class, which class he therefore wished to be strengthened. To do this, he would have a property-qualification for senators, that they might represent the middle class. Then, he thought, there could be no danger from the extreme poor, because the middle class would unite with the extreme rich against them; and no danger from the extreme rich, because the middle class would unite with the extreme poor to defeat their encroachment. The only danger left is in case the extreme rich and extreme poor uniting should overbalance the middle class; against which he seemed to despair of a check and only hoped it would be far removed in futurity, *ib.*, 50–2.

[2] In the reprint in *A Collection of Papers on Political, Literary, and Moral Subjects*, New York, 1843, pp. 269–71.

denied to be monarchies simply so-called, and the
popular odium against which as monarchies he labored
to dispel, as also to dissipate the presumption that republics or democracies must always be free governments,
instead maintaining that they may be as tyrannical as
monarchies, all men being made "with like passions."[1]
And this dictionary-maker and publicist finds in our
government a defect "in the election of senators by
the same constituents as the representatives in the
other branch," and asserts that "the most obvious
method of preserving a proper balance in the Constitution, and creating an effectual check of one branch
upon the other, is to place the election of the two
branches in different hands; and "in this country,
where there are no distinct orders or ranks of men,"
such as "nobles and commonalty," but where "the
distinction of rich and poor does exist" (which "no
human power or device can prevent," and which produces jealousies and rivalship needing to be controlled
by the government), each of these classes ought to have
"power to defend its own rights against the invasions of
the other," and be "equally secured" by having "a
complete check upon every attempt of the other."
This great object of allaying "party strife" must be
"accomplished by constitutional provisions." "The
most simple process would be to separate the electors
into two classes," with age- and property-qualifications
higher in the one than in the other, which "may be
independent of each other in elections, and their representatives compose different houses each with a negative upon the acts of the other." The one set are to be
the general guardians of the rights of persons, equal in
all men; the other, the special guardians of the rights of

[1] *Ib.*, 273.

property, not equal in all men, but superior in the rich, and in them additional to the personal rights, which they have the same motives to protect as the poor, though "the poor have not the same motives to protect" the rights of property "as those have who own it."[1] As for the executive department, he says that most nations, taught by their own or by the experience of Poland, "have a settled conviction that it is better to trust to hereditary succession for a chief magistrate, than to a popular election"; that our people "are making the experiment of electing the chief magistrate and most of the executive officers"; and that "the result of the experiment is not finally determined, and prudence requires that we should not confidently predict what the issue will be." Though he avers that this experiment with a president instead of a king "should be fully tried," he already wishes the mode of election to be reformed, and, because, in his opinion, popular elections to such high office are very "menacing to the purity and stability of our institutions," and are the more dangerous the more frequently they occur, he wishes the President (and the governors, and the judges too) to be appointed by the legislatures,—here departing from Adams, but returning to him in wishing them all to "hold their offices during good behavior."[2] He therefore called upon the great men of the country to unite their efforts to amend the Constitution; and he criticized the original founders as "enthusiasts," whose "crude ideas" hardly reached beyond getting rid of kings and nobles, and who did not perceive, or learn from history, that "the same principles of human nature, and the same disposition to tyrannize, exist in

[1] Ib., 274–6.   [2] Ib., 276–8, 280, 285.

all other men,"[1]—at the very time he was rehashing the teachings of one of them!

Perhaps the most curious avatar of this plan of government by classes was its reappearance in the report of a commission appointed in 1875 by Governor Tilden to deliberate upon constitutional amendments permitting reorganization of the municipal government of New York City. This commission recommended the creation of a board of audit as a sort of second chamber, with absolute veto over all appropriations passed by the aldermen, with the distinctive feature that while all other officers were, as before, to be elected by universal suffrage, the members of this body were to be elected only by those who paid taxes on real estate.[2] Here, however, the system might not be so bad, since, above the contending powers in a municipality, there is a superior power in the State government, capable of separating them when they become deadlocked and restricting them to fighting fairly. But it might be a fatal precedent.

This proposal was, apparently, suggested without any reference to Adams, and possibly without any knowledge of his doctrine. The oblivion into which Adams's teaching has fallen, is strikingly illustrated in the work of a New England jurist and professor. In his *Political Science* (ii. 307–8), Woolsey, commenting on the theory that rich and powerful families are dangerous to the state unless accorded a recognized position in the government, makes no allusion to Adams, as nowhere

---

[1] *Ib.*, 285; 284, *cf.* 273–4.

[2] Bigelow's *Life of Tilden*, i., 266. S. Sterne, who was a member of that commission, makes a distant allusion to some such restriction of the suffrage in his *Constitutional History and Political Development of the United States*, 270–1.

else either, but to some incidental passages in Montesquieu and Guizot![1]

CHAPTER XXII

COMPARISON WITH CALHOUN

THE resemblance deserves to be noticed which exists between Calhoun's theory of government and Adams's, along with their difference.

Calhoun, who placed equal if not greater importance upon a good or bad organization of government as cause of virtue or vice in the people,[2] agreed with Adams that "single or *one power*" constitutes absolute government, whether composed of one ruler, of few, or of many,[3] and found salvation only in an antagonism of interests, by opposing power to power.[4] The state, first of all, contains two contrary interests in those of the governors and of the governed. The governors control the governed, and it is necessary also that the governed should control the governors. This is accomplished by the institution of the suffrage, which converts the governors from masters into representative agents, and constitutes free governments.[5]

[1] So the German-American Lieber, though he quotes an approbative allusion to Adams's work, as counteracting the movement toward a single chamber, yet, combating Adams's main reason for two chambers, assigns it to Brougham, *On Civil Liberty*, pp. 195, 198-9.—The general scheme has appealed to others in Europe, probably without any acquaintance with Adams's views. Thus the Belgian H. Denis has proposed that the lower house should represent labor and the upper house capital, in his *Organization représentative du Travail* (according to Ch. Benoist, *La Crise de l'État moderne*, p. 182 n.).

[2] *Works*, i., 50–1, *cf.* 90, and vi., 34.   [3] *Ib.*, i., 36, *cf.* vi., 229.
[4] *Ib.*, vi., 40, ii., 254, i., 12.   [5] *Ib.*, vi., 64, 190, i., 12–13.

Although such a control of the governors is primary
and indispensable, a great error is committed in supposing it sufficient.[1] Free governments themselves beget
an antagonism of interests between two parties among
the people,—between those who live on the government
and those who live under the government; between
those who profit by the government, "the stockholding
interest," and those at whose expense it is run; between those who are tax-payers only and those who,
although likewise paying taxes, are recouped and even
over-benefited by being tax-consumers and even re-
ceivers of bounties; forming a controlling interest and a
contributing interest, the one bent on increasing, the
other on diminishing, power and expenditure,[2]—in
short, "a governing majority and a governed minority."[3] The rule, in such a government, of the majority
over the minority ultimately becomes as bad as the
rule of the governors over the governed in an absolute
government; for the dominant part of the community
have the same tendency as have absolute rulers to abuse
power and oppress the rest, the minority in a republic
being the ruled exactly as the people at large are in
absolute monarchy or aristocracy.[4]

This is on the supposition that the majority are unchecked, as are the absolute rulers; for then the majority
also are absolute rulers, and their government is an
absolute democracy. Therefore the majority likewise
need to be checked: a new remedy, a second control is
necessary, since the trouble now has a different location,
lying not with the elected representatives, but with the

---

[1] *Ib.*, ii., 245–6, i., 13, *cf.* vi., 138, 191, 265, 269.
[2] *Ib.*, vi., 249; ii., 246 (254), iii., 642; i., 21 (102).
[3] *Ib.*, vi., 136, i., 16.
[4] *Ib.*, i., 22, vi., 138, 229, 265, 190–1; i., 23, *cf.* vi., 75.

electing constituents.[1]   In addition to the suffrage as
an organism of government, there must be an organism
of society, whereby the weaker interest is organized as
well as the stronger.[2]   As the actual governors need to
be held accountable, by the suffrage, to the whole body
of the governed, so the virtual governors, the major
part of society, need to be compelled to consult the
interest of the minor part, the only one that is ultimately governed; which means that both must consult the
interest of each other.[3]   This is to be effected by requiring that the sense of each part should be taken
separately, and thereby requiring, for the passage of
any measure, the consent of both, thus reserving to
each the right of self-protection by giving to each a
negative upon the acts of the other.[4]   Thus, in place
of a mere "absolute" or "numerical majority," which
is alone provided by the suffrage, he substitutes a more
complex system of what he calls the "concurring" or
"concurrent majority."[5]   The former, though mistakenly considered constitutive of free government, is
absolutism and despotism; and it is sure to end in
militarism and absolute monarchy.[6]   In the latter
alone is there maintenance of liberty, and security for
the interests of the whole people—of the minority as
well as of the majority.   No enduring free state has ever
existed "whose institutions were not based on the
principle of the concurring majority."[7]   Against the
abuse of power there never has been, and there cannot
be, devised any other remedy than this.[8]

Thus far, in their theorizing, Calhoun and Adams

[1] Ib., vi., 32, ii., 306; vi., 30.

[2] Ib., ii., 250, i., 26; ii., 254.

[3] Ib., vi., 64, 190.

[4] Ib., i., 25; vi., 64, 66, i., 35.

[5] Ib., vi., 181, ii., 250; i., 28.

[6] Ib., i., 102, 308, 381.

[7] Ib., vi., 182.

[8] Ib., vi., 66, 91.

are in close agreement, Calhoun, the master logician, merely giving a deeper analytical exposition of Adams's system. From now on, in the practical application, there comes in a divergence. Calhoun maintains that it does not matter whether the class interests are divided socially and economically throughout the mass of the people over the whole face of the land, in separate estates, as in England, or whether they are divided locally, sectionally, or geographically, except that in the latter case the danger of conflict is greater.[1] Here in America we have no distinctions of rank, or orders of society, as in England; but here we have the geographical distinction between an agricultural people in the South and a manufacturing people in the North, the latter desiring protection for their industries at the expense of the former, and, being the majority, obtaining it,—the two sections forming, in fact, a sovereign party and a subject party.[2] Therefore, just as Hamilton wished to protect the numerical minority of the rich from the despotic power of the numerical majority of the poor, by giving the rich a negative in the senate,[3] and as Adams wished to protect the intellectual minority (so to speak) of the poor from the despotic power of the intellectual majority of the rich, by giving the poor

---

[1] *Ib.*, vi., 64, 66-7.   [2] *Ib.*, vi., 64-5; 31.

[3] Notice the quotations from "Hamilton," *ib.*, vi., 30, 42, (from *The Federalist*, No. 51, which surely is Madison's. Here it is said: "It is of great importance . . . not only to guard the society against the oppression of its rulers; but to guard one part of society against the injustice of the other." This was always a favorite subject with Madison, evidently original with him. A corrective for this evil in republican governments, distinguished from that in absolute governments of oppression by the rulers, he hoped for, first, in the extent of the country, and, after 1789, also in the composite form of our government: see his *Writings*, i., 325-8, 350-3, iii., 42, 430, 483, 506-7, iv., 21, 23, 27, 51-2, 73, 326-7, (*cf.* 467), also in Elliot's *Debates*, v., 162, and *cf.* 242-3 and i., 450.

a negative in the house of representatives, each at the same time recognizing a similar right in the other class; so Calhoun wished to give the geographical minority of the South a negative to protect them from the despotic power of the geographical majority of the North. Only the means he had to seek elsewhere, since our Federal government was not organized in the first place so as to have these two sectional interests represented as two wholes in the two chambers of the Federal legislature respectively.[1] In our Federal government, he says, the division of the legislature was intended merely to prevent abuse in the administration of the granted powers, not to protect the reserved powers not confided to either of them[2]; and moreover, that division would be ineffectual for this other purpose, since each branch is under the control of the same numerical majority, our Constitution not having taken the further step of making these branches represent different interests of the country.[3] Such a use of the legislative branches to represent different geographical interests he found in his own State of South Carolina, where since 1807 the franchise was so ordered that the senate was mostly in the hands of the slave-holding lowlanders and the house of representatives in the hands of the freer uplanders; and the good effects of this distribution of power he commended as an exemplification of the general principle.[4]

But Calhoun did not venture to advise the adoption of this scheme in the Federal government. Instead, he at first thought he found in the existing arrangement of

[1] In the Convention Madison had made a suggestion in this direction, which received no attention: see Elliot's *Debates*, v., 265, 290.

[2] *Works*, ii., 256–7. He might here have quoted Monroe, Elliot's *Debates*, iii., 219.

[3] *Works*, i., 34.   [4] *Ib.*, vi., 259–64, i., 400–6.

things the desired remedy, since in our country there is
a geographical division into States, in the requirement
of whose majority he detected the principle of the concurrent majority.   For misuse of powers indisputably
granted to the Federal government, he apparently had
no constitutional remedy, beyond persuasion.   But
considering the protective tariff not a granted power,
against this he thought he found a remedy in the States
being the guardians of the reserved powers, as parties
to the compact which instituted the Federal government, so that any State (not its government, but a
convention summoned for the purpose) that felt
oppressed by a measure the constitutionality of which
it disputed might interpose,[1] as the House of Lords in
England interposes between the rulers there represented
by the King and the ruled there represented by the
House of Commons,[2] and annul for a time the action of
the central government, thereby compelling submission
of the disputed question anew to the people of all the
States in convention assembled, where, according to the
terms of the present Constitution, the express grant of
it may be obtained if three fourths of the States are
willing, or else is withheld without possibility of further
dispute.[3]

Being defeated on this project, he later suggested
another remedy, wholly novel, to be inserted in the
Constitution as an amendment, consisting in a division
of the executive department among two Presidents,
who, like the Roman Consuls, were to divide foreign
and domestic affairs between them, but of whom the

---

[1] *Ib.*, i., 308–9.   [2] *Ib.*, i., 103.

[3] *Ib.*, vi., 50, 54–5, 68–9, 101–2, 111, 142, (*cf.* 207); ii., 260.   He did not
care whether this was called nullification, interposition, or State veto,
vi., 159–60, *cf.* 42, 61, ii., 306–7.

one was to be chosen by the North, the other by the South, and each to have an absolute veto over legislation,[1]—a suggestion, which, published after his death, never met with either defense or refutation.

Had he advised that the North and the South should separately be represented, the one in the Senate and the other in the House of Representatives, his suggestion would have fallen equally flat. Yet a geographical is as important as a social or economic contrariety of interest. In fact, it *is* a social or economic contrariety, only instead of the interests being evenly commingled throughout the country, they are separated and collected at opposite poles, whereat being concentrated, their opposition is intensified and, as Calhoun indicated, rendered more dangerous. If, then, contending interests deserve to have separate representation in the one case, they deserve to have it in the other. Let all manufacturers have representation in one house, and all agriculturists in another, each with a negative upon the other. Obviously such a system would not be a good one. But it would be as good as Adams's.

CHAPTER XXIII

THE GENERAL ARGUMENTS FOR BICAMERALISM

ADAMS did much to bring about the introduction of the bicameral system, with the absolute negative in each chamber,—or rather to keep it in the States where it already existed, to extend it to other States, and thereby to secure its adoption in the Federal

[1] *Ib.*, i., 392.

government, after which the few remaining States
that had it not, fell into line.   On this account his
reasons for advocating it are of peculiar interest and
importance.   And not less so are those of other political
writers since his day.

Adams's great reason is the complete system of
mixed and balanced government we have been reviewing, in which the mixture and the balance were sought
not so much in the three departments as in the three
branches of the single legislative department, with their
roots in at least two distinct classes or orders of the
people.   Yet Adams did not confine himself to that
great systematic reason.   In fact, he was not chary of
reasons: he was willing to take them wherever he could
pick them up.   He once wrote of the purpose of appointing two chambers being that "the errors of one
may be corrected by the other" (vi. 212), overlooking
that equally the right positions of the one might be
perverted by the other.[1]   He had early noticed an advantage of a second chamber, similar to one often
dwelt upon in England in defense of rotten boroughs,
that it might make room for distinguished men "omitted by the people in the choice of their representatives"
(ix. 395).   He twisted to his own account an ambiguous simile ascribed to Franklin (iv. 390–1, cf. 440),
ignoring another simile employed by Franklin which

---

[1] Cf. Iredell: "If a measure be right, which has been approved of by
one branch, the other will probably confirm it [sancta simplicitas!]; if
it be wrong, it is fortunate that there is another branch to oppose or
amend it," Elliot's Debates, iv., 38.   Hamilton: "This organization is so
complex, so skilfully contrived, that it is next to impossible that an
impolitic or wicked measure should pass the scrutiny with success,"
ib., ii., 348,—or a good measure either, perhaps.   Maclay soon discovered that "a government with so many branches affords a large
field for caballing," Sketches, 59.

was not ambiguous and could not be so misused.[1]　He adopted from Harrington an argument for two assemblies of a totally different nature from his own, Harrington's being the one to debate and propose and the other to resolve[2]—a system which has its analog now when the legislature propose a law and refer it, by the *referendum*, to the people.[3]　That the result reached differed, did not matter: in this subject everything was grist that came to his mill.

Is not this the case to-day?　Is not the bicameral system such a fetich that any old argument is good enough to prove it, or that it may dispense with any serious argument?　Lieber says it "accompanies the Anglican race like the common law," and "is to us as natural as the jury,"[4]—and this is considered enough. Countenance is thus given to Bentham's stricture that the universal notion about the usefulness of the second chamber "is mere prejudice—authority-begotten and blind custom-begotten prejudice."[5]　The real funda-

[1] The former (of the wagoner with two teams going down hill) is alluded to also by Graydon, *Memoirs*, ch. xi., p. 286, and repeated by Sparks in his *Life of Franklin* in his ed. of Franklin's *Works*, i., 409; both of whom may have taken it from Adams.　The other (of the snake with two heads caught by a twig) is in Franklin's *Works*, i., 521, v., 166-7, (i., 409-10).　　　　　　　　　　　　　　[2] See above, p. 245.

[3] And this system makes the upper chamber superfluous.　"The effect of the Referendum in Switzerland," says McKechnie, "is to add a third Chamber (to wit, the people in their masses) to the two ordinary Chambers of the Legislature," *The Reform of the House of Lords*, p. 94. Consequently, according to S. E. Moffett, "the arguments for a second chamber lose their force when the people retain the right of reviewing legislation through the referendum," *Suggestions on Government*, 2d ed., p. 115.　The people then compose the lower house, and the assembly is their senate.

[4] *On Civil Liberty*, p. 194 and note; followed by Woolsey, *Political Science*, ii., 302.

[5] *Works*, iv., 445B.—On the other side, of course, there have been worthless arguments against bicameralism, as the oft-quoted one of the

mental reason—Adams's—the dread of pure democracy
—still relied on in England, superseded in our country
by another contrivance (the constitution), is backed up
or replaced by trivial reasons that do not go the whole
way, and by appeals to the utterly insufficient test of
experience. Confusion reigns throughout.

To be methodical ourselves, let us notice that there
are really two distinct things argued for, as well as two
distinct lines of argument for them. The two distinct
things argued for are bicameralism in countries without
a constitution set up by the people above the government, and bicameralism where there is such a constitution. The two distinct lines of argument are the *a
priori* and the *a posteriori*, the rational and the historical. The complication does not end here, for what is
said of the two distinct things argued for refers to
bicameralism proper. But there is something also
usually confounded with bicameralism, which is really
short of it, and at best can be called bicameralism
improper.

That bicameralism in a government with a constitution erected by the people at large is a very different
thing from bicameralism in a country without such a
constitution, is apparent from the fact that in the latter
the bisection of the legislature runs down into the ultimate or primary legislature which makes the government itself and its frame or constitution, whereas in the
former the primary legislature is unicameral (except for
the distinction between a drafting body and the accepting or rejecting people). In the former (for the last
time to use Bodin's distinction) the state is bicameral,

Abbé Sièyes, that if the second chamber agrees with the first it is useless,
and if not, it is bad; also one by Condorcet, about a slave being no better
off with two masters, *Œuvres*, xii., 209.

in the latter only the government. In the latter, then, the bicameralism of the government is not so necessary from the standpoint of the upper classes, for defending them from the lower classes and safeguarding their vested special interests, while it can do some harm, from the standpoint of the major people, in going a step in the direction of producing the condition of bicameralism in the state, by fostering special interests and helping to vest and fortify them, in addition to the safeguard already provided by the constitution in its bill of rights, which shields the rich at the same time it protects the poor. This latter safeguard is now often forgotten, and the argument relied upon by the English and other Europeans is also employed by Americans. Adams himself, we have seen, committed this mistake, neglecting the constitution, the full force of which he did not anticipate. He then harped upon what Lecky has still urged, in these sententious words: "Of all the forms of government that are possible among mankind, I do not know any which is likely to be worse than the government of a single, omnipotent, democratic chamber."[1] Whatever the value of this statement, the truth of which may be admitted, it is to no purpose in America, where the legislature is not supreme or "omnipotent." A minor form of this argument, also used by Adams, is that the division of the legislative department is needed to weaken it, or else it would be an overmatch for the executive.[2] In England this

---

[1] *Democracy and Liberty*, opening of ch. iv., vol. i., p. 361.

[2] From De Lolme, see above, p. 233. Similarly Wilson, Elliot's *Debates*, v., 197, Martin, *ib.*, i., 429, King, *Life and Correspondence*, i., 621, and Madison, *The Federalist*, No. 51. "The great use of the two Chambers," said Beaumont, "is to strengthen the Executive by enabling it to play one against the other," in Senior's *Correspondence and Conversations of Alexis de Tocqueville*, ii., 268.

encroachment of the legislature upon the executive, in spite of the former's division into two houses, has in fact been effected, and instead of being deplored as an evil, is extolled as one of the chief excellences of the British Constitution. In America such encroachment would be impossible, even if we had but one chamber, on account of the written constitution. Yet this argument has been used here—by Daniel Webster, for instance, and others.[1]

Both the lines of argument are vitiated by non-recognition of this distinction. When Lecky writes, "The necessity of a second Chamber, to exercise a controlling, modifying, retarding, and steadying influence, has acquired almost the position of an axiom"; and again when he says, "The experience of the past abundantly corroborates the views of those who dread government by a single chamber"[2]; the force of his words is greatly lessened by the fact that what is axiomatic in the one set of conditions may not be in the other, and that experience in the one set of countries may teach no lesson for the other. But let us examine these arguments separately.

[1] Webster's *Works*, iii., 10–11, where he mentions Adams's *Defense* without citing his chief reason, and says: "If all legislative power rested in one house, it is very problematical whether any proper independence could be given, either to the executive or the judiciary. . . . If all legislative power be in one popular body, all other power, sooner or later, will be there also." Thus this "Defender of the Constitution" likewise overlooked the constitution! Again, *ib.*, iv., 110 and 122–3, he associates the separation of the branches with the separation of the departments, upon the maintenance of which boundaries "the continuance of liberty depends," (*cf. ib.*, iii., 27 where the departments are spoken of as "branches"). Also Professor Burgess, reviving this argument, forgets the constitution by speaking of historical cases (not cited) of single-chambered legislatures encroaching upon the executive and through anarchy ending in despotism, *Political Science and Constitutional Law*, ii., 107–8.

[2] *Op. cit.*, i., 363, 364.

The *a priori* or rational argument really should be twofold. In countries without a written constitution superior to the legislature, it should be the familiar one that the second chamber, representing a privileged estate in the country, is needed to prevent the excesses feared from an omnipotent purely democratic assembly —' to oppose," in the words of a Netherlandish commission, "in difficult times, a dyke to the passions" and "to surround the throne with a barrier against which factions shall shatter themselves."[1] The counterargument which we Americans ought to raise to this, is that the privileged second chamber is not the only and necessary means of preventing the excesses of a single assembly, deprived of omnipotence: that education of the people, and a fixed constitution containing a properly drawn-up bill of rights, and establishing a judiciary independent of the legislature, will accomplish the purpose. Having these things ourselves, we may leave the privileged second chamber to surround the thrones and dyke-in the preserves of the aristocrats in the countries which delight in those things.

For us is applicable only another form of the *a priori* argument, which is, that two chambers are needed to prevent hasty and ill-considered legislation—"to provide the safety which lies in sober second thoughts," "to appeal from Philip drunk to Philip sober,"[2] etc.,

---

[1] *Rapport* présenté au Roi par la Commission chargée de la révision de la loi fondamentale des Pays-Bas Unis, July, 1815, in Dufan, Duvergier, and Guadet's *Collection des Constitutions, Chartes, et Lois fondamentales des Peuples de l'Europe et des deux Amériques*, Paris, 1823, vol. iii., p. 159. (This Report is reviewed and criticized by Bentham, *Works*, iv., 427–9.)

[2] J. A. R. Marriott, *Second Chambers*, Oxford, 1910, pp. 4–5. The last simile had been apologetically used by A. Helps, *Thoughts upon Government*, p. 41.

etc. This service of foiling precipitancy is pronounced by Woolsey "the true view of the use of two houses."[1] Yet this reason ignores innumerable other devices, less expensive and less dangerous, which can equally well secure this object. We may point out later that bicameralism improper secures it as effectually as bicameralism proper. Here we should note that this modified *a priori* reason is contained within the preceding absolute form of the *a priori* reason; for if two legislative bodies represent two different interests or classes in society, they will retard legislation and thus have the desired effect of producing deliberation. But that reason contains much more; and to produce deliberation it is not necessary to overdo the matter by granting to the upper chamber more power than is sufficient for this purpose[2]; and especially it is not necessary to grant to one class or to one assembly the power of blocking the deliberate will of the majority of the whole people. Those, therefore, who favor the minor reason without approving the larger one, should be on their guard lest the protection of privilege be effected through desire for deliberateness, and should be suspicious of the insidious machinations of persons who urge the former alone while secretly desiring the latter also.[3]

[1] *Political Science*, ii., 311–12. It was also employed by Webster, *Works*, iii., 10, 487; and again by Burgess, *op. cit.*, ii., 106–7.

[2] Certainly, to exert restraint upon "the sudden impulses and violent passions" of the popular body, there is no need of the senate having a right to initiate legislation, other than repeals, or to amend tax- and appropriation-bills otherwise than by lowering them.

[3] An instance of this may be seen in the argument employed in favor of the bill for revising the Chamber of Peers in France in 1831, both in the *Exposé* of the minister, Casimir Périer, and in the speech of Thiers. This was, that the second chamber is not intended merely for the trifling advantage of correcting the oversights of the other, but "to represent another principle"(or "interest," Thiers said), whereby alone it avoids

At bottom the *a priori* recommendation of bicameralism seems to be its capacity to satisfy clashing claims and to quiet distracted minds. For the essence of bicameralism is compromise. It conciliates opposing theories by making room for both, giving a place to each in each of the halves into which it divides the legislature. The number of diversities that may in this way be reconciled, is truly surprising. If you hesitate between wide and narrow suffrage, you may with Madison stop your embarrassment by leaving the franchise wide for the lower house and restricting it for the upper. If you are equally impressed by the allegations that the representation of districts should be according to their population and according to their wealth, you may solve the problem, as was done in the Massachusetts constitution of 1780, by distributing the so-called representatives on the first principle and the senators on the other. If in the economic world you are undecided between the pretensions to power of opposing interests, as between those of agriculturists and of the mercantile and manufacturing classes, between labor and capital, between free and slaveholding communities, or between the sections of the country occupied by them (as between the hill-dwellers with the small farm system and the plain-dwellers with the large plantation system, between west and east, or north and south), you may end the trouble, as you think (though you may be only renewing it), as Calhoun, Denis, and others would have

being "a useless repetition;" which other principle, or interest, is stability, while that of the first chamber is progress; wherefore the first chamber must itself be mobile (by frequent election by the people) and the other itself permanent (by appointment for life by the king). See Thiers' *Discours parlementaires*, i., 149–50, 158–62. Here the "principles" evidently are the "interests" of the upper and lower classes, though named differently.

liked to do, by giving representation to the one set of interests in the one house and to the other in the other. Or if you generalize more and like Adams are so enraptured with the respective merits of democracy and of aristocracy that you cannot decide which you prefer to see all-powerful, and if also you have a hankering after monarchy, you may put each of the former in a house by itself, and over them set an executive chief with legislative power equal to theirs and affect to believe him a monarch (which indeed he may become, unless one of the others makes itself predominant first). If you do not go so far, or are not so outspoken about your desires, which still are to reserve a place for aristocracy while giving a place to democracy in the legislature, with something of monarchy in the executive, you may copy our Federal Constitution-makers, who did their best in a country without well-marked and hardened classes to fit the one house for aristocracy though leaving the other democratic; and you may go even further, as they could not do all that they desired: you may render the lower house democratic by widening its franchise, making low or no property or other qualification for its members, small and numerous districts, one for each representative, who must be a resident thereof, with short term, small salary, preferably with enforced vacation after every term, all the members coming in and going out together, and so forming a large, heterogeneous, ill-assorted, inexperienced, amateurish assemblage, with open sessions; and you may render the upper house attractive to aristocrats (if there are any, or to plutocrats), and oligarchic in its character, by narrowing its franchise or making the election indirect, raising the property qualification for its members, enlarging the districts, preferably using the general-ticket system, not confining the member to the district, lengthening the term, granting no or large salary, with indefinite re-eligibility, and continuity through the rotation of a fraction going out and coming in at stated periods, so as to compose a small assemblage, compact, homogeneous, experienced, professional, of men who have fallen together at the top and who work in harmony, with secret sessions. The opportunity to do this you will especially seize if you are instituting a federal system composed of large and of small states, the former of which desire their size (whether measured by population or wealth) to tell and the latter wish every state to count alike; for you may settle this dispute by organizing the one house in the one way and the other in the other, adding whatever of the preceding features to each you choose, or are able. All such compromises, we may note, are gratifying to democrats in an aristocratic country, because they are concessions favorable to them; and they are agreeable to aristocrats (or to would-be aristocrats) in a democratic country, because they are the most that can there be obtained. They are, in any kind of country, truly satisfactory only to those who cannot make up their minds and are fond of compromising. But if you are not such, and do not wish to carry out a compromise in the government of your country, you had better not advocate bicameralism; for if you set up two chambers exactly alike, or differing only in size and in length of terms, as in most of our State constitutions, you are simply dividing responsibility and accomplishing no good whatever; and if you introduce distinctions of prominence between the two chambers, you are setting up oppositions and really entering upon a compromise contrary to your intention. To-day true democrats should be on their guard and open their eyes to the fact that in upholding the kind of bicameralism that is most strenuously contended for, they are yielding half their ground to their opponents.

And their opponents try to win their ground by turning the argument aside from the intent and purpose at which they are really aiming, to a mere appeal to history, and making experience their chief weapon and placing upon it their main reliance.[1] In this argument *a posteriori*, it is alleged that experience has everywhere approved the bicameral system and disproved the unicameral. To this the answer is simple: the unicameral system has never had a fair trial in any country with a constitution superior to the single chamber. The experience of antiquity and of the middle ages yields no adverse testimony on the real question at issue, since the bad working of a single omnipotent assembly without a superior constitution would prove nothing about the working of a single-chambered legislature such as we have under consideration. In modern times, since the invention of the constitutional system, the prejudice has been so virulent against unicameralism, tested, if at all, only under the prior defective system, that no government with a single legislative chamber has been constitutionally set up and allowed to work out its destiny under favorable conditions in any large state. Yet in small states and dependencies, and even where there is no written constitution, there is a goodly number of successfully working unicameral governments, some of great age, still existent. Among dependent bodies are the Dutch provinces, the Swiss cantons,

---

[1] *Cf*. Marriott: "The only satisfactory appeal, I venture to submit, is the appeal to history; the only safe guide, that of experience," *op. cit.*, p. 5.

a dozen or more little German states,[1] beside the semi-independent republics of San Marino and Andorra, the isle of Crete, and many tiny British possessions[2] and the Canadian provinces (excepting Quebec and Nova Scotia). Among independent states are a few of the smallest Spanish American countries,[3] three east-European states,[4] and, until their extinction, the Orange Free State and the Transvaal.[5]

These are generally overlooked. But when there were more such states, especially in our Union, comparison was drawn between them and the bicameral. Here we must be on guard against glib and unsubstantiated assertions. A fair example of the genus may be cited in Webster's empirical basis for a reason previously quoted. Webster declared: "If we look through the several constitutions of the States, we shall perceive that generally the departments are most distinct and independent where the legislature is composed of two houses, with equal authority and mutual checks."[6] Poor as this argument would be if it were well based, its basis is not sound. The unicameral constitution of Pennsylvania had almost identical regulations concerning the president or governor and the judiciary with the contemporary bicameral constitution of New Jersey. In the South Carolina ratifying convention Charles

[1] Anhalt, Brunswick, Oldenburg, the two Lippes, the two Reusses, the two Schwarzburgs, the four Saxes, and Gotha. Also Luxemburg.

[2] Among them may be cited the Isle of Man, the Channel Islands, and Jamaica.

[3] Guatemala, Honduras, Costa Rica, Salvador, Santo Domingo.

[4] Greece, Bulgaria, and Servia (this with a legislative council).

[5] The latter since 1890 had an anomalous sort of additional chamber, which could be vetoed by, but could not veto, the first. Both had executive councils; and the presidents, though endowed by the constitutions with little power, personally had great influence.

[6] *Works*, iii., 11.

Pinckney complained that in no States except Maryland, Massachusetts, and New York, were the judicial and executive departments any more independent than in Pennsylvania and Georgia.[1]   Moreover, Webster's statement, made in 1820, implied that there were enough constitutions of both kinds to permit of a "general" comparison.   There was then just one unicameral legislature in all the States.

And when we come to statements about the causes of the abandonment of unicameralism, by which its failure is sought to be proved, we strike no surer footing. In Adams's time there were a few tumults in Pennsylvania, which he at once attributed to "the nature of their government"[2]; and before long, just after the adoption of the Federal Constitution and under its influence, the legislative form of that State was altered,[3]

---

[1] Elliot's *Debates*, iv., 324–5.   *Cf.* above, pp. 184–5 n.   In the Federal Convention also Wilson said that Pennsylvania "had gone as far as any State into the policy of fettering power," *ib.*, v., 424.

[2] IX., 505, in 1779.

[3] "So as to render it more conformable to that of the United States," according to Graydon, *Memoirs*, p. 343; because two houses of assembly were, *inter alia*, "fashionable politics," according to Oliver Wolcott, Jr., in Gibbs's *Administrations*, i., 26. Soon after the adoption of the unicameral constitution in 1776 there had been formed in Pennsylvania an opposition party, who called themselves Republicans and afterwards merged with the Federalists, while the defenders of the State constitution were called Constitutionalists, Graydon, *op. cit.*, 331, 342, (*cf.* Morris in Elliot's *Debates*, v., 430, and Madison, *Writings*, i., 356, 364). The former were the aristocratic element, who evidently were unwilling to wait for the evils they anticipated, and helped to produce them.   The alteration of this constitution from unicameralism to bicameralism has some analogy with the constitutional change made in England by the law of 8 Henry VI (1429) restricting the suffrage.   This is often described as occasioned by disorders occurring at elections, whereas the preamble of the law itself shows that it was occasioned by the *expectation* of such disorders (which "verisemblablement sourdront & seront, si covenable remedie ne soit purveu en celle partie").

whereupon he said that that State "found by experience the necessity of a change"[1]; and his opinion has been adopted abroad.[2] South Carolina and Georgia had already changed, and the infection of example caused Vermont to abandon its isolated position later, in 1836. There was a "rebellion" in Massachusetts, under

[1] VI., 274, cf. ii., 508. Neither the experience nor the necessity is apparent. A Pennsylvanian wrote in 1786: "Pennsylvania hops along on her *one* leg better than I expected," and assigned a fanciful reason for her doing so, F. Hopkinson, in Jay's *Correspondence*, iii., 184.—*Cf.* Lord Rosebery's allusion, not long ago, to unicameral one-eyedness and one-leggedness. The inappropriateness of this time-worn metaphor is well shown by the use made of it by Nevill, who, after speaking of the government during the King's reign without summoning Parliament as "hopping upon one leg," said the kingdom previously (when conducted in the manner desired by Adams) had "marched upon three legs" [like a decrepit old man!], *Plato Redivivus*, p. 116. And the Long Parliament once declared that the two houses were "the eyes in the politic body, whereby his majesty was, by the constitution of the kingdom, to discern the differences of those things, which concern the public peace and safety thereof," Clarendon, *History of the Rebellion*, i., 566. But then the King was the brains of the kingdom! A much better simile was invented by Harrington for *his* two assemblies, which he compared with the two ventricles of the heart, the one greater, the other less, *Oceana*, 161. —The two-legged argument has also recently been revived in support of man-and-woman suffrage, by Mrs. R. L. Venturini in the New York *Sun*, Oct. 16, 1912. And by the way, if we have universal suffrage of women in addition to that of men, this might furnish an equally good principle of division of the chambers, as some of those we have seen. Let the one house represent women, and the other represent men. Yet it might then cause heartburning to decide upon which to call the upper or the lower, or which the first or the second. Without observing this difficulty, G. W. Mullins had already, in an article on *Woman Suffrage: A New Synthesis*, in the Hibbert Journal, January, 1911, advocated a halfway measure of admitting women, on the same terms with men, merely to a "wisdom franchise" for the second chamber.

[2] Thus Stewart cited this change in Pennsylvania as due to the violence of "the factions and disorders which the former Constitution produced," *Political Economy*, ii., 432. Factions and disorders were no greater there than in New York; but that did not matter. See also the next note but one here following.

Adams's own constitution, and a couple more, one of them dignified as a "war," in Pennsylvania under its new régime;[1] but these were never attributed to the bicameral system, nor did Pennsylvania change back again: on the contrary, the Massachusetts trouble specially called forth Adams's defense of that system. The failures since then, of the French unicameral constitutions of 1791, 1793, and 1848, of the Spanish of 1812 and 1820, of the Neapolitan of 1820, of the Portuguese of 1822, have other reasons in plenty to account for them.[2] Some were doomed to fail, however perfect they might have been; and in the same states other bicameral constitutions likewise failed, as, for instance, the French of 1795, which Monroe said was modeled "upon our principle, a division of the legislature into two branches, etc."[3] Those unicameral constitutions contained the defects of leaving the executive magistrate as a distinct power independent of the legislature and either for life or for long terms independent of the people, with no means of appealing to the people to arbitrate between them, and with no authority in the judiciary to pass upon their acts in violation of the constitution.[4] The fact is, they contained too many of the features recommended by Adams.

But the greatest instance, oftenest cited, of course is

[1] For the other, see Adams, x., 47.

[2] Yet Creasy classed these with the Italian republics of the middle ages, and with Pennsylvania and Georgia "for a short period," as not escaping "the miseries which the instability, the violence, and the impassioned temerity of a single legislative assembly, have ever produced," *Rise and Progress of the English Constitution*, p. 178.

[3] *Writings*, ed. by S. M. Hamilton, ii., 269, similarly 283, 297, *cf.* 413–14.

[4] They contained, properly speaking, no bill of rights, only a declaration of rights, saying such and such restrictive laws ought not to be made, but not prescribing that if they were made, they would be voided by the judiciary not observing them.

that model and original of bicameralism—the English government. Whether this be considered in the past, when it truly was bicameral, or in the present, when it no longer is so, and especially whenever its solitary lapse into actual unicameralism is brought into the comparison, this is taken as proof positive of the need of bicameralism.[1] The past we may set aside as superseded by the present. The English government to-day is not an instance of unicameralism proper. Unicameralism proper is where there are two chambers each with a full negative upon the other, equally strong therefore, or coördinate. But the English "two

[1] A recent writer on this subject, Mr. Marriott, seems to take the failure of the English "unicameral experiment" under Cromwell as satisfactory proof of the need of the bicameral system, "at any rate in England," *Second Chambers*, ch. 3, although mentioning that under Cromwell there was also a bicameral experiment, equally unsuccessful, and for the same reason, which is overlooked, that neither rested upon the consent of the people, and was regulated by no constitution properly so called, but both were clear usurpations. Moreover, in them, as in Adams's plan, the executive chief was *in* the legislative department, and the judiciary was dependent upon it. Mr. Marriott, however, recognizes that his argument is especially applicable to countries without a written constitution, p. 87, *cf.* 253. And although admitting that the above instance, and two other experiments by great nations, were tried in conditions not normal, 240–1, he rests his case almost wholly on the consensus of the world, which he follows Burke in thinking we ought to believe to be right, 260. "Experience, no less than philosophy, has declared unmistakably in favor of the bicameral system," 298. "The world, by a sober and considered and unanimous verdict, has affirmed its belief in the necessity of a Second Chamber. Unicameral experiments have been tried and failed," 299.—Another English publicist, H. W. V. Temperley, in his *Senates and Upper Chambers*, London, 1810, lays more stress on "the American experiments," as passing the real condemnation on the Single Chamber system," because they were made in periods of peace and under safeguards of the federal system, p. 34. But he recognizes that of late almost everywhere in unitary states, except the American State legislatures, the tendency prevails to do away with the "checking" power of the upper chamber, pp. 140–2.

Houses are not coördinate, the House of Commons being much the stronger"[1]—and since 1911 the subordination of the House of Lords has no longer been left to custom but has been fixed by law, or, as we should say, made a part of the constitution, its veto on money bills being proscribed and on all other bills rendered merely suspensory. If we wish to employ a distinctive term, as the English system contains, so to speak, a chamber and a half, it may be called sesquicameralism. Now, such a system, lying halfway between unicameralism and bicameralism, is as good an argument for the one as for the other. And so are some other governments usually classed as bicameral.[2] And the strongest English supporters of the second chamber hardly venture to suggest the restoration of its pristine equality with the House of Commons, and hope only to save it from utter annihilation by fixing it in its present subordinate position. Thus Lecky, whose dread of a single House of Commons we have seen, wished the negative of the House of Lords to be limited, and suspensory, extending over one Parliament at least, to be

[1] Bryce, *Studies*, p. 430.

[2] Especially several of the great British self-governing possessions, and most prominently the latest, the constitution of the South African Union, drawn up in 1909 and put in force May 31, 1910, whose senate possesses only a suspensive negative, and disputed bills are to be settled by a simple majority of the two chambers sitting in one. So already, for nearly a century, Norway (see above, p. 314 n.), which political writers have been unable to classify. For an opposite reason, it is difficult to classify the German Empire, since the Bundesrath is not so much a legislative assembly as a conference of executive delegates with legislative functions. The constitution does not directly give an additional veto to the Emperor, and thus departs from Adams's full system and that of our States and of the United States; but Bismarck used a "joker" in the constitution practically to obtain such a veto, by himself, as Chancellor, refusing to promulgate certain measures which he and the Emperor disapproved.

overcome in the next or in the following House of
Commons by a two-thirds majority.[1] It is true that,
desiring something more definite than the present un-
certain position of their upper House, English publicists
often turn with envious eyes to the United States Senate,
and praise it not only as the "masterpiece" of our
Constitution,[2] but as the greatest and best example of
a successful upper chamber.[3] This helps to confirm
American publicists in their satisfaction with our own

---

[1] *Democracy and Liberty*, i., 464–6. So Creasy was glad that the
English Upper House was not (like "the American Senate"!) "elected
solely by the wealthy class of the community," in which case it "would
be infinitely more oligarchical and obstructive to reform than the House
of Lords has ever been," *op. cit.*, p. 305, *i. e.* would exercize an absolute
negative (as desired by Adams), whereas the House of Lords exercises
only a suspensive veto, pp. 348–9. And likewise Herbert Spencer (who
expected the "spontaneous division of the primitive group into the
distinguished few and the undistinguished many" to continue to be
represented in two houses, the one consisting of "the representatives of
directing persons" and the other of "the representatives of persons
directed," because the two aspects of law, as "looked at from above or
from below—by those accustomed to rule or by those accustomed to be
ruled,"—"require to be coördinated") expressly added that "the
representatives of the class regulated must be ultimately supreme,"
Principles of Sociology, § 578.

[2] Bryce, *The American Commonwealth*, i., 109.

[3] "There is perhaps no other equally important second chamber in
the world," Leonard Alston, *Modern Constitutions in Outline*, London,
1909, § 7. "The one thoroughly successful institution which has been
established since the tide of modern democracy began to run, is a
Second Chamber, the American Senate," Maine, *Popular Government*,
p. 181. Cobden had even dreamt of converting the House of Lords
into a Senate, with two members elected from each county (as from an
American State), Morley's *Life of Cobden*, ii., 25. Our Senate is, in fact,
even stronger than the House of Representatives, as it alone has control over treaties, while the mere precedence in taxation accorded the
House is of little importance because the Senate can make its tax-bills
over from the bottom up. Stronger than the lower houses are also the
German Bundesrath and the Austrian Herrenhaus. Only in Switzerland the two chambers have exactly the same functions.

institution, and in return they praise the English system, in this respect, as the prototype and exemplar of all perfection. Thus goes on the log-rolling, in spite of the one country having only a little stick. Yet most plain is it, that if any country needs an upper house co-ordinate with the lower house it is a country like England that allows omnipotence to its legislature, and that if England can get along with a subordinate upper house, the American Federal and State governments, in which the legislatures are restricted, have still less need of coördinate upper houses.

The science of government, as Adams himself and others have maintained, is an experimental science.[1] It is a pity, then, that some of our fifty odd States and Territories do not experiment with unicameralism. An advantage of our Federal system is that it affords opportunity for experiments in political science. Our States ought not all to flock together like so many sheep. Political science is not yet so firmly established as to be able to dispense with experimentation. And nothing has been so little tried as a well-guarded unicameral system. Of course there should be a council, which should be supplementary not only to the legislature, but to the other departments. If this, because of its relation to the legislature, keeps the system from being strictly unicameral, it at all events does not constitute bicameralism. But of this more by itself in a final chapter of suggestions.

[1] E. g. Burke, *Reflections on the Revolution in France, Works*, iii., 311; Macaulay, essay on *Mahon's History*, near end, and on *Mill's Essay on Government*, also near end; Brougham, *Political Philosophy*, i., 71. So in 1774 J. Shipley, "surely the art of government itself is founded on experience," in Niles's *Principles*, 420.

CHAPTER XXIV

TENDENCY OF THE UNITED STATES SENATE, AND SUGGESTIONS

OUR Federal bicameral system was not instituted avowedly on Adams's principles. Indeed, Adams did not at first care to have two chambers in the Federal government. It was adopted ostensibly as a means of effecting a compromise between the confederative and the national systems, between the interests of the small and of the large States. Our "double organization," says President Wilson, "represents no principle, but only an effort at prudence."[1] And there is a curious commentary upon its success in this respect in the remark of an English historian, that in a unitary state like England or France "the question between one or two Chambers in the Legislature is simply a question in which of the two ways the Legislature is likely to do its work best," but "in a federal constitution, like that of Switzerland or the United States, the two Chambers are absolutely necessary."[2] Yet, although bicameralism served this purpose of reconciling the smaller States to the loss of their equality in one chamber by instituting another in which their equality was preserved, bicameralism had already been decided upon for other reasons, which appear to resemble those of Adams. In fact, there was an indirect attempt to attain the same end. Four other differences were established between the two chambers: the Senate was made a small body, with long terms, renewable in rota-

---

[1] *The State,* § 929.
[2] Freeman, *Growth of the English Constitution,* p. 199; similarly Marriott, *Second Chambers,* p. 241.

tion, elected by the State legislatures, while the House was made a numerous body, with short terms, renewable together, elected by the people. These differences, it was hoped, would be sufficient, while leaving the latter a popular or democratic body, to make the former a select and aristocratic body, removed from the fickleness of the popular will, and attractive to men of wealth and position.[1]

The attempt is now succeeding, though in the absence of any true aristocracy in our country the idea

[1] The views of Hamilton, Morris, Madison, and others have already been given, in Ch. XXI. Randolph desired a small Senate, to act as check upon "the turbulence and follies of democracy," Elliot's *Debates*, v., 138. Dickinson, in proposing the motion for making the Senators elective by the State legislatures, had two reasons, one of which was, "because he wished the Senate to consist of the most distinguished characters, distinguished for their rank in life and their weight of property, and bearing as strong a likeness to the British House of Lords as possible; and he thought such characters more likely to be selected by the State legislatures than in any other mode," *ib.*, 166, *cf.* 163. Butler considered the second branch "as the aristocratic part of our government," *ib.*, i., 452, and Gerry referred to the senates in some of the States as "somewhat aristocratic," v., 169. In the ratifying conventions the friends of the Constitution, while repudiating any trace of aristocracy in the Senate or elsewhere, *ib.*, iv., 67 (Davie), 132, 134 (Iredell), 207 (Spaight), 259, 329 (C. Pinckney), frequently spoke of the other chamber as the "democratical branch," *ib.*, ii., 26 (Cabot), 75 (Jones), 251 (Hamilton), iii., 185 (H. Lee), 600 (Randolph), iv., 67 (Davie), 69 (Maclaine): 207 (Spaight); *cf.* also Mason and Randolph, *ib.*, v., 136 and 186 (and i., 393). That the two chambers were intended to represent different *interests*, we have seen avowed by C. Pinckney, above, p. 312-13 n. In public, this was reduced to saying they should have a different *composition*, by Madison in *The Federalist*, Nos. 62 and 63 (*cf.* his *Writings*, iii., 42). Since then also Webster hung between these two doctrines, *Works*, iii., 12-13, 17; and the latter has been preached by Story, *Commentaries*, ii., 179-80, Lieber, *On Civil Liberty*, 198-9, Woolsey, *Political Science*, ii., 312.—The desire of the constitution-drafters to subject democracy to the curb of aristocracy, and the amount of their success, has recently been thoroughly investigated by J. A. Smith in his *The Spirit of American Government*.

"plutocracy" ought to be substituted. The process has been a slow one, and still is incomplete, becoming more manifest, however, as its condition, the differentiation of the rich as a class from the rest of the community, is becoming more pronounced. Already our Federal Senators are mostly rich men; and though they are not elected by rich men solely, yet their affiliations are chiefly with the rich, and they are becoming more and more distinctively the representatives of the rich and the guardians of vested interests and of vested abuses, the conservatives, the blockers of progress. A bicameral system would seem inevitably to lead to this result, as otherwise there appears no sufficient reason for the two chambers—for "the repetition"; and where each has an absolute negative, enabling it to prevent new and to retain old laws, economy of effort enjoins the capture of only one of the chambers, and that the smaller[1] and longer-lasting. The fiction can no longer be kept up of the Senators representing the States that send them. They do not, and never did from the beginning, truly represent the States, any more than the so-called Representatives truly represent their particular districts. Senators would represent the States only if, as in the Confederation, they were delegates or deputies, subject to instructions and liable to recall; which they expressly are not. Much rather do Senators and Representatives alike represent interests, wherever located.

---

[1] *Cf.* Wilson: "It is a lesson we ought not to disregard, that the smallest bodies in Great Britain are notoriously the most corrupt. . . . When Lord Chesterfield had told us that one of the Dutch provinces had been seduced into the views of France, he need not have added that it was not Holland, but one [of the smallest of them," Elliot's *Debates*, v., 196 (*cf.* i., 415). But the lesson was disregarded, and accordingly the seat of corruption throughout our country is in the senates.

And as they form two bodies set in opposition to each other, they are likely to represent opposing interests, which will be the great ones of wealth and poverty, anticipated by Adams and Hamilton, as they grow up in advancing civilization into more prominent antagonism. The prospect, therefore, is, that the end, though deferred, will be just as bad as though Adams's scheme were embodied in the Constitution itself.

In the individual States these evils have not developed yet to quite so appreciable an extent, owing to the lesser importance of these territorially small and sub-ordinate bodies; also because the terms of the Senators are shorter (mostly for four years, rotating by halves), and their districts are not so unequal, with the result that the people can more quickly bring them into agreement with the lower house. But other inherent evils have come to the surface. Bicameralism divides responsibility. Popular measures have been defeated by politicians in the two houses agreeing to differ on details, while all pretended to uphold the principle. Against which no appreciable benefit, not otherwise obtainable, can be discerned.

It is not likely that this system shall last permanently. If deadlocks have not caused much harm in the past, they may in the future, as the homogeneity of the people continues to diminish. If there be a revulsion of sentiment and another wave toward democracy sets in, the possession of the United States Senate by the rich, bought up especially in the small States, may block its advance. We may then come to a pass similar to that in which the English recently found themselves, through the revival there of the unrevoked powers of the House of Lords. Two equal powers in a government are an absurdity,[1] even on Adams's principles. If we do not wish the House of Representatives to kneel before the Senate, we must make the Senate bow to the House of Representatives. Merely making its members elective by the people, advantageous though it will be, will not be enough. The Senate ought to be shorn of some of its functions. To do this, involves reconstructing it. From a branch of the legislature, it should be converted into a distinct member of the body politic—a council.

The idea of the council seems to be passing out of the ken of modern political scientists. It was already obsolescent in Adams's day. It is sometimes lost in that of the cabinet,[2] more often in that of the upper chamber of the legislature. The fact is overlooked that in England, beside the legislative Houses, and beside the Ministry, exists a Privy Council. In truth, a council is one of the earliest of institutions. Primitive states seem to fall naturally into a constitution in the form of a chieftain, a council, and an assembly. The council is a small and continually officiating body, which is effaced upon the occasional, generally annual, meeting of the assembly, or sinks into that large body. In Rome, after the expulsion of the Kings, the council, named the "Senate," while the executive chiefs were called "Consuls" (consulters as well as advisers), inherited the Kings' usurpation of the initiative in legislation, till the people got it back by the institution of the Tribunes and the Comitia Tributa. The English

[1] "My soul aches
To know, when two authorities are up,
Neither supreme, how soon confusion
May enter 'twixt the gap."
Coriolanus, III., i., 108-11.

[2] As for instance was done in the Philadelphia Convention by Morris and others, Elliot's *Debates*, v., 442, 446, 462.

doubling of the assembly was a peculiar phenomenon, which, according to most English historians,[1] arose by accident. For the English House of Lords descended from the Anglo-Saxon Witenagemot, which was the primitive council. But the Anglo-Saxon Folkmot, or popular assembly, had fallen into abeyance, and the Witenagemot or House of Lords had assumed its legislative functions. While this was now filled with the Norman leaders, a new Privy Council was introduced above it from the Council of the conquerors. When later the French Simon de Montfort introduced from abroad the representative system and summoned the shires and boroughs to elect and send braces of knights and burghers, these naturally took the place of the old Folkmot, while the House of Lords was not reduced to its old place as council, which was already occupied by another body, but, by a compromise between conquerors and conquered, remained a companion legislative body—at first superior, then coördinate, at last subordinate. The development was thus different from what took place on the continent, where generally there were three or four estates which normally sat either together or in three or four chambers. In Germany as well as in England the clergy combined with the nobility, but in the German Diet the princes parted into the electoral and the ordinary, and, with the delegates of the cities, still formed three estates or colleges, which had to agree (and with the Emperor too) for any enactment.[2] Four estates continued to act separately,

---

[1] E. g. Freeman, *Growth of the English Constitution*, p. 97.

[2] This single but three-chambered assembly has been replaced in the modern German Empire by two distinct houses, the Bundesrath, containing appointees of the sovereign princes, and the Reichstag, representatives of the people.

in four chambers, with necessary concurrence for enactments, in Sweden and Finland. But in England the
four were reduced to two, by the lower clergy holding
off and meeting only in their own Convocations, while
the upper clergy, as Lords spiritual, united with the
Lords temporal, and the burghers and country knights,
first summoned together, as above said, likewise combined. There this division into two Houses, along with
the development of the Ministers into a Cabinet,
forming a new and active council, segmented off from
the old Privy Council, has relegated the old council
proper to the background.

But most of the American colonies had reverted to
the original type, because they were chartered corporations, in which this kind of organization has been
prevalent. Not only in Connecticut and Rhode Island,
which did not alter their governments on becoming
States, but also in New Hampshire, Massachusetts,
New York, New Jersey, Pennsylvania, Virginia, and
South Carolina, the governments before the Revolution
consisted of a governor with a council, and a legislative
assembly. The council, indeed, had a negative upon
the assembly, and thus a legislative function, but only
as a part of the executive. The legislature was unicameral. Yet these colonies (and the first two States)
are generally treated as having had the bicameral
system (which treatment would make the English
government tricameral).[1] Still, it was, later, but a

---

[1] Thus these colonial governments were not copied from the English
government. They were modeled upon the original type of all government, handed down in corporations everywhere. On the continent
of Europe the tradition of an assembly and a council (or directory)
helped along the willingness to copy the English bicameral system,
which system perverted the old system by supplanting the council with
a second chamber of the assembly. It is really that old system of two

slight transition for the executive council to be made over into a legislative council or senate.[1] Thus, while in England the fissure had taken place in the assembly, in America it occurred in the executive. During the metamorphosis of the councils, these bodies, in many cases, long partook of both natures, the "senates," as they came to be called, having both executive and legislative functions.[2] In the States they have mostly been deprived of the former; but in the United States the Senate is still in the amphibious condition.

In which direction shall it betake itself? Shall it become legislative entirely, or shall it revert to the position of a council? The last is to be recommended. Much of its legislative power ought, therefore, to be reduced. Let it cease to amend tax and appropriation bills, and let its negative on all bills be only suspensive. The first is the English practice, and the second has been adopted in the new Australian as well as South African constitutions.[3] More in detail, let it be required to act on everything coming to it from the House

different whole bodies or houses (a legislature and a council), and not the new system of two half bodies or chambers (composing one legislature), for which there is world-wide approval.

[1] See above, p. 115 n.

[2] But in Massachusetts, by the constitution of 1780, these functions were divided between the senate and a council, the new council retaining the executive functions of the old colonial council, and the senate taking over its legislative functions and being made a coördinate branch of the old assembly. Thus if Massachusetts had before been bicameral, it now was tricameral. But it is more correct to say that it before was only unicameral and now bicameral, yet its legislature before was bipartite, because of the negative in the executive (governor and council) added to the assembly, and now is tripartite, because of the negative in the governor added to the two chambers into which the assembly is divided. *This*, and not *that*, constitution shows the peculiar influence of the English model.

[3] It was also in the Polish constitution of 1791 (art. 6).

within a definite period, say a month, or be passed by,
and let it have the right to return tax and appropriation
bills with recommendations, which the House may heed
or not as it pleases, and to suspend all law bills (unless
the House accept its suggestions) till after the next
election, when the House may pass them without the
Senate's concurrence. In all these cases simple majorities of the whole House should be sufficient.[1] Another
legislative function ought to be taken from the Senate
as not rightfully belonging to it: the House alone should
ratify or reject treaties. The proper function of the
Senate with regard to treaties is to be consulted and to
advise during their negotiation. It ought also to be
consulted by the House in the drafting of bills, to perfect their wording—a function especially needed in our
State governments. Its control over appointments
should be continued, and it might even be extended.
Its confirmation might be required also for dismissals,
in the case of high officials, to be acted on individually,
to prevent wholesale discharges; but with the difference
that the latter should be rendered easier than the former: let the consent of two thirds of the Senators be
necessary for appointments, and of one third for dismissals. But the heads of departments, forming the
Cabinet, ought to be exempted from this control, and
be put under that of the House, where they should have
the right to speak when called upon.[2] Also the judicial

[1] It is at all events indispensable that the Senate should have an absolute negative no further than upon raises in taxes and appropriations
and upon new law bills, while the House should be able to renew and
especially to lower existing taxes and appropriations and to repeal laws
without the consent of the Senate.

[2] And, of course, to vote if they be members; for there is no good
reason why the heads of departments should not be taken from members
of the House. In course of time this might become the exclusive custom,

functions of the Senate may be increased. Impeachment need not require presentment by the House,
especially in the case of judges. The Senate itself ought
to be able to initiate it, except in the case of the President and Cabinet officers; and, the trial being conducted
in the name of the whole Senate, the judges should
be a jury, not too numerous, selected from among its
members, present or past.

These various powers would properly belong to the
Senate as a council—as an intermediate body standing
beside the three great departments, and supervisory
over them all. The doctrine of the total separation of
the three departments is false. There must be some
connecting link between them. But this should be a
distinct body, itself belonging to neither of them alone,
and overlapping each of them. The Senate or Council
would then be the circle of union of them all, the mediator between them, the moderator of their differences,
and the smoother of their roughnesses. As a central
court in which all their functions converge, it would be
a sort of clearing house for the separate departments,
having the whole functions of none of them. And its
justification for having a share in the functions of any
one department, is that it has a share in the functions
of the others also. It is an advisory board, subservient to all the departments. Its sessions need not be
entirely synchronous with those of the House.

With this altered conception of its position, its membership needs reorganization. In the first place, be it
said, as it is a council, whose character is *wisdom*, there
is perfect propriety in the States, large and small,

and it would form an incentive to competent men to seek election. But
before this can be, a citizen must be eligible from any district, at least
of his own State.

sending the same number of Senators each; but this is a monstrosity when they are, as now, endowed with *power*, which in representatives ought to be proportioned to the power of the represented, which itself in a tolerably homogeneous people is proportional to their numbers. Little validity appertains to a perpetual clause in a constitution, and therefore little to the last sentence of Art. V. of ours. Yet, as this is regarded as a compact, there is overwhelming sentiment for respecting it. But while the numbers of the Senators from each State cannot be changed, nothing in the Constitution (or in the compact) prevents taking away their power and leaving them principally influence. Nothing prevents, also, increasing the whole number by admitting others, provided the equal opportunities of the States be observed. Thus all ex-Presidents, and the oldest ex-Governors of the States, the justices of the Supreme Court, and the chief-justices or ex-chief-justices of the States, might be admitted.[1] The actual President should not only be a member, but should be its president, presiding whenever he chooses to attend, and the Vice-President should preside only in his absence. Indeed, the President's action upon the Legislature (save in his messages) should be only in his capacity as member of the Council: his veto should coalesce with its suspensory negative. But if a special veto be left to him, it should have no greater force than to require reconsideration on the part of the Legislature. Whether the extra members should have the right to vote, may be a question; but at all events the justices ought to vote in impeachments, and to vote first; and

[1] Perhaps by special popular election, in reward for their services if approved, with a chance for the punishment of rejection if their conduct has not been satisfactory.

if Cabinet members be admitted, they should only be
ex officio. Eligibility to the Senate should be confined
to men who have gained experience by serving as Representatives—a requirement which would force ambitious men to pass through the House.[1] And in view of
their diminished power, no harm would be done if their
electors were confined to men with a property or educational qualification. Nor would long terms be irrational, when the purpose is guidance through wisdom
gained by experience. The regular Senators (and also
the ex-Presidents) should constitutionally have a
higher salary than the assemblymen (say twice as
high),[2] and should take precedence over them in all
ceremonies, in order to make their position more attractive to men of eminence, and to exact from power the
deference due to wisdom.

The same features would be equally suitable in the
constitutions of the individual States. There, for instance, the counties might send the same number of
such senators or councilors each, while representation
proportioned to population is required for the house.
Ex-governors and certain justices or ex-justices might
be admitted as additional members in the senate. And
here the senate's negative might call for the submission
of law bills to the people in the referendum,[3] if the

[1] And if no one should be eligible to the Presidency except a one-time
member of the Senate, or a State Governor, the incentive would be all
the greater for competent men to devote themselves to politics.

[2] *Cf.* Gorham in the Convention: "Their [the Senators'] allowance
should certainly be higher. The members of the senates in the States
are allowed more than those of the other house," Elliot's *Debates*, v.,
427.

[3] But no measure should pass in the referendum unless it received an
affirmative majority of all the eligible voters, as determined either by
the last census or by the registration at the last general election, or at
the present general election if preceded by registration.

assembly prefer such a direct appeal instead of waiting for the next election—a measure not applicable to the Union merely on account of its unwieldy size. The fact is, these features all belong, in the first place, and most properly, to unitary states. Yet in our new "Federal" (in distinction from the ancient "federative") system the real composition lies in the coexistence of sectional governments for sectional affairs and of a national government for national affairs, the latter being supreme (under the whole people) over the nation in *some* (enumerated) matters, while each sectional government is supreme (under its people) over its section in *other* matters not forbidden to it either by the whole or its own people. The combination which puts into the national government, as coördinate parts of its legislature, both representatives of the people of the nation (in the House) and representatives of the sections (in the Senate), is puerile. The national government, as far as it goes, has as much right to be properly constructed, as has any unitary state.

And with the Senate converted into a council, its control over legislation reduced as here indicated, this sort of sesquicameralism would accomplish all the good of bicameralism and avoid its evils. The only sound argument for bicameralism is the psychological one, that a body of men are put on their mettle and will do their best if they know their work is to be reviewed by another body of men. Especially will this be the case, if the reviewing body be composed of men promoted from the body in question or from equally high positions, and treated with more honor, thus having the reputation of a superior body.

A government so constituted also returns to first principles. In a famous simile Sir William Temple

compared the stable condition of a government to a
pyramid: if it be broadly bottomed upon the whole
people, and terminate above in the authority of one
single man.[1] The foundation should be power and
force; the upper part, wisdom and knowledge. Force
and might should diminish as we go from the base up-
ward; more wisdom, leading in the right, should be
demanded as we approach the apex. If this distribution be attained, the people at the bottom will respect
the persons near and at the top, and will be influenced
by their advice. Then strength will be guided by
knowledge, and wisdom will rule by its own proper
power, which is not force, but persuasion.

[1] *Essay upon the Original and Nature of Government*, in *Miscellanies*,
Part I., 1697, pp. 83-4.

INDEX

Achaian cities, 55 n.
Adams, C. F., 1 n., 14 n., 136.
Adams, H., 28 n.
Adams, J., system of, 2–3; periods of his career, 3–4; dogmatism, 4; early democratic views, 5–12; on Independence, 6 n.; writings, 7 n., 13, 28 n., 261, 262, 273, 281–2, 305 n., 315–16 n.; aristocratic in spirit, 54, 146, 228, 258, 281; pardon of Fries, 104 n.; casting vote, 110 and n.; failure to profit by his model, 142–3, cf. 235 ; reactionary, 224–6; deterioration, 251; thoroughness and originality, 253–5; fondness for balancing, 256; the change, and its cause, 259–61; monarchism, 261, 273–6, 283–4, denial, 282; Federalism, 267–8 and n.; a States'-rights man, 268; not a Tory, 283; election to the Presidency, 284, 288–9 and n.; honesty, 289 and n.; republicanism, 291–5; merit, 304; influence, 304–12, 328; how ignored, 318, 321, 322 n.
Adams, J. Q., 214 n., 288, 292.
Adams, S., 6 n, 9 n., 188 n., 212 n., 216 and n., 224, 253 n., 278 n.
Æschines, 23 n.
Agrarian law, 38 n., 249–51, 258, 272–3.
Agreement of the People, the, 17, 17–18 n., 209 n.
Alston, L., 346 n.
Amendment of constitutions, 160 n., 221–2; of the Federal, 222–4; of the English, 223 n.
American, people, 1, 5, 220 n., 220–1, 221 n., 227; doctrine, 211–15; Whiggism, 215–18.

Ames, F., 112 n., 268 n., 295–6.
Andorra, 340.
Anglo-Saxons, 106 n., 353.
Anhalt, 340 n.
Anti-Federalists, 163.
Appointments, wholly by the executive, 10, 108–16, 150, 177; annual, 12.
Arbiter (or mediator), need of, 10, 54, 56, 58, 59, 62–3, 66, 78–9, 94 n., 152–3; power of, 153–4; proper place of, 166.
Aristocracy, defined, 47 and n., simple, 29, 40; natural, 47–8; by art, 260; needed against the king, 62; encroachments of, 60, 65, 68; difficult to manage, 63; need of control, 65–6, 70, 79; to be segregated, 65–6, 110, 120, 141–2, 151, 308–9; then a blessing to society, 67, 120; opposition of, to the king, 67–8; to be made dependent on the king for appointments, 110–11; Adams's fear of, 270; late definition of, 292, 293; the term, 306 n.; exclusion of, from the lower house, 300.
Aristotle, 25 n., 32 n., 39 n., 49 n., 143, 214 n., 249 n., 254 n.
Army, standing, assigned to the king, 61, 71; dispensed with by the English, 65; not to be granted, 116, 177.
Arragon, 158.
Assembly, single, advocated by others, 3, 9 n., 97; combated by Adams, 9–10, 14–19, 65, 141, 177, 182, 262; by others, 245; though approved by him in confederacies, 12, 263, 265 n.; on his arguments against, 132–5, cf. 251–3, 260, 279.

Index

A Selection from the
Catalogue of

G. P. PUTNAM'S SONS

❦

Complete Catalogue sent
on application